Social History of Africa
WORKING WITH GENDER

**Recent Titles in
Social History of Africa Series**
Allen Isaacman and Jean Allman, Series Editors

Colonial Lessons: Africans' Education in Southern Rhodesia, 1918–1940
Carol Summers

Poison and Medicine: Ethnicity, Power, and Violence in a Nigerian City, 1966 to 1986
Douglas A. Anthony

To Dwell Secure: Generation, Christianity, and Colonialism in Ovamboland
Meredith McKittrick

Genders and Generations Apart: Labor Tenants and Customary Law in Segregation-Era South Africa, 1920s to 1940s
Thomas V. McClendon

"City of Steel and Fire": A Social History of Atbara, Sudan's Railway Town, 1906–1984
Ahmad Alawad Sikainga

"We Were All Slaves": African Miners, Culture, and Resistance at the Enugu Government Colliery
Carolyn A. Brown

Running after Pills: Politics, Gender, and Contraception in Colonial Zimbabwe
Amy Kaler

"The Pygmies Were Our Compass": Bantu and Batwa in the History of West Central Africa, Early Times to c. 1900 C.E.
Karin A. Klieman

Men and Masculinities in Modern Africa
Lisa A. Lindsay and Stephan F. Miescher, editors

Planting Rice and Harvesting Slaves: Transformations along the Guinea-Bissau Coast, 1400–1900
Walter Hawthorne

Landed Obligation: The Practice of Power in Buganda
Holly Elisabeth Hanson

WORKING WITH GENDER

WAGE LABOR AND SOCIAL CHANGE IN SOUTHWESTERN NIGERIA

Lisa A. Lindsay

Social History of Africa
Allen Isaacman and Jean Allman, Series Editors

Heinemann
Portsmouth, NH

Heinemann
A division of Reed Elsevier Inc.
361 Hanover Street
Portsmouth, NH 03801-3912
www.heinemann.com

Offices and agents throughout the world

© 2003 by Lisa A. Lindsay

All rights reserved. No part of this book may be reproduced in any form or by any electronic or mechanical means, including information storage and retrieval systems, without permission in writing from the publisher, except by a reviewer, who may quote brief passages in a review.

ISBN: 0-325-00188-X (cloth)
ISBN: 0-325-00187-1 (paper)
ISSN: 1099-8098

Library of Congress Cataloging-in-Publication Data

Lindsay, Lisa A.
    Working with gender : wage labor and social change in southwestern Nigeria / Lisa A. Lindsay.
    p. cm.—(Social history of Africa, ISSN 1099-8098)
    Includes bibliographical references and index.
    ISBN 0-325-00188-X (alk. paper)—ISBN 0-325-00187-1 (pbk. : alk. paper)
    1. Wages—Nigeria. 2. Sexual division of labor—Nigeria. 3. Nigeria—Social conditions. I. Title. II. Series.
HD5098.L56 2003
306.3′615′09669209045—dc21   2003040682

British Library Cataloguing in Publication Data is available.

Printed in the United States of America on acid-free paper
07 06 05 04 03 SB 1 2 3 4 5 6 7 8 9

Copyright Acknowledgments

I gratefully acknowledge permission to publish the map, which was designed and produced by Karin Breiwitz at the Center for Teaching and Learning, University of North Carolina–Chapel Hill.

I also acknowledge permission from the Bodleian Library, Oxford, to reprint the cartoon from "Nigerail" in chapter 5.

*For Jay, Amelia, and Julian,
and in memory Elizabeth Pennington Taylor*

Contents

	Illustrations	ix
	Acknowledgments	xi
	Abbreviations	xv
1.	Introduction: Gender and Wage Labor in Colonial Africa	1
2.	Wage Labor, Money, and Masculinity in Early Twentieth-Century Yorubaland	31
3.	Families, Jobs, and the State before 1945	53
4.	Domesticity and Difference: The 1945 General Strike	77
5.	The Rise of the "Male Breadwinner" in Postwar Southwestern Nigeria	105
6.	Urban Labor, Extended Families, and the Differentiation of Domesticity	133
7.	Domesticity and Difference Reconfigured: The 1964 General Strike	173
8.	Conclusion: The Fall of the "Modern" Breadwinner?	203
	Bibliography	215
	Index	233

ILLUSTRATIONS

MAP

1.1 Map of Nigeria, c. 1955   2

PHOTOGRAPHS

1.1	Nigerian Railway Corporation headquarters, Lagos	17
1.2	Nigerian Railway Corporation Pensioners' Welfare Association headquarters, Ebute Metta, Lagos	19
4.1	Ibadan market women, 1993	81
5.1	Cartoon from "Nigerail," 1956	113
5.2	Sign on the railway compound, Ibadan, 1994	123
6.1	Apprentice Engine Drivers Training School, Lagos, 1956	135
6.2	Ayo Salako and his shunting engine, Abeokuta, 1966	143
6.3	Railway housing quarters, Ibadan, 1998	149
6.4	Residents of Ayo Salako's compound, Kano, c. 1960	151
6.5	D.A. Owolabi, Ibadan, 1998	159
8.1	Anthony and Hannah Nnodua, Ibadan, 1994	209
8.2	Pensioners' Union sign, Lagos, 1998	210

TABLES

3.1	Permanent Railway Staff, 1930–1941	62
7.1	Railway Staff Allowances, 1957	181

ACKNOWLEDGMENTS

Although this book focuses on a different time and place from where I live, it fundamentally revolves around an issue about which my generation of professional American women (and some men) is very concerned: the relationship between paid work and family life. This was not my intention when I started the project as a Ph.D. dissertation. But as it evolved and my family grew, I learned firsthand the impossibility of separating "home" and "work," regardless of what over a century of Western bourgeois ideology implied about those concepts. In producing this book, I have accumulated debts of a broad range, from those of a very "professional" nature to those that helped me get this project done by sharing some of my familial obligations. The one person who made vast contributions in both of these realms is Jay Kaufman, and so I want to reverse the conventional order of acknowledgments and thank him first. For his consistent companionship, intellectual curiosity, adventurous spirit, statistical expertise, logistical assistance, home-front partnering, and amazing command of African studies, I am eternally grateful.

I owe an enormous thanks to the men and women in Lagos and Ibadan who generously shared their time, insights, and hospitality with me. I conducted the original research for this book during the summer of 1992 and then in 1993–1994. This was a tumultuous period for Nigerians. In addition to massive economic distress, my stay in 1993–1994 coincided with three national governments, two general strikes, countless gasoline shortages, and a military coup. I returned to Nigeria in July 1998, just after the death of the dictator Sani Abacha and in time for the demise of Chief M.K.O. Abiola in prison. While it was fascinating (and horrifying) to see these events unfold, there were moments when I was not sure this project would ever reach completion. In such situations I was all the more dependent upon the goodwill of friends, colleagues, archivists, informants, and patrons.

In Nigeria the University of Ibadan's History Department provided my institutional home. In particular I am grateful to Dr. LaRay Denzer, who not only facilitated my research there but also provided valuable advice on matters both academic and quotidian, introduced me to scores of people, and provided excellent company. I also acknowledge the support of Professors Bolanle Awe and Benson Mojuetan and the comradeship of Andrew Apter, Andrea Cornwall, Gladys Effa-Heap, Donna Flynn, Simon Heap, Robin Derby, and Mimi Wan. Much of the research on which this book is based was gathered with the capable aid of Babajide Oyeneye. 'Jide was involved in most stages of the research, from making contacts with railway pensioners to checking archival sources to transcribing court cases. I am grateful for his meticulous work and good cheer. Funmilayo Carew and Olusanya Ibitoye provided more short-term assistance with interviews, translations, and archival research. Outside of work, my life in Ibadan and Lagos was enriched through association with Anjola Aboderin, Dr. Judith Asuni, Shawna Bucharam, Guido Di Dominico and his family, Dr. Eme Effiong-Owoaje, Drs. Modupe and J.J. Ladipo and their family, Dede Mabiaku, Mrs. H.O. Shitta-Bey, Assaad Zard, and Dr. Raymond Zard.

The most rewarding and pleasurable part of my research in Nigeria involved the Nigerian Railway Corporation (NRC) and its current and former employees. I appreciate the goodwill extended to me by senior officials, including A. Abdulkarim Abdullahi, Assistant Director of Personnel; E.A. Amadi, Assistant Chief Public Relations Officer; F. Bola Kolawole, Chief Industrial Relations and Welfare Officer; and F.M. Ibilaiye, Assistant Director (Pension Fund), all at the Ebute Metta headquarters; and Alhaji M. Lawal, Director of the Pay Office in Ibadan. My day-to-day operations were facilitated through the efforts of Mr. Kolawole, M.O. Nola of the NRC's Ibadan Pension Office, and F.A. Oyenike of the Pension Office in Lagos. Irouje Don-Iroube of the headquarters Pay Office was especially helpful in introducing me to the NRC and its workings. For most of the surveys and interviews with retirees, I relied initially on the Railway Pensioners' Unions in Ibadan and Lagos. The Ibadan branch was led by, among others, J.B. Adekanola, Alhaji S.D. Aderohunmu, A.O. Akindele, J.A. Akinpelu, Afolabi Aremu, and J.J. Jideonwo, whose help facilitating interviews I much appreciate. In addition I came to spend a great deal of time with Mudasiru Folarin, Anthony and Hannah Nnodua, D.A. Owolabi, and A.A. Salako. I am especially grateful to Mr. Salako for sharing his personal photographs with me. In Lagos my contacts with the Pensioners' Union were facilitated by its head, Alhaji Raheem Balogun, and one of its executives, Mrs. Folasade Tade. I thank all of the railway retirees and their wives who patiently answered my questions, shared their insights, and in the process taught me Nigerian history.

Acknowledgments are due to the staff at the various archives and libraries where I have conducted research for this project. At the National Archives, Ibadan, I relied upon the assistance and expertise of staff members, including

Mr. Abioye, Mrs. Aribusola, Mrs. Dada, Lanre Olokede, and Akins Olowe. At the Kenneth Dike Library, University of Ibadan, I was assisted by Sam Odularu and especially by the indefatigable Shina Osunlana in the manuscripts section. Mr. Aderibigbe granted me access to Ibadan court records in the Obafemi Awolowo University Library. Mrs. Owade and others at the Yaba Magistrate's Court in Lagos tolerated my persistent questions and monopolization of one of their desks. I also acknowledge the assistance of the staff of the Nigerian Institute of Social and Economic Research's library in Ibadan. In the United Kingdom, in July and August of 1994 and again in October 2000, I appreciated the efficient personnel at the Public Record Office and Rhodes House Library. Andrea Cornwall in London and Dr. Phyllis Ferguson in Oxford helped with my arrangements and provided academic companionship. The staff at the New York Public Library's Schomberg Collection were also very accommodating, and I appreciate Jaime Sperling's repeated hospitality in New York.

I have been fortunate in receiving funding for the project that became this book. The dissertation research was assisted by a grant from the Joint Committee on African Studies of the Social Science Research Council and the American Council of Learned Societies with funds provided by the Ford, Mellon, and Rockefeller Foundations. Preliminary research during the summer of 1992 was funded by the Rackham Graduate School of the University of Michigan, and an earlier trip to Nigeria in 1991 was made possible by grants from Rackham and from the University of Michigan's Center for Afro-American and African Studies, with moneys partially provided by the Ford Foundation. A grant from Cornell University helped to offset the costs of an intensive Yoruba language course there in the summer of 1993. At the dissertation writing stage, I was supported by a Rackham Predoctoral Fellowship from the University of Michigan's graduate school. The 1998 trip to Nigeria was funded by a junior faculty research grant from the University of North Carolina at Charlotte, and the University of North Carolina–Chapel Hill funded the 2000 trip to the United Kingdom. Fellowships from the National Endowment for the Humanities and the American Council of Learned Societies, administered by the University of North Carolina–Chapel Hill, supported a year of writing in 2000–2001, and the university's History Department granted me another term of leave for the final revisions in 2002.

Even with the time off from teaching, I would not have been able to complete this book without the assistance of a community of friends and relatives, many of whom have provided meals, supplementary child care, and other help at one time or another. Certainly it was easier for me to undertake research trips, or simply retreat to my desk, knowing that Jay Kaufman, Joyce and Sol Kaufman, Dianne Lindsay, Wayne Kaufman, Julie Johnson, Peg Palmer, and Kirsten Kainz were, at various times, covering my domestic responsibilities.

The late Penny Taylor, Dean Taylor, and Gene Taylor provided crucial help with travel arrangements. Most of these people, along with Wendell and Laura Lindsay and other family members, are not particularly interested in the subject of this book, but it is to their credit that they have been supportive nonetheless. My children Amelia and Julian are certainly not interested in this book, except insofar as it competes with them for my attention. Yet they have contributed to it too, both by illustrating to me the connections between paid work and domesticity and, more importantly, by giving me joy which spills into every part of my life.

Working with Gender took initial shape at the University of Michigan, where I began accumulating my many debts to Frederick Cooper. The project initially occurred to me after I read his *On the African Waterfront,* and his *Decolonization and African Society* provides the imperial context for much of what follows. In its emphasis on gender and social history, this book is differently focused than those are, but still his work represents for me a model of sharp analysis, clear writing, and political engagement. I remain deeply grateful, moreover, for Fred's intellectual generosity as a graduate advisor and beyond. David William Cohen deserves credit for steering me toward African history as an undergraduate; years later his line of questioning during my dissertation defense suggested the book's current concern with modernization as experienced in the 1950s and 1960s. Ann Stoler prompted me to look beyond the obvious in studying colonialism, and Sonya Rose urged me to think comparatively about gender and wage labor. Luise White might as well have been on that graduate committee, too: she has offered unflagging support, analytical insights, and advice. I am so lucky to have worked with these people, each of whose brilliance complements the others'.

It would be difficult to come up with an exhaustive list of all the people who have commented on parts of this work in conferences, other presentations, and papers. Without slighting others, I do want to single out those whose suggestions and comments have most stayed with me and influenced the shape of this book. To Karin Barber, Carolyn Brown, LaRay Denzer, Dorothy Hodgson, Kristin Mann, Kenda Mutongi, Scott Nelson, Jane Parpart, Steven Pierce, Pamela Scully, Lynn Thomas, Heather Thompson, and Kerry Ward, I am grateful for readings, comments, ideas, and contributions of materials. For the hard work of reading and providing comments on the entire manuscript, I am immensely grateful to Frederick Cooper, Andrea Cornwall, Stephan Miescher, Luise White, and the two anonymous readers for Heinemann. Their thoughtful comments and much appreciated encouragement made the final version possible. I also thank the Social History of Africa series' editors, Allen Isaacman and Jean Allman, along with Jim Lance for their important roles in getting this book to press. Whatever deficiencies remain after all this help are, of course, my own doing.

ABBREVIATIONS

ACSTWU	African Civil Servants Technical Workers Union
AG	Action Group
AHR	*American Historical Review*
ALDFAWN	Association of Locomotive Drivers, Firemen, and Allied Workers of Nigeria
ANRCS	Association of Nigerian Railway Civil Servants
CJAS	*Canadian Journal of African Studies*
CME	Chief Mechanical Engineer
CO	Colonial Office
cola	cost of living adjustment
ComCol	Commissioner of the Colony (Lagos)
CRB	Criminal Record Book
CSG	Chief Secretary to the Government
CSO	Chief Secretary's Office
CSSH	*Comparative Studies in Society and History*
CvRB	Civil Record Book
DO	Dominions Office
DS	*Daily Service*
DTN	*Daily Times of Nigeria*
GM	General Manager
GML	General Manager (Labor)
GMS	General Manager (Staff)
HMP	Herbert Macaulay Papers
HMSO	Her/His Majesty's Stationery Office
IJAHS	*International Journal of African Historical Studies*
JAC	Joint Action Council
JAH	*Journal of African History*
JHSN	*Journal of the Historical Society of Nigeria*
JSAS	*Journal of Southern African Studies*

LC	*Labour Champion*
LEDB	Lagos Executive Development Board
MP	*Morning Post*
NAI	National Archives, Ibadan
NCNC	National Council of Nigerian Citizens
NLA	Nigerian Labor Archive
NNDP	Nigerian National Democratic Party
NPA	Nigerian Ports Authority
NRC	Nigerian Railway Corporation
NT	*Nigerian Tribune*
NTUC	Nigerian Trade Union Congress
NUR(F)	National Union of Railwaymen (Federated)
PRO	Public Record Office, London
PWD	Public Works Department
RHO	Rhodes House, Oxford
RWU	Railway Workers Union
RWUN	Railway Workers Union of Nigeria
SLRO	Senior Labor Relations Office
TUC	Trades Union Congress
TUCN	Trade Union Congress of Nigeria
UAC	United Africa Company
ULC	United Labour Congress
WAISER	West African Institute of Social and Economic Research
WAP	*West African Pilot*

1

INTRODUCTION: GENDER AND WAGE LABOR IN COLONIAL AFRICA

The Yoruba-speaking women of southwestern Nigeria are renowned for their history of active market trading and financial independence from men.[1] Yet colonial interventions in Africa, particularly after World War II, were often based upon and promoted notions of men as primary household providers and women essentially as dependent homemakers. Throughout colonial Africa in the postwar period, British and French planners attempted to differentiate and control African workforces by offering metropolitan-style wages and benefits, creating well-defined career trajectories, and recognizing trade unions.[2] These policies were implicitly about gender, because they assumed that stable urban labor would be male and would be reproduced by wives sharing their urban residences. What happened when such measures met with very different gender norms in Nigeria?

This book attempts to answer this and related questions. Through a focus on railway workers, it examines the dynamics of family structure and gender ideology in the large towns of southwestern Nigeria as affected by the colonial wage economy. Although the material here reaches back to the late nineteenth century, the book is primarily concerned with the period from about 1930 through the early 1960s. These were years of rapid economic growth and social change, fueled both by colonial initiatives and African ambitions. The late colonial and early independence periods were the era of "modernization," in which planners as well as Nigerians from many walks of life— and often with different meanings in mind—aspired to bring "progress" to economic, political, and social institutions. As I demonstrate, such modernization ideals bore important relationships to wage labor and gender relations. And although the country had not yet been transformed by the petroleum industry, the dreams of the 1940s, 1950s, and early 1960s continue in many ways to shape contemporary Nigerian life.

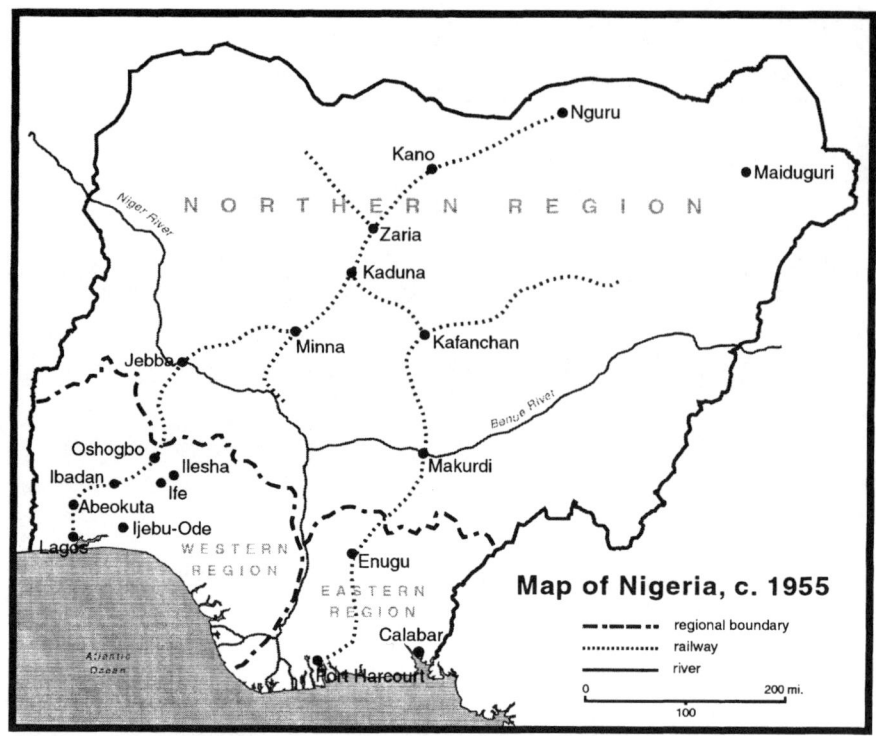

Map 1.1 Map of Nigeria designed and produced by Karin Breiwitz, Center for Teaching and Learning, University of North Carolina–Chapel Hill.

The title of this book—*Working with Gender*—reflects in multiple ways the intersection of wage labor, gender, and family life in colonial southwestern Nigeria and more broadly. On one hand, colonial administrators and employers worked with gender in the sense that they based policies on their assumptions about the ideal roles and attributes of men and women. As Frederick Cooper has written, "The gendering of the African worker was so profound it was barely discussed."[3] Yet colonial policies about labor and gender were also contradictory. As we will see, some officials eventually advocated family wages and other measures to help create "stabilized" domestic groups. But others continued to argue to Nigerian trade unions that African gender and family structures made many potential labor reforms, social welfare measures, and urban planning schemes impractical. In an era in which such initiatives were increasingly held to be universally applicable and part of a large-scale process of modernization, local gender and domestic arrangements became markers of cultural differences (and "backwardness") that colonizers used to justify racial discrimination in wage-fixing and other benefits. Thus, while idealistic colonizers hoped to *work with*, or transform, African gender relations for the purposes of raising labor productivity and increasing urban stability, European administrators and employers also *worked with* African gender by selectively using it as a foil for potentially expensive or undesirable colonial reforms.[4]

That is one part of the narrative of this book. Greater attention, however, is devoted to the numerous ways *Africans* worked with gender. The men readers will meet in this book brought gender with them when they went to work. Luise White pointed out over ten years ago that historians of Africa need to take male gender as seriously as we have come to take gender in women's lives. "Men were motivated by land shortages, poverty, and decreasing real wages," in typical historical portrayals, "but not by their qualms and anxieties about the changing rights and obligations of fatherhood."[5] Why should we assume that women were the only people for whom gender was decisive in shaping goals, constraints, and opportunities? The notion of male privilege is a familiar one, but we must go beyond this in examining the ways male lives have been bound up with expectations about how "real men" should conduct themselves. I argue in this book not only that men undertook wage labor for reasons largely having to do with their sense of themselves as men and their obligations and goals as sons, husbands, fathers, and relatives (as has been argued for a variety of contexts),[6] but also that workers' struggles and collective action were similarly motivated. As American historian Ava Baron has put it, "In learning to work and in working, in struggles between workers and employers over the nature and meaning of work, both sides construct and contest definitions of masculinity and femininity."[7] Agitation for wage increases, improved job security, and benefits obviously were about the material conditions that people lived and worked within. But those conditions related crucially to male (and female) workers' positions within their households and relations within communities—contexts that were fundamentally gendered. As a trade unionist noted during a 1963 strike threat, "It is this institution of extended family which is the root of labour unrest in Nigeria."[8] In the 1990s one labor commentator wrote that Nigeria "has a workforce that is most committed in terms of taking care of its families," and another noted that "the Nigerian worker is going to work for the upliftment of his [family] . . . his children are part of his stake in the work place."[9] Cooper has stressed that the new labor policies of the post–World War II era represented the intersection of metropolitan designs and African trade union activism.[10] This activism, I suggest, was motivated by assumptions and aspirations about gender and family life, just as the policies of colonial planners implicitly were. All sides of the colonial encounter were bringing gender to their notions of work.

In another meaning of the title of this book, I argue that wage earners actively manipulated, or *worked with*, gender in relation both to their colonial employer and to members of their households and families. Gender can be understood and explored in at least three different but overlapping ways: through discourse (that is, how people talk), through actions and practices (what people do), and through subjectivities (how people think about themselves).[11] Although interview material and other types of testimonies have allowed me to make some tentative assertions about wage earners' self-conceptions as men, the nature of the evidence means that this book contains vastly more material on gendered discourse and practices. Transformations in *discourse* about labor and gender were radical during the late colonial period. Steady wage earners increasingly defined themselves as financial providers for their wives and children, both at home in assertions of power and in union representations calling for a family wage and other social safety nets. Yet gendered *practices* were more complex. A former locomotive driver told me that career railway workers "had family lives just like those of other Nigerians, except that they traveled more," but the evidence I gathered only partially substantiates this.[12] Steady paychecks, along with ideas about the nature of "modern" families, and sometimes travel around the country, often focused railway households on the nuclear family and on a man's wage. Still, extended family and community concerns remained important for many, and wage earners did not assume that the image of a male provider could not coexist with wives' income earning. In fact, unions defended women's access to wage employment in the face of colonial government efforts to confine women to home and markets, and labor struggles over leave time and transfers made clear employees' commitments to their extended families. How can we account for the tensions between self-representation and practice, not to mention subjectivity? As the title of this book indicates, I assert that workers actively and strategically used arguments about gender to advance claims to a dignified and stable working life. These arguments bore *some* resemblance to actual practices, but did not neatly overlap with them.[13] Such men were *working with* gender.

LABOR AND GENDER IN COMPARATIVE CONTEXT

This book's underlying concern is with a broad issue: what effect does the expansion of wage labor have on relationships between men and women and on understandings about how women and men structure their lives? Is the normative pattern that emerged in Western Europe and North America, with men working for wages and women reproducing the household in unpaid labor at home, a universal one? Does long-term wage labor necessarily become a male preserve over time? What does this mean for working-class families?

Introduction

Fundamentally, these are questions about the social reproduction of labor.[14] In Great Britain, Nigeria's colonizer, a consensus had emerged by the early twentieth century that working-class households should generally be supported by "family" (or "breadwinner") wages. Ideally, employers were to pay for the reproduction of the labor force through wages disbursed to men (although these often were not in fact sufficient to support women and children). In return, wives' unpaid domestic work enabled men to sell their labor outside the home. This gendered allocation of labor was the result of many local struggles, but by the 1900s, it represented the strength of trade unions, the state's reluctance to intervene actively in the labor market, and employers' interest in social stability.[15] Trade unionists, for their part, tended to favor family wages because they raised income levels and because they buttressed working men's power and status within the household.[16] Family wages both reflected and reinforced a gender ideology encompassing separate spheres for men and women and a male breadwinner ideal.[17]

Although colonizers often did seek to impart their notions of gender to African elites and mission converts,[18] they did not initially expect African workers' households to replicate those of Europeans. In the areas with concentrated wage labor forces—the mining centers of southern and central Africa, along with port cities and railways throughout the continent—the original model was migrant labor, with men leaving their rural families to work for bounded periods of time. Colonial policy makers favored migrant labor as a corollary to indirect rule, in which Africans were to live and be governed through rurally based "tribes." Trade unions were weak until the 1940s, and the state often backed employers' low wages through extra-economic means of labor recruitment. In southern Africa, female-headed rural households in effect subsidized the reproduction of the male labor force, whose wages were otherwise too low to sustain itself.[19] In Nairobi, the state depended on urban labor for administration and services but refused to pay adequate wages or to commit itself to housing Africans permanently. Prostitutes stepped into the breech, earning their living by providing migrant workers with accommodation, food, and bathwater in addition to sexual services.[20] In the 1920s some mine owners in Zambia and the Belgian Congo began to move away from the migrant labor model, calculating that workers would be more enthusiastic and productive if they were allowed to bring their families to the mining compounds, where wives could garden and cook for their husbands. But rural African elders complained about their loss of control over women and long-term migrants, prompting conflict between a state that supported "native authorities" and companies seeking to ensure the most efficient maintenance of their workers.[21]

Compared with the "new" cities of the colonial era such as Johannesburg, Nairobi, and the urban parts of the Copperbelt, where the relationship between wage labor and gender has been studied more extensively, Nigeria had little migrant labor and several well-established urban areas already peopled with African families. West Africa's economic focus on peasant agriculture meant that wage labor was less developed than farther east or south, yet the state and commercial enterprises did need workers in administrative centers and along transportation and communication routes. It was a foregone conclusion that such wage earners would be male, but where women earned income in their own enterprises, as in southern Nigeria, employees were paid cheaply on the grounds that they had no need to support wives and children (as I detail in chapter 3). Thus, even though the specific circumstances varied throughout Africa, nowhere did colonial officials before World War II believe that "family" wages were appropriate or necessary to reproduce an African working class. African workers were not like European workers, nor were their families comparable to European families.

This type of thinking was challenged during the "second colonial occupation" of the postwar era.[22] In the 1940s and 1950s, Britain's and France's shortages of hard currency and the loss of many of their Asian colonies made them all the more dependent on African economies. But colonial promises of reform after the peace, intensified nationalist aspirations, and Africans' frustration with continued hardship led to the most intense series of urban disturbances the governments had yet seen—including the 1945 strike in Nigeria, which is examined in chapter 4. This was the context for a new emphasis on "development," which was intended both to prime colonial economies and to illustrate that imperial rule was actually beneficial for Africans. Ambitious planners attempted to rationalize peasant agriculture to increase production, stabilize wage labor to improve efficiency, and reshape African cities to make them less disorderly. They hoped that given the proper institutions and incentives Africans would work in industries, commercial undertakings, and agricultural enterprises in a manner comparable to Europeans. Although many colonial officials continued to see Africans as "backward" or mired in tradition, reformers in this period argued that Africans could and should become "modern."[23]

What effects did labor stabilization measures have on urban African families? Researchers have been considering this question for decades. In the 1940s and 1950s, a number of sociologists and anthropologists conducted studies on the links between social and economic changes in urban Africa and the home lives of wage workers, particularly on the Zambian Copperbelt but also in the urban areas of Kenya, South Africa, and elsewhere. The results of this research both reinforced and complicated the views of bureaucrats and labor officers. Many of the urban anthropologists were sympathetic to the stabilization/modernization project, insisting that Africans could and were entitled to participate in "progress" just as others were, and their reports indicated that urban Africans were becoming increasingly "modern" in their lifestyles and outlooks. But they also stressed the social costs of urbanization and stabilization: African cities were sites of terrible poverty and insecurity; while crime, juvenile delinquency, and unstable marriages were (supposedly temporary) results of Africans' separation from their rural communities. The urban African research of the postwar era made it clear that "modernization" was happening in complicated ways shaped by local cultures and that change could occur in one part of a worker's life but not necessarily in others.[24] Studies of urban women from this era further destabilized the stabilization model, showing them as financially independent from men or else impoverished by their reliance on men's wages.[25]

Colonial-era researchers often distinguished between more or less educated Africans and pointed to a reworking of ethnic and other affiliations in towns. But the major innovation in more recent studies has been their explicit attention to the differentiation of urban African populations along lines including access to resources, skill, and gender, and the intersection of that differentiation with both official efforts and personal strategies. On the Copperbelt, in southern Rhodesia, and in Nairobi, officials worked to control urban families in the postwar period by regulating access to housing. Women frequently were denied rights to live in the city except as dependents of working men, and independent women faced harassment and regulation by colonial officials in collusion with rural African patriarchs. Yet women also worked creatively to earn their living by offering the goods and services urban men needed and forming strategic alliances, sometimes of a temporary nature, with men who had access to housing. "Respectable" urban families, composed of elites or of steadily employed urban workers, often jockeyed to differentiate themselves from the informally and unemployed around them.[26] On the Zambian Copperbelt, the relatively fluid marital arrangements of the 1930s had become less frequent by the 1950s, when the government became committed to more permanent urbanization for African workers. Various influential groups—state officials, rural patriarchs, and missionaries—had a stake in tightening control over marriages and female mobility, but this change may have had more to do with the rising influence of urban elites and their concerns with respectability. As Jane Parpart argues, in Zambia "the move towards stabilized, urban family life involved struggles between Africans as well as alterations in colonial policy."[27] But similar struggles could also lead in other directions, away from any ideal of nuclear families living together, relying on a husband's wage. Even in Zambia, as James Ferguson points out, most domestic units were *not* nuclear households formed around married couples.[28] In Accra (Ghana), when some men became skilled workers or educated professionals in the colonial and postcolonial periods, this did not necessarily improve the lives of their wives or other women with whom they were associated, who struggled to balance financial interests with personal autonomy. Indeed, as the numbers of skilled and literate male workers in Accra increased, so did sex segregation in housing.[29] Thus, it is difficult generalize about how late colonial initiatives reshaped the home lives of urban workers, because the differentiation of the labor force had uneven effects across urban populations, because labor stabilization and other associated policies were incompletely realized, and because these official efforts were shaped by the agency of the people to whom they were directed, and this agency in turn was rooted in local contexts.

WAGE LABOR, GENDER, AND COLONIALISM IN SOUTHWESTERN NIGERIA

At first glance, Nigeria seems an unlikely setting for any study of wage labor, since the vast majority of its economically active population has always been, and still is, engaged in nonwage activities. An International Labor Organization report from the mid-1950s listed Nigeria as the African colony least involved in a wage economy, with 4 percent of the able-bodied adult male population working for wages (as opposed, e.g., to 7.9 percent in French West Africa, 18.3 percent in the Gold Coast, 29.9 percent in Kenya, and 38.3 percent in the Belgian Congo).[30] But even though Nigeria's colonial economy was based on the export of agricultural produce, wage labor was vitally important in creating and maintaining transport and communications infrastructure, as well as staffing mercantile firms and the state bureaucracy. Wage-earners were concentrated in southern Nigeria, particularly in the administrative and commercial center Lagos and along ports and railway depots. In 1950, 13 percent of the population of Lagos (or 30,544 people) earned wages.[31]

Differentiation was a central feature of the stabilization of wage labor in Nigeria as elsewhere, as we see in chapter 6. But the relationship between differentiation and the overt actions of the state—as through housing policies and influx controls—was more tenuous in Nigeria than in Zambia or Zimbabwe, largely because the cities of southwestern Nigeria predated colonialism.[32] Lagos and Ibadan, the two cities with the greatest numbers of wage earners, serve as examples. Lagos was founded in the fifteenth century and became a center of the Atlantic slave trade in the late eighteenth century. In the 1800s it developed into West Africa's leading center of international trade and colonial capital, with a rapidly growing population consisting of local immigrants seeking economic opportunities and physical security from the Yoruba wars in the interior, as well as liberated slaves from Sierra Leone and Brazil. By 1866, the town's population had grown to 25,000.[33] During this period, commerce in palm products replaced the slave trade, missionaries promoted Christianity and western education, and European interference in local commerce and politics increased. Annexed by Britain in 1861, Lagos became the capital of southern Nigeria and then of the colony and protectorate of Nigeria after the expansion of colonial rule in the 1890s. In comparison to Lagos, Ibadan is a relatively young city, but it still was well established by the period of European conquest. Ibadan was founded during the Yoruba wars of the late eighteenth and early nineteenth centuries. In 1829 it became a military garrison and center for refugees, where free men were trained for war and slaves and captives did the farming. By the mid-nineteenth century, Ibadan was the preeminent Yoruba city-state, with control over numerous other towns, an active army, and a unique political structure based on rotating leadership. In 1893, when it became part of the British Protectorate of Southern Nigeria, Ibadan's population was estimated at 150,000.[34] During the colonial period, Ibadan continued to expand as a center of cocoa production and marketing, becoming in 1946 capital of the western provinces and then the Western Region. Until it was surpassed by Lagos in the 1960s, Ibadan was the largest city in sub-Saharan Africa, with a population of 387,359 in 1931, swelling to 460,000 by 1952. Lagos, Nigeria's commercial and administrative center, grew from 126,108 in 1931 to 267,407 in 1950 and 665,246 in 1963.[35]

In Salisbury, Nairobi, or the mining towns of the Zambian Copperbelt, the goal of stabilization required relocating workers' families to urban environments, where the labor force could be replenished and a new generation reproduced in a stable milieu, separated from the rural extended family and other "disorderly" elements. Influx controls and urban housing were key to such a transformation. In Yorubaland, with its long history of urbanism, planners rarely even considered such measures. Many wage-earners were already established with their families near their places of employment, along with extended kin and countless social and economic networks. Even most migrants tended to stay within their own region, where their social connections were relatively nearby. It thus proved practically impossible to separate a class of workers from the informal sector, the unemployed, or numerous relatives. With their long-established populations and institutions, Lagos, Ibadan, and the smaller Yoruba cities could exert counter-pressure on colonial planners and adapt to new developments within some preexisting urban structures. Their history has the potential to modify Africanists' understanding of colonialism's influence on gender and domestic life among wage-earning populations, since no such research has been based in the "old" cities of West Africa. How much did different historical, geographic, and cultural contexts matter in shaping African life to colonial designs?

Yoruba culture would seem to both hinder and facilitate gender changes associated with wage labor. On one hand, in southwestern Nigeria the gendered ideals implicit in colonial policies met an equally powerful but very different body of assumptions about the respective roles of men and women. Yoruba women have a history of economic independence from men, typically based on careers in market trading. Married couples historically have not pooled their incomes, and in the past there was very little expectation that husbands would act as exclusive, or even primary, providers for wives and children.[36] In fact, many of Lagos's Christian elites around the turn of the twentieth century did form so-called "Ordinance marriages," that is, legally binding monogamous marriages in which husbands were expected to financially support their wives. But so many of these husbands took "outside wives" and/or neglected their "legitimate" spouses that within a generation the trend had reversed. Even elite Christians then trained their daughters for a profession under the assumption that women must be financially able to take care of themselves. The rise of a male breadwinner ethos among many southwestern Nigerians, which I describe in chapter 5, thus represents a significant departure in the region's social history.

Part of the explanation for such a transformation, I argue, relates to other local cultural currents. First, as is covered in chapter 2, Yorubaland's longstanding commercialization has meant that people there placed, and continue to place, special importance on money. By undergirding processes that contribute to status and personal relationships, money in Yoruba culture is and has been fundamental to social life and identity.[37] Stable wage labor offered men new access to money, which in turn had important implications for their places in homes and communities, as well as their self-definitions as men. Further, since at least the nineteenth century, individuals and Yoruba communities have equated "enlightenment" with the selective incorporation of ideas and materials from outside their boundaries. The specific pathways to "progress" have changed over time, but for many, they entailed converting to Christianity or Islam, imbibing Western education, acquiring development goods, and migrating at least temporarily in pursuit of these.[38] I take up this theme in greater detail below, but here I note that mid-twentieth-century wage and salary earners' engagement with what were perceived as "modern" family forms and gender relations rested at least in part on long-term, local trends. And, finally, workers and trade unionists frequently *talked about* changing family forms and gender relations with more intensity than they actually *lived* and *practiced* them. Local culture may help to explain this as well. In realms as diverse as economic decision making, religious change, and theatrical production, southwestern Nigerians have embraced "potentiality."[39] In essence, leaving one's options open has been an important, culturally valued strategy in many contexts. We should not be surprised, then, that wage and salary earners made similarly creative and flexible moves in their use of gender discourses vis-à-vis employers and the state.

UNDERSTANDING (MALE) GENDER

One of the most basic assumptions behind this study is that work—both what people put into it and get from it—has some bearing on gender, just as gender has shaped the kind of work that variously defined people do. By now it has become commonplace in academic circles to write of the constructedness of gender and its malleability in historical context. Gender is a multidimensional concept, carrying descriptive and prescriptive elements. At is most basic, gender is a social category imposed on bodies, an understanding about what it means to be male and female. But it also signifies relationships between and among men and women and their relative positions in society. As a fundamental aspect of social relations—including economic ones—gender forms a major component of personal identity and subjectivity. Even when they are not necessarily followed, gender norms provide people with ways of understanding and leading good or bad lives as men and women. This description positions gender relations as a structure of society, but they are also historically contingent and continually transforming. In a continual cycle, gender norms form the social apparatus within which people operate, while that structure is modified through the practices of individuals shaped by it.[40]

How does that work? A persuasive answer is that gender is "performative," that is, "constituted by the very 'expressions' that are said to be its results." People "do gender," in a sense, by acting in particular ways for particular reasons, some of which have to do with existing gender ideologies but some of which can be improvisations for specific ends. Yet these improvisations do not come from thin air. As Judith Butler puts it, they are produced under "situations of duress," in response to social and economic constraints. These new practices can then influence what people consider to be normative behavior for (certain groups of) men and women. When people engage in actions that they define as male or female, or when they attribute male or female characteristics to particular actions overtly or through the subtleties of language or symbolism, they help to create or maintain ideologies and structures of gender. Similarly, people challenge and transform notions of gender by engaging in behavior seen as transgressive or unseemly.[41]

Although there are relatively few studies of labor and gender in Africa to draw conclusions from, a richer literature from other areas provides examples of how changes in work and its remuneration have had important implications for how male workers have related to women and to each other. Sonya Rose has argued that British capitalism developed as a gendered set of practices through industrial structures, state policies, and political activities. These, in turn, were significantly shaped by the ideologies of the bourgeois and laboring classes. In this way, gender was constitutive of economic and class relations, even as it was shaped by them.[42] In Europe and North America, male workers have often engaged in two interrelated struggles: to resist the power of capitalists over workers and to extend or defend male dominance over women. Because of preindustrial norms linking men's gender identity to independent production, industrialization brought on what some historians have identified as a "crisis in masculinity," and artisans often defended their autonomy and respectability in terms of male prerogatives. But the meaning of masculinity on the job was transformed during the transition from craft to mass production: what workers used in the late nineteenth century as a tool in workplace struggles and in claims to respectability was by the twentieth century turned against them, as employers used claims about what manhood was supposed to mean to exhort workers to greater production and identification with industrial work. At the same time, there were fierce struggles between working men and women within households and communities over who should earn income, in what types of jobs, and how that income should be allocated.[43]

The same double dynamic can be applied in African labor history: workers and employers often framed their conflicts in terms of the rights and obligations of manhood, while wage labor facilitated transformations in gender relations within homes and communities.[44] The racialized structure of African colonialism adds an extra dimension to these relations as well, even though class divisions were often expressed in racial terms in Europe, too. In their construction of the "African worker," Carolyn Brown notes, colonial officials and employers feminized and infantilized African men. She argues that gender was constantly created and recreated both through the work experience, where African men had their closest contact with a racialized European masculine power, and, at the same time, in the roles that these men were able to assume because of their work (and pay) in the broader society. The same worker could be a "man" in the village and yet, in the parlance of colonial officials, a "boy" in the workplace.[45] This doubly gendered identity was a particular feature of domestic work. African servants in expatriate homes both entered a public sphere to earn wages that could be used to expand their own households—something adult men did—and engaged in "women's work"; for Europeans, they could be both less than full men and also sexually threatening.[46] In other contexts, steady wage work may have offered some men material benefits and access to the trappings of colonial power at the price of making them feared and stigmatized as men in their home communities. Through the colonial and postcolonial periods, east and central African firemen, policemen, game wardens, and health workers were the subjects of pervasive rumors about vampirism, and Luise White suggests that these rumors reflected ambivalent attitudes toward colonial power and the men and physical objects associated with it.[47] Thus the same situations that provided new expressions of adult masculinity could also undermine some men's masculine standing, and vice versa.

As these examples indicate, gender must be seen as a relational and situational concept, and not only about relations between men and women. In this book, I show the ways that wage earners and their trade unions articulated ideals and expectations of men within marriages; within families as fathers, sons, brothers, and other relatives; and within hierarchies of men in workplaces, communities, and politics. It makes no sense to assume a kind of monolithic "African" masculinity that confronted an equally monolithic "European" or "colonial" one.[48] Similarly, I find the notions of "hegemonic" and "subordinate" masculinities only partially useful in colonial Africa, although they have become popular elsewhere. The sociologist R.W. Connell has outlined four categories or levels of masculine privilege—hegemonic, complicitous, marginalized, and subordinate—which represent various abilities to enjoy what he calls the "patriarchal dividend," or the "advantage men in general gain from the overall subordination of women." Connell argues that at any given time "one form of masculinity rather than others is culturally exalted" and defines this dominant, hegemonic masculinity "as the configuration of gender practice which embodies the currently accepted answer to the problem of the legitimacy of patriarchy." Subordinated masculinities are located at the bottom of the power hierarchy because they are the ones most intensely opposed by hegemonic masculinities. Connell stresses that the four forms of masculinity are not identities or personalities and that insofar as an individual's set of practices fits any (or a combination) of these categories, that person will experience a related level of access to social validation and power.[49]

The concept of plural masculinities rightly emphasizes that maleness and femaleness can carry multiple meanings within a society, and that power relations affect which definitions become normative. Certainly such an insight applies to colonial situations, which included gender norms imposed from outside as well as (perhaps competing) indigenous values and practices. But in such cases, how can we call one vision hegemonic and others subordinate? The limited reach of colonial ideologies, combined with the social flux created by new constraints and opportunities, meant that a "multiplicity of competing masculine identities" interacted with more complexity than in Connell's original formulation.[50] Stephan Miescher's work with retired Presbyterian teachers in Ghana suggests that these men creatively and consciously adapted their strategies and self-presentations in an environment of plural gender ideologies, which they did not perceive as ranked according to a particular hierarchy.[51] Similarly, I show in this book that Nigerian wage and salary earners consciously grappled with their roles as men, engaging with, adopting, and discarding various aspects of what were perceived as European, Yoruba, Nigerian, "modern," elite, or working-class masculinities. They were *working with gender*.

GENDER AND MODERNIZATION

The people studied in this book were engaged in a similarly active and eclectic process with the concept of *modernization*. Postwar plans for remaking colonial Africa were based on assumptions that were by the late 1950s being articulated in modernization theory: that directed social change was possible, that it would move "less developed" countries along a path previously traveled by "more developed" countries, and that it involved a bundle of traits that automatically appeared together—including status based on achievement rather than ascription, secular instead of religious forms of authority, and (importantly for this study) more nuclear, stable families. Scholars are now more skeptical about the analytical value of abstractions such as modernization and modernity than a generation or two ago, but it is important to remember that these were also categories deployed and internalized by the actors involved.[52] Critics in and from Europe's colonies were deeply engaged with questions of how their modernity intersected with or challenged Western-directed social, political, and economic transformations, but as Cooper points out, focusing on a specific issue like labor (or, I would add, gender) helps us "to draw out the complexity of these issues in ways that generalized debates over colonialism and westernization did not necessarily allow."[53]

The idea of "enlightenment" or "civilization" (Ọ̀lajú—from the verb meaning "to open the eyes") was an old one in Yoruba communities. As John Peel has detailed, the term ọ̀lajú was first used to describe the cultural package brought by European missionaries, including technical, medical, and clerical skills as well as Christianity. By the 1920s it became a popular ideology, largely because Western education was clearly identified as a springboard for success in the colonial economy. Ọ̀lajú also referred to those who were not necessarily well educated, but who gained worldly knowledge by pursuing trading opportunities away from the hometown. Either way, the central idea was to use knowledge or experience derived from beyond the local community to advance individual careers and, through the combined efforts of many, bring the material benefits of "progress" back home. By the 1940s, as opportunities for the educated multiplied, new elites provided the leadership of urban associations and challenged chiefs for positions of authority in the towns. Ọ̀lajú described both their personal qualifications and their association with the universally held value of communal aggrandizement.[54]

It was in this context that the postwar Western ideology of modernization had local saliency, since, like ọ̀lajú it implied progressive change on both individual and societal levels. Many of the skilled workers and trade unionists described in this book saw the concepts of modernity and modernization as both representative of the changes they observed in the world around them and useful for demanding concrete benefits like family wages, pensions, and other aspects of honorable and stable working-class life. "Modernization" also helped people describe home lives that included spousal co-residence, a male breadwinner ideal, and infrequent hometown visits. Indeed, where "modernization" most differed from ọ̀lajú was in the former concept's assumptions about family life. Modernization theory's rational individual was not only implicitly male, but provided financial support to a nuclear family and was otherwise unencumbered by kin and communal ties.[55] But through their continued aspirations to "big man" status, maintenance of relatives, and participation in local patronage networks—all of which European commentators saw as "traditional," and all of which were consistent with *ọlajú*—workers asserted that the attributes of modernity did not form a "package" to be adopted completely or not at all. Even as they attempted to claim and make use of "enlightenment," workers and others were wary of abandoning so-called traditional ways completely. According to a recent theoretical overview, "Everywhere, at every national/cultural site, modernity is not one but many; modernity is not new, but old and familiar; modernity is incomplete and necessarily so."[56] For the colonial workers in this book, multiple modernities were based on configurations of imported values, *ọlajú* (itself a changing mix of imports and local influences), and new material circumstances. These ideals about modernity intersected with multiple masculinities as an array of possibilities for leading lives of dignity and progress.

For a time, roughly between the late 1950s and the early 1980s, the concrete manifestations of modernization seemed to be coming to career workers. Incomes and benefits were on the rise—albeit more slowly and unequally than many wanted—and as chapters 5 and 6 show, family lives were in transformation. The change in gender and domesticity that the postwar initiatives suggested made family relations central to what modernization was supposed to mean.[57] But this ideal could also unravel, in Nigeria and elsewhere. In Zambia, according to James Ferguson, workers' hopes for better lives with stabilization and unionization were defeated by the fall of copper prices in the 1970s and the failure of mining companies and the state to create the conditions for the working class to reproduce itself.[58] In Nigeria by the 1990s, the economy had declined drastically, and the state had lost its political legitimacy. Many, particularly older, Nigerians interpreted the loss of the modernization dream as a tragedy and a betrayal. Political and economic crises took away much of what an entire generation or two of Nigerians had sought and thought they had done something to attain. In the end, the stabilization and modernization project worked to redefine the male role for a particular group of people in a way that cannot be fulfilled in the conditions of contemporary Nigerian life.[59]

WORKERS ON THE NIGERIAN RAILWAY

This book is part labor history, part social history, part the history of ideology, and part demographic history. While archival research revealed some of these pieces, the social and demographic history components necessitated a case study of workers who could stand reasonably well for career wage earners in general and whose family lives could be traced over time. Railway workers were the obvious choice. The Government Railway was the largest single employer of Nigerian wage labor throughout the colonial period. Railway employment began in 1896 with the massive project of clearing land and laying hundreds of miles of track. The 123-mile link between Lagos and Ibadan opened in 1901, at a time when the railway workforce numbered over 10,000.[60] The rail system took shape over the next sixty-five years, ultimately including a western line from Lagos beyond Kano to Nguru in the north, and an eastern line from Port Harcourt to Maiduguri, with links between the two at Kaduna and Zaria. In 1938, 30 percent of an estimated 182,000 wage earners in Nigeria worked for the government. Of those, 19,153 were railway employees, who comprised 11 percent of the wage labor pool.[61] The railway workforce exceeded 20,000 by 1943 and topped 30,000 in 1952.[62] In 1965, railway workers, still at about 30,000, accounted for 5 percent of all wage earners in Nigeria.[63] The largest group of railway employees were based in Lagos, where in 1950, 15 percent of the 30,544 wage earners counted by the census (or 4,579) were railway employees.[64] There were also large concentrations at the regional railway hubs of Ibadan, Enugu, and Zaria.

Although the Nigerian Railway drew its workforce from all over the country, the majority of its employees in the southwest and significant numbers in the other regions were from Yoruba communities. A 1934 survey of station staff identified 90 percent in the western provinces, 45 percent in the north, and 15 percent in the east as Yoruba. Its author suggested that because of their longer access to Western-style education and job training, Yoruba and Igbo workers predominated on the railways even in northern Nigeria, particularly as clerks and artisans.[65] A random sample of personnel files from the railway's Western District showed that between 1920 and 1984, 51 percent of the employees, in all job categories, were Yoruba, with other southern Nigerians forming the majority of the remainder.[66] And a 1958 survey of workers in the Ebute Metta railway workshops indicated that 63 percent were from western Nigeria, with 30 percent from the eastern region and 7 percent from the north.[67] In the Western Region particularly, Yoruba culture was instrumental in shaping workplace interactions.

Moreover, the Railway was intimately involved with twentieth-century urban development in Nigeria (as elsewhere). In remote areas or small towns, railway stations became centers of communities peopled by wage-earners, traders catering to them, and various hangers-on.[68] Ebute Metta, on the mainland opposite Lagos island, is the city's second-oldest neighborhood, originally settled in the nineteenth century by Christian refugees from Abeokuta. The site of Railway workshops, much employee housing, and wage-earner socializing, Ebute Metta grew into the lively and congested neighborhood

Introduction

Photo 1.1 Nigerian Railway Corporation headquarters, Ebute Metta, Lagos.

described, among other places, in Cyprian Ekwensi's book of stories, *Lokotown*.[69] In Ibadan the railway stimulated commerce and made the city a collecting and trading center for the surrounding agricultural lands. Physically and socially, Ibadan developed into two cities: an old district in the eastern half, separated by a ridge of hills from the new settlement centered on the railway on the western side. There, a business community composed of European enterprises and local traders developed along with residential settlements primarily inhabited by immigrants from other parts of Yorubaland and Nigeria.

Railway work entailed diverse occupations and levels of skill. Permanent way employees, led by gangers (so-called because they were in charge of work gangs), ensured that the track was maintained and saw to any necessary construction or earth work. Train crews included those who actually ran the machinery—engine drivers assisted by firemen and engine cleaners—and those who saw to passengers, traffic, and baggage—guards (conductors), ticket collectors, and brakemen. Although they were subject to serious disruptions of their social and family arrangements, engine drivers and guards enjoyed high prestige among railway men and passengers. Station masters were also something of an elite. Often the products of mission schools or well-established families, they were the lords of their domains, supervising traffic, paperwork and ticketing, and the movement of trains and vehicles within the station limits. Inside they were assisted by clerks, telegraph operators, and signalmen; outside a number of yard personnel like shunters and switchmen worked at all hours. The large railway workshops, housed at Ebute Metta (Lagos), Enugu, and Zaria, provided employment for artisans who maintained the rolling stock and manufactured tools and parts. Finally, a relatively small number of clerks at the Ebute Metta headquarters and the divisional hubs kept records and staffed the Railway Printer.[70]

From early in the twentieth century, the railway represented modernity to administrators, workers, and the general public. The Nigerian Railway's 1935 annual report noted proudly that " 'progress' emanates, so to speak, from every train from Lagos that steams into Kano."[71] The railway introduced regulated concepts of time, helped promote the use of currency, and spread the English and pidgin languages, according to historian Wale Oyemakinde. Moreover, railway employees were differentiated from others in Nigeria by their familiarity with industrial technology and relatively high skill levels, as well as a cosmopolitan outlook resulting from long-distance travel and a multiethnic workforce.[72] Wole Soyinka's father, according to the writer, was amazed on his first voyage, probably in the 1920s, to observe "this railway world of iron and steel and fat wooden slippers; nothing could match the flag in the hand of the station guard, his censorious eye sweeping up and down the platform, flag upraised, smartly dropped, followed by a nod of acknowledgment from the grimy, sweat-soaked engine driver who leant so casually, so confidently, so fully 'in control' of this monster in which they could actually stretch their legs and walk. . . . Everything was excessive!" He continued to marvel, "this was not a market nor was it Isara. This was THE WORLD. The railway denizens are different from the rest of humanity."[73]

The railway pioneered labor stabilization in Nigeria, both because its labor force was vital to the colonial economy and because its powerful trade unions demanded improvements in job security, wages, and benefits. Although casual workers remained the majority until the 1960s, beginning in the 1940s increasing numbers of railway personnel were transferred to the "permanent establishment." The railway's long-term employees were among the best-remunerated in Nigeria, earning regular pay increases, fringe benefits, and pensions in exchange for providing dependable service wherever they were sent. They also were subject to concerted official attempts to reshape and control the labor force. Nevertheless, railway employees, like others occupying the "middle levels" of colonial African societies, remained rooted in their home communities even as they were influenced by official projects.[74] Career workers, who were crucial to the operation of the late colonial economy, were also in a position to shape the nature of wage labor and to impose their own ideas of gender and domesticity on colonial structures.

In order to construct a social and family history of highly stabilized workers, I pursued two types of research. The heart of the investigation consisted

Introduction

Photo 1.2 Nigerian Railway Corporation Pensioners' Welfare Association headquarters, Ebute Metta, Lagos.

of an extensive survey and more open-ended interviews with retired railway men and their wives in Lagos and Ibadan in 1993–1994. One hundred sixty-seven railway pensioners and fifty-three of their wives were located through meetings of the pensioners' union and referrals. A Yoruba-speaking research assistant and/or I asked them a series of questions about their backgrounds, education, work and marital histories, contacts with different types of relatives, residences, and associations.[75] We followed these questionnaires with longer interviews with approximately thirty of those in the initial pool. To obtain information on a larger group of railway men, with whom those surveyed could be compared statistically, I also made a random sample of 434 personnel files from the Ibadan and Lagos pension offices of the Nigerian Railway Corporation (NRC). These files were classified according to whether the retiree had been a "pensioner," who retired from a pensionable appointment, or an "annuitant," who received a lump-sum payment upon completion of a set minimum number of years' service in a "nonpensionable" job. A comparison of pensioners and annuitants points to some of the ways the lives of long-term, stable workers differed from those of other wage earners. These groups, in turn, could be compared with other members of the population portrayed in other sources.

Using railway men to study the effects of stable wage labor is problematic in the sense that railway work is not entirely like other types of wage earning. As elsewhere in Africa and the world, Nigerian railway workers were both integrated into and isolated from larger communities, both similar to and different from other workers.[76] The necessities of travel, irregular hours, and particular skills and job trajectories set railway life apart and helped to create close communities among railway men that often cut across ethnicity, religion, and occupational specialty. But railway men did maintain links to wider communities. To set the experiences of railway families within the larger context of urban wage work in southwestern Nigeria, I have drawn on information about other groups of wage earners and urban residents generally from court records, administrative reports, newspapers, and fictional accounts produced in Nigeria in the late colonial period.

This study necessarily privileges a male point of view in regard to gender and domestic relations, primarily because of the research methods I used. While I began with the intention of spending roughly equal time with (male) former wage-earners and their wives and family members, a number of considerations made this difficult. I located the women through their husbands, since that was the only way I could tell which women in the population were wives of wage-earners. Often my having talked to their husbands first made women reluctant to tell me "their side" of stories. Sometimes husbands even discouraged me from contacting their spouses or made themselves part of the conversations between myself and their wives. But the most important consideration was something that is crucial to the story told in this book: retired men had the time to talk, whereas their wives' hectic schedules of income earning (generally through market trade), housework, and child (or grandchild) care gave them little time to indulge a researcher's questions. Most of the men I interviewed considered themselves "retired," even if they were engaged in some income-generating activities for some part of their days. Not only did they have time for conversation, but also many seemed to feel neglected and underappreciated by the wider public. Most were delighted that I was interested in their pasts and seemed likely to publicize their previous contributions to building Nigeria. They were also eager to know about my world and to discuss politics, the economy, and relations between the United States and Nigeria. Most of the time in these interviews I felt like I had become to some degree or another an "honorary man," participating (marginally, of course) in these male retirees' world of railway work, trade unionism, and armchair politics. This status, I think, also prevented me from becoming closer to many of the women I interviewed. Still, it is utterly crucial to recognize gender as a *relational* category and not to analyze men without women and vice versa. Thus I have worked to keep women's concerns and agency as part of my narrative, even as a primary concern of this book is masculinity.

Meeting and talking with retired workers and their family members in the mid-1990s raised the issues that are central to this book. Generally everyone was struggling to make ends meet in the harsh economic and political environment of structural adjustment policies and military rule. Under the circumstances, it makes sense that older people would describe the past as a time of prosperity and stability. But what I found striking was the *terms* these pensioners used to idealize the past, nearly all centering on masculinity and modernity. Thirty to fifty years ago, the general narrative went, they had prided themselves as skilled workers, earned steady salaries, counted on a government pension, and structured their social and family lives accordingly. They were "modern men" and important family providers. Now the railway corporation is virtually bankrupt, and the pensioners are forced, in the main, to live from the continued trading income of their wives. They speak now of literal "postmodernism": that is, in the past, they and Nigeria were on the road to progress, but now that progress has been derailed by poor leadership and economic downturn. These interviews brought up the central themes of this study: the complex history of a male breadwinner norm among working southern Nigerians, the partial reconfiguration of family forms and relations associated with urban wage-earning, and the conceptual linkages between wage labor, changing family life, and modernization.

The next chapter of this book lays the groundwork for later discussions of changing social relations associated with stable wage labor by describing various masculinities in early twentieth-century Yorubaland and their close associations with money. I trace the development of wage employment and the factors that led some young men to choose it. Finally, I show that although money was crucial for status and personal relations, within marriages as well as in other contexts, men were not expected to be exclusive financial providers for their wives and children.

Chapter 3 reveals official thinking about wage labor and African life between the 1930s and 1940s and the ways that these top-down views intersected with workers' own experiences and concerns. During the decades before World War II, administrators and employers justified a lack of attention to labor conditions by insisting upon the marginality of wage labor to African life. Yet many wage-earners did make long careers, and their organizations agitated for concessions to workers' family commitments. This agitation helped to change officials' views of African workers' families. Whereas during the depression administrators in Nigeria viewed hometown connections as important safety nets that justified a lack of labor reform, by the early 1940s they saw chain migration, based on hometown connections, as the root of urban overcrowding and unemployment. As in the earlier period, colonial officials justified their reluctance to institute labor reforms through reference to wage-earners' extended families, even though the ways of understanding African family life had shifted over the previous decade.

Chapter 4 deals with the 1945 general strike, a massive labor demonstration that reveals the gendered nature of colonial discrimination and opposition to it. During the six-week agitation, working men demanded wages and benefits by referring to themselves as family breadwinners, even though most married women contributed to household budgets and the support of market women was critical in the strike's success. Further, trade union leaders demanded that the government pay family allowances to workers, not only because these were necessary to facilitate social reproduction, but also because European officials in Nigeria received them and Nigerian activists claimed that they were family providers just as the British men were. This debate—which centered on racial equality, colonial citizenship, and workers' dignity—was articulated in terms of domestic life and especially fatherhood.

Chapter 5 traces the expansion of the "male breadwinner" into a potent cultural ideal in Nigeria in the decades following that strike. Here I particularly stress an understanding of gender as performative. I argue that wage-earners actively manipulated ideas about gender in relation both to their colonial employer and to members of their households and families, while government officials and Nigerian women worked with gender for their own ends as well. Moreover, struggles over women's formal-sector employment show that the male breadwinner ideal contained crucial ambiguities and contradictions.

If chapter 5 is about the history of an ideology, chapter 6 seeks to answer the question of what labor stabilization actually did to workers' home lives and gender relations. As the labor force became increasingly differentiated, so did wage and salary earners' domestic lives. At the same time, family relationships were often described through the language of modernization, even if that term carried complex meanings in practice. Ironically, those upwardly mobile, career workers who were the objects of colonial labor stabilization policies were able to use the perquisites of their jobs—salaries, housing, medical and other benefits—to support large households and become important patrons, rather than form the small, nuclear families of official fantasies.

The differentiation of the labor force and of working people's family lives helped to fuel the general strike of 1964, the subject of chapter 7. In the face of galling inequalities between the elites of newly independent Nigeria and the mass of workers, unions not only demanded increased wages and improved conditions, but they called for the *abolition* of family allowances and other benefits that top officials had inherited from the colonial era. In other respects, too, the 1964 strike seemed an inversion of the general strike of 1945. A comparison of the general strikes of 1945 and 1964 highlights the increasing identification of wage labor as a male preserve, even as greater numbers of women undertook paid employment; the inseparability of labor differentiation from domesticity and masculinity; and the malleability of ideas about gender in changing political contexts.

NOTES

1. See, for instance, Niara Sudarkasa, *Where Women Work: A Study of Yoruba Women in the Marketplace and in the Home* (Ann Arbor, MI: Museum of Anthropology, 1973). The Igbo women of southeastern Nigeria also have a history of formidable political and economic power. See Ifi Amadiume, *Male Daughters, Female Husbands: Gender and Sex in an African Society* (London: Zed Books, 1987).

2. The seminal work is Frederick Cooper, *Decolonization and African Society: The Labor Question in French and British Africa* (Cambridge: Cambridge University Press, 1996).

3. Ibid., p. 266.

4. For a similar process in a different context, see Mrinalini Sinha, *Colonial Masculinity: The "Manly Englishman" and the "Effeminate Bengali" in the Late Nineteenth Century* (Manchester, England: Manchester University Press, 1995).

5. Luise White, "Separating the Men from the Boys: Constructions of Gender, Sexuality, and Terrorism in Central Kenya, 1939–1959," *IJAHS* 23 (1990):1–25; reworked as "Matrimony and Rebellion: Masculinity in Mau Mau," in Lisa A. Lindsay and Stephan F. Miescher (eds.), *Men and Masculinities in Modern Africa* (Portsmouth, NH: Heinemann, 2003).

6. Examples include William Beinart, *The Political Economy of Pondoland, 1860–1930* (Cambridge: Cambridge University Press, 1982); Bill Bravman, *Making Ethnic Ways: Communities and Their Transformations in Taita, Kenya, 1800–1950* (Portsmouth, NH: Heinemann, 1998); Patrick Harries, *Work, Culture, and Identity: Migrant Laborers in Mozambique and South Africa, 1860–1910* (Portsmouth, NH: Heinemann, 1994); T. Dunbar Moodie with Vivienne Ndatshe, *Going for Gold: Men, Mines and Migration* (Berkeley: University of California Press, 1994); and contributions in Lindsay and Miescher (eds.), *Men and Masculinities*. Jane Parpart has argued that conflicts over family resources fueled worker demands on the Copperbelt in the 1950s, while Carolyn Brown makes a similar case for Igbo coal miners in eastern Nigeria. See Jane L. Parpart, "The Household and the Mine Shaft: Gender and Class Struggles on the Zambian Copperbelt, 1926–64," *Journal of Southern African Studies* 13 (1986): 36–56; and Carolyn A. Brown,

"A 'Man' in the Village Is a 'Boy' in the Workplace: Colonial Racism, Worker Militance and Igbo Notions of Masculinity in the Nigerian Coal Industry, 1930–1945," *Men and Masculinities,* ed. Lindsay and Miescher. For the same argument in a European context, see Laura L. Frader and Sonya O. Rose, "Gender and the Reconstruction of European Working-Class History," in *Gender and Class in Modern Europe,* ed. Frader and Rose (Ithaca, NY: Cornell University Press, 1996).

7. Ava Baron, "Introduction" to Baron (ed.), *Work Engendered: Toward a New History of American Labor* (Ithaca, NY: Cornell University Press, 1991), p. 37.

8. James Ojiako, "More Money: Do Workers Deserve It?" DTN, October 29, 1963.

9. The first quote is by Stephen Faulkner of the Commonwealth Trade Union Council; the second is by Chidi Uzor; both are in Uzor, "Between Workers' Welfare and Their Productivity," the *Guardian* (Lagos), December 7, 1993, p. 13.

10. Cooper, *Decolonization.*

11. This distinction is drawn out more fully in Stephan F. Miescher and Lisa A. Lindsay, "Men and Masculinities in Modern African History," introduction to Lindsay and Miescher (eds.), *Men and Masculinities.*

12. D.A. Owolabi, January 20, 1994, Ibadan.

13. I am grateful to Luise White for suggesting this point in her comments on a panel on masculinity in African history, African Studies Association annual meeting, 1999, Philadelphia.

14. I follow Robertson and Berger in interpreting "the sphere of reproduction" as including "household labor, the care and socialization of children, and the reproduction of class-related attitudes that create both a new generation of workers and the value system necessary for the social order to survive." Claire Robertson and Iris Berger (eds.), *Women and Class in Africa* (New York: Africana Publishing Co., 1986), p. 9.

15. An overview is in Colin Creighton, "The Rise of the Male Breadwinner Family: A Reappraisal," *CSSH* 38 (1996): 310–37. Anna Clark, in *The Struggle for the Breeches: Gender and the Making of the British Working Class* (Berkeley: University of California Press, 1995), traces the origin of the breadwinner wage demand in Britain to trade unionists' political weakness in the 1830s.

16. See Sonya O. Rose, *Limited Livelihoods: Gender and Class in Nineteenth-Century England* (Berkeley: University of California Press, 1992).

17. The literature is best summarized in the excellent introductory essays in Baron (ed.), *Work Engendered* and Frader and Rose (eds.), *Gender and Class.* But these patterns were varied, although similar, elsewhere in Europe, as the contributions to the Frader and Rose volume make clear.

18. For instance, Kristin Mann, *Marrying Well: Marriage, Status and Social Change among the Educated Elite in Colonial Lagos* (Cambridge: Cambridge University Press, 1985); Christine Oppong, *Marriage among a Matrilineal Elite* (Cambridge: Cambridge University Press, 1974); Pamela Scully, *Liberating the Family? Gender and British Slave Emancipation in the Rural Western Cape, South Africa, 1823–1853* (Portsmouth, NH: Heinemann, 1997); and Karen Tranberg Hansen (ed.), *African Encounters with Domesticity* (New Brunswick, NJ: Rutgers University Press, 1992). An exception is Nancy Rose Hunt, "'Le Bebe en Brousse': European Women, African Birth Spacing and Colonial Intervention in Breast Feeding in the Belgian Congo," *IJAHS* 21 (1988): 401–32.

19. Harold Wolpe, "Capitalism and Cheap Labour-Power in South Africa: From Segregation to Apartheid," *Economy and Society* 1 (1972): 425–56; Colin Murray, *Families Divided: The Impact of Migrant Labour in Lesotho* (Johannesburg, 1981).

20. Luise White, *The Comforts of Home: Prostitution in Colonial Nairobi* (Chicago: University of Chicago Press, 1990).

21. George Chauncey Jr., "The Locus of Reproduction: Women's Labour in the Zambian Copperbelt, 1927–1953," *JSAS* 7 (1981): 135–64; Jane Parpart, "Class and Gender on the Copperbelt: Women in Northern Rhodesian Copper Mining Communities, 1926–1964," in *Women and Class,* ed. Robertson and Berger.

22. D.A. Low and J.M. Lonsdale, "Introduction: Towards the New Order, 1945–1963," in D.A. Low and Alison Smith (eds.), *History of East Africa,* vol. 3 (Oxford: Oxford University Press, 1976).

23. Cooper, *Decolonization.*

24. Much of this research is represented or summarized in C. Daryll Forde (ed.), *Social Implications of Industrialization and Urbanization in Africa South of the Sahara* (Paris: UNESCO, 1956); and Aidan Southall (ed.), *Social Change in Modern Africa* (London: International African Institute, 1961). Overviews tracing the study of urban Africa can be found in Peter C.W. Gutkind, "African Urban Family Life: Comment on and Analysis of Some Rural-Urban Differences," *Cahiers d'etudes africaines* 3 (1962): 149–217; Sally Falk Moore, *Anthropology and Africa: Changing Perspectives on a Changing Scene* (Charlottesville: University Press of Virginia, 1994), ch. 3; Cooper, *Decolonization,* 370–74; and, for the Copperbelt in particular, James Ferguson, *Expectations of Modernity: Myths and Meanings of Urban Life on the Zambian Copperbelt* (Berkeley: University of California Press, 1999).

25. Tanya Baker and Mary Bird, "Urbanisation and the Position of Women," *Sociological Review* NS 7 (1959): 99–122.

26. Among others, see Nancy Rose Hunt, "Noise over Camouflaged Polygamy, Colonial Morality Taxation and a Woman-Naming Crisis in Belgian Africa," *JAH* 32 (1991): 471–94; Timothy Scarnecchia, "The Politics of Gender and Class in the Creation of African Communities, Salisbury, Rhodesia, 1940–56," (Ph.D. dissertation, University of Michigan, 1993); White, *Comforts*; Chauncey, "Locus"; Parpart, "Class and Gender" and "'Wicked Women' and 'Respectable Ladies': Reconfiguring Gender on the Zambian Copperbelt, 1936–1964," in *"Wicked" Women and the Reconfiguration of Gender in Africa,* ed. Dorothy L. Hodgson and Sheryl A. McCurdy (Portsmouth, NH: Heinemann, 2001); and Elizabeth Schmidt, *Peasants, Traders, and Wives: Shona Women in the History of Zimbabwe* (Portsmouth, NH: Heinemann, 1992).

27. Jane L. Parpart, "'Where is your Mother?': Gender, Urban Marriage, and Colonial Discourse on the Zambian Copperbelt, 1924–1945," *IJAHS* 27 (1994): 241–71, 269 quoted.

28. Ferguson, *Expectations,* ch. 5.

29. Claire C. Robertson, *Sharing the Same Bowl: A Socioeconomic History of Women and Class in Accra, Ghana* (Bloomington: Indiana University Press, 1984), pp. 16–17, 57.

30. International Labour Organization, *African Labour Survey* (Geneva: ILO, 1958), p. 666. Similar figures are cited in All-Nigeria Trade Union Federation, "Paper on Need for Increasing Wage-Earning Employment in Nigeria," 1956, NLA/21.

31. Nigeria, *Lagos Census* (1950), pp. 83–84.

32. For the distinction between "old" and "new" colonial cities, see A.W. Southall, "Introductory Summary," in *Social Change,* ed. Southall.

33. Pauline H. Baker, *Urbanization and Political Change: The Politics of Lagos, 1917–1967* (Berkeley: University of California Press, 1974), p. 33. I find Kristin Mann's history of Lagos in chapter 1 of *Marrying Well* particularly useful.

34. Gilbert Carter, *Dispatch from Sir Carter Furnishing a General Report of the Lagos Interior Expedition* (1893), p. 54, cited in R.A. Akinola, "The Growth and Development of Ibadan, the Largest Yoruba Town," *Bulletin of the Ghana Geographical Association* 11 (1966): 48–63.

35. 1931, 1952, and 1963 Censuses.

36. N.A. Fadipe, *The Sociology of the Yoruba,* ed. by Francis Olu. Okediji and Oladejo O. Okediji (Ibadan: Ibadan University Press, 1970 [orig. 1940]), p. 88; Eleanor R. Fapohunda, "The Non-Pooling Household: A Challenge to Theory," in *A Home Divided: Women and Income in the Third World,* ed. Daisy Dwyer and Judith Bruce (Stanford, CA: Stanford University Press, 1988); Peter Marris, *Family and Social Change in an African City: A Study of Rehousing in Lagos* (Evanston, IL: Northwestern University Press, 1962), ch. 4; Sudarkasa, *Where Women Work.*

37. Karin Barber, "Money, Self-Realization, and the Person in Yoruba Texts," in *Money Matters: Instability, Values and Social Payments in the Modern History of West African Communities,* ed. Jane I. Guyer (Portsmouth, NH: Heinemann, 1994); Toyin Falola and Akanmu Adebayo, *Culture, Politics and Money among the Yoruba* (New Brunswick, NJ: Transaction Publishers, 2000).

38. J.D.Y. Peel, "*Ọlajú*: A Yoruba Concept of Development," *Journal of Development Studies* 14 (1978): 139–65; and *Ijeshas and Nigerians: The Incorporation of a Yoruba Kingdom, 1890s–1970s* (Cambridge: Cambridge University Press, 1983). Ferguson's brilliant book on Zambia (*Expectations*) reveals local investment in modernization ideologies there as well.

39. Sara S. Berry, *Fathers Work for Their Sons: Accumulation, Mobility and Class Formation in an Extended Yoruba Community* (Berkeley: University of California Press, 1985); J.D.Y. Peel, *Religious Encounter and the Making of the Yoruba* (Bloomington: Indiana University Press, 2000); Karin Barber, *The Generation of Plays: Yoruba Popular Life in Theater* (Bloomington: Indiana University Press, 2000). The term "potentiality" comes from Barber's book.

40. Joan Wallach Scott, "Gender: A Useful Category of Historical Analysis" in *Gender and the Politics of History* (New York: Columbia University Press, 1988).

41. Judith Butler, *Gender Trouble: Feminism and the Subversion of Identity* (New York: Routledge, 1990), quotation on p. 25; and Ferguson's use and modifications of Butler's concepts in *Expectations*, pp. 94–99. For African challenges to established gender norms, see Hodgson and McCurdy (eds.), *"Wicked" Women.*

42. Rose, *Limited Livelihoods* and "'Gender at Work': Sex, Class and Industrial Capitalism," *History Workshop* 21 (1986): 113–31.

43. Rose and Frader (eds.), *Gender and Class;* Michael Roper and John Tosh (eds.), *Manful Assertions: Masculinities in Britain Since 1800* (London: Routledge, 1991); John Tosh, "What Should Historians Do with Masculinity? Reflections on Nineteenth-Century Britain," *History Workshop* 38 (1994): 179–202, and *A Man's Place: Masculinity and the Middle Class Home in Victorian England* (New Haven, CT: Yale University Press, 1999); Keith McClelland, "Time to Work, Time to Live: Some Aspects of Work and the Re-Formation of Class in Britain, 1850–1880," in Patrick Joyce (ed.), *The Historical Meanings of Work* (Cambridge: Cambridge University Press, 1987), and "Some Thoughts on Masculinity and the 'Representative Artisan' in Britain," *Gender and History* 1 (1989): 164–77; Clark, *Struggle for the Breeches.* My summary draws from Steven Maynard,

"Rough Work and Rugged Men: The Social Construction of Masculinity in Working-Class History," *Labour/Le Travail* 23 (1989): 159–69.

44. For one formulation of this, in an earlier period, see Scully, *Liberating*.

45. Carolyn A. Brown, "A 'Man' in the Village"and *"We Were All Slaves": African Miners, Culture and Resistance: The Enugu Government Colliery, Nigeria, 1914–1950* (Portsmouth, NH: Heinemann, 2003).

46. This dynamic is best captured in Ferdinand Oyono's tragic novel, *Houseboy* (London: Heinemann, 1966). Also see Karen Tranberg Hansen, *Distant Companions: Servants and Employers in Zambia, 1900–1985* (Ithaca, NY: Cornell University Press, 1989); Schmidt, *Peasants*; and Norman Etherington, "Natal's Black Rape Scare of the 1870s," *JSAS* 15 (1988): 2–53; and Diana Jeater, *Marriage, Perversion, and Power: The Construction of Moral Discourse in Southern Rhodesia, 1894–1930* (Oxford: Clarendon Press, 1993).

47. Luise White, *Speaking with Vampires: Rumor and History in Colonial Africa* (Berkeley: University of California Press, 2000).

48. This is a point made by Nancy Rose Hunt in her introduction to *Gendered Colonialisms in African History,* ed. N.R. Hunt, T.P. Liu, and J. Quataert (Oxford: Blackwell, 1997).

49. R.W. Connell, *Masculinities* (Berkeley: University of California Press, 1995), pp. 79 and 77 quoted. Earlier formulations of this model are in Tim Carrigan, R.W. Connell, and John Lee, "Toward a New Sociology of Masculinity," *Theory and Society* 14 (1985): 551–604; and Connell, *Gender and Power: Society, the Person and Sexual Politics* (Stanford, CA: Stanford University Press, 1987).

50. Andrea Cornwall and Nancy Lindisfarne, "Dislocating Masculinity: Gender, Power and Anthropology," in *Dislocating Masculinity: Comparative Ethnographies,* ed. Cornwall and Lindisfarne (London: Routledge, 1994), p. 4.

51. Stephan F. Miescher, "The Life Histories of Boakye Yiadom (Akasease Kofi of Abetifi, Kwawu): Exploring the Subjectivity and 'Voices' of a Teacher-Catechist in Colonial Ghana," in *African Words, African Voices: Critical Practices in Oral History,* ed. Luise White, Stephan F. Miescher, and David W. Cohen (Bloomington: Indiana University Press, 2001) and "The Making of Presbyterian Teachers: Masculinities and Programs of Education in Colonial Ghana," in *Men and Masculinities,* ed. Lindsay and Miescher.

52. See, for instance, Dilip Parameshwar Gaonkar, "On Alternative Modernities," *Public Culture* 11 (1999): 1–18, along with other contributions in that issue.

53. Cooper, *Decolonization,* p. 592, fn 56.

54. Peel, "*Ọlajú*."

55. Rita Felski, *The Gender of Modernity* (Cambridge, MA: Harvard University Press, 1995).

56. Gaonkar, "On Alternative Modernities," p. 18. For an examination of Yoruba engagement with ideas about modernity, see Barber, *The Generation of Plays*.

57. For this point more generally, see Dorothy L. Hodgson (ed.), *Gendered Modernities: Ethnographic Perspectives* (New York: Palgrave, 2001).

58. Ferguson, *Expectations*.

59. I am grateful to Fred Cooper for articulating this point.

60. Wale Oyemakinde, "Railway Construction and Operation in Nigeria, 1895–1911: Labour Problems and Socio-Economic Impact," *JHSN* 7 (1974): 303–24.

61. G. St. J. Orde Browne, *Labour Conditions in West Africa* Cmd. 6277 (London, 1941), p. 79; Nigeria, *Annual Report on the Government Railway for the Financial Year Ending 31st March 1939,* p. 49.

62. Nigeria, *Annual Report on the Government Railway for the Financial Year 1943–44,* p. 58; *and Annual Report on the Government Railway for the Financial Year 1952–53,* p. 36.

63. Nigerian Railway Corporation (NRC), *Report and Accounts for the Year Ended 31st March 1965,* p. 35. There were approximately 565,000 Nigerian wage-earners in 1965 according to Tayo Fashoyin, *Industrial Relations in Nigeria* (London: Longman, 1980), p. 13.

64. Nigeria, *Lagos Census* (1950), pp. 83–84.

65. G.A. Oldfield, "The Native Railway Worker in Nigeria," *Africa* 9 (1936): 379–402. Of the 167 railway retirees that Babajide Oyeneye, Olafunmilayo Carew, Olusanya Ibitoye, and I surveyed in Lagos and Ibadan in 1993–1994, 84.4 percent identified themselves as Yoruba.

66. Based on a random sample of 434 personnel files from retired, terminated, and dead railway workers from the western region of Nigeria located in the pension offices of the Ebute Metta (Lagos) headquarters and the Ibadan regional hub of the Nigerian Railway Corporation. Ethnic designations were either listed in the files or surmised on the basis of the employees' names.

67. T.M. Yesufu, *An Introduction to Industrial Relations in Nigeria* (London: Oxford University Press, 1962), p. 119.

68. Fadipe, *Sociology,* pp. 91–92; Oyemakinde, "Railway Construction."

69. Cyprian Ekwensi, *Lokotown and Other Stories* (London: Heinemann, 1966).

70. Oyemakinde, "Railway Construction"; J.O. Oyemakinde, "A History of Indigenous Labour on the Nigerian Railway, 1895–1945" (Ph.D. dissertation, University of Ibadan, 1970); Francis Jaekel, *The History of the Nigerian Railway,* 3 vols. (Ibadan: Spectrum Books Ltd., 1997).

71. *Annual Report of the Nigerian Railway for the Year 1935,* pp. 7–8.

72. Wale Oyemakinde, "The Railway Workers and Modernization in Colonial Nigeria," *JHSN* 10 (1979): 113–24. In this article, as among colonial-era observers, time discipline, the use of money currency, language continuity, travel, and heterogeneous social contacts are unambiguous markers of modernity.

73. Wole Soyinka, *Isara: A Voyage around Essay* (Ibadan: Fountain Publications, 1989), pp. 12 and 18.

74. On colonial "middles," see Nancy Rose Hunt, *A Colonial Lexicon of Birth Ritual, Medicalization and Mobility in the Congo* (Durham, NC: Duke University Press, 1999).

75. Most of these surveys were conducted by Jide Oyeneye or myself; Olafunmilayo Carew and Olusanya Ibitoye did a handful of others.

76. For African railway workers, see Richard Jeffries, *Class, Power and Ideology in Ghana: The Railwaymen of Sekondi* (Cambridge: Cambridge University Press, 1978); R.D. Grillo, *African Railwaymen: Solidarity and Opposition in an East African Labour Force* (Cambridge: Cambridge University Press, 1973); Anton Rosenthal, "Controlling the Line: Worker Strategies and Transport Capital on the Railroads of Ecuador, Zambia and Zimbabwe, 1916–1950," (Ph.D. dissertation, University of Minnesota, 1990); Paul Pheffer, "Railways and Aspects of Social Change in Senegal, 1877–1933," (Ph.D. dissertation, University of Pennsylvania, 1975). The literature on railway labor elsewhere is huge. Some examples include James H. Ducker, *Men of the Steel Rails: Workers on*

the Atchison, Topeka and Santa Fe Railroad, 1869–1900 (Lincoln: University of Nebraska Press, 1983); R.S. Joby, *The Railwaymen* (London: David and Charles, 1984); Walter Licht, *Working for the Railroad: The Organization of Work in the Nineteenth Century* (Princeton, NJ: Princeton University Press, 1983); Scott Nelson, *Iron Confederacies: Southern Railways, Klan Violence, and Reconstruction* (Chapel Hill: University of North Carolina Press, 1999).

2

Wage Labor, Money, and Masculinity in Early Twentieth-Century Yorubaland

For Nigerian men, the expansion of wage labor in the early twentieth century brought more than paychecks and time discipline. Men's new relationship with money and work had implications for their most fundamental social ties—with their natal families, conjugal groups, and wider communities. This was true in many parts of colonial Africa: in spite of local variations, young men generally took advantage of agricultural commercialization and the expansion of wage labor to become increasingly autonomous from their elders.[1] "Target labor," or temporary participation in colonial wage economies, by and large allowed juniors to marry and set up their own households with less input than before from older generations. In such cases, money was the medium through which young men sped up their attainment of adult masculine status.

In early twentieth-century Yorubaland, as everywhere, men's roles and status were largely determined by their position in the life course and their access to resources. The most important resources have been, and continue to be, mutually reinforcing: "wealth in people" and money.[2] While these are typical sources of influence worldwide, southwestern Nigeria's long tradition of economic diversity and commercial activity has meant that Yoruba peoples historically have placed special importance on money. Citing the proverb, "I know her/him/it as one knows money," (*Mo mò ón bí ení mowó*), Karin Barber has suggested that money represents the most intimate and familiar relationships a person could have. By undergirding processes that contribute to status and personal ties, "money in Yoruba culture is conceived of as constitutive of individual self-realization."[3] According to Toyin Falola and Akanmu

Adebayo, "[N]othing sums up the Yoruba view of money better than *kose-e-mani*, the idea that money is the 'Indispensable One.'"[4] Much of the extensive research on Yoruba women has acknowledged the connection between money, status, and identity, stressing female traders' economic independence and drawing attention to separate, gendered spheres of social life.[5] But what about men? What relationships have existed between men and money, and how have these been implicated in economic changes over time?

Any attempt to describe gender (or other) relationships in the past is plagued with problems: the risk of treating social relations as unchanging; the implication that sources such as ethnographies and court cases accurately describe the lifestyles of most people in a given community; the tendency to generalize within and across groups. It is even more difficult to elicit people's ideas about gender, since all we can really know is what individuals said and, sometimes, how they acted—certainly not what they were thinking or how they necessarily saw themselves. I confront these obstacles by focusing here on the normative framework—that is, the set of rules and general expectations—of social and gender relations in colonial Yorubaland, particularly in the 1930s and 1940s. This is not to say that people always followed what was generally expected, or even that the same expectations held for everyone. Indeed, life could be quite different for members of the emergent educated elite, men from traditionally powerful families, or ordinary men seeking their fortunes; or for men of coastal versus hinterland origin; or for men of different generations. But there are enough commonalities in what the historical sources say about marriage, money, and gender to support the impression of a set of relatively stable ideals, however loosely defined and interpreted. In later chapters I trace conflicts over gender ideals between African workers and European employers, but it is important to point out first that such contests came in the context of a set of contingent practices that provided people with ways of understanding and leading good lives as men and women. The ideas about gender discussed here were most salient not necessarily as reflections of behavior but as (changing) norms for explaining the world and guiding expectations.

This chapter elaborates some of the ways that money exchanges helped to "make men" in colonial Yorubaland and thus lays the groundwork for later discussions of changing social relations associated with stable wage labor. I first delineate the early history of wage labor in southwestern Nigeria, pointing out its initial associations with slavery and degraded status. Within a generation or two, however, young men were taking advantage of opportunities for independent earning to establish themselves as adults. The next section of the chapter places "target labor" in the context of gender and generational relations in Ibadan and other Yoruba towns in the first half of the twentieth century. I show that money worked to establish adult masculinity by facilitating marriage and the establishment of independent households. Later in life, adult men could become more senior, and some even attained the status of "big man." The third section of this chapter shows that ideals associated with "big men," though changing over time, continued to link social power to idioms of masculinity through the nexus of money. Yet, as I discuss in the last section, even big men were not expected to provide exclusive financial support to their wives, although money and other gifts clearly could smooth domestic relations. As we will see in later chapters, the normative notion of a "male breadwinner" was born in the interaction of colonial efforts, labor struggles, and household politics.

THE DEVELOPMENT OF WAGE LABOR IN SOUTHWESTERN NIGERIA

Wage labor does not have a long history in Nigeria.[6] Throughout the nineteenth century most work for African-directed trade and production was carried out by family members, slaves, and clients.[7] With the arrival of European traders in the Niger Delta and Lagos in the early nineteenth century, small numbers of Africans were hired as laborers, porters, interpreters, and clerks, a process that continued after Lagos was made a British colony in 1861 and the Royal Niger Company was chartered to administer the Niger Delta in 1886. In Lagos, Calabar, and the Niger Delta, where Christian missions established schools from the 1840s, firms engaged primarily in the palm oil trade competed for employees among students and graduates. The few with elementary and secondary education had little difficulty in finding prestigious white-collar jobs. But manual labor was more difficult to recruit. In the late nineteenth century, European merchants frequently hired laborers from the Gold Coast, Liberia, and Sierra Leone for work on the Nigerian coast.

The demand for wage labor increased with the formalization of British rule over what was by 1900 called the Protectorate of Southern Nigeria, although the numbers of employees remained small. With few attractions for European settlers and long-standing commercial connections with international mercantile firms, West Africa's colonial economy was based from the start on the export of cash crops or raw materials developed by African producers and locally marketed by African traders. Nigeria's main exports during the colonial period were cocoa and rubber in the southwest; palm oil throughout the south; groundnuts, cotton, and shea products from the north; tin from the middle region of the country; coal and other minerals. Yet railway lines, roads, and harbors were necessary in order to export these items, and these required workers. Further, in this land of few Europeans, without a cadre of clerks and other civil servants, a bureaucracy could not function. Thus there was growing demand for manual laborers, skilled artisans, and literates, especially in

Lagos. In 1881 roughly 9 percent of the city's total population, or 2,357 people, were employed in the formal sector of the economy; those figures increased to 13.7 percent and 6,388, respectively, by 1911.[8]

Officials hoped and assumed that by bringing an end to regional warfare and undermining the institution of slavery, colonial rule would "free" the necessary able-bodied men for wage employment. However, labor supplies remained low in the early twentieth century. In southwestern Nigeria, the end of the Yoruba civil wars, which had lasted from 1817 to the 1890s, allowed people to move out of fortified cities and into the countryside. The end of slavery also led to population losses in the towns. Abundant land and markets for cash crops meant that ex-combatants and former slaves could make their living farming and trading. A.G. Hopkins's assertion that "the transition from slavery to freedom was accomplished relatively smoothly" masks the complexities of demographic movements during this period, but most ex-slaves did continue to work in agriculture, either for their former masters or on new farms that they developed themselves.[9] Independent farmers also were not attracted to wage labor, which was considered degrading and fit only for those of servile status.[10]

Thus the developers of the state's largest project, the Government Railway, initially confronted labor shortages, in the southwest and elsewhere in Nigeria. Construction on the first segment, between Lagos and Ibadan, began in 1896. Over the following years thousands of laborers were recruited both by the administration and local contractors for the massive efforts of clearing land and laying track. Administrative reports from the late nineteenth and early twentieth centuries consistently complained about the difficulties of getting and keeping workers. Particularly in northern Nigeria, railway builders relied on conscription until the 1930s. In some parts of the south, unskilled labor for government projects was compulsory, but paid, through the 1910s and into the 1920s. In the context of this labor shortage, the government was forced to pay 9 pence per day for public works, a wage administrators considered too high for Africans.[11]

By 1919, Frederick Lugard, the first governor of a united Nigeria, could gloat that "the Government rule that every labourer must be paid up fully in cash, at short intervals, and without the intermediary of any middle man or Chief, has done more than anything else to popularize the system of labour, and to create a free labor market."[12] Yet there were abundant opportunities outside of wage labor for earning the cash necessary to pay taxes and buy consumer goods. In southwestern Nigeria, farmers planted a new cash crop, cocoa, and thereby initiated sweeping changes in the agricultural economy. Cocoa cultivation spread to Ibadan in the 1890s, Ilesha soon thereafter, and Ife, Ondo, and Ekiti between the 1910s and 1930s, bringing prosperity to some rural farmers and supporting a system of produce buyers, local and regional markets, and—as time went on—hired agricultural labor.[13] One of many new economic opportunities of the era was for young men to work as itinerant traders. These *oṣomaalo* took advantage of expanding transportation routes and local markets to sell cloth and other items throughout Yorubaland, earning significant incomes in the process. In fact, so many young men left Ilesha to work as *oṣomaalo* that food crop production there suffered, contributing to a famine in 1905.[14]

With these opportunities for cash-cropping and trade, why would anyone work for wages? The explanation lies in the dramatic social transformations that accompanied the expansion of the colonial economy. First, ever greater numbers of people qualified for and aspired to employment as clerks and technicians. From early in the twentieth century, western education and its frequent partners Christianity and migration came to be seen as routes to social and economic advancement. Cocoa farmers and others with the means invested in their children's education and fueled a massive popular demand for schools. Dissatisfied with the relatively small numbers of government and government-assisted mission schools (150 in 1912 and 195 in 1922), independent African churches and other private organizations founded their own primary schools, which numbered more than 3,000 by 1926. That year, government and mission schools served 28,000 students, while the unassisted schools had 122,000 enrolled pupils. This "veritable explosion of unassisted schools"[15] produced graduates ready to take up "clerkly" employment in the expanding colonial economy. At the same time, "[t]he establishment of civil order and the inauguration of the work of laying down the railway lines," as the Yoruba sociologist N.A. Fadipe wrote, "meant the opening up of prospects of employment for men of varying grades of literacy whether in the civil service, on the railway line, or in the mercantile service." Through the first two decades of the century, "prosperity came to the literate class."[16]

Second, young people and other dependents sought wage work and other new opportunities as ways of challenging parents and patrons for social autonomy. In the early years of railway construction, workers' wages enabled them to purchase their freedom, if they were slaves, or often to marry if they were free.[17] Women sought new opportunities as well, trading at railway construction camps and "defy[ing] both their parents and public opinion [to] become attached to some clerks or artisans as mistresses."[18] Even before the turn of the century, female slaves gained their freedom by taking as their lovers railroad workers or other government employees, who provided "presents" to the women's owners. District Commissioners then recognized these transactions as severing the owners' rights to the women.[19] Similarly, according to correspondence between the Alake (traditional ruler) of Abeokuta and local Railway Commissioners, twenty-nine Egba women ran away to the railway camp between 1899 and 1901. Of their new partners, seventeen were laborers, seven were head laborers, one was a carpenter, and one was a steward.[20] The "Report on the Yoruba," written by a committee of educated Lagosians in 1910, suggested that "In consequence of the rapid opening up of the country ... [y]oung people easily find employment; they earn considerable wages and emancipate themselves from the control of the family."[21] Wage labor, then, helped to facilitate marriage and social independence. This chapter now turns to the context in which such transitions occurred.

MONEY, MARRIAGE, AND ADULT MASCULINITY[22]

In southwestern Nigeria in the early twentieth century, the organization of households, relations between generations, and the social and economic independence of young men all related to control over labor. Junior men formed a dependent labor force for their elders' farms or trading enterprises, and as long as they remained unmarried, they could not claim a share of the compounds' land or control their own labor. Unlike in many other African societies, in Yorubaland there was no specific coming-of-age ritual for either sex.[23] Rather, a boy would learn farming or a trade or craft from his father or other senior men, and gradually his responsibilities and community standing would increase. The break point, marking a young man's definitive attainment of adult masculinity, was marriage, although marriage itself could be a protracted affair. When a man married, he set up his own household, either in a senior kinsman's compound or, eventually, in his own house. He acquired his own dependent domestic labor force and became the *baálé* (literally, "father of the house") in relation to his wife and children. A wife also brought economic help, crucial in maintaining an independent household. "Without her aid (economic)," the missionary Edward Ward noted in 1938, a man "is just a 'small boy' without a home of his own." Further, he reported that domestic work was seen by all as "unmanly," and marriage saved an adult man from the stigma of doing it himself.[24] Thus, a man's "first marriage was the foundation of his future existence as a social being."[25]

Such a change in status required money, and transactions in cash, goods, and labor formalized marriage ties between individuals and families.[26] In spite of colonial officials' and anthropologists' efforts to make the rules for Yoruba marriage more rigid, "custom" was never hard and fast, and it varied over time and by locality.[27] Marriages were contracted in several stages, often extending over a period of years, almost always requiring transfers of money and goods. In the precolonial period, exchanges between the families of the marrying parties took the form of refreshments, agricultural produce, services, and small amounts of currency, but certainly by the 1930s, if not sooner, money was the primary object of exchange.[28] Court records indicate contestation and negotiation in the amounts involved and the rights and obligations associated with each stage of marriage, but nevertheless money was crucial to both obtaining and keeping a wife, and thus to adult standing.

Ideally, regardless of whether the parties practiced Christianity, Islam, or Yoruba religion, without bride-price (*owó-gbéyàwó*, literally, "money to carry the wife"), there was no marriage. The amount involved proved formidable for most men. Ward wrote that in Ondo Province in the early 1930s a new bride could fetch £10.12, plus "dashes" to herself and her family, for a total of about £20. By 1938, the minimum he reported comprised about £14.10, compared with an average daily wage of 9 pence; marriage fees in this case represented about sixteen months' labor. These figures correspond with amounts given in Ibadan court cases from the 1930s. Karin Barber's informants indicated that between 1920 and 1950 bride-price in the town of Okuku was between £6 and £7, plus other expenses comprising up to £40. In fact, the average bride-price there was greater than the entire cash value of a household's yearly food consumption. In cocoa growing areas of the 1950s, a survey team estimated total marriage expenses at £50, or about one year's agricultural wages.[29]

As this suggests, bride-price was only a part of the total cost of marriage. While courting, a suitor was usually expected to visit his fiancée's parents regularly and to give small gifts of money to them and their daughter. Once or twice a year during the engagement and as long as the marriage lasted, the suitor and his relatives or age-mates had to perform free labor for his father-in-law, which involved clearing farm land or repairing the house. Although this practice was dying out by the mid-1930s, payments were not. Several Ibadan court cases even in the 1950s mentioned money spent to help a prospective father-in-law build a house.[30] As the bride-to-be's consent was necessary for marriage, she typically received payments as well. At least half, and perhaps more, of the total expenditures were made to her in the form of "friendship money," gifts, or *ibowó* (dowry). A virginity fee could also be paid to the bride and her parents.[31]

Many more expenditures had been required around the turn of the century, when a suitor could be called upon to help defray extraordinary expenses incurred by any of his prospective in-laws as well as his future father-in-law's debts. "This almost unlimited liability for the financial commitments and obligations of others," Fadipe wrote, was one reason why it was so important to make careful inquiries about the family before the betrothal. Some payments persisted into midcentury: Lapide testified in his divorce from Selia in 1949 that when they married he loaned £5 to Selia's father to prevent him from pawning his cocoa farm. And in 1958 an Ibadan man sued to break the engagement of his daughter because he claimed the suitor had provided neither money nor labor.[32] In an Ibadan case from 1954, a jilted boyfriend named Muraina Alabi sued to recover the marriage expenses he had paid on Amuda Anike, testifying:

When I first befriended the defendant, she got £2 from me to consult a mallam about our marriage. One month later, I gave her £3 to return to her former friend who was keeping her [i.e., her former fiancé who had made payments on her]. A week after that she got 10/- from me to cook food for her friend who was married. I gave her £1 when she was going to see her mother who had an injury. I gave her £2.10 to buy a pair of shoes, £9 friendship money, 10/- when her brother named a child, £1.2.6 to buy another pair of shoes, £1.15 on seven occasions when I visited her.[33]

In addition to the amounts, the careful accounting of marriage expenses is itself noteworthy. Suitors usually passed payments and gifts through at least one, and ideally more, intermediaries, who could be called upon to confirm the amount spent. This was important in the case of divorce and repayment, as well as serving as a sign of the man's commitment to the relationship and his affection for his betrothed. Letting the community know how much he spent on her was a man's way of announcing to the world that he was serious about marriage. Money meant married status; listing expenses advertised that status and emphasized its earnestness.[34]

The idea of marrying solely for love, without the appropriate money to back it up, was not part of public discourse. Since men were required to make a number of payments to prospective brides and their families, any of the parties could derail marriages on grounds of insufficient finances. And the protracted nature of marriage proceedings meant that marriages could be disputed or dissolved even after the couple had already lived together.[35] In 1937 an Ibadan woman named Lanlehin was betrothed to someone else, but she married Salami "because he promised to give me money." He never paid her or her parents, though, and they forced her to leave him after a week. In 1941, a woman named Adefunmi asked for divorce because of an unpaid balance on her bride-wealth, in spite of the fact that she had lived with her husband for fifteen years. After three years of courtship with no money paid to her, Silifatu Ajile brought Layiwole Amoo to court for divorce, citing "neglect."[36] Probably there were other contributing factors in these breakups, but what is significant for this discussion is that financial insecurity threatened men's ability to get or to stay married.

In this context in which marital status could be indefinite, children were clear markers of marriage and created lifelong connections between the parents. Through the payment of bride-price, men became the "owners" of their wives' children. Conversely, without bride-price a man's status as a father could always be questioned: "One who does not own a kola tree cannot have its fruit" (*Enì ti kò ní igi obi ki ìní eso*). Men and women valued children as additions to their lineages, markers of their fertility, and potential sources of wealth and security: this is the basis of proverbs like "Children are the clothes of men" (*Ọmọ l'aṣo èdá*) and "Children are the profit of life" (*Ọmọ l'ère aiyé*).[37]

Ideally, young men expected money for marriage to come from their fathers. In fact, though, fathers could delay funding their sons' marriages on the grounds that the money was not available, thereby prolonging their access to the young men's labor. Ijesha men born in the first two decades of the twentieth century, for example, generally were in their thirties before they were able to marry. In many cases, the fathers of this cohort did not live up to their obligations at all. Sons then were forced to fend for themselves, and conflict about the availability of marriage money produced tensions between different generations of men.[38]

Marriage expenses comprised a primary "target" for early twentieth-century labor migration, as they did throughout Africa.[39] With the expansion of such opportunities, young men were increasingly able to "abbreviate the period of their juniority"[40] by earning cash away from home. Early *oṣomaalo* recalled that they had undertaken itinerant trade because "*Mo fẹ́ gbéyàwó*" (I wanted to get married).[41] By the 1930s the pattern of migrant trade or wage labor in order to raise marriage funds was well established, and men's typical age at first marriage had fallen to the mid-twenties.[42] Fadipe linked bride-price inflation to the railway, wage labor, and commercial expansion. As the rail line extended to Northern Nigeria, he explained, unskilled government labor allowed a man to earn in one year what it would take three years of farming to save, and this money was frequently used by young men for getting married. "The introduction of wage employment also meant a modification of the custom that a son remained directly under his father in whatever occupation he followed from about the age of six until his marriage, and that the father should, thereafter, get a wife for him," Fadipe wrote. "The latter custom, with regards to those in salaried or wage employment, no longer holds since a young man is now responsible for finding the money for paying the bride-price for his fiancee."[43]

Paying their own marriage expenses allowed young men to choose their own spouses more frequently than they had before. Women, too, started to demand more influence in their choice of husbands, often favoring young earners with cash over older men or nonmigrants.[44] By the 1930s, Fadipe charged that footloose young women looked for boyfriends or husbands on the railway line or other places where men were "away from home and beyond the watchful eyes of parents, extended family, neighbors and friends."[45] The marriage story of Tubosan and Oke, recounted in a 1939 Ibadan court case, follows this pattern. The two had met in 1927 at the Afonta railway station, where Tubosan worked as a policeman. Oke was staying with her cousin Selia, who may have moved in with a railway gateman herself. When Tubosan's job sent him to Oshogbo, Oke went with him and bore two children. Later Tubosan sent a bride-wealth payment and some gifts to her relatives through Selia.[46] A government official denigrated such relationships: "It is in the native reservations of Townships and similar cosmopolitan settlements along the railways and in mining camps that there is general laxity. In these places many unions are contracted which are not marriages at all, but simply cohabitation."[47] As a man who had come of age in the town of Ado-Odo in the late 1930s, and who had felt free to make his own marriage choices, recounted, "They [our fathers] were not able to control us . . . if we liked things we did them in our own way."[48]

This statement applied to more than marriage. Unskilled workers in the 1930s and into the 1940s typically worked at least five or six years before they saved the money necessary to marry.[49] In the meantime, steady wages allowed a young man to begin to accumulate possessions and run his own affairs away from home. According to his memoirs, when Oba Daniel Anirarẹ Aladesanmi became a railway clerk in 1930 he was able to support himself for the first time: "When I received my salary I was launched into a new orbit whereby I got my own accommodation, furnished it moderately and equipped it with cooking utensils."[50] Most began their careers living with an older relative or friend and after earning some money gradually took on more expenses. After railway pensioner M.O. Shofekun finished school in 1941, he lived in a room in Lagos with his brother, who helped support him while he looked for work. He secured a clerkship in Ibadan and then was able to rent a room of his own. His Oke Awo neighborhood was full of railway workers, he said, especially single men who held debating meetings, met for drinking and socializing, discussed the events in the *West African Pilot*, and sometimes attended church.[51] The hero of the novel *Blade among the Boys,* Patrick Ikenga, entered railway traffic training in the early 1940s. In Lagos, he "spent his evenings either reading or enjoying himself in many different ways" such as attending parties, dancing at night clubs, or participating in nationalist political rallies. Castigated by a relative, he retorted, "This is Lagos and not Ado [his hometown]. I am no longer a child who must be dictated to."[52]

Some members of the older generation resented this independence. Fadipe criticized the clerks who took advantage of their positions to usurp the powers and prerogatives of their elders. In addition to "sharp and fraudulent practices in relation to workers and their pay, victimisation and the bringing of false accusations against enemies," he listed "violation of the chastity of unmarried girls and seduction of married ones, [and] disrespect and defiance of local functionaries" as "some of the characteristics of the 'writer' (clerk)" early in the century. Some parents feared that paychecks, along with living in a new place, "would make their sons too independent to be controlled." A front-page newspaper headline in 1941 confirmed such anxieties: "Son Sues His Father for Debt of £188. 15s." The son in question was a salaried employee in the Treasury Department, who won the case.[53]

But for every young man whose independence brought tensions with his parents, there were many others who made their families proud by sharing their earnings with people in the home community. The memoirs of Chief

Simeon Adebo, who much later became head of the United Nations Commission for Economic Affairs, state matter-of-factly that when he was a young man working as a railway accounts clerk in the 1930s he considered his discretionary income to be that which was left after his monthly contribution to his parents at home. According to a 1941 government report, "The young men go out to seek paid employment not entirely for themselves but very largely also for the benefit of the family and much of the money earned is sent home in order to educate the younger members of the family. Family custom again compels those in employment to support their less fortunately situated brothers." Parents and other relatives who had funded a young man's education would expect him to share with his family the wages earned by virtue of that education. This would then provide for the kin group in lean times, or perhaps fund the schooling of another family member. Young employees had to strike a balance between two types of spending that would contribute to their community standing: toward marriage and personal accumulation, and toward their family obligations in order to be good sons and hometown members.[54]

By the 1940s, then, a new generation was able to take advantage of expanding opportunities to achieve autonomous adulthood through their own efforts. Those who entered the wage economy of the towns were regular earners of a wage that they could spend largely as they liked. For them, paternal authority no longer held the same weight as before. Yet most of these men remained embedded—financially and otherwise—in family and hometown networks. Retirees who had gone to work for the railway in this era stressed that what had appealed to them most about their jobs was the steady pay and their ability to address both types of concerns. "When you have a [wage] job at hand it's then your relatives know your value and respect your opinion," one retired railway man noted. Another summarized the benefits of working on the railroad this way: "I married, I got children, I built this place [his house]."[55]

SENIOR MASCULINITY AND THE "BIG MAN"

These comments indicate that social adulthood was only the beginning of men's aspirations. Temporary "target workers" eventually returned home to establish themselves in their own farms or businesses, growing and marketing a cash crop like cocoa or forming other types of enterprises. As Fadipe put it, the migrant worker "who has done well abroad returns home an important man in his little community."[56] Even when wage labor provided the cash that gave a man his start as an independent adult, his "real career of self-aggrandisement . . . could only be conducted on home ground, and was based on the expansion of the household his earnings had helped to found."[57]

While the first step in settling down was getting married, eventually men hoped to gain renown by fathering and educating children and exercising influence in lineage and community affairs. As a man gained in age and wealth, his advice would be sought in disputes, he would be asked for help by the less fortunate, and he would bestow gifts upon patrons and clients. His social position would be reflected in the number and rank of the individuals who associated with him, and particularly who accompanied him about town. His associations might include church, mosque, or other religious groups, and certainly he would be expected to contribute to local civic development projects. Such a senior man might accumulate the resources to build a house, preferably a two-story brick structure with a corrugated iron roof, or compete for chieftaincy titles.

Through these and other means, some men became prosperous and influential enough to be known as "big men." Ward observed in 1937 that "[e]very young Yoruba boy . . . has an ambition to become a 'big' man sooner or later in life. A 'small boy' (a poor man) is very much looked down upon."[58] Since at least the early nineteenth century, Yoruba men have competed with each other for followers, wealth, and reputation. Aspiring big men struggled to establish themselves at the center of a circle of people, whose labor was invested in the expansion of their farms or trading enterprises. Material wealth enabled them to acquire yet more people through marriage and the production of children, patronage and hospitality, slavery and pawnship (in the nineteenth and early twentieth centuries), and hired labor (in the twentieth century). A large household and wealth thus reinforced each other: a big man attracted dependents by his ability to provide for and protect them; in turn, they supported his claims to be "big" by contributing labor or productive resources, serving him personally, or enhancing his reputation.[59] As the still extant proverb states, "I have money, I have people, what else is there that I have not got?" (*Mo lówó, mo lénìyàn, kí ló tún kù tí mi ò tíî ní?*).[60]

Although being a big man remained an ideal through the twentieth century, changing political and economic circumstances affected the ways people pursued and displayed such status. In the late nineteenth century, seniority and a large household were crucial for social standing. A senior man, supported through the economic contributions of his dependents, headed a large kinship group, became eligible for titles, and gained political influence by representing his lineage and participating in royally recognized associations with other senior men. Over time, another kind of big man emerged in circles more closely articulated with the colonial political economy. By the 1930s the spread of education and the growth of the cocoa industry resulted in the development of a group of predominantly Christian (but some Muslim) literates and wealthy businessmen in many towns, who exercised growing influence on local politics. In spite of the fact that many eventually lived or operated outside of their towns of origin, these "new" elites remained connected to their homes, building houses, investing money, and providing the leadership of new progressive unions being formed. In this arena, seniority could help a man's position but was not as necessary as education, ability, and networks of influence through which one could advance both individual clients and local communities. As opposed to the world of "wealth in people" inhabited by big men in the former model, the emergent educated elite focused on the world of "enlightenment." "New" big men were still associated in the public mind with personal magnificence, generosity, self-reliance, and power; but they also reflected values associated with education, such as Christianity, literacy, and public spiritedness.[61]

Differences between old and new big man ideals were also expressed in marriages. For men concerned with "having people," polygyny was highly valued, not least because it helped them produce many children and form multiple networks of in-laws. Kings and important chiefs in the nineteenth century reputedly had scores, perhaps even hundreds, of wives—a fact that helps to account for young men's difficulties in making their own marriages.[62] By the mid-twentieth century, polygyny was an attainable goal for many Yoruba men. Galletti and others' 1951–1953 survey of cocoa-farming areas reported polygyny rates of 58.5 percent in Ibadan, 73.5 percent in Ife, 65.8 percent in Ondo, and 50.7 percent in Abeokuta. Overall, 62.6 percent of the men surveyed were polygynous, with the majority of those having two wives.[63] But these numbers also reveal monogamous marriages in significant numbers, given the value placed on large households and the relative prosperity of the cocoa region at that time. It is no surprise that Abeokuta, with its large Christian population, had the lowest proportion of polygynous marriages. Muslims and adherents of Yoruba religion had no ideological opposition to polygyny, and some African Christian churches tolerated it as well. But Christians and others who received western education increasingly saw monogamy as part of the package of "enlightenment" to which they aspired.[64] The new elites were less concerned with building large households than their predecessors were and instead based their careers on opportunities and networks *outside* lineage and hometown structures. Yet big men of both varieties held this common assumption about marriages: husbands and wives should each largely provide for themselves.

HOUSEHOLD ECONOMIES AND MARRIAGE RELATIONSHIPS

As in many West African societies, Yoruba marriages in the first half of the twentieth century were not predicated on a male breadwinner norm.[65] Women were expected to work and earn money just as men were. Husbands and wives typically controlled their own separate resources and expenditures, and household members did not pool their incomes. Still, men's (and women's) financial resources had important implications for spousal relationships. Already we have seen that men needed money in order to get married, and that some of the money went to the bride in the form of gifts and other payments. This means of expressing sentiment and jockeying for privileges did not come to an end once a couple lived together and produced children. Although men were not expected to provide exclusive financial support for their wives and children, spending money was a culturally valued way of expressing love and care.[66] It could smooth marital relationships and boost a husband's attractiveness and prestige. In later chapters I use this background to explore changing marital relationships among men with long careers and steady paychecks.

Yoruba spouses in the first part of the twentieth century ideally had distinct economic obligations to one another. Husbands were expected to provide their families with a place to live, give their wives capital to begin trading, meet their obligations to extended families, and contribute to their children's feeding and education. Wives were to help support themselves and their children and to fulfill responsibilities to their husbands' and their own kin. Beyond these obligations, spouses enjoyed considerable autonomy. Each could pursue independent income-generating activities and accumulate wealth beyond the interference of the other.[67]

These ideals were interpreted and practiced in multiple ways. Although nearly all Yoruba women engaged in trade or food processing, for instance, they were often expected to help their husbands with farm tasks as well.[68] Women's independent earning thus occurred more in some areas than others. Women's contributions to household budgets also varied, although nearly all provided at least some food and clothing. A 1952 survey of households in cocoa-producing areas showed that three-fourths of the wives were working on their own accounts. One-fifth of the women provided all their own food and clothing, while half clothed themselves and provided part of the household's food. Five percent were totally dependent on their husbands.[69] Similarly, men liberally interpreted the obligation to provide a new wife's trading capital. In a 1935 Ibadan divorce case, for example, Lamidi wanted to reclaim money he had given his wife to start a trade. Moriamo, however, testified that the money had never been used for trade; instead, she had used it to feed the family when Lamidi was jobless. A woman in a 1949 case testified that contrary to her husband's claims, he never gave her a penny for trade in the eleven months they were married. Witnesses testified in 1950 that one Sabitiyu had divorced her husband of fifteen years because she was unsatisfied with the amount of money he was able to give her for trade.[70]

Regardless of their wealth relative to each other, women tended to have some cash on hand more frequently than their husbands did, simply because of the differences between trading and farming. While women's trade provided them with liquid capital (and indeed, most traders made no distinction between personal and business money), farmers had to wait until they sold their crops to gain access to cash. Further, because of the heavy social demands on those holding cash money, many farmers preferred to sell their crops a little at a time, keeping nearly no currency, to avoid having their money disappear into the pockets of friends and relatives.[71] This meant that women often were the ones to maintain domestic budgets, especially when a man's wealth was limited. Women became exasperated with husbands who were not financially responsible or who channeled too much of their incomes outside of the household. Their most common complaint in divorce cases was lack of sufficient financial maintenance.[72]

Court records are full of cases in which husbands and wives quarreled over money, sometimes in the context of divorce and sometimes not. The web of debts and other financial transactions between spouses not only reiterates that separate economies coexisted within households but also shows that money and other exchanges were deeply connected to emotions and status within relationships. As long as couples were getting along well, debts and payments might represent affectionate presents or even business transactions worthy of little comment. If there were disputes, however, the same exchanges might become sources of conflict only resolved in the courts.[73] In a case from 1930, for instance, Moboroje testified that she had frequently given her husband Yesufu money, some of which she had obtained from her mother, for business expenses. But when Yesufu showed himself to be both a poor businessman and a poor husband, Moboroje filed for divorce. Not only did Yesufu not make a profit with her investment; according to Moboroje's mother, he just went "about drinking and dancing till he consumed the whole money."[74] In another example, S.A. Adebo, two years after divorcing Ladisun, listed over £20 in debts accumulated by his wife of sixteen years. He would not have sued for recovery, he stated, if not for the fact that she had left him for another man.[75]

One of the ways men could attempt to resolve marital disputes outside of court was through the payment of "begging fees." Men paid their wives to win favor after an argument, to atone for physical abuse, and to apologize for having spent too long away from home. In 1933, Lamuni paid his wayward wife Rihonatu Foyelle £2.10 "that she might not leave me again." After paying £12.10 in marriage expenses, Lamidi still could not convince his new wife Raji to accept him as her husband. He gave her an additional £13 in an effort to sway her. Current or future mothers, fathers, and brothers-in-law received begging money in exchange for favorable intervention, consent to the marriage, or forgiveness for an offense.[76] Similar payments could be required by lineage elders and customary courts as a form of dispute resolution.[77]

Exchanges such as these represented men's attempts to maintain marital harmony. Although their efforts to become "big men" often were directed outside of the household, keeping a wife was crucial for masculine status and identity, and spending money was an important way to do so. This is not to imply that payments were cynical attempts to "buy" favor in the absence of underlying affection. The relationship between marriage and money in colonial

Yorubaland suggests the limits of distinguishing between a presumptive amoral economic sphere and a noneconomic emotional sphere. An itemized list of payments made by a man to his betrothed likely showed his commitment to and affection for her just as a love poem might in another context. Money, as an integral part of individual identity and status, had the power to show sentiment as nothing else could.[78]

CONCLUSION

Money was linked to masculinity in colonial Yorubaland in a number of ways. The expansion of wage labor early in the twentieth century was propelled by young men's aspirations to marry and embark upon their adult lives—transitions that required cash. By marking marriage and helping to reconcile marital differences, money symbolized and facilitated social agreements between parties; and by making payments, a male suitor was able to become a husband and father. Later in life, money allowed adult men to take on the attributes of seniority by providing for children's education, assisting lineage members, investing in the community, and building a house. Even more money could translate into greater social influence, patronage, and the status of "big man." A history of the social implications of wage labor needs this understanding of the importance of money for identity and status.

Yet the normative ideals linking money and masculinity did not include the notion that men should be the sole financial providers within their households, or that wives should not earn money as well. As a group of female traders expressed it to political authorities in 1938, "Although we are women, we have responsibilities, same as our menfolk; we feed our children, send them to school, and support our old mothers and fathers, and pay taxes for our old or unemployed menfolk. It is not the practice in this country as it may be elsewhere, that husbands support wives; here wives must work, and maintain not only themselves but their children and other dependents."[79] In the next chapter, I begin to explore the interactions between this version of gender and labor and one understood and acted upon by colonial administrators and employers. In the 1930s, officials embraced the notion of wives as earners, especially because it fit nicely with their conceptions of male workers as casual employees with limited monetary needs. Ultimately this view would be challenged by trade unions and twisted into something else by employers—but that story comes in later chapters.

NOTES

1. Stephan F. Miescher and Lisa A. Lindsay, "Men and Masculinities in Modern African History," in Lindsay and Miescher (eds.), *Men and Masculinities in Modern Africa* (Portsmouth, NH: Heinemann, 2003).

2. See Jane I. Guyer (ed.), *Money Matters: Instability, Values and Social Payments in the Modern History of West African Communities* (Portsmouth, NH: Heinemann, 1995); and Jane I. Guyer, "Wealth in People, Wealth in Things—Introduction," *JAH* 36 (1995): 83–90.

3. Karin Barber, "Money, Self-Realization, and the Person in Yoruba Texts," in *Money Matters*, ed. J.I. Guyer, pp. 205 and 207 quoted. Similarly in Asante, "Money provides the building blocks of social solidarity. . . ."; Gracia Clark, "Gender and Profiteering: Ghana's Market Women as Devoted Mothers and 'Human Vampire Bats,'" in Dorothy L. Hodgson and Sheryl A. McCurdy (eds.), *"Wicked" Women and the Reconfiguration of Gender in Africa* (Portsmouth, NH: Heinemann, 2001), p. 298.

4. Toyin Falola and Akanmu Adebayo, *Culture, Politics, and Money among the Yoruba* (New Brunswick, NJ: Transaction Publishers, 2000), p. 51.

5. The best study of Yoruba women and the link between trade and gender identity is Niara Sudarkasa, *Where Women Work: A Study of Yoruba Women in the Marketplace and in the Home,* Anthropological Papers No. 53 (Ann Arbor: Museum of Anthropology, University of Michigan, 1973). For more on Yoruba women, see Bolanle Awe, "The Economic Role of Women in a Traditional African Society: The Yoruba Example," in *La Civilisation de la Femme dans la Tradition Africaine* (Paris: Presence Africaine, 1975); LaRay Denzer, "Yoruba Women: A Historiographical Study," *International Journal of African Historical Studies* 27 (1994): 1–39; Cheryl Johnson, "Towards a Conceptual Framework for the Study of African Women: A Case Study of Pre-Colonial and Colonial Yoruba Women," *Red River Historical Journal of World History* 55 (1979): 52–63; Wambui M. Karanja-Diejomaoh, "Perceptions of Marriage, Family and Work in Nigeria: A Study of Lagos Market Women" (D.Phil., Oxford University, 1980).

6. This section is based primarily on the following sources: Wogu Ananaba, *The Trade Union Movement in Nigeria* (New York: Africana Publishing Corp., 1970), ch. 1; Arnold Hughes and Robin Cohen, "An Emerging Nigerian Working Class: The Lagos Experience, 1897–1939," in *African Labor History,* ed. Peter C.W. Gutkind, Robin Cohen and Jean Copans (Beverly Hills, CA: Sage, 1978); A.G. Hopkins, "The Lagos Strike of 1897: An Exploration in Nigerian Labour History," *Past and Present* 35 (1966): 133–55; and T.M. Yesufu, *An Introduction to Industrial Relations in Nigeria* (London: Oxford University Press, 1962).

7. Kristin Mann, "Owners, Slaves and the Struggle for Labor in the Commercial Transition at Lagos," in *From Slave Trade to "Legitimate" Commerce: The Commercial Transition in Nineteenth-Century West Africa,* ed. Robin Law (Cambridge: Cambridge University Press, 1995).

8. Hopkins, "Lagos Strike," p. 147.

9. Ibid., p. 143. Wale Oyemakinde disagrees that there were labor shortages in southwest Nigeria, arguing that the end of the Yoruba wars and the abolition of slavery yielded ex-soldiers and ex-slaves looking for employment. "Railway Construction and Operation in Nigeria, 1895–1911: Labour Problems and Socio-Economic Impact," *JHSN* 7 (1974): 303–24 and "A History of Indigenous Labour on the Nigerian Railway, 1895–1945" (Ph.D. dissertation, University of Ibadan, 1970), ch. 2.

10. T.M. Yesufu, *The Dynamics of Industrial Relations: The Nigerian Experience* (Ibadan: University Press Ltd., 1984), p. 15.

11. This is the alleged "backward bending supply curve," in which employment was defined as "target labor" and supposedly was in greater supply the lower the wages. Hopkins, "Lagos Strike."

12. Lugard, *Political Memoranda* (London: HMSO, 1919), p. 243, cited in Yesufu, *Dynamics,* p. 19.

13. Sara S. Berry, *Cocoa, Custom, and Socio-Economic Change in Rural Western Nigeria* (Oxford: Oxford University Press, 1975); J.D.Y. Peel, *Ijeshas and Nigerians: The Incorporation of a Yoruba Kingdom, 1890s–1970s* (Cambridge: Cambridge University Press, 1983), ch. 7.

14. Peel, *Ijeshas,* ch. 8, p. 106.

15. Karin Barber, *The Generation of Plays: Yoruba Popular Life in Theater* (Bloomington: Indiana University Press, 2000), p. 455, n. 3; A. Babs. Fafunwa, *History of Education in Nigeria* (London: George Allen and Unwin, 1974), pp. 97, 112, 115.

16. N.A. Fadipe, *The Sociology of the Yoruba,* eds. Francis Olu. Okediji and Oladejo O. Okediji (Ibadan: Ibadan University Press, 1970 [1940]), p. 322.

17. Oyemakinde, "Railway Construction," p. 305.

18. Fadipe, *Sociology,* p. 92.

19. Governor MacGregor to Secretary of State Chamberlain, December 27, 1899, CO 147/145, cited in Kristin Mann, *Marrying Well: Marriage, Status and Social Change among the Educated Elite in Colonial Lagos* (Cambridge: Cambridge University Press, 1985), pp. 172–73, fn. 21.

20. Judith Byfield, "Women, Marriage, Divorce and the Emerging Colonial State in Abeokuta (Nigeria), 1892–1904," *CJAS* 30, 1 (1996): 32–51, 40.

21. Anthony G. Hopkins, "A Report on the Yoruba, 1910," *JHSN* 5 (1969): 67–100, 79, quoted in Mann, *Marrying Well,* p. 113.

22. Some of the material in this and the following sections also appears in Lisa A. Lindsay, "'No Need . . . to Think of Home'? Masculinity and Domestic Life on the Nigerian Railway, c.1940–61," *JAH* 39 (1998): 439–66, and "Money, Marriage and Masculinity on the Colonial Nigerian Railway," *Men and Masculinities,* ed. Lindsay and Miescher.

23. William Bascom, *The Yoruba of Southwestern Nigeria* (New York: Holt, Rinehart & Winston, 1969), p. 56. On labor and adult masculinity, see Karin Barber, *I Could Speak until Tomorrow: Oriki, Women and the Past in a Yoruba Town* (Washington, DC: Smithsonian Institution Press, 1991), pp. 214–16.

24. Edward Ward, *The Yoruba Husband-Wife Code,* Catholic University of America Anthropology Series, No. 6 (Washington, DC: Catholic University of America, 1938), p. 62.

25. Barber, *I Could Speak,* p. 216. Also see Peel, *Ijeshas,* p. 119.

26. These exchanges should be understood in the context of the generalized circulation of presents in Yorubaland, which as Peel notes for the nineteenth century, "signified and established moral relationships. They served to define community and . . . to reassert the donor's membership of it." J.D.Y. Peel, *Religious Encounter and the Making of the Yoruba* (Bloomington: Indiana University Press, 2000), p. 86.

27. Jane I. Guyer, "Lineal Identities and Lateral Networks: The Logic of Polyandrous Motherhood," *Nuptiality in Sub-Saharan Africa: Contemporary Anthropological and Demographic Perspectives,* ed. Caroline Bledsoe and Gilles Pilson (Oxford: Clarendon Press, 1994). In *Marrying Well,* Mann argues that the early twentieth century was a particular period of flux in Yoruba marriages.

28. Mann, *Marrying Well,* ch. 2, based on the experience in Lagos. Peel (*Ijeshas,* p. 118) notes that in Ilesha, because of the combined effects of the cocoa economy and indirect rule, marriage required cash from early in the twentieth century. For the similar

monetization of marriage expenses in Ghana, see Jean Allman and Victoria Tashjian, *"I Will Not Eat Stone": A Women's History of Colonial Asante* (Portsmouth, NH: Heinemann, 2000).

29. Ward, *Code,* p. 64; Barber, *I Could Speak,* p. 217; R. Galletti, K.D.S. Baldwin, and I.O. Dina, *Nigerian Cocoa Farmers: An Economic Survey of Yoruba Cocoa Farming Families* (Oxford: Oxford University Press, 1956), pp. 214 and 265. Relevant court cases include CvRB, Bere (Ibadan District) II Native Civil Court B6, vol. ? [torn cover], 15/30, Odunola vs. Salami, October 9, 1930, p. 47; and CvRB, Bere vol. ?, 633/35, Lamidi vs. Moriamo, September 18, 1935, pp. 160–62.

30. For example, Ojaba II Native Court, Oke Are (Ibadan), vol. 35, 124/55, Lamidi Adegbimdin vs. Yesufu Alamu, March 21, 1955, pp. 1–3.

31. Bascom, *The Yoruba,* 60–62; H.U. Beier, "The Position of Yoruba Women," *Presence Africaine* 1 (1955): 39–46.

32. Fadipe, *Sociology,* p. 76; CvRB, Ojaba Native Court II, Oke Are, vol. 12, 428/49, Lapide vs. Selia, December 7, 1949, pp. 93–94; CvRB, Customary Court Grade B No. 6, Mapo (Ibadan), vol. 2, 2419/58, Matthew Awoniyi vs. Lasupo Ajadi, December 5, 1958–February 6, 1959, 56ff. Other relevant cases are CvRB, Bere I Native Court, vol. 30, 83/51, Ladejo vs. Yekinni, May 25, 1951, p. 1 and Customary Court Grade C, Agodi (Ibadan), vol. 5, 3/64, Wosilatu Adoke vs. Lamidi Iyanda, April 10, 1964, p. 137.

33. CvRB, Ojaba I Native Court, Oke Are (Ibadan), vol. 92, 12/54, Muraina Alabi vs. Amuda Anike, January 21, 1954, pp. 66–69.

34. For an analogous situation in Ghana, see Allman and Tashjian, *"I Will Not Eat Stone,"* ch. 2.

35. John C. Caldwell, I.O. Orubuloye, and Pat Caldwell, "The Destabilization of the Traditional Yoruba Sexual System," *Population and Development Review* 17 (1991): 229–62, 239; Mann, *Marrying Well,* p. 42.

36. CvRB, Ojaba Native Court, Oke Are, vol. 10, 63/37, Salami vs. Lanlehin, August 12, 1937, pp. 21–24; Bere I Native Court, vol. 18, 326/41, Adefunmi vs. Akinyemi, April 8, 1941, pp. 243–44; Bere II Native Court, vol. 138, 904/58, Silifatu Ajile vs. Layiwole Amoo, May 28, 1958, pp. 155–57.

37. Guyer, "Lineal Identities"; Bascom, *The Yoruba,* p. 60; E. Ward, *Marriage among the Yoruba* (Washington, DC: Catholic University of America, 1937), p. 30; Bernth Lindfors and Oyekan Owomoyela, *Yoruba Proverbs: Translation and Annotation,* Papers in International Studies, Africa Series No. 17 (Athens: Ohio University Center for International Studies, 1973).

38. Peel, *Ijeshas,* pp. 118–19; Barber, *I Could Speak,* pp. 216–7.

39. Among others, see Luise White, *The Comforts of Home: Prostitution in Colonial Nairobi* (Chicago: University of Chicago Press, 1990), ch. 2; William Beinart, *The Political Economy of Pondoland, 1860–1930* (Cambridge: Cambridge University Press, 1982), ch. 3; Bill Bravman, *Making Ethnic Ways: Communities and Their Transformations in Taita, Kenya, 1800–1950* (Portsmouth, NH: Heinemann, 1998); Peel, *Ijeshas.*

40. Peel, *Ijeshas,* p. 118.

41. J.D.Y. Peel, "*Olaju*: A Yoruba Concept of Development," *Journal of Development Studies* 14 (1978): 130–65, 151, and 162, n.27.

42. Peel, *Ijeshas,* p. 119.

43. Fadipe, *Sociology,* pp. 92 and 325.

44. Peel, *Ijeshas,* p. 119; Peel, *Religious Encounter,* p. 245.

45. Fadipe, *Sociology,* p. 67.

46. CvRB, Bere I Native Court, vol. 8, 61/39, Oke vs. Ladepe [Ladipo?], January 19, 1939, pp. 246–50.

47. E.S. Pembleton, Secretary of the Northern Provinces, to Chief Secretary to the Government, July 25, 1936, CSO 26/30004.

48. Andrea Cornwall, "Wayward Women and Useless Men: Contest and Change in Gender Relations in Ado-Odo, S.W. Nigeria," in *"Wicked" Women,* ed. Hodgson and McCurdy, pp. 73.

49. The same could be said even for highly educated employees like Simeon Adebo, who married in 1940 at the age of twenty-seven, eight years after beginning employment as a railway accounts clerk. Chief Simeon O. Adebo, *Our Unforgettable Years* (Lagos: MacMillian Nigeria Publishers Ltd., 1983), p. 56.

50. Daniel Anirarę Aladesanmi, *My Early Life: An Autobiography* (privately published in Nigeria, 1977), p. 49.

51. M.O. Shofekun, April 4, 1994, Ibadan.

52. Onuora Nzekwu, *Blade among the Boys* (London: Heinemann, 1962), pp. 123 and 125.

53. Fadipe, *Sociology,* p. 323; "African Civil Service Union," *WAP,* September 11, 1941; *WAP,* October 18, 1941.

54. Adebo, *Unforgettable Years,* pp. 42 and 56; Nigeria, *Annual Report of the Department of Labor* (Lagos: Government Printer, 1943), p. 3; M.C. Adegbulu, "That Inhuman Bridal Price," *LC,* March 24, 1950. Also see Buchi Emecheta's novel, *The Joys of Motherhood* (New York: George Brazillier, 1979), for the horror experienced by parents living in Lagos in the 1940s and 1950s, when their eldest sons refused to work toward the family's support.

55. Bernard Aruna (former locomotive driver), December 28, 1993, Ibadan; M.O. Adegbite (who rose from railway laborer to foreman blacksmith), December 28, 1993, Ibadan.

56. Fadipe, *Sociology,* p. 325.

57. Barber, *I Could Speak,* p. 218 quoted. Also see Sara Berry, *Fathers Work for Their Sons: Accumulation, Mobility, and Class Formation in an Extended Yoruba Community* (Berkeley: University of California Press, 1985).

58. E. Ward, *Marriage among the Yoruba* (Washington, DC: Catholic University of America, 1938), p. 29.

59. Barber, *I Could Speak,* ch. 6. For the life history of an urban "big man," see Kristin Mann, "The Rise of Taiwo Olowo: Law, Accumulation, and Mobility in Early Colonial Lagos," in *Law in Colonial Africa,* ed. Kristin Mann and Richard Roberts (Portsmouth, NH: Heinemann, 1991). For the continuity of the big man ideal through much of African history, see Miescher and Lindsay, "Men and Masculinities."

60. Barber, "Money, Self-Realization," p. 213; Barber, *I Could Speak,* p. 183.

61. Barber, *Generation of Plays,* p. 21; Barber, *I Could Speak,* p. 243. Also see Peel, *Ijeshas* and *"Olaju"*; and Berry, *Fathers Work.*

62. Peel, *Ijeshas,* p. 81.

63. Galletti, *Nigerian Cocoa Farmers,* pp. 72–73; Bascom, *The Yoruba,* p. 65.

64. Barber, *Generation of Plays,* p. 283.

65. For southern Ghana, which in many ways seems similar to Yorubaland, see inter alia Claire Robertson, *Sharing the Same Bowl: A Socioeconomic History of Women and Class in Accra, Ghana* (Bloomington: Indiana University Press, 1984); Gracia Clark, *Onions Are My Husband: Survival and Accumulation by West African Market Women*

(Chicago: University of Chicago Press, 1994); and Allman and Tashjian, *"I Will Not Eat Stone."* In Nigeria, most marriages are still based on separate incomes and spending, as I discuss in subsequent chapters.

66. I thank Andrea Cornwall for this insight.

67. Mann, *Marrying Well,* p. 40; Sudarkasa, *Where Women Work.*

68. Berry, *Fathers Work.* Galletti noted that more female trading was done in Ijebu, Abeokuta, and Ibadan than Ondo or Owo. *Nigerian Cocoa Farmers,* p. 76.

69. Galletti, *Nigerian Cocoa Farmers,* p. 77. Also see Sudarkasa, *Where Women Work.*

70. CvRB, Bere Native Court, vol. ?, 633/35, Lamidi vs. Moriamo, September 18, 1935, pp. 160–62; CvRB, Ojaba II Native Court, Oke Are, vol. 12, 408/49, Salami vs. Rabi, November 6, 1949, pp. 1–4 and 33/50, S.A. Akinfanda vs. Sabitiyu, February 7, 1950, pp. 231–37.

71. Jane Mason Guyer, "The Organizational Plan of Traditional Farming: Idere, Western Nigeria" (Ph.D. dissertation, University of Rochester, 1972), ch. 6.

72. Nigeria, *Annual Report of the Federal Social Welfare Department for the Year 1955–56* (Lagos: Government Printer, 1956), p. 10 and innumerable divorce cases involving financial "neglect."

73. For examples, see CvRB, Ojaba I Native Court, Oke Are, vol. 21, 1693/30, Ayi vs. Lawani, September 8, 1930, pp. 231–37; CvRB, Bere I Native Court, vol. 23, 233/42, Foyeke vs. Obasawi, February 24, 1942, pp. 125–26.

74. CvRB, Ojaba 1 Native Court, Oke Are, vol. 21, 340/30, Moboroje vs. Yesufu, September 1, 1930, p. 216.

75. CvRB, Ojaba IIB Native Court, Oke Are, vol. 14, 591/50, S.A. Adebo vs. Ladisun, November 1, 1950, pp. 279–286. Similar cases include CvRB, Bere II Native Court B6, vol. ? [torn cover], 45/30, Salami vs. Ibidun, October 7, 1930, p. 30; CvRB, Ojaba Native Court, Oke Are, vol. 47, 529/33, Lamuni vs. Rihonatu Foyelle, March 20, 1933, pp. 2–9; CvRB, Ojaba Native Court, Oke Are, vol. 49, 471/34, Ogundike vs. Eboade, July 19, 1934, pp. 356–58; CvRB, Bere I Native Court, vol. ?, 655/38, Oyekunle vs. Adegoke, June 7, 1938, pp. 283–91; CvRB, Ojaba Native Court, Oke Are, vol. ?, 107/47, Yawerera Agbaje vs. Gbadamosi Alabi, March 22, 1946, pp. 43–44; CvRB, Ojaba II B Native Court, vol. 7, 56/49, Adeyemo vs. Rabi, February 16, 1949, pp. 148–51.

76. CvRB, Ojaba Native Court, Oke Are vol. 47, 529/33, Lamuni vs. Rihonatu Foyelle, March 20, 1933, pp. 2–9 and Ojaba I Native Court, Oke Are, vol. 83, 64/51, Lamidi vs. Raji, May 11, 1951, pp. 103–04. Other examples include CvRB, Bere Native Court, vol. ?, 912/36, Selia vs. Lajide, April 16, 1936, pp. 321–23; Bere I Native Court, vol. 18, 286/41, Barikisu vs. Yesufu, March 27, 1941, pp. 200–202; Bere I Native Court, vol. ?, 816/37, Ayi vs. Salau, May 25, 1937, pp. 53–55; Bere Native Court, vol. ?, 517/36, Adenike vs. Johnson, August 27, 1936, pp. 311–13; Bere I Native Court, vol. 23, 193/42, Joseph Abioye vs. Ainke, February 12, 1942, p. 88; Oke Are Customary Court No. 4, Grade B, D946/60, Bolatito Adunni vs. Gabriel Ayoade, July 11, 1960, pp. 527–30.

77. Kristin Mann, "Women's Rights in Law and Practice: Marriage and Dispute Settlement in Colonial Lagos," in *African Women and the Law: Historical Perspectives,* ed. Margaret Jean Hay and Marcia Wright (Boston, MA: Boston University, 1982). "Begging fees" seem to parallel the gifts vulnerable Ibadan chiefs in the nineteenth century gave to "appease anger." Peel, *Religious Encounter,* p. 86.

78. Maurice Bloch and Jonathan Parry, "Introduction," in J. Parry and M. Bloch (eds.), *Money and the Morality of Exchange* (Cambridge: Cambridge University Press, 1989);

John Comaroff, "Introduction," in *The Meaning of Marriage Payments,* ed. J.L. Comaroff (London: Academic Press, 1980); Barber, "Money, Self-Realization."

79. Petition from Sarah Abeo and the Union of Women Cotton Goods Traders of Ibadan to the Olubadan [traditional ruler] and Council, August 26, 1938, Provincial Records, Ibadan Division, 1/1 1651, NAI.

3

FAMILIES, JOBS, AND THE STATE BEFORE 1945

In 1934 Mrs. Genevieve Oldfield, described simply as "a resident of Nigeria, where she has lived for several years," undertook a survey of Nigerian railway workers. Her report, published two years later in *Africa,* epitomizes wage labor in the 1930s. On one hand, a long section describes the training and salary scales of an array of occupations, from the highly paid first-class clerks, station masters, and locomotive drivers to the hourly paid manual laborers, who nonetheless were required to have a Standard VI education as a condition of their employment. Nearly half of the 2,288 railway men surveyed "expressed the desire to advance in the railway service to higher positions." On the other hand, Oldfield was mainly concerned with "the extent to which contact with a foreign civilization is responsible for the state of native society one finds to-day in the Colony of Nigeria." The basic demographic and employment information collected then prompted discussion of questions such as "Does the native think for himself?" and assertions that "Essentially a happy-go-lucky race, they [Nigerians] would gladly reap the benefits of others' work, accept—if possible—the inventions and luxuries of other lands without stirring a hand to be worthy of them." The workplace realities of African labor—the qualifications necessary for each job, salary scales, promotion prospects, career ambitions— were there, but the questions that this European researcher chose for analysis were of a different order, concerned instead with the "racial" differences between Africans and Europeans and, to a lesser extent, the social and economic implications of those alleged differences.[1]

Oldfield's survey was unusual in the sense that few analyses of Nigerian employment before World War II were produced at all. Indeed, administrative reports from the 1930s contain hardly any information about the wage labor force. Rather, the government merely reported in successive annual reports that "the vast majority of the population do not work for wages, being cultivators farming their own ground, traders or craftsmen working for themselves and their own profit."[2] Although early in the twentieth century officials had been concerned with finding enough workers for government projects, by the depression years that concern had evaporated. Further, colonial administrators were not particularly concerned with wages and job conditions given that the numbers in formal employment were relatively low and that, in their estimation, dissatisfied workers could simply return to family farms. Most labor was defined as casual and understood to be staffed by "target" workers seeking quick returns from temporary labor migration. Officials' understanding of African family life was deeply tied into this conception of labor: extended families functioned as safety nets, the thinking went, obviating the need for pensions or unemployment provisions; similarly, since wives provided for themselves and their children, wages need only support a single man.

Yet even as officials insisted on the marginality of wage labor to African life, thus justifying the lack of reforms, they were also confronted with evidence to the contrary. Certainly wage laborers did generally combine their employment with other forms of income generation, and certainly they did rely on wives and kin for material contributions: these strategies were fundamental to social and economic life. But at the same time, they also used their wages to *support* family members, an aspect of the much lauded (at the time) extended family that officials generally ignored until later. Moreover, the assumption that all wage labor was temporary and to meet specific targets overlooked significant numbers, particularly by the 1930s, who made long careers in wage employment. As trade unions came into being during the depression, they immediately focused on the status of these long-term, yet "daily-paid," workers. They also began to argue that African systems of family and gender could not be used to justify low wages and poor conditions.

Moreover, trade unions and individual workers attended to the pressures faced by wage earners trying to balance urban labor with involvement in the hometown. Although southern Nigeria's cities predated the colonial period and were home to established urban families, many urban wage earners were migrants from small towns or rural areas. With little access to paid leave or affordable transport, such workers had a difficult time maintaining close contact with their hometown relatives. In the absence of pensions and unemployment insurance, such contacts were vital elements in wage earners' long-term survival strategies. Such considerations helped to propel labor activism from the earliest years of union activity. After wages, the most common issue of contention was annual leave, which allowed a worker to spend time with his family without giving up his job. As union activities intensified during World War II, they focused not only on wages and the cost of living, but also on benefits considered necessary for migrants away from their extended families.

During this period, we can also see a shift in the way officials interpreted African workers' kinship ties. Although during the depression administrators in Nigeria had viewed hometown connections as important safety nets that justified a lack of labor reforms, by the early 1940s they saw chain migration, based on hometown connections, as the root of urban overcrowding and unemployment. Now, particularly in the face of labor activism around the family needs of urban migrants, they no longer praised local systems of extended family supports but instead saw workers' family connections as a problem. Wage increases and improvements in urban amenities might be appropriate for urban workers, the thinking went, but they were impractical in Lagos and elsewhere because the benefits would just be diffused through workers' social and familial networks. As in the earlier period, colonial officials justified their reluctance to institute labor reforms through reference to wage earners' extended families, even though the ways of understanding African family life had shifted over the previous decade.

FAMILIES, LABOR, AND THE STATE DURING THE DEPRESSION

For Nigerian workers, wage labor before the 1940s offered monetary incentives but few other benefits and little long-term security. Since their inception, the Nigerian Railway, Marine, and Public Works departments and other large employers had relied on a large casual labor force to ensure flexibility and low labor costs. When budgets tightened, workers were simply sent home, a profitable system but one that gave workers no income reliability. According to Luke Emujulu, a leader of the Railway Workers Union in the 1940s, before the beginnings of union agitation, "men had no vacation leave, old age pension, gratuity and all the perquisites of the Civil Service were dreams of an Utopia for a privileged few. . . . It was the rule rather than the exception to grant workers a periodical forth-night [sic] leave of absence without pay."[3] In response to a query sent from the secretary of state to all of the British colonies, Nigeria's administrative officer summarized the labor laws in force as of 1931, all of which had been passed in a Labor Ordinance two years previously. Ten hours of work for laborers were set per day, with a two-hour break, but the "laborers" to whom this referred were strictly defined; wages and overtime rates were unregulated; labor contracts were enforceable through fines and imprisonment; limited housing and medical facilities were available in a few, mostly remote, locations; and a few welfare measures, including very limited workman's compensation, were in effect.[4] Moreover, real wages declined in the 1930s relative to previous levels. Although early in the twentieth century officials had been worried about finding enough workers, by the 1930s that concern was gone. The poor prices paid for produce and massive retrenchments in the public sector meant that the supply of wage labor greatly exceeded demand. Cost-cutting measures on the railway included layoffs and a new system of payments based on hourly, rather than daily, calculations, instituted in 1931. In effect, when workers were idled because of broken machinery or delays on the system, they were not paid. Average wages for casual labor in 1935 were 3 to 8 pence per day, compared with 9 pence per day when workers were scarce at the turn of the century. Although their grievances were many, employees were in a weak position to protest the new measures given the gross disparities between the demand for jobs and available positions. In 1931 the Railway Workers Union split off from the Association of Nigerian Railway Civil Servants, founded in 1919, because of outrage over the new hourly wage payment system. The new union protested the wage calculations but lacked official recognition and remained weak throughout the decade.[5]

A slight improvement in the economy in the late 1930s created the space for new agitation for better conditions of service. After a 1938 meeting at the Ebute Metta railway compound was broken up by police, the union approached Sir William Geary, a British solicitor resident in Lagos, to be its official advocate. For the next several years, Geary urged General Manager J.H. McEwen, Governor Bourdillon, and eventually Secretary of State Malcolm MacDonald to reform the railway payment system, reclassify certain categories of workers as part of the permanent establishment, and institute provisions for sick leave, vacations, and pensions. Geary argued that Nigerian railway workers should be subject to the same working conditions—though not rates of pay—as their British counterparts, and that it was racist not to extend such benefits to them. Such inaction might be dangerous as well, he suggested: "Now my clients have not votes . . . but they might strike . . . [so] why not have some such legislation [covering conditions of service] as a safety valve?" McEwen maintained that British and Nigerian workers were "not comparable," and that the only railway men similar to Nigerians were those in other colonies. Bourdillon and MacDonald backed the general manager on this point, especially since they felt the government could not afford the concessions Geary was requesting. "[I]n Nigeria any improvement in conditions of service must be dependent on finance," Geary was informed, and "there were certain very desirable reforms which the Government would not be able for financial reasons, to afford for a long time."[6]

In addition to the financial argument, government officials during the 1930s maintained that labor reforms were not necessary because relatively few Africans were entirely dependent on wage labor and because their families provided financial safety nets. A 1935 government commission pointed to family ties as decisive in supporting the 120,000 unemployed in the colony's capital: "non-Lagos-born unemployed seem to be maintained and housed by relatives and friends in employment in Lagos and also wives and mothers of Lagos-born unemployed who are engaged in petty trade form solid support of unemployed men."[7] Jobless Lagosians managed to subsist "entirely [through] the goodwill of their relations and friends who are in good employment."[8] Annual social and economic reports made the same case year after year through the 1930s: labor improvements and welfare provisions were not necessary because extended families took care of their members. "The terms of employment of Africans are generally satisfactory and their system of living in family compounds or tribal groups by which many can live for long periods of unemployment, even in Lagos, without acute distress will always tend to prevent natives from having to accept employment under bad conditions merely in order to exist."[9] In 1937, at the instigation of the Colonial Office, the Nigerian government constituted a committee on conditions of labor in Lagos. The committee rarely met over the next two years, although in 1939 its members each investigated housing in different Lagos districts. Their reports contain references to severe poverty and unemployment, yet the inhabitants of these working people's slums were said to be "happy, healthy, and contented with their lot."[10]

Such arguments about African family life justified a lack of official attention to workers' retirement needs. For the first two decades of wage labor in Nigeria, neither government nor private employers offered any provisions for workers whose employment ended due to old age or incapacity. In 1904 the railway traffic and clerical staff went on strike in part because the government reneged on its promise to institute a Provident and Guarantee Fund.[11] After 1915 many government departments and larger firms offered minimal provident funds, to which employees were required to contribute a set percentage of their wages. The employer matched the workers' contributions, interest accrued, and the whole account was available in a lump sum when the employment ended. Officials considered provident funds to be superior to pension schemes for Africans largely because they were inexpensive to maintain. From the start, though, workers and their representatives protested their forced contributions and the fact that benefits were insufficient to sustain retirees.[12] These were the luckier ones: daily-paid workers complained that they were not even eligible for provident funds.[13] Still, officials assumed that pensions were not necessary because retired employees would be supported by their relatives or by farming. "The people of Nigeria have not advanced to that stage of civilization where it has become necessary for the state to make provision for its destitute members. The family or clan is still a very vital force and its members look after and support one another, in sickness, old age or any other misfortune."[14] Similarly, there was no workman's compensation for injuries, which were frequent.[15] Moreover, migrant workers were often compelled to take unpaid annual leave, even if they did not have the means to visit their hometowns.[16]

In the 1930s only about 10 percent of the railway workforce was classified as part of the "permanent establishment," subject to monthly salaries and certain fringe benefits. Other government departments with large workforces, such as Public Works and Marine, did not differentiate between permanent and casual workers in their annual reports, but the vast majority of their employees were considered "unestablished" as well. In actuality, as Geary pointed out, there was a much greater proportion of stable railway labor, since many employees of all categories made the railway their career and served it for up to thirty years. The fact that they were classified as "daily-rated" or "daily-paid" meant that they were theoretically rehired on a casual basis every day of their long careers. As the Railway Workers Union gained strength, this system became a principal focus of protest.

In spite of official rhetoric that all labor was casual, or temporary "target" work, there is evidence of long-term careers from the early twentieth century. Such evidence is fragmentary because of the lack of official reporting on labor during this period, but it does point to the existence of "stabilized" workers long before that term was used by colonial bureaucrats. A.G. Hopkins has identified, in addition to the Public Works Department strike of 1897, six other strikes in the Lagos area between 1886 and 1904. In addition to low wages, workers also complained about their lack of job security and the absence of a provident fund for retirement, indicating that even at this early date a segment of the Nigerian workforce was willing to consider long-term wage employment.[17] Israel Fleming Johnson began his maritime career in the engineering section of the Royal Niger Company, where he worked from 1910 to 1913. The next year he joined the Marine Department and worked there as an engineer until his retirement in 1937. Johnson became the first African to captain a ferryboat from Apapa to Lagos wharf, in 1924.[18] In 1932, A.M. Taylor, a railway pay clerk, petitioned the Colonial Office because he felt he had been unjustly fired. He had been hired in 1920 and was earning a high salary; he had no intention of leaving his job.[19]

Less educated workers also made long careers, sometimes—but not always—advancing through promotions. In 1933, the *Daily Times* announced the retirement party of David Jaiyeola Dosunmu, African foreman artisan, who had spent thirty-one consecutive years in government service, the first eight (1902–1910) of which were as daily-paid, that is, so-called "casual" labor. Just over 10 percent of the retirees in my random sample of railway personnel files had been hired before 1940 (45 out of 434). They all made long careers, retiring between 1957 and 1980. In a 1940 petition for improved wages, promotion prospects, and leave benefits, Michael Imoudu (about whom more will be said later) represented the grievances of workers in the railway mechanical department, whose average length of service was said to be twelve to fifteen years. A 1945 editorial in the *West African Pilot* complained that "men with over twenty years meritorious service to their credit should go by the paradoxical nomenclature of daily paid workers."[20]

The economic ties between such employees and their extended families were both more complex and more significant than the way officials in the

1930s portrayed them. While it was generally true that a man in urban employment could look to his hometown relatives in times of distress, it was also the case that he would make important contributions to the upkeep of his parents, siblings, and other relatives. In addition to the costs of education for young relatives or food for aged parents, there could be other claims on a worker's paycheck:

> A letter from his peasant parents domiciled amidst farm yards in his home informs him of the approach of the tax-collection season when he is to pay the tax of an unemployed brother, nephew, etc. Then comes a plaintive request that the family house at home must be saved from decrepitude. An enterprising uncle wants some money with which to start off as a petty trader or private blacksmith. Yet these are but few of the catalogue of problems the Nigerian worker has to face—so important is he to the rest of his community.[21]

The greater his earnings, the more a man would be expected to contribute to his relatives, as the Colonial Office's labor advisor, Major G. St. J. Orde Browne, noted on his tour of West Africa in 1941. "There is a custom, general throughout West Africa," he wrote, "whereby any man in permanent employment is expected to maintain not only his own wife and family (and he may of course be a polygamist), but also various relations and dependents. The better his pay, the larger the number that he is required to support." As examples, Orde Browne mentioned a Nigerian clerk earning £27 per month who maintained a household of nineteen members plus two domestic servants, along with a man living on an allowance of £2.10 per month from his brother-in-law who nonetheless refused the offer of a job at £4 per month.[22]

The Great Depression brought out the tensions between the big man ethic of dispensing patronage and supporting followers, family members' assumptions that kin would always help each other, and individuals' pressures to balance their budgets. For instance, in 1938, I.O. Robert, who worked in the Ebute Metta locomotive workshops, attempted to ease his own financial situation by requesting help from an influential patron in getting his brother a government job. Robert's brother and sister-in-law were currently living with him, and unless the brother got a job Robert would have to continue supporting them indefinitely.[23] A 1934 newspaper column described the bind faced by wage earners trying to live within their means during austere times, but still supporting numerous family members. "The African who has not the least intention of jettisoning . . . communal life and selfless devotion to the ideals of sires is to be applauded." The article acknowledged that extended family responsibilities were often "self-imposed" and related to the fact that a man's "importance or status in his community is assessed more from what he appears to be than what he really is in the private recess of his house." Yet it asserted that "life is not worth all that is claimed for it if the man . . . who could afford it, shunned this age-long spirit of altruism, instead of facing it manfully within reason." This column explicitly linked masculine valor with supporting relatives, at least to the best of one's ability, and even during hard times.[24]

LABOR AGITATION AND EARLY REFORMS

The outbreak of World War II in 1939 had dramatic repercussions for Nigerian labor and the economy.[25] By 1941, 16,000 Nigerians were in the army, and hundreds of thousands of others were mobilized for a rapid expansion in the production of raw materials and the construction of infrastructure. As the war spread to North Africa, the Middle East, and India, Nigeria gained strategic importance to Britain and its allies as a staging post for troops and for the organization of supplies to these places. Military camps, airports, and roads to connect them were rapidly constructed in or around such towns as Ibadan, Lagos, Kano, Enugu, Maiduguri, and Jos. Railway and harbor traffic increased dramatically. New production demands vastly expanded the wage labor force in Nigeria's cities, particularly Lagos, although continued migration kept the numbers of unemployed people high. Skilled workers were at a premium: defense regulations compelled those in essential services to work compulsory overtime, so that many Railway and Public Works employees were putting in seventy-seven-hour weeks.[26]

Trade unions took advantage of their bargaining position to press for improved wages and conditions. As Frederick Cooper has detailed, empire-wide developments in the 1930s and early 1940s also gave rise to a greater recognition of the importance of African labor within the Colonial Office.[27] In 1930, Secretary of State Lord Passfield had urged all colonial governments to legalize and encourage the existence of trade unions. In Nigeria, such a move occurred at the prompting of Geary's agitation, along with public outrage at the 1938 police breakup of a Railway Workers Union meeting.[28] Nigeria's Trade Union Ordinance, which took effect in 1939, officially recognized unions but required them to register with the government before negotiating with employers or taking industrial action. In January 1940, the Railway Workers Union became the first recognized union when Michael Imoudu filed the appropriate paperwork, at the last minute replacing another man who had lost his nerve. Imoudu, then a railway turner in his early thirties, later earned the nickname "Nigeria's Labor Leader Number 1," both because of his forceful leadership over the next two decades and because his was the first name on the official list of recognized unions.

The Railway Workers Union's registration gave it further impetus to press the demands it had been expressing for years, namely, for improved wages in the face of rising costs of living, a return to daily rates of pay instead of the hourly rates that had been introduced in 1931, and the transfer of certain job categories to the permanent establishment. Union officers organized provincial branches and addressed memoranda to railway management and the government. For over a year, officials gave them no satisfaction, even suggesting that it was too much trouble to answer their letters because of the war.[29] Tensions between the railway administration and the union mounted as labor leaders faced victimization and union meetings debated the merits of striking. In a May 1941 compromise, the government announced its acceptance of all the requested conditions except the cost of living adjustment, which other groups of workers were demanding as well and which would be referred to a commission of inquiry. With these concessions, 1,900 formerly casual railway workers (out of a total of nearly 16,000) were to be moved to the permanent establishment.[30]

Railway officials were charged with implementing the reforms, but they procrastinated for months, prompting the union and the nationalist Lagos newspaper, the *West African Pilot*, to demand management's proposals through much of the rainy season. When the plans were finally released in late September, they fell short of the RWU's expectations. The union attributed their deficiencies to the influence of Chief Mechanical Engineer W.G.W. Wilson, who for years had poor relations with employees and was particularly hated for his intransigence and blatant racism. On September 29, the *Pilot* published a union resolution condemning the management, especially Wilson. He apparently was so intimidated that the next morning he had the gates to the Mechanical Workshops locked, barring entry to the men who came to work and thereby violating a wartime injunction against strikes and lockouts. The workers, numbering about 3,000 and led by Imoudu, marched in protest to Government House. Along the way, they were joined by other railway men and cheered by crowds lining the streets. The protesters only dispersed after Governor Bourdillon met them at the Lagos Race Course, expressed regret about the lockout, and promised to announce concessions the following day.

By the end of the week, Wilson had been fired, the day of the lockout had been declared a paid holiday, and an immediate interim cost of living award was made to all government labor and lower paid clerical and technical staff. From October 1 (which henceforth was celebrated as "Freedom Day" and years later became Nigeria's independence day), the hourly pay rate was abolished, and 1,270 employees in the mechanical workshops and 530 in the running shed were transferred to the permanent establishment, which guaranteed fifteen days paid leave per year with free transport, sick leave, regular annual increments, improved promotion prospects, and membership in the Provident Fund.[31] As a result of these concessions, the

Table 3.1 Permanent Railway Staff, 1930–1941

Date	Established Staff (African)	Total Staff	% Established
1930	2,348	23,640	9.9
1933/34	1,792	16,745	10.7
1936/37	1,891	18,923	10
1939/40	2,027	17,658	11.5
1940	2,019	16,312	12.4
1941	4,735	15,994	29.6

proportion of permanent African workers within the Nigerian Railway more than doubled, as Table 3.1 shows.

The enactment of the Trade Union Ordinance and the example of the RWU encouraged workers in other industries to form unions and seek registration, and by end of 1941, forty-one unions represented 17,521 workers. The number of strikes in Nigeria jumped from one in 1940 to six in 1941 and eleven in 1942.[32] Trade unionists were encouraged by the nearly constant support for their causes in the *West African Pilot*, a daily newspaper based in Lagos and edited by the nationalist politician and businessman (and later, Nigeria's first president) Nnamdi Azikiwe. Zik's daily column, "Inside Stuff," repeatedly indicted the colonial government and individual businesses for their poor labor practices and called attention to the gross disparities in working conditions between Nigerians and expatriates.[33]

In July 1941, as the Railway Workers Union was pressing its demands for labor reforms, it joined with other unions of government workers to form the African Civil Servants Technical Workers Union (ACSTWU). This organization's agitation for a cost of living adjustment resulted by November in the appointment of a commission to address government wages and the cost of living in Lagos. The Bridges Commission was composed of African majority, including prominent trade unionists, and its report was published in July 1942, after an interim award had already been granted. The commission largely agreed with union demands and called for increased minimum wages, a 50 percent boost in the cost of living allowance to government workers, and the adoption by commercial employers of labor practices similar to those of the government. Confirming Nigerians' complaints about rising inflation, Bridges suggested that the price control apparatus be strengthened, especially regarding food, and that the government consider the provision of quarters or assisted housing schemes for poorer inhabitants. Finally, the commission recommended that a Labor Advisory Board be established to set wages for Lagos.[34]

In spite of the eventual adaptation of some of Bridges's recommendations, including the cost of living award, government adjustments lagged behind inflation. Labor agitation—spearheaded by the RWU—persisted, prompting increasing anxiety on the part of government officials. In fact, implementation of Bridges's recommendations was accelerated when government workers only *threatened* to demonstrate.[35] The Railway's general managers, J.H. McEwen and then C.E. Rooke, wrote frantically to the Colonial Office between 1941 and 1943, begging for the appointment of a welfare officer to deal with railway union grievances. As Rooke warned in 1942, "the absence of a full time labour officer can no longer continue without disadvantageous and possibly serious repercussions." After wartime needs had prevented such an appointment into the next year, the governor sent a telegram to the secretary of state firmly requesting intervention: "Railway labour still restless and requires urgent wholetime attention [of] one officer and it is of vital importance . . . for whole future of labour questions in Nigeria that we should be able to deal promptly and effectively with labour problems."[36] Meanwhile, the Colonial Office's labor advisor, Orde Browne, emphasized the need to create an agency to handle labor matters in Nigeria generally, and the Department of Labor was formally inaugurated in 1942. Although the Railway finally got its labor specialist, union-government tensions continued to mount with production increases, inflation, dissatisfaction with the government, and official controls. Amid rumors of possible strikes and industrial sabotage, Imoudu was dismissed from the Railway and detained as a threat to security. He spent the next two years under house arrest in Auchi.

MIGRATION, EXTENDED FAMILIES, AND LABOR ACTIVISM

Union demands and other complaints about Nigerian employment conditions during the war years clearly stressed wages and the cost of living. But another theme also ran through the arguments about labor during this period: workers demanded recognition of their links to their extended families and the extent to which labor migration threatened these connections.[37] This had been a concern from the earliest days of migrant wage labor, but with the expansion of urban employment during the war, the calls for official recognition of workers' families became increasingly intense.

Migration had long been a feature of economic activity in southern Nigeria. Traders moved around for favorable markets, craftsmen took out-of-town apprenticeships, and early wage workers went where their jobs took them. The mid-twentieth century, particularly the 1940s, saw a dramatic increase in both interregional and intraregional migrations, fueled by the expanding urban economies and demands for wage workers. These migrants swelled the populations of southern Nigeria's cities. Between the censuses of 1931 and 1952–1953, six southwestern Nigerian towns (Abeokuta, Ibadan, Ilesha, Oshogbo,

Iwo, and Oyo) experienced population increases of at least 40 percent. Lagos's population more than doubled during that period, from 126,000 to 267,000, while Ibadan's rose from 387,000 to 459,000.[38]

Moreover, while thousands of workers, particularly those without qualifications, migrated voluntarily, others—generally with education or skills—moved to places not necessarily of their choosing, because job transfers were a regular feature of employment in government or other large-scale enterprises. Most young entrants into the civil service were soon transferred away from their hometowns, and government servants generally were transferred with each major promotion.[39] Officially justified through the goal of matching qualified labor with demand wherever it happened to be, transfers were also used as a means of labor discipline. Posts in favorable locations became rewards for good service; transfers to faraway or unpleasant stations punished troublemakers and union organizers.[40]

Labor migration, either voluntarily or through transfers, created a host of issues relevant to family life. A long-standing ideal had been for migrants to retain links with their hometowns, where they would spend holidays, find a mate, attend the death or serious illness of a relative, and celebrate public holidays. Workers attempted to time their vacation leave in order to plant crops, build houses, marry, and perform burial or other ceremonies at home. When they were earning, workers would send some of their income to their parents; when they were unemployed or retired, they would find social and economic support there among kin and longtime friends. But lack of frequent contact put strains on personal relationships and disrupted the system of safety nets by which wage earners contributed to family resources in exchange for care in old age or disability. If a worker were to maintain hometown contacts from his new location, how would he find the necessary time, money, and transport for visits? And if he allowed hometown connections to lapse, how would he provide for his retirement in the absence of a significant system of social security? Further, if a worker were to live away from his family's home, either in a big city or in a more remote area, how would he find housing for his spouse(s) and children? Worker activism, both individual and collective, repeatedly returned to these themes.

The most striking case in point comes from a series of columns published in the *West African Pilot* in 1941, entitled the "Manifesto of Nigerian Wage Earners."[41] This twelve-part article drew on arguments from British labor relations experts and social reformers to make a forceful case for sweeping labor reforms in Nigeria. It began, "No government can justify its existence in any community which has a majority of wage-earners in its population, unless it is convincingly demonstrated that the lot of the wage-earners under its aegis is desirable, judged by the general level of the standard of living of the whole community." In return for their citizenship obligations, workers were entitled to education; vocational training; protection from the exploitation of their employers; "wages which will improve our standard of living beyond the minimum subsistence level"; regular pay; healthy working conditions; "relief from fatigue by being allowed regular vacations, sufficient leisure, and opportunities for recreation"; protection from occupational diseases; "appropriate traveling facilities whilst on vacation or in the prosecution of our duties"; adequate notice prior to termination; a substantial honorarium if terminated after five years in any particular establishment; a pension or gratuity after serving any employer at least ten years; an old age pension from the state after at least twenty years of employment; unemployment insurance; workman's compensation for injuries; overtime pay; rights of collective bargaining and strikes; and state protection if any employer violated these rights. Many of these provisions were in keeping with progressive labor norms throughout the western world at the time, although they were not standard in Nigeria. But the demand for vacation leave with free transport as well as for economic provisions upon retirement, unemployment, or physical incapacity also reflected the particular Nigerian context, in which wage labor was usually associated with migration and hometowns were the source of financial security.

Throughout the colonial period, railway workers petitioned for favorable postings and protested transfers to areas undesirable to them. In particular, employees from southern Nigeria resisted transfer to the northern region.[42] Most of the requests about transfers mentioned family obligations, like shunter Abraham Falade's repeated entreaties in the 1950s that he be transferred closer to his hometown of Abeokuta so that his children could go to school there and he could care for his grandmother.[43] In a 1938 staff circular responding to complaints about the inconvenience of some transfers, the railway's general manager stressed that workers' opinions were of no relevance. Transfers were not a right, he insisted, and the needs of the railway, not personal preferences, determined who would be sent where. After seven years in one district (changed to five in 1951), a worker could petition for a transfer, but it would be contingent on convenience and good conduct. Nothing was guaranteed.[44] Into the 1950s, workers requesting transfers on the basis of their family needs were informed that "domestic affairs are not taken into consideration when postings are made."[45]

When employees lived away from their hometowns and families, they could only visit them when on leave from work. Moreover, they needed access to transport, which could be costly. From the formation of the Civil Servants Union in 1912 until about 1920, its petitions to the governor and secretary of state frequently called for improved "leave rights" to facilitate staff members' contacts with their hometowns.[46] But in the 1930s and early 1940s, only a small minority of government civil servants and other members of the "permanent establishment" were eligible for annual paid leave, with free transport to the hometown provided through their employers. These perquisites were part of the package of demands that Geary had made on behalf of the Railway Workers Union in the late 1930s.[47] In 1941, as thousands were added to the government permanent establishment, new regulations made them eligible for fifteen days per year of paid leave. But at the same time the administration suggested that existing second-class train coaches would be insufficient for the increased numbers going on annual leave and moved to cut that benefit. The outcry from the African Civil Servants Union was tremendous, indicating a determination to defend their abilities to visit home and forcing the administration to back down within a week.[48] In Lagos, United Africa Company motor drivers complained that they could not visit home at all because of their conditions of service and low pay. Laborers for the UAC in Burutu went on strike over pay and working conditions, as well as their isolation from their hometowns. "Some of them [were] said to have worked for upwards of 20 years without ever visiting their homes owing to lack of money" for transport. Ultimately, the company's management conceded free round-trip passage to any laborer going on leave.[49] It was not until 1944 that government daily-paid workers received one week per year of paid leave, without free transport, since it was assumed that they were employed in their hometowns.[50]

These demands for transport and leave reflect the potentially intense pressures of combining migrant wage labor with hometown responsibilities. In 1929, Assistant Chief Signaler Simeon Adewuyi Payne reluctantly resigned from the railway after thirteen years' employment in order to deal with family difficulties at home.[51] In 1946, John Adeyinka Adeboye resigned because his father had died and he needed to look after his junior siblings and elderly mother.[52] Other workers regularly faced disciplinary measures for lateness or absence from work, even in circumstances of family emergencies. Paul Opara, a coal man at Iddo station (Lagos), for instance, protested in 1948 that he was fired after missing half a day's work. He argued that his absence was justified because he needed to see his ill and pregnant wife.[53] In a more poignant example from the same year, J.O. Makinde, a mason in the Engineering Department, tried to save his job by writing the following message on the back of his pink slip:

> In fact I ask for a week leave without pay; but when I reach home I could see that the condition of my wife was very serious, she is in pregninance [*sic*] and was about to deliver, but it was not possible until 7 days, before she can delivered, but the child was deliver in dead body. During these time, there were nobody to help me in order to look after her beside me, my father which she lived with was seriously sick too.
>
> I am the only one he born and I have nobody to look after him. I have to look after the two of them after some days when my wife had delivered

she died. When I beread [buried] her, on my returning to work I was told that I have been dismissal, when I am trying to explain all these matter, I got the telegram from Idogo village that my father has died.

When I received the telegram, I have to go in order to beread [bury] him, I return on Saturday 2/1/48.

I beg the Administration to please pardon me for my lateness and to give me benefit of doubt, first let this be to me, sir, my first warning.[54]

Workers and their sympathizers also continued to protest, as they had done previously, the lack of provisions for long-term workers who had neither pensions nor strong hometown support to provide for their retirements. Azikiwe's 1941 "Manifesto" charged, "Today, there are many 'old men' at 40 who are unemployed or who are unemployable and they constitute a public charge by virtue of the fact that some of them have no savings and made none in their heyday." The article went on to record the case of a man in government employment for thirty-three years and discharged without any pension or gratuity because he was "nonpensionable."[55] The next month, the *West African Pilot* championed the cause of a widow whose husband had been an employee of the Lagos Town Council for forty-two years. After his death, the woman was entitled to the equivalent of three months of his wages, or just over £6.[56] Such agitation brought some successes: on the railway and in other government departments, pensions replaced the old provident fund in 1943. Additionally, a lump-sum gratuity was paid to the recorded next of kin when a worker died in the government's employ.[57] The amounts of these pensions and gratuities continued to be insufficient to support a retired worker and his dependents, however, reinforcing the continued necessity of outside sources of income, including the extended family.[58]

The precarious situation of those without such sources of security can be seen through the experiences of the West Indians and Africans from outside of Nigeria who had been recruited to work on the Railway in the 1910s and 1920s. They came to Nigeria as engine drivers and other skilled workers in an era in which railway officials looked to non-Europeans to cut costs but were unwilling to hire Nigerians for such important jobs. Many of them married and raised families in Lagos, staying there after retirement. In 1948, a group of such retirees, who had been hired in 1913–1914, requested additional benefits because their provident fund allocations were insufficient to sustain them during the period's economic inflation. Describing themselves as "a body of men who are advancing in life with no pecuniary assistance from any source," they argued that "The management of a family with children, with no cola [cost of living allowance], was and is a problem distressing in imagination and galling in experience." Although they continued to agitate, collectively and individually, until at least 1952, no additional benefits were ever granted to them.[59]

Whenever the government considered more general schemes of social security, these were rejected out of fear that they would bring more migrants to the cities and on the grounds that extended families could take care of their own.[60] For instance, in response to the 1944 circulation of a Colonial Office document entitled "Social Security in the Colonial Territories," Nigeria's government considered it "dangerous" to offer social security benefits in Nigeria because they would apply only to the small percentage of the population totally dependent on wage earning. This in turn would create imbalances between rural and urban areas, which would create political unrest. "There is a distinct risk that by providing compensating economic advantages, any extensive schemes of social security may result in the people modifying their customs and abandoning their traditional restraints."[61]

OFFICIAL ATTITUDES TOWARD EXTENDED FAMILIES AND HOMETOWNS IN THE 1940s

Whereas depression-era colonial administrators had pointed to workers' extended families as sources of support, which allegedly made higher wages and better benefits unnecessary, officials by the 1940s generally remarked upon African kinship networks more negatively. As the foregoing discussion of social security indicates, they still used African family structures as excuses for low wages and a lack of welfare provisions, but now the rationale worked differently: family members consumed urban wages and strained urban amenities, making any improvements inconsequential for workers.

Buchi Emecheta's novel, *The Joys of Motherhood*, provides a more visceral picture of Lagos in the 1940s than does any historical work.[62] The story traces the heroine's struggle to maintain her family in crowded conditions and in the face of constantly rising prices. Between her husband's wage as a laborer and her own irregular income from trading, they barely make ends meet; when he is forcibly conscripted into the Allied army, she finds it impossible to pay the escalating costs of housing and food. But like Emecheta's Nnu Ego and her husband Nnaife, people from all over southern Nigeria continued to migrate to Lagos in search of jobs in the formal sector or some kind of living from trade. In 1945, the commissioner of the Colony estimated that there were 20,000 unemployed out of Lagos's 220,000 population.[63]

In order to reduce unemployment and overcrowding, and to encourage rural agricultural production, during the war the administration created a labor exchange in Lagos. In December 1943, officials began to register unemployed men in Lagos; the next year the unemployed in Ibadan were registered as well. Thereafter, labor officials urged employers to register their job openings with the labor exchanges so that these positions could be matched with job seekers. By 1946, the labor exchanges ran a series of trade tests and certifications in order to ensure to employers that those matched with jobs were actually qualified. Although touted as a service to workers and employers, the Lagos labor exchange's most ambitious function was as influx control: initially only those who had been in Lagos six months or more were allowed to register, and registration was required by law for all those employed in the formal sector. In 1945, the extreme conditions in Lagos resulted in a tightening of controls, excluding from legal employment those "normally resident outside the township."[64] In practice, this system of controls was often evaded, as even the government acknowledged, although it remained in place until the mid-1950s.[65]

From the administration's point of view, Lagos's problems would have been easier to ameliorate if not for the willingness of its residents to support those who were jobless. "Few of the migrants are unable to find relations or friends willing to house and feed them while the search for employment continues. It is obvious however that although destitution is likely to be rare in such a community the loss of productive capacity in the agricultural areas from which many of the migrants come and the strain put upon the resources of their temporary hosts will tend to cause a general lowering of living standards."[66] Reports from the 1940s frequently contained complaints that workers were using their wages to maintain a "number of dependents which by European standards would be regarded as excessive."[67] Such drains on workers' wages were thought to give them little incentive to earn more and to counteract the possibility that raising salaries would lead to improved standards of living. The March 1942 *Colonial Review* suggested that labor legislation was of little use in improving urban living standards because there were relatively few wage workers, higher wages would cause higher rents, and "an African's household frequently consists of far more than his wife, or wives, and children. If he is in permanent employment, he is expected, and willingly agrees, to support a whole range of sisters, cousins, and aunts as well; and the more prosperous he is, the more dependents he will maintain."[68]

But trade unions argued that wages needed to rise and that supporting family members was logical in a situation with few government welfare provisions. As the Nigerian Civil Servants Union argued in 1941,

> When considering the African cost of living it is necessary to bear in mind that in Nigeria there is no free education, unemployment dole, old age pension, Widows and Orphans' pension scheme, insurance and such other social schemes as exist in Europe. The social need of the African life demands that he should assist unemployed relatives by housing, feeding and clothing them and their children and even paying their poll tax thus saving Government the expenditure of thousands of pounds every year in poor relief as is the case in Europe. And while it may be true that in Europe no employer could be expected to consider this as a determining factor in fixing wages for his employees . . . in Nigeria this is the main reason why unemployment

with its gruesome effect has not constituted such a grave problem to Government as it has in Europe.

Two years later the union argued that "[t]he general condition of poverty among the labouring classes in Nigeria . . . is largely due to the prevailing low wages rather than, as is erroneously thought in some quarters, to the African communal mode of life."[69]

HOUSING DEBATES AND VIEWS ABOUT THE AFRICAN FAMILY

The clash between migrants' and officials' views of extended families was reflected in debates over housing.[70] Access to housing in Lagos had long been starkly stratified, "from the stately cement or stucco mansions of the professional and business men to the primitive huts or tenements of the poorer classes." In areas where poor Lagosians lived, "narrow and tortuous alleys wind through a labyrinth of crazy shacks with dark, cavernous rooks, each of which may house several families: every inch of space is utilized."[71] The problem was that the supply of housing in Lagos never kept up with demand—particularly during the war years—causing high rents and limited availability even when a worker was able to pay. Members of established urban lineages housed their spouses and dependents in family houses, often becoming landlords for tenants as well.[72] But even workers from Lagos were often happy to be posted elsewhere, since their money went further in other towns.[73] For new migrants, housing was a constant struggle. "Many landlords complained that the people occupying their houses are not those to whom the house was originally let. Tenancies are transferred and the new occupier continues to pay rent in the name of the original tenant without the knowledge of the landlord. . . . . In consequence, a newcomer to Lagos, transferred with little warning, cannot even compete on equal terms in the open market since the houses have not the appearance of changing hands and, of course, never stand empty."[74] In inaugurating its housing committee in 1947, the Trades Union Congress resolved to urge authorities in Lagos and other major cities to erect "tenements" for workers at affordable rates, as well as to provide suitable accommodations for workers on transfer. "This will obviate unnecessary embarrassment and safeguard against losses usually experienced by transferred employees who are compelled to hand indefinitely on friends and co-workers."[75]

Officials seemed to share the concern of the press and the general public about crowded conditions in Lagos, but through the 1940s, they stressed that African family life made housing schemes impractical. In 1941, the relatively liberal Bridges Commission recommended that the government consider provision of quarters or assisted housing schemes for the poorer population. Yet the Lagos Housing Committee concluded in 1945 that a government housing scheme would be expensive and would not solve Lagos's problems. A pressing issue, according to the committee, was "surplus population, several thousands of which are in non-gainful occupation," and the committee recommended their removal. The difference between the Bridges Report and that of the Housing Committee would be repeated in subsequent years: labor representatives emphasized the needs of working people for affordable accommodation, whereas town planners stressed that urban housing shortages were caused by jobless migrants, many of them housed by sympathetic relatives. According to the secretary of the Lagos Town Council, "The real remedy [for housing shortages and overcrowding] lies in devising some scheme as early as possible for getting rid of people from the Provinces—especially undesirables and unemployed. Their name is legion and there are large distinct areas of the town given over to the housing of groups from specific parts of the country. Many of the men are unemployed and are, I am afraid, supported and housed by their compatriots out of loyalty in the hope that they may eventually find jobs."[76]

This stark contrast is well represented by two different reports issued in 1946. The first, analyzing the 1945 general strike (which is described in the next chapter), asserted that "the great majority of the lower paid workers in Lagos are compelled to live in slums. . . . This presents . . . a serious social problem which can hardly fail to cause discontent and dissatisfaction with the existing order of things social and economic."[77] Thus, slums resulted from the poor purchasing power of Nigerian workers and could spill over into political trouble. In contrast, Commissioner of the Colony T. Hoskyns-Abrahall, who made recommendations for town planning in Lagos the same year, was pessimistic about the possibility of improvements because of what he saw as African culture. "Fundamentally Lagos remains a Yoruba village with a village mentality," his report stated, continuing that all its inhabitants wanted was a room for sleeping, a spot for trading, and a tree for gossiping underneath. He identified the major impediment to slum clearance as the large proportion of residents who could not afford to live in a "modern house." Of these, "[q]uite a large proportion are not natives of Lagos, giving no benefit to Lagos, and they should be got rid of. Others with whom we are concerned here can claim to be Lagosians, though the mere fact of their being unable to pay a reasonable rent proves them to be of no great value as citizens." Hoskyns-Abrahall thus made it clear that those without regular incomes, or who hoped to live rent free in family houses, were not welcome in a replanned Lagos.[78] Shortly after this report was submitted, the Colonial Office asked for the Nigerian government's plans for clearing slums and creating new housing in Lagos, prompting a discussion on the subject within the administration. Nigeria's chief secretary to the government, G. Bereford Stooke, compared Lagos with the "new" cities of East Africa, where immigrant communities subsidized the urban housing of their workers in efforts to reproduce the labor force without raising wages. In contrast, he asserted that southwestern Nigerian towns were "essentially African." The tax base would not support subsidized housing, and he did not see so much need of it. Besides, Stooke argued, cheap housing would just attract more people to the cities: "The current saying in Lagos is that whenever a room in a tenement in Lagos becomes vacant, ten families immediately move into the town from Ijebu-Ode."[79]

CONCLUSION

Wartime hardships in the early 1940s, along with official recognition of trade unions, propelled a dramatic increase in labor activism. In addition to the cost of living, much of the unions' attention focused on issues affecting workers because of migrant labor—leave with transport, pensions in the absence of hometown safety nets, and affordable housing for newcomers. Under these challenges, and in the context of wartime overcrowding in Lagos, government officials articulated a new stance in relation to African extended families. Although at times they still referred to kin and hometown networks as sources of support for workers, as they had done during the depression, administrators now mostly described such groups as practically parasitical, leading to urban overcrowding and unemployment and mitigating the potential benefits of labor reforms and increased housing. During the general strike of 1945—the subject of the next chapter—workers would find little sympathy for their claims as members of extended families. Instead they would depict themselves as breadwinners for nuclear families, in spite of women's continued economic importance, even to the strike itself.

NOTES

1. G.A. Oldfield, "The Native Railway Worker in Nigeria," *Africa* 9 (1936): 379–402.

2. Quoted in T.M. Yesufu, *An Introduction to Industrial Relations in Nigeria* (London: Oxford University Press, 1962), pp. 12–13. The Marine Department recorded no labor statistics in its annual reports from 1937 to 1951/2. The Public Works Department did register the number of clerks, skilled artisans, and unskilled laborers in its employ each year, but did not differentiate between the permanently and casually employed. Until 1934, railway annual reports contained employment statistics only for track laborers; thereafter, all employees are accounted for.

3. L.M.E. Emejulu, *A Brief History of the Railway Workers Union* (Lagos: Railway Printer, 1949), pp. 1–2.

4. G. Hemmant, Officer Administering the Government to Lord Passfield, Secretary of State for the Colonies, January 29, 1931, ComCol 1/1097.

5. Geary to CSG, March 15, 1939; McEwen to CSG (confidential), March 6, 1939, both in CSO 26/32851, vol. 3; MacDonald to Bourdillon, June 21, 1939, CSO 26/32851, vol. 4. Also see Emejulu, *Brief History*, pp. 16–17.

6. C.W. Leese (chair), *Report of the Committee Appointed by His Excellency the Governor to Enquire into the Question of Unemployment*, Nigeria Legislative Council Sessional Paper No. 46 of 1935 (Lagos: Government Printer, 1935), para. 8.

7. Nigeria, *Annual Report on the Social and Economic Progress of the People of Nigeria* (Lagos: Government Printer, 1936), para. 179. The same sentiment was echoed in the 1938 report as well.

8. Commissioner of the Colony to CSG, January 18, 1936, ComCol. 1/1097.

9. Report by Dr. Akinola Maja, Acting Secretary, Lagos Town Council, in Minutes of the first meeting of the Committee on Conditions of Labor–Lagos Municipal Area, September 27, 1939, ComCol. 1/2159.

10. Oyemakinde, "Railway Construction and Operation in Nigeria, 1895–1911: Labour Problems and Socio-Economic Impact," *JHSN* 7 (1974): 304–25, p. 313.

11. Wale Oyemakinde, "The Railway Workers and Modernization in Colonial Nigeria," *JHSN* 10 (1979): 113–24.

12. Geary to Secretary of State, April 11, 1939, CSO 26/32851 vol. 3.

13. Nigeria, *Annual Report on the Social and Economic Progress of the People of Nigeria* (Lagos: Government Printer, 1936), p. 66.

14. See "Protect Our Workers" (editorial), *WAP*, March 19, 1938.

15. E.O. Renner, L. Belo, et al., Chargemen and Master Artisans, Locomotive Workshop, Ebute Metta to Chief Mechanical Officer, June 20, 1938, HMP 36/1.

16. A.G. Hopkins, "The Lagos Strike of 1897: An Exploration in Nigerian Labour History," *Past and Present* 35 (1966): 133–155, p. 155. Also see Wogu Ananaba, *The Trade Union Movement in Nigeria* (New York: Africana Publishing Corp., 1970); Hughes and Cohen, "Emerging Nigerian Working Class."

17. David Omoruyi, "Long Day in the Life of a Pensioner," *Drum* (December 1962): 31–33. I am grateful to Kenda Mutongi for sending me this article.

18. "Petitions: A.M. Taylor," CO 583/186/8.

19. *DTN*, August 11, 1933; Michael Imoudu, President of RWU to CSG, July 22, 1940, CSO 26/32851, vol. 4; "Security for Daily Paid Workers" (editorial), *WAP*, November 7, 1945.

20. "Beguiling or Aiding the Nigerian Worker?" *WAP*, April 9, 1946.

21. G. St. J. Orde Browne, "Labour Conditions in West Africa," *Parliamentary Papers* Cmd. 6277 (1941), p. 23.

22. I.O. Robert to Herbert Macaulay, September 3, 1938, HMP 91/3.

23. "Lagos Day by Day," by "Diarist," *DTN*, February 17, 1934.

24. See G. O. Olusanya, *The Second World War and Politics in Nigeria, 1939–1953* (Lagos: Evans Brothers, 1973); and, more generally, David Killingray and Richard Rathbone (eds.), *Africa and the Second World War* (New York: St. Martin's Press, 1986).

25. ACSTWU to CSG, March 22, 1945, in W. Tudor Davies (chair), *Enquiry into the Cost of Living and the Control of the Cost of Living in the Colony and Protectorate of Nigeria*, Colonial No. 204 (London: HMSO, 1946), pp. 66–68.

26. Frederick Cooper, *Decolonization and African Society: The Labor Question in French and British Africa* (Cambridge: Cambridge University Press, 1996).

27. Emejulu, "Brief History," p. 17; Ananaba, *Trade Union Movement*, p. 21.

28. Emejulu, "Brief History," pp. 25–31; Secretary of State to Governor Bourdillon, October 21, 1940, CSO 26/32851, vol. 4.

29. "1,900 Loco Workers Are to Get Permanent Appointment," *WAP*, May 8, 1941. For details of the new designations, wages, and benefits, see Railway circulars "Improvement

of Conditions of Service of Daily-Paid Employees," "Improvements of Conditions of Service of Daily-Rated Employees," CSO 26/39230, vol. 1, and "Improved Conditions of Service of Railway Employees," *DTN*, October 6, 1941.

30. Ananaba, *Trade Union Movement*, pp. 20–25; Emejulu, *Brief History*, pp. 32–36; Wale Oyemakinde, "Michael Imoudu and the Emergence of Militant Trade Unionism in Nigeria," *JHSN* 7 (1974): 541–561.

31. Nigerian Railway *Annual Reports*, 1933–34, 1936–37, 1940–41; *Blue Books*, 1940–41.

32. Ananaba, *Trade Union Movement*, p. 26; Robin Cohen, *Labour and Politics in Nigeria, 1945–71* (London: Heinemann, 1974), p. 194.

33. For example, "Our Low Standard of Living," *WAP*, November 1, 1941. For Azikiwe's ideological and managerial goals for the *Pilot*, as well as his prolabor views, see Nnamdi Azikiwe, *My Odyssey: An Autobiography* (London: C. Hurst & Co., 1970).

34. A.F.B. Bridges (chair), *Report on the Cost of Living Committee* (Lagos: Government Printer, 1942).

35. J.O. Oyemakinde, "A History of Indigenous Labour on the Nigerian Railway, 1895–1945" (Ph.D. dissertation, University of Ibadan, 1970), ch. 5; and Timothy Sander Oberst, "Cost of Living and Strikes in British Africa, c. 1939–1948: Imperial Policy and the Impact of the Second World War" (Ph.D. dissertation, Columbia University, 1991), pp. 183–84.

36. Rooke to CSG, December 22, 1942, and Governor to Secretary of State, Confidential Telegram, February 27, 1943, both in CSO 26/38928.

37. Also see Lisa A. Lindsay, "'No Need . . . to Think of Home'? Masculinity and Domestic Life on the Nigerian Railway, c.1940–61," *JAH* 39 (1998): 439–466.

38. R. Olufemi Ekundare, *An Economic History of Nigeria, 1860–1960* (New York: Africana Publishing Co., 1973), p. 355.

39. "African Civil Service Union," *WAP*, September 11, 1941.

40. Michael Omolewa, Gbolagade Adekanmbi, Larinde Akinleye, Kemi Adeola, and MBM Avose, *Michael Imoudu: A Study in the Nigerian Labour Movement* (Ilorin: Michael Imoudu Institute for Labour Studies, 1992), p. 38; Ananaba, *Trade Union Movement*, 22; Bernard Aruna, December 28, 1993, Ibadan.

41. Nnamdi Azikiwe, "Manifesto of Nigerian Wage Earners," *WAP*, Aug. 16–30, 1941.

42. Secretary General, Association of Nigerian Railway Civil Servants to General Manager, January 4, 1950, GMS 28/47, vol. 1; minute by Assistant General Manager (Staff) to GM, February 28, 1955, GMS 335, vol. 1; S.O. Akintola, May 2, 1994, Ibadan.

43. Personnel file of Abraham Adepoju Falade, WP 6689, Ibadan pension office, NRC.

44. General Manager's Circular No. 766/SR492, September 22, 1938, GMS 28/47, vol. 1; GMSC No. 38/51, September 19, 1951, GMS 335, vol. 1.

45. For example, District Superintendent to Jebba Garuba, September 23, 1953, in Jebba Garuba's unnumbered personnel file (Ibadan Pension Office, NRC).

46. T.M. Yesufu, *An Introduction to Industrial Relations in Nigeria* (London: Oxford University Press, 1962), p. 35.

47. The group of demands is summarized in General Manager (McEwen), Nigerian Railway to Geary, November 28, 1939, CSO 26/32851, vol. 3.

48. "Manifesto of Nigerian Workers (7)," *WAP*, August 25, 1941.

49. "U.A.C. Motor Department" (editorial), *WAP*, October 20, 1941; "U.A.C. Labourers, Burutu" (editorial), *WAP*, October 15, 1941; "U.A.C. Labourers in Burutu Town Obtain Redress and Call Off the Existing Strike," *WAP*, November 12, 1941.

50. "Improved Conditions of Service of Railway Employees," *DTN*, October 6, 1941; GM to Heads of Departments, August 20, 1943, GMS 337/16, vol. 1. In 1947, the Miller Commission on wages of unestablished workers reiterated the expectation that they worked in their hometowns, but then went on to indicate the numerous exceptions to this generalization by awarding a lump sum in addition to wages to offset the costs of travel on leave. E.A. Miller (chair), *Report on Unestablished and Daily-Rated Government Servants* (Lagos: Government Printer, 1947).

51. Correspondence from July 1929, HMP 36/1.

52. Adeboye to District Engineer through Labor Officer, May 19, 1947; and Adeboye's Certificate of Service, unnumbered file on recruitment, NRC.

53. Paul Opara to Chief Mechanical Engineer, July 30, 1948, in unnumbered NRC file on recruitment.

54. J.O. Makinde (mason) to District Engineer, October 4, 1948, GMS 33/2.

55. Nnamdi Azikiwe, "Manifesto of Nigerian Wage Earners (8)," *WAP*, August 26, 1941.

56. "Lagos Town Council Gratuity Scheme" (editorial), *WAP*, September 1, 1941.

57. Olukemi Alabi, April 12, 1994, Ibadan.

58. The inadequacy of pensions is discussed, inter alia, in J.F.S. Paulissen (Honorary Secretary of Government Pensioners), "Government Pensioners and COLA," *WAP*, November 14, 1946; Luke M. Emejulu, "Railway Pensioners—Lord Help Them!" *WAP*, June 28, 1946; and Alfred Dosumu-Ainnah, "Retired Railway Officials Ex-Provident Fund Scheme," *LC*, June 16, 1950.

59. Joseph B. Arthur to CSG, April 14, 1950; Association of Retired Railway African Officials to Governor McPherson, June 3, 1948; and other correspondence in SL 696.

60. See minute from Inspector-General of Medical Services (SLA Manuwa) to Secretary of State, July 20, 1953, on Social Insurance in Nigeria, CO 888/10; T.C. Stephens, Ministry of Pensions and National Insurance, to D. Bishop, Colonial Office, February 19, 1954, CO 859/739.

61. OAG [Officer Administering the Government], Nigeria to Secretary of State, April 17, 1945, CO 859/246/1. For postwar discussions about social security in the African colonies more generally, see Cooper, *Decolonization*, pp. 333–35.

62. Buchi Emecheta, *The Joys of Motherhood* (New York: George Braziller, 1979). The novelist was born in Lagos in 1944, the daughter of a railway porter and petty trader, and her fiction often addresses themes from her mother's and her own life. Historical treatments of Lagos in this period include Pauline H. Baker, *Urbanization and Political Change: The Politics of Lagos, 1917–1967* (Berkeley: University of California Press, 1974); Sandra T. Barnes, *Patrons and Power: Creating a Political Community in Metropolitan Lagos* (Bloomington: Indiana University Press, 1986); Akin Mabogunje, *Urbanization in Nigeria* (London: University of London Press, 1968); Olusanya, *Second World War*; and James S. Coleman, *Nigeria: Background to Nationalism* (Berkeley: University of California Press, 1971).

63. Appendix XVI, Memorandum of the Commissioner of the Colony on Unemployment in Lagos, in Tudor Davies, *Enquiry*, p. 199.

64. Nigeria, *Annual Report on the Department of Labor and on the Resettlement of Ex-Servicemen* (Nigeria: Government Printer, 1945).

65. Minutes of the Seventh West African Labor Officers' Conference, Accra, May 1951, CSO 26/44041/S.4.

66. Nigeria, *Annual Report on the Department of Labor for the Year 1949–50* (Lagos: Government Printer, 1950).

67. Appendix I "Statement by the Chief Secretary to the Government, G. Beresford Stooke" in Tudor Davies report, 51–2. Also see Department of Labor *Annual Reports* for 1943, 1944, and 1949–50.

68. "Labor in the Colonies," *Colonial Review* 2, no. 4 (March 1942).

69. African Civil Servants Union, "Memorial Submitted to the Secretary of State Praying for the Amelioration of Salary and Other Service Conditions of the African Staff," May 1, 1943, and Appendix A: Nigerian Civil Servants Union to CSG, September 19, 1941, NAI.

70. Housing was an issue of central importance to urban labor and took on particular salience in the era of stabilization. For two important cases, see Luise White, *The Comforts of Home: Prostitution in Colonial Nairobi* (Chicago: University of Chicago Press, 1990); and Timothy Scarnecchia, "The Politics of Gender and Class in the Creation of African Communities, Salisbury, Rhodesia, 1940–56" (Ph.D. dissertation, University of Michigan, 1993).

71. Both quotations are from E.A. Carr, Commissioner of the Colony, *Annual Report on the Colony for the Year 1946*, S.P. No. 28/1947.

72. Ebute Metta Magistrate's Court CvRB, vol. 62B, 1285/50, Bakare v. Alabi, May 9, 1950, pp. 222–24. Numerous other cases made reference to Lagos wage and salary earners who were also landlords.

73. D.A. Owolabi, January 20, 1994, Ibadan.

74. D.E. Faulkner, Colony Welfare Officer to R.J. Hook, Commissioner of the Colony, December 16, 1943, HMP 14/4.

75. "Resolution: Housing of Workers (TUC)," May 16, 1947, in NLA/6.

76. E.A. Carr (chair), "Report of the Lagos Housing Committee," (n.d. [1945]), Campbell Leach Waide papers, MSS.Afr.s.757, RHO; memo by C. Martin, December 21, 1943, HMP 14/4.

77. Memorandum on Strike of African Civil Servants' Technical Workers' Unions, June–August 1945, Resident's Office, Oyo Province, 2/3/C.328, NAI.

78. T. Hoskyns-Abrahall, *Report of the Lagos Town Planning Commission with Recommendations on the Planning and Development of Greater Lagos* (Lagos: Government Printer, 1946), pp. 1, 29.

79. G.B. Stooke, CSG to A.B. Cohen (Colonial Office), October 7, 1947, CO 583/295/4.

4

DOMESTICITY AND DIFFERENCE: THE 1945 GENERAL STRIKE

From June 22 to August 6, 1945, around 40,000 Nigerian workers—mostly civil servants and railway men in the southwest—stayed off their jobs to protest the government's refusal to raise wages after years of acute inflation.[1] Scholars have seen the general strike as a turning point in Nigerian labor history, as well as part of a larger movement of African nationalism, in which workers achieved a remarkable degree of class unity, broad segments of the population openly defied the colonial regime, and the government was forced to live up to some of its war-era developmentalist rhetoric.[2] Although historians have stressed the importance of community support in explaining the strike's ultimate success, none have noted a crucial irony: male workers demanded wage increases and even family allowances on the basis of their status as breadwinners, yet they survived during the course of the strike in large measure because of their wives' economic independence and market women's importance to local economies. Furthermore, in the poststrike debate over family allowances, trade unionists used gendered language and claims about respectability to talk about racial equality within the colonial order and to constitute the colonial worker and citizen as a male household head.[3]

The 1945 general strike in Nigeria was part of a wave of strikes across colonial Africa during and after the war. As Frederick Cooper has detailed, these disturbances prompted British and French officials to question the "particularity of the African."[4] Colonial governments moved toward extending more European-style benefits to certain groups of African workers in exchange for more productive, uninterrupted service. But as I will show, Nigerians' calls for family allowances, as a counterpart to increasingly lucrative "separation allowances" paid to expatriate workers, were rejected on the grounds that African families were too different from European ones to justify similar entitlements. Current scholarship emphasizes that colonialism both included subject peoples into *and* excluded them from metropolitan political, economic, and cultural communities, at times simultaneously.[5] In this case, it was the family and gender relations of southern Nigerian workers that complicated the engagement of universalistic notions of labor: women worked outside the home, especially after marriage; spouses generally did not pool their incomes; polygyny was widespread; and households were often composed of "families" much larger and more extended than those of the European bourgeoisie. In an era in which industrial relations practices were increasingly held to be universally applicable, local gender and domestic arrangements became markers of cultural differences that colonizers used to justify racial discrimination in wage fixing.

Gender and domesticity have been fundamental in demarcating boundaries between colonizers and the colonized and in formulating the very identities of Europeans at home and abroad.[6] Yet we know less about how the gendered exclusions of colonialism intersected with African identities and the political strategies of the colonized. Like colonial administrators, Nigerian trade unionists confronted tensions between universalizing impulses and African particularities. During and after the strike, they demanded cost of living increases through reference to a universal male breadwinner model and family allowances on the basis of equality with expatriate men. At the same time, however, they also depended on the economic and political activities of women. The vast majority of African women in southwestern Nigeria earned money through trade. Individually and in guild organizations, they provided crucial support for strikers by lowering prices on goods they sold, extending credit, and contributing to the strike fund. For them the issue was not male wages or racial equality, it was their own breadwinning capacities. During the four years of trade unionists' cost of living agitation (1941–1945), the government instituted price controls and then took on food distribution itself in an attempt to curb inflation from the supply end. These actions threatened market traders' livelihoods, and they engaged in political protest, isolated acts of sabotage, and vigorous black marketeering to thwart the official scheme. When workers struck over the cost of living issue and protested the unfairness of the colonial order, market women could see that their own interests were at stake as well. But wage-earners' claims to be their families' primary providers undermined their support for traders' struggles and helped to define "worker" as a masculine category.

DISCRIMINATION, SEPARATION ALLOWANCES, AND THE COST OF LIVING

Tensions leading to the 1945 strike had been building since at least 1941, when the government issued new salary scales for the civil service. After strenuous complaints from the press and the African Civil Service Association that wage levels were still too low, it then withdrew the proposals and appointed the Bridges Commission to investigate the cost of living in Lagos (see chapter 3). The commission's report was not released until mid-1942, after months of agitation on the part of the African Civil Servants Technical Workers Union (ACSTWU), an umbrella group representing most government employees. When it finally emerged, the Bridges report called for increased minimum wages, a 50 percent boost in the cost of living allowance to civil servants, and the adoption by commercial employers of labor practices similar to those of the government.[7] The administration accepted most of Bridges's recommendations, including the cost of living award. Governor Bernard Bourdillon also promised that if inflation continued, a new cost of living adjustment would be made in the future.[8] Prices kept rising as the war demanded manpower, limited imports, provided incentives for farmers to export their crops, and lured potential agriculturalists to the cities in search of work.[9] The cost of living index had increased 74 percent between 1939 and October 1943. ACSTWU called for cost of living allowance (cola) revisions in 1943 and 1944, but Governor Arthur Richards, the more intractable official who had replaced Bourdillon, refused on the grounds that money was not available and that efforts were being made to control prices.[10]

This argument struck trade unionists and their supporters as disingenuous given that the Nigerian government continued to increase the allowances paid to European civil servants. In May 1942 the administration had introduced the payment of "separation allowances" to those whose wives did not live in Nigeria. A ruling in late 1943 increased the amount of the separation allowance and made it payable for other dependents—including children, siblings, and parents—as well as wives. The next year the government introduced "local allowances" for European expatriates whose wives were with them in Nigeria. Further, it announced that the earnings of an officer's wife would not be considered in assessing local or separation allowances, since when European wives did work outside the home, their economic contributions were assumed to be insignificant. The small number of Africans holding what were known as "superior posts" also became eligible for local allowances, but they were paid only three-quarters of the amount that a European received.[11]

The unions alleged that racism accounted for the differentials in payments and that Britain's calls for "equality of sacrifice" during the war were hypocritical. According to a memorandum from the Nigerian Civil Servants Union, 1,631 European officials in Nigeria were earning a total of £1,077,390 while 14,866 African civil servants' yearly wages amounted to £998,640.[12] Under these circumstances, it seemed patently unfair that African government employees were refused a cost of living increase. According to Michael Imoudu, leader of the Railway Workers Union, the chief secretary to the government had told him in a meeting before the release of the Bridges Report that "he agreed to all our feelings but where did we think government could get two shillings for every worker? The delegates asked him where government got separation allowances for non-Africans?"[13] In other words, if the state could help support European families, it could do so for Africans.

PRICE CONTROLS AND MARKET WOMEN'S POLITICS

Workers particularly resented government officials' concern with providing for their own dependents given how difficult it was to feed families in Lagos during the war years, and the standard of living became a major theme in political and labor activism. Women mobilized against government interference in market trading, which deprived them of earnings; men suggested that their inability to secure food for their families diminished their masculine status. Meanwhile, colonial officials blamed their own inability to control inflation on southern Nigeria's system of gender and family relations.

By 1940–1941, markets were running out of supplies, and prices were skyrocketing. Reluctant to increase wages, the government attempted to control inflation from the supply side. The Pullen price control scheme, named after the commissioner of the colony, began in 1941 when the government attempted to set prices on selected foodstuffs sold in Lagos and nearby markets. Critics argued that the mandated prices were often lower than the combined costs of production and transportation. The scheme's ineffectiveness was quickly apparent, as market women refused to sell at prices that would deprive them of even meager profits.[14] But still the administration clung to price controls, a decision that mobilized an opposition coalition of elite women, market traders, and nationalist politicians. The *West African Pilot* ran frequent articles criticizing the scheme. Groups such as the Lagos Women's League and the Oyingbo Market Women's Association held public meetings and lodged formal protests. Madam Alimotu Pelewura, leader of the 8,000-member Lagos Market Women's Association, charged that the government was depriving the women of their livelihoods and that the authorities who set price controls had no knowledge of local markets and trading practices. With the assistance of veteran nationalist Herbert Macaulay and his Nigerian National Democratic Party (NNDP), they employed a variety of protest strategies, including storming a local town council meeting and petitioning the governor, the Lagos Chamber of Commerce, the commissioner of the colony, and the Legislative and Town Councils.[15]

Pelewura and Macaulay, along with most Lagos chiefs, had been political allies since the 1920s. Most recently, Macaulay had provided support to the Lagos market women's anti-tax campaign. In 1940, in an effort to raise revenues, the government had extended the income tax to women earning over £50 per year. Although the tax only applied to a few of them, market traders

Photo 4.1 Market traders, Ibadan, 1993.

feared it would provide an opening for more pervasive female taxation to come. Lagos chiefs, meeting in December 1940, stressed that the taxation of women ran counter to local custom, an argument echoed by Pelewura and thousands of her followers during a protest march and mass rally later that month. Furthermore, Pelewura told the commissioner of the colony that women were already bearing the brunt of wartime hardships: "Lagos women have not only to feed and clothe their unemployed husbands and relatives but also to pay their income tax for them, lest they are sent to prison for defaulting."[16] Sustained pressure from the women, supported by the NNDP and the chiefs, convinced the government to raise the minimum taxable income to £100. This was enough of a compromise for the moment, and traders' concerns about taxes were replaced by more pressing issues of inflation and price controls.

By October 1943, faced with huge difficulties in enforcement, widespread protests, and the perceptible risk of starvation among Lagos's poor, the administration intensified its efforts to reduce food prices. Under a new plan, the government, working through mercantile outfits like the United Africa Company, bought selected foodstuffs directly from producers, subsidized transport costs, and distributed the items to certain traders who were to sell them at fixed, low prices in specially designated "Pullen" market stalls. In order to buy food at these centers, people were supposed to queue in areas cordoned off by barbed wire; queue-breakers were at first fined, then imprisoned. Although the government could not possibly market all of the produce reaching Lagos consumers, officials hoped that its own low prices would force down prices in the rest of the economy. Few were happy with this new arrangement. Farmers hid their stocks from officials and instead sold to local merchants who paid more. Some market women are said to have organized missions to intercept government supply lines. And the Pullen stalls became chaotic. In order to secure a good position in the long queues, people had to line up in the evening in anticipation of early morning supplies the next day. Even after spending a night in line, prospective buyers would reach the front only to be told that supplies had run out, especially as food was being diverted to the more profitable black market. Such frustrations only induced more people to shop elsewhere. By 1944 about two-thirds of Lagos consumers got their food supplies from black markets.[17]

With their incomes at stake, the market women, aided by other women's groups and Lagos politicians, kept up the protests. At a meeting with the deputy controller of native foodstuffs and Commissioner of the Colony Pullen early in 1944, Pelewura stated indignantly that market trading was not the government's "line of business but was the concern of the Lagos market women who had maintained their families for many years through the sale of these foodstuffs."[18] At work and on protest marches, market women sang satirical songs like the following:

> Strange things are happening in Lagos.
> Europeans now sell pepper,
> Europeans now sell palm oil,
> Europeans now sell yam,
> Though they cannot find their way to Idogo
>   [an outlying food supply source]
> And yet Falolu [the king of Lagos] is still in his palace and alive.
> Europeans are not wont to sell melon seeds.[19]

The protesters continued to hold mass meetings and petition the government, heating up their efforts by mid-1945, when food scarcity had reached crisis proportions. Traders and consumers faced a serious shortage of *gari*, a cassava product that formed a staple of the African diet. In early August 1945, over 1,000 Lagos market women staged a demonstration against price controls, shouting in Yoruba, "Pullen market must go."[20]

Throughout the period of price controls, government officials maintained that they were having some effect, citing a reduction in the cost of living index to 162 in October 1944. To the extent that they acknowledged difficulties with the Pullen scheme, they blamed traders, especially market women, alleging that they were earning high profits by selling through the black market while other segments of the population suffered.[21] Some observers, although not exactly exonerating women, did point to other culprits in the letters pages of the *West African Pilot*: one described unemployed men who reportedly earned so much buying at the Pullen stalls and then selling on the black market that they "have sworn never to be employed"; another noted that many black market customers were bachelors who had to work all day and were unable to shop when Pullen stalls were open.[22] Officials also blamed unruly African women for the chaos at the markets and exhorted them to behave like British ladies, who, they claimed, stood peacefully in ration lines during the war.[23] In response, women and their allies accused the government of having little sympathy for market traders or African housewives because Europeans did not have a taste for *gari*.[24]

By June 1945, the *West African Pilot* was running stories on the *gari* crisis nearly every day, describing people spending nights in queues or sustaining injuries from the barbed wire, pregnant women fainting from exhaustion, and whip-welding government officials trying to enforce discipline.[25] Trade unionists, in mass meetings and in official representations, also complained about the food shortage and the Pullen scheme. But the press and workers nearly always took the point of view of the male consumer and household head rather than the market trader.[26] Workers never reiterated traders' claims to support their families; rather, they pointed to men's inability to provide food for their children because of scarce supplies. An editorial from June 20 is a case in point: "Imagine a working class father returning home at dusk to find his little ones turned out of school for lack of stationery and languishing with hunger because mother had failed to secure some food from the Pullen stalls that morning!" Three days before the general strike began, the chair of a meeting of mercantile unions told the crowd that "the present food situation is a manifestation of the sufferings of the Nigerian wage earner and his poor salary." The next speaker expressed his humiliation and frustration when "one of his children almost fainted because of having no food, and he had to run to a nearest neighbor, an old woman, who gave him a small quantity of *gari*, which he gave to his children."[27] Even if this story were made up or exaggerated for effect, what is significant is that these images—of hungry children, frustrated fathers, and women as the ones with a few supplies—were the ones chosen to strike a chord with the audience. Although some may have sympathized with female traders, what men saw as most critical was that a wage-earner with money in his pocket was dependent on the generosity of an old woman to feed his family. The economic crisis was also, for many workers, a challenge to men's domestic positions.

THE STRIKE

Trade unions began calling for a revision of the 1942 cost of living adjustment in 1943 and continued to do so for the next two years as prices kept rising. But as the preceding section suggests, it was in 1945 that the situation reached a climax. On March 22, 1945, the technical workers' association addressed a letter to the government citing rising prices and compulsory overtime and demanding a minimum daily wage of 2 shillings 6 pence for laborers and a 50 percent increase in the cost of living allowance. The union called particular attention to workers' children, who "subsist on mere existence levels. The repercussion on the health and future of these innocent children can well be left to imagination." The government's reply acknowledged the inflation, but again seemed to blame market women: high prices were due to the public's unwillingness to cooperate with price controls. No benefit would come from a cost of living adjustment, the chief secretary argued, unless people were willing to repudiate the black market by purchasing goods at controlled prices or doing without them.[28]

At a mass meeting on May 19, government employees drafted an ultimatum to the government: if ACSTWU's demands were not met by June 21, they would go on strike.[29] Then at a meeting with the chief secretary to the government on May 30, ACSTWU representatives reiterated the union's previous stand on increased cola and minimum wages, and for the first time added the demand for family allowances as a counterpart to European separation allowances. Workers argued that by granting separation allowances to European staff, the government had admitted that salaries were inadequate to cover children's education and certain household expenses. Family allowances to African employees, they suggested, were even more logical in nationalist terms than separation allowances for the relatives of European officials "who not being resident in the country neither spend there nor benefit the country in any way."[30]

While government officials were dealing with ACSTWU's ultimatum, the situation became even more charged by the re-emergence of a popular labor hero. On June 3, Michael Imoudu was released from detention in eastern Nigeria and returned to Lagos. As mentioned in chapter 3, the fiery former head of the Railway Workers Union had been arrested in 1943 under wartime security legislation. When the laws were repealed at the end of the war in Europe, there was no excuse not to free Imoudu. It was unfortunate timing for the government: Imoudu's return by rail to Lagos provided workers and their allies with something of a warm-up to the general strike. An estimated 50,000 supporters throughout the region rallied as Imoudu's train passed through, and his arrival in Lagos culminated in a daylong extravaganza in which thousands lined the streets to welcome him. Macaulay, Azikiwe, and Pelewura were featured speakers at the homecoming rally, reinforcing the ties between organized labor, nationalist politics, and the market women's association.[31] A poem written by Moses S. Ekpeyong celebrated Imoudu's release and also emphasized the gendered dimensions of union agitation: "Two and a half years in exile \ We're sure you're now more virile \ To fight the cause of the worker."[32]

The next week the unions received a negative response to their ultimatum. An increased cost of living allowance would lead to inflation, the chief secretary wrote, and furthermore the suffering caused by the war must be shared across the population. The June 11 letter's most audacious point implied that male workers should exercise more control over their women and extended families: it suggested that the unions use their influence to thwart black marketeering and to curtail the influx of unemployed relatives into Lagos![33] At a meeting a few days later, 800 workers reaffirmed ACSTWU's strike threat; the same day four Lagos chiefs joined a mass procession of market women to the Nigerian Secretariat to protest restrictions on *gari* sales.[34] On June 18, however, the commissioner of labor announced that the strike would be illegal, and ACSTWU's leaders were persuaded to postpone it while filing formal notice of a trade dispute. Under Imoudu's influence, rank and file members repudiated the moderates—led by J.O. Erinle, J. Marcus Osindero, and T.A. Bankole—and vowed to go ahead with the work stoppage. The morning of June 22 began with railway men blowing their train whistles to announce the government employees' strike. They would not mount their platforms again for six weeks.

The strike spread along the railway lines to northern and eastern Nigeria, but it was strongest in the southwest. Government officials, who had previously argued that increased wages would put nonsalaried workers at a relative disadvantage, noted with surprise the level of community support, even in rural areas. Many strikers were able to leave the cities and return to family farms, or their relatives sent produce to them and their allies.[35] A government report after the strike complained that the support received by strikers in the southwest could be attributed to the nature of Yoruba families:

> A man who is lucky enough to be in Government service is expected to, and in fact does, assist a large number of his relatives, either by paying school fees or by sending remittances to his home. All the members of the family—and the term covers a far wider field of relationship in Africa than it does in Europe—are anxious to see the person who is very likely their main financial prop get more for the family funds and therefore support him in his efforts to squeeze more out of Government.[36]

As workers well knew, their wages reverberated through the economy, helping to maintain relatives and friends, fueling market transactions, and providing business for a range of people employed in the informal sector: "the interests of wage-earners and those of other Nigerians are one and indivisible."[37]

During the month of July, government officials debated the relative merits of offering immediate concessions to stop the crippling strike or holding out on the principle of discouraging future unrest. Although they threatened strikers with dismissal, they admitted privately that many of the striking workers, particularly those from the railway, were highly trained and could not easily be replaced.[38] In an attempt to maintain transportation of export goods, the railway administration ran a skeleton service with a motley assortment of European managers, Port Harcourt prison labor, and 900 blackleg workers. But transport was largely paralyzed, telegraph and telephone wires were dead, and even night soil men and grave diggers stopped working.[39] Meanwhile, Azikiwe's newspapers, the *West African Pilot* and the *Daily Comet*, were banned from July 8 to August 15 in retaliation for their support of the most militant trade unionists. Finally, in early August the strike was called off in exchange for a promise of no victimization, no prosecution for arrested strike leaders, and negotiations toward a settlement. Work resumed in Lagos on August 7, just days before the war in Japan ended. Peace brought a relaxation in price controls by September. Although prices were still high, Lagosians noted a palpable sense of relief.[40]

Negotiations between ACSTWU and the government on the cola issue broke down again, months after the strike, when the union rejected the government's offer of a 20 percent cost of living increase in favor of submitting the question to a commission of inquiry. Imoudu exhorted union members to keep up the pressure, again linking the wage struggle to male power: "[A]s we are now nine-tenths of our step [*sic*] to manhood, we must see that we workers are granted social justice."[41] The Tudor Davies Commission heard evidence in late 1945 and issued its findings the following year. The report largely concurred with the unions that workers' standard of living needed to rise, and it dismissed the government's warnings about inflation. It called for a 50 percent retroactive cost of living increase for government workers, improved industrial relations machinery and worker welfare, and some recognition of the needs of workers' families. Such policies, Tudor Davies suggested, were necessary to ensure labor stability, prevent future unrest, and thus increase productivity. The Commission concluded that

> labour, be it black or white, should be adequately paid in accordance with the standard of efficiency and results of work performed, and . . . with the monetary results of that labour the consumer goods available should be purchasable. . . . By this means the colonies can become busy hives of activity, filled with eager, ambitious and loyal workers; this is the ideal of an ever-expanding Colonial development.[42]

Workers and their representatives quibbled with some details of the Commission's report, but ultimately they saw it as a hard-fought victory.

WOMEN AND THE STRIKE

Perhaps no group's support was more important to strikers than that of Lagos market women, although their influence seems to have been understated in most contemporary and subsequent accounts of the event.[43] They were involved from the beginning: T.A. Bankole, the ex-chairman of ACSTWU's Joint Executive, suggested that market women were part of the rowdy group that repudiated him in the final days before the strike. On June 20, a last-minute meeting was held in the market adjacent to the locomotive yard. Persuaded by Imoudu that Bankole had capitulated to the administration, the crowd of workers and traders turned on him, shouting, "Thief, thief, you have been bribed; the government has bribed you." According to Bankole's account, "Then followed the showering on me of an appreciable quantity of 'gari' (farina)—an act which, in my opinion, savoured of rank impudence."[44] Once the strike was on, traders offered credit and lowered the prices charged to strikers, demonstrating to Pullen and other officials that they would regulate prices when their own interests were involved. They and a group of elite Lagos women contributed generously to the Workers' Relief Fund.[45]

Market women's support was motivated by a number of overlapping considerations: intense frustration over the Pullen scheme, community and family ties with strikers, and a solid political alliance between market leader Pelewura, trade unionist Imoudu, and nationalist journalist Azikiwe.[46] Since at least 1941, Imoudu had been working formally to link market traders and wage-earners. In May of that year, he wrote to Pelewura to ask for credit and political support in the event of a strike over cost of living allowances:

> The Yorubas have a common adage which says that "There is nothing that affects the eyes that will not affect the nose." . . . The monthly income we are earning now is hardly sufficient for our wives to engage in trade and also to cook, much less to buy clothes or pay our children's school fees. . . . There is no language which the Europeans understand more clearly than that the workers should go on strike. We know the implication of this for the people throughout Nigeria. . . . God help us unless we unite our voices to enable the Europeans to increase our monthly pay as they should. It is your co-operation that we seek in this matter and the co-operation of our wives, children, senior and junior siblings and our relatives, many of whom are members of the Women's Marketing Association in Lagos and all its environs. We are asking you to devise a means by which you our mothers can make the white men realize that we their workers did not just descend from heaven, and also that our progress at work is the progress of our people in the markets and in the country; our strike is also your own strike. Whatever effects the eye will also affect the nose, in fact, you, our mothers. God help all of us.[47]

Using repeated images, eloquent Yoruba turns of phrase, and respectful references to women as mothers, Imoudu reminded Pelewura of the kinship and economic connections between wage earners and market women. Supporting trade unionists would pay off for them in their own businesses as well as in their households. As Pelewura pointed out to wage-earners at a mass meeting on May Day 1944, "We [market women] are your mothers and your wives. We live and educate our children from your earnings."[48]

Such a remark was intended to reinforce solidarity around what was actually a starkly gendered division of labor and resources, which was itself in transformation by the mid-1940s. As previously emphasized, the vast majority of women in Yorubaland, including wives of wage earners, engaged in trade of some sort.[49] According to my survey of retired railway men in Ibadan and Lagos, for instance, 80 percent who had been working in the 1940s were at that time married to market traders. Yet in this context, trade unionists and market women emphasized their common interests as Nigerians oppressed by colonialism and as household members in need of economic relief. Trade unionists in particular seized upon the strategy of representing themselves as key providers in household economies, downplaying women's incomes as they made claims on the basis of their "breadwinner" status. As a supportive newspaper put it before the strike ended, "Now it is time for the Nigerian government to put on its thinking cap for the sake of thousands of dependents who look unto the strikers for bread and butter."[50]

This reference to bread contrasts sharply with women's continued agitation around a different edible commodity—*gari*. Indeed, one can almost trace the gendered fault lines in the strike through the references to these two foods. Neither of them, or rather neither wheat for making bread nor cassava for producing *gari*, was indigenous to Nigeria. But cassava had become the starch staple of the urban diet throughout southern Nigeria. It was grown, ground, soaked, resoaked, scrubbed, dried, and usually sold by women, and it was thoroughly identified as a women's crop. It was therefore *gari* that galvanized the market women's protests, making it logical that *gari* was the product poured over Bankole's head when women saw him as a government stooge. In contrast, wheat had to be imported, thus linking bread to the colonial cash economy. Nigerian elites and upwardly mobile workers viewed wheaten bread as one of many desirable western commodities that had to be purchased with cash. In Wole Soyinka's account of his 1940s childhood, for instance, it is his father rather than his mother who eats bread. One of his rural relatives even chides him by saying, "The teacher's children don't eat things like that [snakes]. They eat bread and butter."[51] The rhetoric about bread and "breadwinning," then, referred not only to gendered patterns of household earning, but also to changing systems of production and consumption in the urban areas. But in spite of the tensions between what bread and *gari* each stood for, breadwinner discourse featured prominently in the debate between workers and the government over family allowances.

THE DEBATE OVER FAMILY ALLOWANCES

By 1945, there had been roughly a century of debates in Europe and North America over wage policy and the extent to which the state should pay for the social reproduction of labor.[52] In Britain, the male breadwinner norm had emerged from a variety of struggles involving men and women's positions in households, trade union and employer strategies, and state interests in stability and economic growth.[53] This ideology was firmly entrenched by the early twentieth century, even if in many cases male wages were not in fact sufficient to support households, and it in turn shaped the assumptions of policy makers and labor advocates. As Susan Pedersen's comparison of Britain and France has shown, even where patriarchal ideologies were similar, though, twentieth-century wage policies could differ since they were based on the relative powers of employers and trade unions and the nature of their relationships to the state. In the 1920s, 1930s, and 1940s, the British government's commitment to a free labor market and trade unions' concerns that family allocations would allow for lower wages ultimately converged in opposition to feminist- and socialist-backed proposals for widespread family allowances to be paid to women. Although the 1943 Beveredge Report recommended family allowances in an attempt to provide social insurance to families without encouraging inflation by raising wages, the government's policy, adopted in 1945, favored male, breadwinner wages as the route to household maintenance, supplemented by very low allowances paid to women with children. In 1930s France, by contrast, pronatalist concerns, the greater economic necessity for female workers, employers' desires to keep base wages low but to tie workers to their jobs, and the relative weakness of trade unions yielded a system of family allowances paid on a per-child basis to workers who otherwise earned low rates of pay.[54]

Nigerian trade unionists tended to gloss over the distinction between family allowances and breadwinner wages, insisting broadly that some kind of pay increase was necessary to fund the social costs of reproducing labor. Since the first cola agitation in 1941, labor leaders had argued that working men spent at least part of their paychecks on the support of their families. Wages, then, should in some way reflect men's family obligations. By the time they testified before the Tudor Davies Commission in 1945–1946, union leaders were demanding family allowances comparable to the separation allowances paid to European officials. Clearly the most important issue of the 1945 strike centered on wages and the standard of living, but the argument about family allowances was significant. In Nigeria, as in industrializing Britain, male members of an emerging working class based their demands for increased wages and equal rights on claims to respectability presented in terms of a patriarchal household.[55]

Trade unionists argued for family allowances in terms they thought would be favorably received by government officials—men's household responsibilities, social order, and the stabilization of urban labor. But administrators would only accept these arguments to a point. First, as described earlier, family allowances had been a contentious issue in Britain itself. Then there were financial considerations, which were always of utmost importance to bureaucrats. But the basic ideological objection to paying Nigerians family allowances centered on two specific "problems" of the African family: "[t]he wife does not make a vocation of house-keeping as is done in the western cultures"[56]; and wage-earners supported not just a wife and children, but often a "number of dependents which by European standards would be regarded as excessive."[57] The particularities of Nigerian social structures seemed to make family allowances for Africans impractical, ideologically incongruous, and conducive of the types of social relations colonizers ultimately hoped to change.

Who would bear the costs of socially and biologically reproducing the labor force? Until the 1940s, and especially during the Great Depression, the answer was clear to officials: workers' wives supported themselves and their children, so wages could be kept low. Reports from the 1930s, and later, further argued that wages could be kept low because wives supported themselves and children. "The average woman is self-supporting" was a statement repeated in social welfare reports through the 1930s.[58] According to this view, it would be both artificial and impractical to pay family wages in southern Nigeria, as "the wives of wage-earners and of those on low salaries are petty traders and their profits are sufficient to pay for their own food and that of their children."[59] The first statement of official wage policy for government employees, published in 1935, declared that "no account is taken of the cost of maintaining a labourer's wife and children, as the wife in such cases normally contributes to the family income a sum equal to the expenses so involved."[60] In the 1940s, however, trade unionists began to argue that higher wages were necessary to keep urban households financially viable. African labor leaders argued that marketing was only a supplement to men's earnings, so male wages should reflect their family obligations. In 1941 the Bridges Commission, composed of an African majority, suggested that even though workers' "wives to a considerable extent support themselves . . . in the light of its knowledge of local conditions, however, [the Commission] is unable to accept the opinion, sometimes advanced, that such women are wholly self-supporting." Bridges estimated that the average laborer spent at least a quarter of his earnings on the support of wives and children, and thus suggested factoring the costs of dependents in wage calculations. The government, however, rejected that part of the Bridges Report.[61]

The introduction of separation allowances for European officials refocused labor leaders' arguments about the family wage. Now the issue was not only household maintenance but also racial discrimination and with it working-class masculinity: that Europeans, but not Africans, could be recognized as supporting their families. Nigerian trade unionists argued that family allowances were needed to foster social reproduction, especially in the absence of a welfare state, and that men's wage-earning was related to the prerogatives of citizenship. In a 1944 radio broadcast, I.S.M.O. Shonekan, a Trade Union Congress undersecretary, pushed this point:

> Some employers forget that his [a worker's] children are not given free education, but he tries his best . . . to educate them. They forget that his children are a valuable contribution to society who in the future, will assist mentally or physically in developing the wealth of the nation and defend the State. He is not paid any family allowance by either the State or the employer for these. He is forced to distribute his scanty wages on these important items which go to make him and his family good citizens. But at what price? The health of himself and his family.

Eight months later, Shonekan raised the issue at the annual congress of the Federated Trades Unions of Nigeria. Arguing that "many of us have wives and children to support" and that wage levels were insufficient, Shonekan drew his audience's attention to arguments in favor of family allowances made by politicians in Europe and South America. His motion, "That the Government of Nigeria be requested earnestly to formulate schemes for family allowances, and to enact an Ordinance sanctioning their payment by all employers to all married African workmen throughout the country," passed unanimously amid cheers.[62]

Union leaders then brought up family allowances in their submissions to the Tudor Davies Commission. The Supreme Council of Nigerian Workers, a new umbrella organization which represented union members before the tribunal, made several broad arguments in favor of extending family allowances to African workers, but they all centered on a European point of reference. First, because of the low levels of housing and amenities in Nigerian cities, the majority of Nigerian workers were compelled to maintain two homes, one in the city and one for wives and children in a separate town or village. Thus, their conditions of service were analogous to those of expatriates with jobs in Nigeria and families in Europe. Second, since in Africa there was no free education, poor relief, or general pension scheme as in Europe,

Nigerian workers were forced to support their young, old, infirm, and unemployed relatives. Family allowances, then, would take the place of metropolitan-style social insurance. To thwart the argument that such benefits were not intended for the colonies, the Council pointed to allowances in New Zealand for laborers' wives, children, and elderly parents. And to discount the importance of wives' independent incomes, it noted that the earnings of European wives were not considered in the calculation of expatriates' local allowances.

It was in its discussion of family responsibilities and citizenship that the Council most closely linked universalist claims and Africa's specific needs.[63] The memorandum asserted that "It is the duty of the African worker to maintain parents and relatives," and then went on to suggest that this could be related to European norms. Perhaps referring to the recent plan for social insurance in Britain, it argued that "The right of a citizen to raise and maintain a healthy family . . . is becoming more and more recognised as a measure of public economy and should be more so in the new social order for which we all had fought and suffered so much in the last war." Then, the Council applied these universalistic notions to African circumstances, where the slave trade had led to population losses: "The average African sincerely regards polygamy and the rearing of children as a social duty inseparable from citizenship. And [because of depopulation caused by the slave trade] he may well be right."[64]

Tudor Davies's report did not go as far as the labor leaders had hoped, but it did recognize, in theory, that they had a point. Although it suggested "that family allowances shall not be granted to Nigerian workers on the same principles as separation allowances granted to Europeans," it did conclude "that the principle of separation allowances which already exists for certain African Civil Servants who are required by the nature of their duties to live away from their families and thus to pay for two homes shall be extended." The extension was to apply to single men required to live away from their homes, as well as to married civil servants in the lower grades. Tudor Davies recognized that African workers helped to support a range of relatives but tried to strike a balance with official concerns about the costs of extended family ties. The report recommended that the government base its cost of living indices on "a reasonable assumption regarding the size of the normal family: e.g. on the assumption that the normal family comprises husband, wife, one other adult, and five children." Tudor Davies also stressed his approval of a male breadwinner norm for Nigeria: "The sooner the male ceases to rely upon the economic contribution of the female to the family exchequer, the sooner will the wage structure be founded upon a more correct basis."[65]

Trade unionists saw the report as an opening, and in October 1946, Luke Emejulu, the general secretary of the ACSTWU, wrote to the governor to inquire as to what would be done to implement and extend such benefits. This prompted a flurry of correspondence within the government, concerned with thwarting the union's demand. Citing a 1944 circular, one official minuted that separation allowances only applied to senior officials, and only those for whom "the wife and/or family of the officer concerned is resident in a different country or colony to that in which the officer himself is residing," that is, only Europeans were eligible. "It would appear," the minute continued, "that the recommendation made by Mr. Tudor Davies was made under a misapprehension" about the current eligibility of Africans for such allowances. Tudor Davies's suggestion that payments be extended was derided as ridiculous: because Nigerians could be expected to move their families to any place within the territory, they would never be eligible for separation allowances. Tudor Davies's other recommendation, that separation allowances be extended to single men working away from home, was described as "curious," since it seemed to assume that unmarried government employees all lived with their parents.[66]

By December 1946, ACSTWU still had not received a reply to its first letter and complained to the commissioner of labor. "Unless an early pronouncement is made by the Government," Emejulu wrote, "my organization will feel compelled to relax its hold on its member-unions in this important and delicate matter." This was a typical threat, to yield to the volatile masses, but here it did imply concern with the issue of separation allowances. The government knew this: "We are in a very weak position I am afraid, and we can expect trouble on this issue," one official commented in January 1947. But that month the union did receive a reply. Since its original letter, the Harragin Commission had reported on labor conditions among civil servants in British West Africa, and the chief secretary to the government reported that its recommendations, rather than Tudor Davies's, would be followed on the issue of separation allowances.[67]

Harragin's report insisted on separate salary scales for European and African civil servants and rejected the claim for African separation allowances completely. It justified such allowances for expatriates on the grounds that "[t]he raising of a family is the normal and natural function of human beings and every salary scale must visualise and make some sort of provision for such a contingency. Thus, in the case of the expatriate officer, one of the chief considerations justifying a grant of expatriation pay is the necessity to provide for children who must live in temperate climates." In contrast, although the report acknowledged that "it is a custom of the West Coast African for a young man to start making a contribution to the family coffers from the day he receives his first month's salary," this "is not a practice which Government can take into account when deciding the salary that any particular post should carry." Not only should wage setting be left to collective bargaining rather than government mandate, but it would be too complicated in a West African context, where "the word 'family' may be taken to mean not only a wife and children but every near relative." "In a country [*sic*] such as West Africa," Harragin wrote, "where polygamy is freely practiced, marriage is easy and divorce simple, a children's allowance is not a practicable position if applied to the whole Service and invidious if only applied to a portion."[68] Here again, African family life was too different from that of bourgeois Europeans to justify universalist claims to entitlements.

Union officials realized that they had little hope of allowances along Tudor Davies's guidelines after Harragin's report was published. Still, they used the threat of a disorderly rank and file to press for some compromise. In January 1947, the government financial secretary reported a "long but friendly meeting" with trade unionists. "As we know," he minuted, "the Union has a fair case in this instance, but while they admitted that in our shoes they would take the same action as Government has done, they state, and I believe them, that their members who are vocal but not literate will not accept the situation." If this is to be believed, it seems the union leaders saw family allowances as symbolic, and were quite willing to compromise on their actual implementation, given the 50 percent cost of living adjustment they had already won. The workers' representatives suggested a measure to appease their members while still allowing the government to resort to Harragin's terms: retroactively implement Tudor Davies's recommendations for the period of August through December 1945, and then abolish them when the Harragin recommendations were implemented, also retroactively, for January 1, 1946.[69] Although the financial secretary favored this arrangement, the secretary of state, in response to calls for intervention from both the union and the governor, came down firmly on the side of the Harragin recommendations. In February the governor announced the adoption of the Harragin Report, with certain modifications: "The Secretary of State has given particular attention to the conflict between the recommendations in . . . the Tudor Davies Report regarding separation allowances, and . . . the Harragin Report regarding compensatory allowances generally, and has decided that the Tudor Davies recommendation shall not be implemented."[70]

Nigerian trade unionists, politicians, and the press denounced the apparent racism of the Harragin report. An irate column in the *West African Pilot* accused Harragin of "abandon[ing] economics for sentiment" on the issue of family allowances and asserted that in reality less than 1 percent of civil servants were polygamous because the urban wage economy made large families too expensive. Harragin's arguments about African domestic life, the correspondent opined, were "not reasons but frivolous excuses."[71] The main concern of the unions, however, was Harragin's defense of separate salary scales for Europeans and Africans. A March 1947 demonstration by over 500 railway workers, which was dispersed with tear gas and fire hoses, focused on pay rates and job classifications, not family allowances.[72] Although union officials did not completely drop their demands for separation allowances after 1947, other struggles took precedence given the government's insistence that African and European workers would not receive equal employment benefits. Moreover, debates over family allowances became subject to piecemeal negotiation as colonial governments—Nigeria's among them—worked to contain labor disputes in a formal structure of industrial relations and to avoid any future widespread demonstrations.

In December 1950, at the recommendation of a government-sponsored arbitrator, Nigerian senior officers of the civil service became eligible for children's allowances comparable to those paid to expatriates.[73] Three years later the government again considered family allowances as part of a wider investigation into possible schemes of social insurance for Nigeria's major cities. The minister of social services, inspector-general of medical services, commissioner of labor, permanent secretary of the Ministry of Health, and the director of the West African Institute of Social and Economic Research (WAISER) collectively determined that old age pensions and widow's benefits were unnecessary because African extended families took care of their elderly; unemployment insurance was not relevant because of seasonal and migrant labor; maternity benefits might be considered at some future time; and family allowances would favor the "registrable few," promote inflation, and be too expensive. WAISER's Professor W. Hamilton Whyte "generally considered it dangerous to attempt to impose social services as organized in a fully developed community like Britain upon a country such as Nigeria which is still in a relatively early stage of development."[74] Again, African social structures provided the rationale for the status quo. Other observers noted that in cases where wage-earners were married to market traders, "it often happens that the wife makes enough profit to support herself and the children, if any, and even her husband when he is unemployed," and "[w]ith polygamy and large families, the cost of introducing a [universal] scheme of family allowances in this country would be prohibitive."[75]

Still, in 1954 the All-Nigeria Trade Union Federation included children's allowances in its grievances to the Gorsuch Commission on conditions in the civil service. The Commission's report, which revised Harragin in arguing that wages for expatriate and African civil servants should both be based on local conditions, did contain some recognition of family obligations. Gorsuch mentioned the usual criticisms of African kinship, but added that family demands for support were not unique to Africa: "[A]s happens elsewhere in the world also, a member of a rapidly developing society who becomes endowed with what appears to be a handsome cash income is quickly confronted with the demands or expectations of his kin." Unlike the Harragin report, which argued that such obligations were irrelevant to government calculations, Gorsuch, writing nearly a decade later, stressed the importance of understanding labor in its social context. Family demands "may be expected to lessen as the general level of living rises, but at present it is a factor that must be recognized, though there are obviously limits to the extent to which it can be taken into account."[76]

By the time the Gorsuch Commission met, family allowances had been overshadowed, at least in the Colonial Office, by family wages. Prompted by agitation throughout the African colonies, including the 1945 strike in Nigeria, British officials by the mid-1950s were rethinking their plans for African labor. Earlier they had argued that their family structures made African workers ineligible for family wages or allowances, but now they believed that the only way to make Africans modern was to change entire families. Family wages were a means to help create the type of domestic units officials thought African workers should have. At the Inter-African Labor Conference in 1950 and 1953, French representatives had highlighted family allowances as part of their moves to stabilize wage labor in French Africa. Although the British colonial establishment was also in favor of tying workers more firmly to their jobs, there was still no interest in applying family allowances to British colonies, both because of the alleged peculiarity of African families and because of a general preference for collective bargaining rather than government wage fixing. The latter, it was argued, would provide incentives for political demonstrations in efforts to increase wages. Nevertheless, in a series of meetings of the Colonial Labour Advisory Committee in 1953, British officials affirmed the importance of family wages in the creation of a stable and controllable labor force, and they suggested that although wages should be related to productivity and based on collective bargaining, they should take reasonable account of domestic responsibilities in a general way. A 1954 circular dispatch informed African governors of the committee's report and asked for relevant information from their colonies. Nigeria's reply asserted that wage fixing, effected mainly through government commissions, included attention to workers' families. "The bachelor wage is unknown in Nigeria," it asserted.[77]

CONCLUSION

In hindsight, Nigeria's resolution to the family allowances/wages issue looks rather similar to Britain's. In both metropole and colony, the state was unwilling to interfere, at least overtly, in the labor market; and a relatively strong trade union movement did not find it useful to insist upon family allowances. In Britain this was for fear that such payments would facilitate a lower basic wage rate; in Nigeria by the early 1950s government workers' pay increases came in the form of cost of living adjustments, and the Harragin Commission had made it clear that metropolitan-style supplements would not be forthcoming. In French West Africa, in contrast, family allowances were granted to civil servants after the 1946 Dakar general strike and to all wage-earners in 1956.[78] The difference likely has to do with the nature of British colonialism in Africa. In the absence of official rhetoric stressing the unity of metropole and colony and a centralized political structure for all of British West Africa—as in the French case—there were few grounds for arguing that African workers should get exactly what those in Britain did. Particular unions could confront specific issues, but there was little possibility of organizing on a West Africa–wide basis for universalistic, British-centered claims as Francophone trade unionists were able to do. Furthermore, family allowances were much more central to French domestic policy than breadwinner wages were to British.[79]

Nonetheless, one should not assume that similar wage policies represented an automatic transfer of metropolitan ideas about labor reproduction to the colonies. As in French West Africa, Nigeria's trade unions and their allies fought pitched battles over the cost of living, which explicitly included the support of workers' families. Although family allowances were not granted to most Nigerian employees, the government's promotion of family wages represented a political victory. Furthermore, unlike in Britain, workingmen in Nigeria never directly opposed women's paid work as part of their own claims to breadwinner status, as I show in the next chapter. Whether in attempts to keep wages high by preventing the employment of lower-paid female workers, or to defend a putative masculine identity based on certain types of work and income earning, male trade unionists in many British industries pursued exclusionary policies in the nineteenth and twentieth centuries.[80] In Nigeria, the sexual division of labor ran so deeply that women never posed a serious threat to men's wage jobs. Nevertheless, women did (and do) earn significant incomes, giving the lie to many men's claims of supporting their households. Nigerian men agitated for family allowances and family wages in spite of their continued acceptance of, and reliance upon, women's economic contributions.

The 1945 strike reveals the uses of gender both in colonial discrimination and in opposition to it. In Nigeria, as in the rest of the continent, the question of applying universalistic principles to colonial workers was related to what kind of men they were and what kind of households they should live in. The debate about family allowances, which so much centered on racial equality and the recognition of workers' dignity, was articulated in terms of domestic life and especially fatherhood. Trade unionists gambled that the demand for family allowances would fall on sympathetic colonial ears because it entailed men asking men to support supposedly common ideas of gender and domesticity. The sticking point—in addition to a tight-fisted administration—was that all sides recognized this particular notion of masculinity as much more tenuous in West Africa than in most of postwar Europe.[81]

Colonizers used local gender relations and household structures as justifications for racial discrimination in wage setting. At the same time, working men claimed political rights in gendered terms. Wage increases and other allowances were said to be necessary in order for workers to "live a decent life."[82] What did such a life entail? According to the Supreme Council of Nigerian Workers,

> As an essential part of the economic life of this country, every workman must be given a minimum just wage. This should be such as to enable him to buy proper food, to keep himself and family in good physical health, to live in decent healthy homes. . . . Education must be provided for the children. . . . Added to this the workman's wages should allow him to enjoy lawful recreations and a few of the luxuries of life regarded as necessary in particular places. Old age must be provided for, so the workman's remuneration must guarantee that, if he is thrifty, he is in a position to lay aside a little for the time when he can no longer work.[83]

In other words, wages should allow men to build respectable households in which they provide for their children and maintain themselves in retirement. The ultimate reward for wage increases would be a stable, respectable family life ostensibly geared to the social vision of colonial planners.

As I argue in the rest of this book, such a stance was at least in part strategic. This is not to say that workers did not aspire to the kind of life articulated in the Supreme Council's statement. But that statement, and others like it, highlighted certain aspects of workers' family lives and muted others. Given colonial officials' overt hostility to workers' extended family ties and a long history of European interest in African men's relationships with wives and children,[84] it made the most sense for trade unionists to emphasize working men's roles within nuclear families in their claims for improved wages and benefits. With a different target audience for their claims, labor activists could emphasize other aspects of workers' family responsibilities—a point to which I return in chapter 7, on the general strike of 1964.

NOTES

1. James S. Coleman, in *Nigeria: Background to Nationalism* (Berkeley: University of California Press, 1971), 259, estimates that 30,000 workers struck; the Department of Labor's 1945 Annual Report put the figure at 42,951, including 34,000 government employees. This chapter is a modified version of my article, "Domesticity and Difference: Male Breadwinners, Working Women, and Colonial Citizenship in the 1945 Nigerian General Strike," *AHR* 104, no. 3 (1999): 783–812.

2. Wogu Ananaba, *The Trade Union Movement in Nigeria* (New York: Africana Publishing Corp., 1969), ch. 7; Robin Cohen, *Labour and Politics in Nigeria* (London: Heinemann, 1974); Coleman, *Nigeria*, ch. 11; L.M.E. Emejulu, *A Brief History of the*

Railway Workers Union (Lagos: Railway Printer, 1949), pp. 5–62; Wale Oyemakinde, "The Nigerian General Strike of 1945," *JHSN* 7 (1975): 693–710.

3. On the construction of (exclusively) male workers as legitimate citizens in Britain, see Anna Clark, "Manhood, Womanhood, and the Politics of Class in Britain, 1790–1845" and Keith McClelland, "Rational and Respectable Men: Gender, the Working Class, and Citizenship in Britain, 1850–1867," both in Laura L. Frader and Sonya O. Rose (eds.), *Gender and Class in Modern Europe* (Ithaca, NY: Cornell University Press, 1996).

4. Frederick Cooper, *Decolonization and African Society: The Labor Question in French and British Africa* (Cambridge: Cambridge University Press, 1996). Aside from those in Nigeria, wartime and postwar strike movements and urban riots occurred in Kenya (1939, 1942, 1947), Northern Rhodesia (1940, 1945), the Gold Coast (1941, 1943, 1947, 1948), Uganda (1945), Tanganyika (1947), Zanzibar (1948), Cameroon (1945), Senegal (1946), and along the French West African Railway (1947–1948). Also see Timothy S. Oberst, "Cost of Living and Strikes in British Africa, c. 1939–1948: Imperial Policy and the Impact of the Second World War" (Ph.D. dissertation, Columbia University, 1991).

5. See Frederick Cooper and Ann Laura Stoler (eds.), *Tensions of Empire: Colonial Cultures in a Bourgeois World* (Berkeley: University of California Press, 1997).

6. Ann Stoler, "Rethinking Colonial Categories: European Communities and the Boundaries of Rule," *CSSH* 31 (1989): 134–61; and *Race and the Education of Desire: Foucault's History of Sexuality and the Colonial Order of Things* (Durham, NC: Duke University Press, 1995). Also see Cooper and Stoler (eds.), *Tensions of Empire*.

7. A.F.B. Bridges (chair), *Report on the Cost of Living Committee* (Lagos: Government Printer, 1942). Also see Cooper, *Decolonization*, pp. 131–34.

8. Appendix XX, Copy of script of broadcast by Sir Bernard Bourdillon on July 24, 1942, in W. Tudor Davies (chair), *Enquiry into the Cost of Living and the Control of the Cost of Living in the Colony and Protectorate of Nigeria*, Colonial No. 204 (London: HMSO,1946), pp. 220–22.

9. G.O. Olusanya, *The Second World War and Politics in Nigeria, 1939–1953* (Lagos: Evans Brothers, 1973).

10. Ananaba, *Trade Union Movement*, ch. 7. For the larger African context, see Cooper, *Decolonization*, ch. 4; and David Killingray and Richard Rathbone (eds.), *Africa and the Second World War* (New York: St. Martin's Press, 1986).

11. Tudor Davies Report, pp. 108, 214–20. Family allowances had been first introduced for British soldiers during World War I. See Susan Pedersen, "Gender, Welfare, and Citizenship in Britain during the Great War," *AHR* 95 (1990): 983–1006 and *Family, Dependence, and the Origins of the Welfare State: Britain and France, 1914–1945* (Cambridge: Cambridge University Press, 1993). On the wives and children of colonial officials in Nigeria, see Helen Callaway, *Gender, Culture and Empire: European Women in Colonial Nigeria* (Urbana: University of Illinois Press, 1987), esp. pp. 18–22.

12. Cited in Nnamdi Azikiwe's column, "Inside Stuff," *WAP*, July 4, 1945.

13. "Artokhamen Imoudu Concludes Dramatic Series on Events Preceding 1942 COLA," *WAP*, June 12, 1945. For background on Imoudu, see Robin Cohen, "Michael Imoudu and the Nigerian Labour Movement," *Race and Class* 18 (1977): 345–62 and "Nigeria's Labour Leader No. 1: Notes for a Biographical Study of M.A.O. Imoudu," *JHSN* 5 (1970): 303–8; and Wale Oyemakinde, "Michael Imoudu and the Emergence of Militant Trade Unionism in Nigeria, 1940–1942," *JHSN* 7 (1974): 541–61.

14. Wale Oyemakinde, "The Pullen Marketing Scheme: A Trial in Food Price Control in Nigeria, 1941–1947," *JHSN* 6 (1973): 413–23.

15. Cheryl Johnson, "Madam Alimotu Pelewura and the Lagos Market Women," *Tarikh: Grass Roots Leadership in Colonial West Africa* 7 (1981): 1–10; Nina Emma Mba, *Nigerian Women Mobilized: Women's Political Activity in Southern Nigeria, 1900–1965* (Berkeley: University of California Press, 1982), 226–31. For decades Macaulay provided political assistance to the Lagos market women, who under Pelewura's leadership supported his NNDP. Some of their correspondence is in the Herbert Macaulay Papers, Kenneth Dike Library, University of Ibadan.

16. Mba, *Nigerian Women*, pp. 200–204; Johnson, "Madam Pelewura," pp. 4–6, 6 quoted.

17. Oyemakinde, "Pullen," p. 423; Ananaba, *Trade Union Movement*, pp. 46–47; Mba, *Nigerian Women*, pp. 227–28.

18. Johnson, "Madam Pelewura," pp. 7–8.

19. Olusanya, *Second World War*, p. 64.

20. Johnson, "Madam Pelewura," pp. 7–8.

21. Appendix VI, Memorandum of Director of Supplies on Measures Taken to Keep Down the Cost of Living, and Appendix VIII, Reply by Director of Supplies to Appendix 7, in Tudor Davies Report, pp. 121–25, 131–32. Oyemakinde did the same thing, writing that "market women took advantage of the prevailing scarcity to profiteer." "Nigerian General Strike," p. 695. Also see Oyemakinde, "Pullen," p. 415.

22. E.O. Oyefeso, "Cost of Living and Nigerian Workers," *WAP*, June 16, 1945; J. Ola Oluwole, "Regarding Food Crisis in Lagos," *WAP*, July 2, 1945.

23. Editorial, "So London Women Can't Take It!" *WAP*, August 24, 1945. Pullen had also raised the English comparison in regard to women's income tax, arguing at a mass meeting with market women that women in England paid tax. Pelewura retorted that such a comparison was not fair, since "England is where the money is made." Mba, *Nigerian Women*, p. 203; Johnson, "Madam Pelewura," p. 5.

24. Ben Oluwole, "The Pullen Market Must Go!" *WAP*, August 21, 1945.

25. Examples are "Food Scarcity Heightens Again," June 1, 1945; "Market Women Want Elimination of Gari Control," June 18, 1945; "Stories Told by Working Class Mothers," July 4, 1945.

26. "The Gari Situation in Lagos," *WAP*, June 19, 1945; "Human Approach to the Labour Crisis," *WAP*, June 20, 1945; Azikiwe, "Inside Stuff: History of the General Strike (3)," *WAP*, September 5, 1945. The exception to this trend was Macaulay; see "Madam Pelewura & 2 Lagos White-Cap Chiefs Will Join NCNC Delegation," *WAP*, June 25, 1945.

27. "Human Approach to the Labour Crisis," *WAP*, June 20, 1945; "20,000 Mercantile Workers Endorse All Demands of Technical Workers' Union," *WAP*, June 19, 1945.

28. ACSTWU to Chief Secretary to the Government, March 22, 1945, reprinted in the Tudor Davies Report, pp. 66–68; W.R.T. Milne, Ag. CSG to ACSTWU, May 22, 1945, reprinted in Tudor Davies Report, pp. 68–69.

29. ACSTWU Resolution, May 19, 1945, reprinted in Tudor Davies Report, pp. 69–70.

30. J.O. Erinle, General Secretary of ACSTWU to CSG, June 1, 1945, reprinted in Tudor Davies Report, pp. 70–71.

31. "MAO Imoudu Returns to Lagos after a Period of 2 Years in Detention: 50,000 Accord Him Fitting Welcome," *WAP*, June 4, 1945; Oyemakinde, "Nigerian General Strike," p. 698.

32. Quoted in Ananaba, *Trade Union Movement*, p. 39.

33. G.F.T. Colby, Ag. CSG to T.A. Bankole, President of ACSTWU, June 11, 1945,

reprinted in Tudor Davies Report, pp.71–73. The *West African Pilot* ran an indignant editorial, "Repatriation of the Unemployed," on June 21, 1945.

34. "Technical Workers Resolve to Order General Strike at Midnight on June 21" and "Market Women Want Elimination of Gari Control," *WAP*, June 18, 1945. Ananaba has inflated the number of attendees at the workers' meeting to 8000. *Trade Union Movement*, p. 52.

35. M.O. Shofekun, April 4, 1994, Ibadan; Francis Soetan, April 12, 1994, Ibadan.

36. Memorandum on Strike of African Civil Servants' Technical Workers' Unions, June–August 1945, Resident's Office, Oyo Province, 2/3/C.328.

37. Appendix II, Memorandum of Supreme Council of Nigerian Workers, Tudor Davies Report, p. 54; also see Oyemakinde, "Nigerian General Strike," p. 699.

38. Memorandum on Strike of African Civil Servants' Technical Workers' Unions June–August 1945, Oyo Prof 2/3/C.328. Coleman made the same point; *Nigeria*, p. 259.

39. "Servicemen Drafted to Strikers' Posts: Grave Diggers & Night Soil Men on Strike," *WAP*, June 25, 1945.

40. See "Govt. Control of Gari Ceases Today but May Reappear if Profiteering Creeps In," *WAP*, August 27, 1945; and "Pullen Scheme Must Now Go," *WAP*, February 7, 1946.

41. "Imoudu Urges Workers to Reject August Pay Unless Calculated from Aug. 5," *WAP*, August 25, 1945.

42. Tudor Davies Report, p. 17. Also see Ananaba, *Trade Union Movement*, ch. 8; Emejulu, *Brief History*, pp. 64–68; Cooper, *Decolonization*, p. 136.

43. Even Azikiwe's seventy-four-part "History of the General Strike," serialized in the *West African Pilot* in the fall of 1945, failed to acknowledge the significance of market women's support. One likely explanation for the omission relates to gendered patterns of newspaper production and consumption; that is, most writers and readers were men who saw women's participation as either insignificant or not newsworthy.

44. T.A. Bankole, "The June 1945 Unauthorized General Strike," memorandum serialized in the *WAP*, September 1945. Relevant sections are in "Mr. TA Bankole Describes the Meeting with Labour Commissioner Two Days before the June 1945 Strike," September 12, 1945; and "Mr. Bankole Says Workers Were Incensed by Mr. Imoudu to Revolt Against Their Leaders," September 13, 1945.

45. Oyemakinde, "Nigerian General Strike," p. 704; Johnson, "Madam Pelewura," p. 9.

46. This is evident from press reports of meetings and joint activities in the first half of the 1940s. Also see Mba, *Nigerian Women*, ch. 7; and Johnson, "Madam Pelewura," p. 9. Similarly, Azikiwe backed the strike for nationalist reasons, but also because he actively sought the political support of wage workers. Thus, nationalist and class interests are difficult to disengage from the practical stuff of price controls, wages, and political alliances between local power brokers.

47. Imoudu and Adediran, Railway Workers Union to Mesdames Pelewura and Lagunju, President and Vice President of the Female Market Leaders Association (*Ẹgbé awọn ọlọjà obinrin*), May 1, 1941, original in HMP 34/2. Translation assistance by Jide Oyeneye is gratefully acknowledged.

48. "Workers' Week Celebrations," *The Nigerian Worker* (published by the Federated Trades Union of Nigeria) 1, no. 5 (April 1944): 5.

49. See N.A. Fadipe, *The Sociology of the Yoruba*, edited by F.O. Okediji and O.O. Okediji (Ibadan: University of Ibadan Press, 1970 [1940]), pp. 88, 152–57.

50. *Nigerian Statesman*, August 4, 1945, quoted in "History of the General Strike (43)," *WAP*, November 8, 1945.

51. Wole Soyinka, *Aké: The Years of Childhood* (New York: Random House, 1982), pp. 115, 133 (quoted). For more about bread, see Peter Kilby, *African Enterprise: The Nigerian Bread Industry* (Stanford, CA: Hoover Institution on War, Revolution, and Peace, 1965). I am grateful to one of the anonymous reviewers for the insights in this paragraph.

52. Much of the relevant literature has been summarized in Colin Creighton, "The Rise of the Male Breadwinner Family: A Reappraisal," *CSSH* 38 (1996): 310–37. Also see Pedersen, *Family, Dependence*; Rose, *Limited Livelihoods*; Laura L. Frader, "Engendering Work and Wages: The French Labor Movement and the Family Wage," in Frader and Rose (eds.), *Gender and Class*; and Martha May, "Bread before Roses: American Workingmen, Labor Unions, and the Family Wage," in Ruth Milkman (ed.), *Women, Work, and Protest: A Century of U.S. Women's Labor History* (Boston: Routledge and Kegan Paul, 1985).

53. Rose, *Limited Livelihoods*; A. Janssens, "The Rise and Decline of the Male Breadwinner Family: An Overview of the Debate," *International Review of Social History* 42 (1997): 1–23; Anna Clark, "The New Poor Law and the Breadwinner Wage: Contrasting Assumptions," *Journal of Social History* 34 (2000): 261–81.

54. Pedersen, *Family, Dependence*; John Macnicol, *The Movement for Family Allowances, 1918–45: A Study in Social Policy Development* (London: Heinemann, 1980). Also see Frader, "Engendering Work and Wages."

55. British examples include Clark, *Struggle for the Breeches*; Rose, *Limited Livelihoods* and "Respectable Men, Disorderly Others"; and Keith McClelland, "Masculinity and the 'Representative Artisan' in Britain, 1850–1880," in Michael Roper and John Tosh (eds.), *Manful Assertions: Masculinities in Britain since 1800* (London: Routledge, 1991).

56. Minute by D.E. Faulkner, Social Welfare Officer, to Commissioner of Lagos Colony, July 31, 1947, Comcol 1/3236.

57. Appendix I, Statement by the Chief Secretary to the Government, G. Beresford Stooke, in Tudor Davies Report, p. 52.

58. Nigeria, *Annual Report on the Social and Economic Progress of the People of Nigeria* (Lagos: Government Printer, 1931–1938).

59. Nigeria, *Annual Report on the Social and Economic Progress of the People of Nigeria* (Lagos: Government Printer, 1936), p. 62.

60. G.C. Whiteley, "Memorandum: Rates of Pay of Laborers and Employees in the Southern Provinces," Acting Chief Secretary's Office, Lagos, September 3, 1935.

61. Bridges Report, p. 101.

62. Excerpt from April 26, 1944, speech on Lagos Radio Distribution Service, in *The Nigerian Worker* 1, no. 5 (April 1944): 4; excerpt from speech entitled "Family Allowances" in *The Nigerian Worker* 1, no. 7 (December 1944): 2. James Coleman points out that the TUC was in contact with a number of foreign organizations, including the Fabian Society and the British Trade Union Congress, either of which could have supplied Shonekan and other Nigerian labor leaders with information on British debates and policies relevant to family allowances. Coleman, *Nigeria*, p. 257.

63. For the conceptual links between the family wage and public citizenship in Britain, see Rose, *Limited Livelihoods*, ch. 6; and Pedersen, *Family, Dependence*, ch. 6.

64. Appendix II, Memorandum of the Supreme Council of Nigerian Workers, Tudor Davies Report, pp. 63–64. That Nigerians were aware of the Beveridge proposals and compared them with Nigerian welfare provisions is clear from "Interim Relief for Unemployed

Workers" (editorial), *WAP*, January 28, 1946. For a letter to the editor stressing the links between citizenship and family allowances, see J.O. Lawanson (from Ile-Ife), "Family Allowances for Nigerian Worker," *WAP*, January 23, 1946.

65. Tudor Davies Report, pp. 17–18, 48.

66. Minute by Deputy Financial Secretary S.R. Marlow, November 7, 1946, CSO 26/46820/S.1.

67. LME Emejulu, General Secretary of the African Civil Servants Technical Workers Union, to Commissioner of Labour, December 10, 1946; Minute by Marlow to the Governor, January 9, 1947, both in CSO 26/46820/S.1.

68. Walter Harragin (chair), *Report of the Commission on the Civil Service of British West Africa, 1945–46* (Accra, Ghana, 1946), p. 19 (first and third quotations), p. 8 (second quotation).

69. Minute to CSG from Financial Secretary, January 17, 1947, CSO 26/46820/S.1.

70. Public Announcement, n.d. [February 1947], CSO 26/46820/S.1.

71. "The Excuses of Harragin for Refusing Africans Marriage Allowance," *WAP*, December 11, 1946.

72. "Hell Is Let Loose: Tear Gas and Water Hose Are Used to Disperse 500 Loco Workers," *WAP*, March 13, 1947; "Railway Men Are Hopeful after a Long Meeting with Officials over Harragin," *WAP*, March 15, 1947. Emejulu wrote that 3,000 railway men and other workers were involved; *Brief History*, pp. 71–74.

73. General Manager's Staff Circular No. 11/50, December 6, 1950, GMS 335 vol. 1.

74. C.J. Mabey, Permanent Secretary, Ministry of Health, to Civil Secretaries of Northern and Eastern Regions and Permanent Secretary, Ministry of Public Health, Ibadan, November 16, 1953, CO 554/1340.

75. Nigeria, *Annual Report of the Labor Office, Ibadan, 1951–52*, 5, Oyo Prof.1 1589/1; minute from S.L.A. Manuwa, Inspector-General of Medical Services, to Secretary of State, July 20, 1953, CO 888/10.

76. L.H. Gorsuch (chair), *Report of the Commission on the Public Services of the Governments in the Federation of Nigeria, 1954–55* (Lagos, 1955), p. 41. Also see Cooper, *Decolonization*, p. 448.

77. Colonial Labour Advisory Committee, Report of the Sub-Committee on Wage Fixing and Family Responsibilities, CO 859/810; Cooper, *Decolonization*, pp. 331–33.

78. Frederick Cooper, "From Free Labor to Family Allowances: Labor and African Society in Colonial Discourse," *American Ethnologist* 16 (1989): 745–65; "The Senegalese General Strike of 1946 and the Labor Question in Post-War French Africa," *CJAS* 24 (1990): 165–215; and *Decolonization*, ch. 6–7.

79. Cooper, *Decolonization*, ch. 8, and personal communication; Pedersen, *Family, Dependence*.

80. For instance, Rose, *Limited Livelihoods*; Wally Seccombe, "Patriarchy Stabilized: The Construction of the Male Breadwinner Wage Norm in Nineteenth-Century Britain," *Social History* 2 (1986): 53–76; Laura Lee Downs, *Manufacturing Inequality: Gender Division in the French and British Metalworking Industries, 1914–1939* (Ithaca, NY: Cornell University Press, 1995).

81. Of course it was often contentious in Europe, too. Jane Mark-Lawson and Anne Witz, "From 'Family Labour' to 'Family Wage'? The Case of Women's Labour in Nineteenth-Century Coalmining," *Social History* 13 (1988): 151–74; Pedersen, *Family, Dependence* and "The Failure of Feminism in the Making of the British Welfare State," *Radical History Review* 43 (1989): 86–110; Rose, *Limited Livelihoods*; John Tosh, "What Should Historians

Do with Masculinity? Reflections on Nineteenth-Century Britain," *History Workshop Journal* 38 (1994): 179–202.

82. "All We Ask for is Fairplay!" *WAP*, November 28, 1945.

83. Appendix II, "Memorandum of the Supreme Council of Nigerian Workers," in Tudor Davies Report, p. 61.

84. As in Kristin Mann, *Marrying Well: Marriage, Status and Social Change among the Educated Elite in Colonial Lagos* (Cambridge: Cambridge University Press, 1985).

5

THE RISE OF THE "MALE BREADWINNER" IN POSTWAR SOUTHWESTERN NIGERIA

During the 1945 strike, working men described themselves as providers for their wives and children in their agitation for improved wages and for family allowances, in spite of most households' dependence on women's incomes, and despite the fact that the strike itself would have been less successful if not for the financial support of market women. Wage-earners' self-depiction as breadwinners was at least in part instrumental, a strategy to appeal to the gendered notions that European administrators and employers held about labor and families. But the "male breadwinner" expanded into a potent cultural ideal in Nigeria in the decades following that strike. In the most radical treatment of Yoruba gender history to date, Oyèrónké Oyewùmí has argued that the unitary category of "woman" was not indigenous to southwestern Nigeria, and thus the notion of dependent wives was premised first on the colonial construction of Western gender categories. Wage labor in Nigeria was gendered as male from the start, since the colonial state almost always hired men (even for work that would have been quite familiar to women). Oyewùmí argues that "The combination of male wage labor and migration produced a new social identity for females as dependents and appendages of men." Later, in a wonderful insight, she notes, "The symbolism of bread is particularly apt since both bread and the male as sole breadwinner are colonial infusions into Yorùbá culture."[1]

I do not dispute that the breadwinner ideal came to southwestern Nigeria as a result of colonialism. But in this chapter I would like to complicate the story, and to bring in Nigerian workers, husbands and wives, as active agents in the process, in a context in which the colonial state also operated with mixed motives. The creation of a male breadwinner image entailed two simultaneous moves: (1) to construe male earnings as supportive of wives and children and

(2) either to ignore women's income earning or to define it as something other than remunerative work. As we will see, neither colonial officials, trade unionists, individual male earners, nor their wives embraced both of these moves, although they participated in various parts of the overall process. The result was the construction of a male breadwinner image, but an ambiguous one. The ambiguities require that we see Yoruba gender as flexible—which will not surprise anyone who studies gender in Africa—and also as performative.[2] People *work with* gender, in a sense, by acting in particular ways for particular reasons, some of which have to do with existing gender ideologies but some of which can be strategic improvisations. These practices can then influence what people consider to be normative behavior for (certain groups of) men and women.

Although gender as performance is a concept with wide applicability, it seems particularly appropriate for southwestern Nigeria, where keeping one's options open has been and remains a highly valued strategy. Karin Barber describes this as a premium on *potentiality*: "everything is continually emergent, continually requiring to be *worked out* afresh in the light of new circumstances."[3] The ever-popular slogan "no condition is permanent" applies equally well to economic and political strategies, entailing movement between multiple networks and opportunities, as to self-representation within different contexts.[4] Moreover, the colonial situation—including Western education, missionaries, and new types of careers—provided a range of discourses and practices for people to choose from. This is not to say that people simply put on new gender identities as the situation demanded: material conditions, social positioning, and individual alliances made some choices fit better than others.[5] Yet within such parameters, and in certain contexts, people actively fashioned themselves as particular kinds of men and women.

As I pointed out in this book's introduction, gender can be understood and explored through discourse, practices, and personal subjectivities. There were dramatic transformations in *discourse* about labor and gender during the late colonial period. Wage earners increasingly defined themselves as financial providers for their wives and children, both in the context of labor struggles and at home. Even employees' wives, themselves income earners, often referred to their husbands as breadwinners. As this suggests, discourse did not neatly reflect gendered *practices*. While steadily employed wage-earners provided increasing proportions of household resources, working wives remained crucial to domestic economies. The colonial state justified men's low wages by pointing to women's incomes, even as they limited the ability of women to gain formal employment.[6] And some activists defended Nigerian women's access to wage employment in the face of official efforts to limit it. How can one account for the tensions between discourse and practice? I argue that wage-earners actively manipulated ideas about gender in relation both to their colonial employer and to members of their households and families, while government officials and Nigerian women worked with gender for their own ends as well. A male breadwinner discourse allowed trade unionists to claim benefits from the state on the basis of men's family obligations and supported individual men's power and prestige in relation to women. Workers' wives and other women at times used the language of male providers in order to claim portions of men's paychecks for the support of themselves and their children. The Nigerian government emphasized women's contributions to workers' household budgets in order to resist the labor movement's demands for improved wages and benefits, even as it attempted to squeeze women out of formal sector employment. And at least some trade unionists resisted this gender discrimination, seemingly contradicting the male provider norm others worked to construct.

MALE PROVIDERS AND COLONIAL EMPLOYERS

Chapter 4 already traced the ways trade unionists used images of male providers in the cost of living agitation of the early 1940s and during the 1945 general strike. In addition to labor unions, individual workers based claims for jobs, wages, and benefits on their putative status as breadwinners for wives and children. In 1931, for instance, a letter carrier named J.D. Offili argued to the secretary of state that he should not be fired from his job (even though he had lost a sack of mail) through reference to his "wife and two children all in a dilapidated and deplorable state."[7] More petitions like this survive from after World War II. A group of railway retirees requesting improvements in their benefits petitioned in 1948 that "The management of a family with children, with no cola [cost of living adjustment], was and is a problem distressing in imagination and galling in experience."[8] The same year, a group of port workers calling themselves the "Painting Gang" wrote to the executive engineer of the Apapa (Lagos) wharf requesting increased wages to help them deal with the high costs of "house rentage, food allowances, luxuries, and also family expenses generally. Bachelors play only a fair show on this subject, whilst married men are especially having the heavy burden to carry. . . . Our wives who are in a very delicate condition look on us every time to have p[ocket] money in case of emergency, or times to buy other stuffs of food, etc. This is in most cases particularly pregnant women."[9] A former railway fireman pressed his case for improved retirement benefits by arguing that "I have a wife, a school going child and an aged mother to look after."[10] Even though it was not always successful, discourse about men's family responsibilities represented a useful strategy for trade unions and individual workers in dealing with employers and the state.

Breadwinner discourse circulated even when workers were not making particular demands upon their employers, especially by the 1950s. The Nigerian Railway Corporation's publicity department began publishing

"Nigerail: The Journal of the Nigerian Railway Corporation" for employees in 1956. The second edition of "Nigerail" introduced a page called "Claypot Club: For the Benefit of Wives and Daughters of Railwaymen." "No railwayman can be efficient and happy without the fullest co-operation of his wife (his better self)" began the introduction, "and it is to this end that this column is reserved for the benefit of our womenfolk." The editor then invited women to submit their letters for future publication. Although no call for letters had been issued previously, a note from a "Stationmaster's Wife" appeared in that very issue, most likely written by Sam Epelle, the paper's editor. Under the headline "Mrs. Stationmaster Says—Let's Give Our Menfolk Happy Home Life," the letter described salary-earners' wives as economic dependents. "Mrs. Stationmaster" wrote, "My friends and I know what goes on in the Railway where our husbands, fathers and relatives make their (and our) living.... The progress of the Railway is our progress; its future is our future, for the livelihood of our men and their families depends on the successful and profitable operation of the railway system."[11] Yet nearly all married women—even wives of station masters—earned incomes in their own rights. So what was this article, and others like it, about? Was the editor of "Nigerail" simply parroting what were seen as European gender values? Was he voicing the (largely unfulfilled) aspirations of a certain segment of the labor force? Or did the postwar period see major changes in household economies among some wage earners? Probably all of these were true.

REGULAR EARNERS MAKE GOOD HUSBANDS

My surveys and interviews with retired railway pensioners located in Ibadan and Lagos, along with other evidence, suggest that waged employees did to some extent see themselves as family providers. From the early years of wage labor in Nigeria, the relatively small numbers of steady earners could be relied upon more frequently than farmers or the irregularly employed for daily household needs as well as periodic payments like school fees. Whereas otherwise wives might have covered food expenses without being repaid, they expected steadily working husbands to reimburse them after the paycheck came. In the 1930s and 1940s, for example, a foreman in the railway mechanical department maintained a household with three wives and their children. Although the man's wives earned money from trading, he was "bound to set aside some kind of food allowance every month." According to his son, "the system [of providing money for the family's food] is not tampered with, especially for a man doing government work." During the same period, the foreman of a track maintenance gang typically reimbursed his wife if she had bought food between his pay periods.[12] "It is true that most husbands in this country do not entrust the handling of their earnings to their wives," a 1945 newspaper column began, but then pointed out that men with steady jobs provided their wives with allowances for food purchasing and other household needs.[13] Indeed, by the 1940s, educated men as well as some artisans and well-placed laborers came to define regular payments of *owó onjẹ* (food money) as part of "being a man."[14]

As salaries and benefits improved throughout Nigeria after World War II and ever greater numbers made long careers in wage employment (a process described more fully in chapter 6), steadily employed men seem to have become responsible for increasing portions of the household budget. For example, most market traders began their careers before or immediately after they married, but the women in my survey (who married between about 1940 and 1965) began working three to five years after marriage. Combined with the fact that most of these women lived with their spouses away from the couple's hometown(s), this means that they were largely relying on their husbands' incomes during the period when they were likely to have young children. A railway man's budget, presented in a Lagos debt case from 1950, indicated that he provided most of his household's support. This thirty-two-year-old machinist shared two rooms with seven dependents. With a monthly salary of £12, his expenses totaled £12.13.6. Even when he earned an extra £1 per month in overtime, he could barely scrape by without borrowing and help from his wife. But if this budget is to be believed, such contributions were much less significant than those many other women made to their households.[15] This was not an exclusively Yoruba phenomenon, as a story by Flora Nwapa about the Nigerian Civil War suggests. In "A Soldier Returns Home," an Igbo train guard tells the protagonist about his work for the Railway beginning in 1941. "I first went to Jos," the man related.

> . . . I saved money and went home and married a wife. . . . And we had all our children there in Jos. . . . In those days, at the end of each month, I would give my wife ten shillings for food. It was more than enough. . . . My colleagues told me ten shillings was too much, but I did not worry. I let her have it. She was such a lovely girl, and I did not want to appear stingy.[16]

Their financial potency, real or exaggerated (an issue raised below), contributed to wage-earners' masculine self-esteem and their sense of importance relative to women and kin. Divorce cases from the 1940s and 1950s show that women became exasperated with husbands who did not meet their material obligations, and lack of sufficient financial maintenance was the most frequent reason women gave for leaving their husbands.[17] In contrast, wage-earners who brought home steady paychecks were often seen as good mates because they could be good providers. Discussing her reasons for marrying a railway clerk in the 1950s, one woman noted, "If anybody who works in the railway comes your way you would like to marry him. At that time, railway paid very well . . . so people loved them [the employees] and liked to mix with them."[18] According to the women's column in the *West African Pilot* in 1946, "A thrifty man stands a good chance of being a likeable husband" because he is able to "provide good meals, proper clothing and every comfort for his family" as well as draw on his savings "when ill health or accident occurs." The same columnist published a letter from a young woman undecided about marrying a third-class clerk. A Mr. Lotus Lily of the Nigerian Railway, Offa, responded that a steadily employed husband, even of the lowest salary grade, "promises you comfort and perhaps some occasional luxuries."[19] Such a man's paycheck allowed him not only to contribute to household expenses, but also to offer loans, presents, or "begging fees" in the event of disputes with his wife.

This sense of steady earners' financial importance and masculine allure—represented by the discourse of male breadwinners—nevertheless coexisted with women's contributions to domestic budgets. The 1950 Lagos census identified 31,926 (76 percent) out of a total of 41,492 women as traders.[20] Eighty-five percent of the railway pensioners I surveyed who had been hired before 1960 were married to traders.[21] A 1950 study of 207 mothers of primary school girls in Lagos found that 96 percent of those married to artisans, laborers, and petty traders were market women, as were 84 percent of those married to clerks and middle-level businessmen.[22] Urban Consumer Surveys from Lagos, Ibadan, and Enugu reported that in the mid-1950s a laborer's wage provided no more than 60 percent of his household's income. The wage contributed about two-thirds of household income for artisans.[23] The wife of a railway clerk spoke for many when she explained that she started trading after marriage "to help my husband because he could not carry the household alone."[24]

As was expected of a good husband, employed men often supported their spouses' enterprises by donating initial trading capital. Less frequently, some even engaged in joint ventures with their wives—a practice that, by contrast, was exceedingly rare among rural farmers.[25] Felicia Adeyemi, for instance, had been a seamstress in Ibadan before her marriage in 1953. She relocated to Lagos to join her new husband, a railway storekeeper, and the two of them opened a shop together in Lagos to sell uniforms. Over the ensuing years, they used their combined income for children's education, housekeeping, and "family affairs." "For instance, if it is the time for school fees and his salary is ready he paid it and I will take care of feeding; but if not, if I have the money I would pay the school fees and vice versa."[26] In locomotive driver Bernard Aruna's household, he paid for rent, ceremonies, and school fees, but his wife contributed money for food, her own clothes, and children's expenses. When he got extra money from overtime, he invested it in her trade. "When I was in grade II [as a locomotive fireman, 1958–1962] I was earning a monthly salary of 12 pounds 4 shillings. I had a child and a wife. Do you think that money can feed us? I have no money to keep somewhere else. . . . We eat the whole thing and wait for the next month's salary." Working overtime brought in some extra money, which Aruna invested in his wife's trade. "That 12 pounds 4 can fetch us about 23–24 pounds up to 27 pounds [if invested in trade] so when we come home [from driving a long-distance route] we can reimburse the wife maybe 10 pounds for her to buy some things to sell."[27]

In spite of such financial cooperation and women's contributions (and regardless of what women thought), the retired railway men whom I interviewed made it clear that they considered themselves financial heads of the households. Although a husband would be reluctant to interfere in his wife's trade, Aruna said, he still makes the major economic decisions: "the husband runs the home's affairs."[28] The ideology of male economic supremacy was voiced even in the face of men's financial shortcomings, as Buchi Emecheta illustrates in *The Joys of Motherhood*, about the wife of an Igbo railway worker in 1940s Lagos. Testifying separately in a court case, both the heroine, Nnu Ego, and her husband claimed to pay their children's school fees. Pressed to explain the discrepancy, Nnu Ego related, "Nnaife is the head of our family. He owns me, just like God in the sky owns us. So even though I pay the fees, yet he owns me. So in other words he pays."[29] Ibadan court cases from the 1930s on confirm that men and women often publicly asserted that husbands were to be primary household providers, even if in practice this was not the case.[30] In the Nadele family, one of those Dan Aronson studied in Ibadan in the mid-1960s, a building contractor and his wife fought bitterly over money and authority. The husband wanted his wife to be known as a full-time housewife, yet she alleged that he did not provide enough money to make this possible.[31] Similarly, an assistant station master was transferred in the late 1960s to a location where he and his new wife had no social connections. After a year of marriage, he gave her some money to start a trade. Once children started coming, although she had no one to help her, she had to continue working because his salary was not enough to support their growing family. The husband's income was crucial, she knew, as was help she secretly solicited from an uncle back home. But she did not tell her spouse for fear of offending his masculine pride and his sense of himself as the sole earner. "He would be thinking that the money he gave is enough but it is not so I have to add to it."[32]

The spouses of such women usually were unaware of exactly how much money their wives earned and spent. In interviews, few railway pensioners were clear about their wives' earnings, generally dismissing them as insignificant. Amona Shofekun, married to a railway ticket collector, was employed at the Ministry of Works from the early 1960s, but her husband considered her earnings to be none of his business: "I didn't bother about that. All that I know is that they weren't paid substantial salary."[33] Interviewed women also hesitated to discuss their finances. Part of the reason was that personal money and trading receipts are generally kept together, making separate accounting difficult; but the most important motivation seems to have been to keep husbands ignorant of exactly how much their wives earned. This way, men's paychecks (or rather, some agreed-upon portion of them) tended to be spent on specified household needs first, supplemented by women's contributions. In the late 1950s and early 1960s, railway shunter Michael Odede's wife "used to assist me in buying foods, books, pencils and cloth for the children before my arrival [i.e., while he was at work out of town] or before I received my salary, and when I take my salary I refunded her."[34] Women knew how much was in their husbands' pay packets, and which days were paydays. They actively laid claim to parts of their husbands' earnings, especially for school fees and other expenses associated with raising children. Women lauded their spouses by referring to them as breadwinners, even when they were earning incomes unacknowledged by their husbands, and when the men spent money on their own extended families. Thus, women were also involved in the creation and dissemination of a male breadwinner discourse, which they used to expand their own options and resources.[35]

Shortly after the 1945 general strike, a series of newspaper articles debated the extent to which wives should depend on husbands for support. A male letter-writer suggested that men's ability to channel money from their paychecks to their wives represented a crucial component of masculinity: "Let the woman hold the purse strings and soon after the man will become a puppet of the woman."[36] As this suggests, the links between men's incomes and their relationships with women brought anxiety as well as pride. As with marriage expenses (see chapter 2), men expected women's affections in return for the money spent on them. For instance, in 1946 a Mr. Justice Smith complained in the women's column of a Lagos newspaper about "the conduct of his girl who despite his humble efforts to assist her financially and to give her every possible comfort was found to be very inconsistent in her love." "To be candid," Smith continued, "she in turn does not give me full services for the money spent on her."[37] Court records contain numerous cases in which boyfriends were disappointed in their expectations of social obligations and physical affection from women to whom they had given money or presents; in some cases, men justified rape on the grounds that they had given gifts or money to the victim and therefore were entitled to sexual relations.[38]

While men relished the power and prestige associated with contributing money to wives, girlfriends, and children, these could diminish as women claimed men's paychecks as a matter of course. A joke from the mid-1950s lampooned this scenario, indicating that it had become rather common:

Said an employee to his employer, "Do you think, sir, I might have a rise?"
"But I put a rise in your pay packet last week."
"Oh, I'm very sorry sir, my wife never tells me anything."[39]

The Rise of the "Male Breadwinner"

Photo 5.1 Cartoon form "Nigerail," 1956. Photo courtesy of the Bodleian Library, University of Oxford.

An advertisement for a railway cooperative store boasted that the scheme would allow a worker "to look up more courageously to your wife when she argues about the house-keeping money," painting an image of a sheepish, dominated husband.[40] In print, popular culture, and interviews, men often alleged that women were selfish, looking only for mates who could provide them with consistent maintenance as well as gifts.[41] In Cyprian Ekwensi's story "Lokotown," both a railway fireman and his engine driver exchange money and presents for the affections of a beautiful, flashy woman named Konni. While the men enjoy their ability to win Konni's attention, they also know that it is their paychecks that attract her: "You have come to Lokotown to seek your fortune, and to empty men's pockets," the engine driver tells her.[42] A 1963 newspaper story reported that men were particularly successful with their girlfriends during the pay week: during that time, women "have special privileges. The boy friend who may range from a teen-age messenger to a sixty-five year old Accountant digs out cash like mad. . . . He pays the house rent, buys the new 'fashion' and takes her out for some nice time. The girl friend co-operates admirably. . . . She understands that for her part, she may be required to pay in kind."[43] A cartoon in "Nigerail" suggested not only that wives spent paychecks without consulting their husbands, but that the women took for granted the hard work associated with earning the money: a woman with a baby on her back says to her shocked husband, "But if I spend more than you earn, it's just as good as if you were earning more."[44] A fictionalized railway man in "Lokotown" complains, "We fight for bonus, wage increase, and all the rest. . . . We go on strike. They give us more money—and what happens? These women take all we get."[45] These representations may well be the mirror image of women's appropriation of the discourse about male providers, reflecting a mixture of male pride over earning wages and the suspicion that being a "breadwinner" did not tip the domestic balance so dramatically in favor of men after all.

Still, it seems clear that by the 1950s some segment of the Nigerian labor force was able to contribute substantially to their household budgets, and that this ability often facilitated relatively smooth relations with wives and a sense of steady earners as important providers. This was the case even though wage earners' wives earned money on their own and made significant contributions for children's economic needs. In fact, such women seem to have used the discourse of male breadwinners as well, as a strategy for increasing the amounts their husbands contributed to family upkeep. But such an image, combined with colonial preferences and persistently gendered spheres of labor, helped to preclude women from earning wages themselves.

WOMEN MAY WORK, BUT THEY ARE NOT BREADWINNERS

"There is a lot of grumbling among the wage-earners about how their wives help them," a 1947 newspaper editorial reported. "Too many demands come on the family purse, and too few hands fill it. And the worse of it all is that most of these housewives, some of them with some wonderfully new-fangled idea of civilization, are unduly lazy and incapable of making the least contribution to the family coffer."[46] This article went on to argue that women should work to provide economic security for children and households, something that most southwestern Nigerian women were already doing. Like much of the public discourse about women and wage earning in the postwar period, it linked women and work (or an alleged refusal to work) with modernization, and it ignored the financial needs and contributions of women in their families. Even supporters of women's wage employment based their arguments less on household economics than on the idea that Nigeria's progress included an expansion of women's opportunities. In other words, many men wanted women to work outside the home, and some articulated this as part of a process of modernization, but they did not want women to translate their employment into a new status within the family or society.[47] Whether they concurred about which specific jobs were or were not suitable for Nigerian women, male commentators (and some women) agreed that women were not breadwinners.

In contrast to the 1947 article cited above, generally when journalists or African elites—particularly women—used the language of civilization and modernization to discuss female roles, they suggested that women's education and employment would lead to greater social progress. "Jeune Moderniste" wrote in a 1930 *Daily Times* article that women should be educated and work outside the home. A decade later, a Native Administration official lectured that although women were primarily mothers and he did not consider them suitable for national leadership, they should be educated for wage employment and responsible citizenship. In a 1944 "Brains Trust" forum held in Lagos, several highly accomplished women argued that given the proper training women could do any job done by men, equal work should earn equal pay, and marriage should not prevent women from continuing with their careers. Nnamdi Azikiwe, radical nationalist and publisher of the *West African Pilot*, editorialized that Nigeria would remain "in a cave man condition" until women had equal opportunities to men. The editor of the *Pilot*'s woman's column opined that "Nigeria cannot afford to be backward by trampling on her women." In the early 1950s, an argument in favor of women politicians again linked women's rights with modernization: "The great principle that actuates modern social thought is that birth is no barrier to a person's advance."[48]

On the other hand, wage labor was, from the start, gendered as male. Girls' education lagged behind that for boys, and the colonial government was extremely reluctant to hire women. Few wage jobs were available for women until the 1940s, and most of these were in the private sector as nurses, lady doctors, teachers, telephone operators, and clerks. In the 1920s and 1930s, the Lagos Women's League and the press frequently called for more young women to be hired as telephone operators in government departments, while the administration answered that qualified women were not forthcoming.[49] A major expansion in girls' education from the late 1930s meant that ten years later there was no shortage of qualified female job seekers. But a government report from the mid-1940s shows that most of the women employed in the public sector earned very low salaries and had few opportunities for advancement. Administrators consistently resisted the inclusion of women in the civil service, which was theoretically gender neutral since entrance to all departments except education and medical services was based on examinations. Officials feared that once a woman entered the standard clerical grade, she then would become eligible to take the qualifying exams for promotions to the next level, where her position might involve the supervision of men. "British men balked at the idea of a female boss; they assumed, perhaps rightly, that Nigerian men would too."[50]

As the demand for workers skyrocketed during World War II, the government and some private employers looked to women as cheap labor, much as they did in Europe and the United States.[51] Male trade unionists opposed these gender discrepancies in wages and benefits, in part on grounds of fairness and in part because they feared employers would replace male workers with lesser-paid women. The 1944 inaugural meeting of the Trades Union Congress (TUC) included a discussion of discriminatory pay to female employees. The resulting letter to the government stated that the unequal treatment of women workers "definitely indicate[s] a tendency to cheapen and exploit labour."[52] Trade unionists had to tread carefully in defending women's paid employment, given that they were at the same time engaged in arguments with the government about family allowances and men's roles as household breadwinners. Indeed, a 1945 TUC progress report followed a summary of negotiations over family allowances with a resolution requesting the government to investigate the employment conditions of female workers.[53]

Deputy Financial Secretary C. Watts reported on women in government service later that year. His committee's recommendations shaped official policy for the postwar era, essentially allowing for the creation for more posts for women—especially as the education, social welfare, and medical bureaucracies expanded—but limiting their prospects for promotion and restricting their employment after marriage. Among other provisions, the government created a separate grade for women typists instead of integrating women into the standard clerical grade.[54] This move effectively removed female workers as a threat to male wages and jobs, and in that respect it may have been a response to TUC pressures. With the elimination of female workers as potential competition, the labor unions were then in a position to mount a vocal defense, on principle, of women's paid employment.

This does not mean that they were inclined to do so, however, and in fact a woman raised the issue within the TUC. At its December 1945 annual convention, Miss E.E. Duke, a representative of the Postal Workers Union, resolved "that in view of the relatively small number of women in the civil service, women must be employed in all government services, especially in the clerical sections." She argued that women's permanent jobs need not be given up upon marriage, and that women should be considered equally with men in regard to salary and promotions. Duke argued that "because African men were very poorly paid, and because some husbands find it difficult to maintain a comfortable living together with their wives, women, if employed after marriage, could help in the economic stand of their husbands, and thereby contribute more substantially to the comfort of the family." Elsewhere in the world, she continued, clerical posts were often held by women, and some females were even employed in workshops. Trade union leaders J. Marcus Osindero and A.O. Omagle, fresh from the debate with the government over family allowances, argued to the contrary that "the woman's place is the home." Duke countered that there was little hope for national development if women were not active participants. Siding with her, Mr. S.A. George stated that "it would be an abuse of Nigerian womanhood if they were not given the chance to try, as were women in other parts of the world." Omagle and Osindero then moved that the section of Duke's motion urging that women be employed after marriage be deleted, with Omagle arguing that "because women were bent on jobs, they have not been able to give proper home training to their children." After much debate, T.A. Bankole, former president of the TUC and ally of Osindero's, succeeded in tabling Duke's motion.[55]

The matter remained public for months. Immediately after the vote, the *West African Pilot* editorialized that "[t]he TUC lost a great opportunity to make history. . . . Nigerian workers cannot oppose racial discrimination and condone sexual discrimination."[56] Yet this ignores the gendered implications of the recently concluded general strike: male workers had specifically argued that they were entitled to metropolitan-style benefits because they were men like European men, that is, that they supported wives and children. An editorial in the *Daily Service*, the newspaper of the radical Nigerian Youth Movement, stated, "Until men are *treated as men and paid as men* on the basis of the services they render irrespective of their race and colour, no Nigerian would be stupid enough to regard himself sincerely as a member of the British Commonwealth of Nations."[57] In 1945 Nigeria, one way of opposing racial discrimination was to embrace a certain notion of masculinity that, if not exactly condoning sexual discrimination, implied women's exclusion from formal employment. To then support Duke's motion would have undermined the trade union leaders' tenuous claims to that very politically salient masculinity. Moreover, some trade unionists may have favored the exclusion of poorly paid females from the labor force as a strategy to enforce generalized male breadwinner wages.[58]

In contrast, Azikiwe devoted two of his daily columns to defending Nigerian women's claims to equality in the workplace, stressing that national development and even political independence depended on equal rights between the sexes.[59] Later, he continued that gender equality in the workplace was necessary to avoid discontent among women and to further "social progress."[60] But the official journal of the Nigeria Civil Service Union criticized female clerical workers for "being lazy and irresponsible." "They observe no manner of discipline and give African sectional heads a lot of headache," the article continued, convincingly enough for the *Pilot* to warn that "[w]e want really serious girls in our working classes."[61] In January, the newspaper's columnist on women's issues opined that although marriage was a "natural" condition, women needed education and jobs for their economic security. Notions that women belong only in the home "will never help the country," Miss Silva asserted.[62]

Government policy on the employment of women, revised and formalized in 1948, forced all women to resign from permanent government posts upon marriage or pregnancy, unless personally exempted.[63] Some indication of female employees' reaction to this comes from a letter sent to the Railway Labor Officer. Elizabeth Offili protested her termination, along with seven other "girls" from the Railway Printer's office, describing herself as an important family breadwinner: "My parents are poor and at present I am supporting both my aged mother and a younger who is attending school and to whom I am sending regular monthly remittances." She stressed that she had no relatives in Lagos and thus was particularly vulnerable. "But now, with unemployment staring me in the face like a monster," she wrote, "my plight can be better imagined than told."[64]

In contrast, as the notion of a male breadwinner became increasingly normative among steady earners and major employers, it carried with it the obverse assumption: that women's wages were *not* necessary to support families. As early as 1944, in response to a request from the Women's Party for vocational schools for girls, increased opportunities for women in the civil service, and equal pay for equal work, the chief secretary to the government replied that "women don't make good saleswomen and since women don't have the same financial responsibilities as men they should not receive equal salaries."[65] A 1954 Colonial Office report asserted that African women's employment "impedes educational advance and diverts maternal attention from the home and family needs." Still, such work was regarded as insignificant: "While wives and families in West Africa do work, their earnings are thought to be less a necessity than a useful supplement to the income of the man."[66] African managers allegedly hired women clerks rather than men not only because they were more easily manipulated, but also because they could be paid lower wages on the grounds that, instead of supporting their own dependents, they were "fed by their parents."[67]

It seems paradoxical that an administration that continually insisted that the wives of male employees contributed to household budgets would also work to exclude women from formal employment. Through the postwar period, official statements about southern Nigerian women remained similar to those from the 1930s: "Where the wage economy is being established . . . the African wage-earner, although he may be earning sufficient [*sic*], does not expect his salary to be used to maintain his wife—he still expects her to support herself as he does on the farm." The Department of Labor reported in 1951 that "[t]he overwhelmingly great majority of women throughout the country undertake profitable activities of one kind or another in addition to their purely domestic duties." Three years later the Ibadan labor officer reported, "It is a characteristic feature of the economy of this area that the wages earned by the working class are often augmented by the incomes accruing from petty trading of wives of the workers."[68] But they opposed this work: a 1953 report on juvenile delinquency in Lagos, for example, blamed "parental neglect" for the maladjustment of young offenders: "fathers habitually fail to maintain their children and mothers spend the whole day in the markets trading. Children are the last consideration not, as in so much of the Western and Asian world, the first." The residential separation occasioned by trading also came under fire for disrupting family life and depriving children of mothers at home. As the Lagos welfare officer noted, "The separation of the parents or their lack of common purpose respecting their children, robs the home of the tranquility and reassurance which must be present for home-training to be effective."[69]

Gladys Plummer, in charge of women's education within the Nigerian government, was one of the few European officials who concluded from women's financial independence that they should be offered more educational and professional opportunities. In 1948, she conducted inquiries among women welfare workers throughout southern Nigeria to find out how much women depended on their own incomes. The replies confirmed her conviction that men's contributions alone would not support women and children. Alison Izzett, the woman's welfare officer for Lagos, divided women into income and educational categories. Across all groups, she reported, women were expected to provide significant sums for food, clothing, and the needs of children. In fact, the illiterate woman was reported to be happier than others: "[A]s she has always been brought up to feel that it is her duty to maintain both her husband and her children, and to expect nothing from him, she is not disappointed when she receives nothing." Although the Welfare Office worked "on the assumption that a man should contribute something towards the cost of his child's maintenance and schooling[,] [i]n no case do we even attempt to try and make him bear the whole cost." In her draft report, Plummer pointed to the discrepancy between some versions of household economics and prevailing norms in southern Nigeria. "It is frequently taken for granted that a married man supports his wife and family," she reported. "This appears to be true in very few instances." Plummer argued that women's financial responsibilities made education and job opportunities for them crucial. She suggested an expansion, not contraction, of women's employment, so as to assist them with their household financial burdens. In addition, as Izzett noted, "If the women could be financially more independent, then the men would have to improve their marital behaviour."[70]

Yet most other administrators discouraged women's formal employment. Even when they referred to women's financial earnings, officials in Nigeria dismissed trading as something other than real work. A 1944 report on Social Welfare lamented the limited political and economic opportunities for women and was unusual in recommending female industrial labor. But this report suggested that Nigerian women needed a means of earning independent incomes other than prostitution, as if that were their only profit-making occupation! "If some enterprising agency would establish a factory for the making of matches or the tailoring of cheap shirts and cloths, streams of girls would be given a chance of independence, and the idea of woman as a mere household drudge and sleeping partner might be transformed." In 1950, the Department of Labor's annual report mentioned small numbers of women in clerical work, teaching, soap and tobacco manufacturing, printing in the south, and tin mining in the north. But "[s]o far . . . there are few options for the employment of women, unless petty trading can be regarded as such."[71]

These opportunities began to expand, albeit still on a relatively small scale, in the 1950s. A 1948 report on the prospects for filling senior civil service posts with Nigerians included in its recommendations that "[w]omen should be encouraged to take a larger share in Government work." In particular, it suggested that special training schemes help women qualify for "certain posts, such as nursing, secretarial and certain other specialist appointments, in which a larger number of skilled Nigerian women officers is urgently required."[72] While the transition of these formerly male-dominated occupations to female realms accelerated, some young women also began to pursue posts designated as "male," such as engineers, photographers, drivers, police, and factory workers. The gender designations of certain jobs became increasingly contested during this period, as an exchange in the *Daily Times* illustrates. One letter to the editor called for the employment of women as bus drivers and conductors, because "Nigeria is now looking for self-government and we shall need everyone to help in the day to day struggles."[73] An outraged reader retorted: "This is stupid! Bus driving is the job of a man—a HE MAN. It is alright to see women joining the police force, but there must be a limit to what they can do in other activities. It needs a very strong man . . . to control the wheel of a bus. . . . Let women drive taxi cabs if they are very anxious to drive something." Another male reader asserted that women were too lazy to work as bus conductors, which required long periods of standing and climbing; an angry woman responded that "any job a man can do, a woman can do also."[74]

Trade unionists' public pronouncements generally supported women's access to wage employment, although—as in Britain and elsewhere[75]— not in jobs or wage scales seen as the preserve of men. On International Women's Day (March 8) in 1950, the *Labour Champion*, edited by the radical trade unionist Nduka Eze, again linked women's employment to national modernization. "The emancipation of Nigerian womanhood must be one of the major tasks of all progressive minded elements in this country." But this doesn't mean just lipstick and western habits, he went on. "It is rather social equality with men, equal pay for equal work, equal educational opportunities, freedom of thought and action, ample opportunities to contribute as much as possible to the social, economic, political and intellectual life of the nation."[76] On the railway, where out of over 33,000 employees there were only thirty-seven women in the mid-1950s,[77] male trade unionists made claims on behalf of their female colleagues. At the 1949 conference of the Association of Nigerian Railway Civil Servants (ANRCS), motions addressed female clerks' pay rates and maternity leave, among other issues. In 1954–1955, the ANRCS considered a report that female railway employees were frequently terminated and replaced by men. The union's motion called such actions "retrograde" and advocated "a change of attitude on the part of the Management [to] encourage both the training and education of Nigerian girls as future mothers of the Nations."[78]

The ANRCS addressed women's conditions of employment throughout the next year in a series of meetings with the railway's general manager, Ralf Emerson. The biggest stumbling block was management's contention that "it is not advantageous to employ women because of the high incidence of sickness among female employees." The union implored its female members to improve attendance and insisted that inefficient women be replaced with other women workers rather than with men (thus keeping men's and women's pay scales separate). Meanwhile, Emerson agreed to reexamine the matter with the heads of departments.[79] The departmental reports made three main arguments against the employment of women: their attendance record was poor, they required costly separate facilities, and they were desirable only when men were not available. These reflected presumptions about women based both on biology (they were less hardy than men) and social relations (men were more suited to regular work). The chief engineer summed up the general views on the matter: "until either the supply of men servants becomes difficult, or the opportunity should arise to staff a new grade suited to female labour (e.g. light repetitive work), it is not recommended that the present policy should be changed."[80] The acting chief accountant added his opinion that men would object to being supervised by women. Since hiring women would entail the obligation of promoting them, men's aversion would necessitate all-female sections, which were impractical. The acting chief mechanical engineer was the most open-minded, conceding that hiring women as typists and telephone attendants was "not entirely unsuccessful," although he added that this was because the jobs did not require regular attendance. He echoed his colleagues' preference for male staff, unless they were unavailable.[81]

Although the civil servants' union continued to defend female employees, management deferred negotiation on the issue because of the transition in the Railway's status to a parastatal corporation, which took place in mid-1955. The National Union of Railwaymen (Federated) opposed the creation of the Nigerian Railway Corporation (NRC) on a variety of grounds, mainly centered on justified fears that new conditions of service would be worse than the old. Included in the NUR(F)'s complaints was the allegation that under the new contracts, married women employees would be dismissed or placed on temporary contracts and would lose their pensions. Such action, the union alleged in a press release, would "create social problems" by depriving women of the opportunity to earn decent incomes. "If Nigerian girls cannot be employed in the Civil Service of our country on the ground that they are married," it asked, "of what avail is their education?"[82] In 1956, the railway civil servants' union even voted for the inclusion of women delegates to its annual conferences, based on the argument that "we can try to represent their feelings, but we can never feel like them." The conference agreed that women's branches should be created in districts with more than fifteen female members.[83]

The Corporation's conditions of service, finally published in 1957, did discriminate against female employees as the union feared. "No woman who is married . . . may be employed by the Corporation except in a temporary capacity on monthly terms," it stipulated. "Immediately on her becoming a married woman . . . a woman officer shall resign or her services may be otherwise terminated." Women employed before 1955 and retained by the Corporation were exempted and able to hold pensionable appointments. Their husbands and children, however, were not eligible for the same benefits as were dependents of male staff.[84] Female employees in other establishments faced analogous conditions, which some women and unions continued to protest. "On almost every day of the week women are forced to listen to, in theory, such rattling nonsense as 'no nation can progress without its women marching side by side with its men,'" one female columnist wrote. "But we all know how much of this sweet 'nonsense' is put into practice. . . . Give married professional women a chance. They are just as good as anybody."[85] In 1961, the Maritime Trade Union Federation resolved that female employees on permanent appointments not be reverted to temporary grade upon marriage.[86] Through the 1960s, the public continued to debate women's access to wage employment.[87]

It seems an interesting contrast that trade unionists and others would defend women's wages and working conditions during the very era in which the

The Rise of the "Male Breadwinner" 123

Photo 5.2 Sign prohibiting women and children, Ibadan railway compound, 1994.

male breadwinner stereotype was making its greatest gains. This is one more piece of evidence for the complexity and fragility of this particular aspect of working class masculinity. It is also important to remember the extremely small numbers of Nigerian women actually working for wages, although those numbers continued to grow. In 1950, less than 2 percent of all paid employees in Nigeria were women. A decade and a half later, that proportion had risen to 7.2 percent.[88] Although there were exceptions, women tended to be clustered in relatively low-paying jobs defined as female. Thus, male employees could defend women's employment without serious threats to their own jobs and wages. Indeed, as elsewhere in the world, this occupational structure allowed higher, "breadwinner" wages to be exclusively earmarked for men. Further, the agitation on behalf of women railway workers occurred in the context of general opposition to new employment terms, not necessarily as a discrete set of grievances.

Finally, even though male unionists made representations on behalf of female employees, individual men and trade unionists also talked about women's work as if it were insignificant, and they relegated women to the sidelines of the labor movement. As we have seen, male wage earners often did not acknowledge their wives' importance to household economies. And within the civil service, male resentment against their married female colleagues, particularly around the issue of maternity leave, ran deeply.[89] A 1963 article on the woman's page of the *West African Pilot* reminded readers that market women were in fact workers: "While others rage over women working or not working she [the market trader] goes about her business in her quiet way. . . . A career woman indeed!"[90] Female employees in the railway and the Nigerian Ports Authority occasionally received union overtures, but they seem to have gotten the most widespread attention when they competed in beauty pageants for the titles of "Miss Nigerail" and "Miss Port Authority."[91] A sign erected on the Ibadan railway compound (and still standing) clearly defines industrial work as male: "Women and children are not allowed in the workshops during the working hours." In 1960, the Maritime Trade Union Federation president called for organizing the female staff of the Ports Authority. Although he emphasized that they should be involved in general union activities, he directed that "[t]hey [female employees] should be organised into a Special Auxiliary Unit responsible for the Social Programme of the Federation."[92]

CONCLUSION

Given the persistently small proportions of Nigerians engaged in wage labor at all,[93] it seems appropriate to point out that the notion of a male breadwinner, supporting wives and children through steady wage employment, has never comprised any "hegemonic masculinity" in southwestern Nigeria. Stephan Miescher and I have argued elsewhere (as have other people) that the concept of "hegemonic masculinity" is not particularly useful for colonial Africa, where so many ideologies mixed and mingled with varying degrees of power.[94] In spite of that caveat, there is no question that a male breadwinner model emerged in colonial Nigeria and that in some contexts it remains an ideal.[95] For instance, after the financially troubled Nigerian Railway Corporation suspended the payment of salaries to current workers and pensions to retirees in 1993, a group of women identifying themselves as railway men's wives brought children and cooking pots to the Ministry of Transport, where they held a noisy and disruptive sit-down strike. The women eventually addressed the minister, demanding that the payments be reinstated on the grounds that they were used to support wives and children.[96] In fact, the male provider stereotype is so potent that my research assistant even inserted the word "breadwinner" when translating and transcribing our tape-recorded interview with a railway pensioner's wife, even though the word was never uttered. Our informant, Olukemi Alabi, told us that when her husband was working for the Nigerian Railway she had sometimes loaned him money, and sometimes he had given her money. "He was the breadwinner," somehow made it into the transcript, although the recording contains neither that English sentence nor any Yoruba equivalent.[97]

How did these notions come to southwestern Nigeria? I have argued in this chapter that attributing their emergence to colonial impositions only tells part of the story. While the colonial state created the conditions under which nearly all wage jobs were filled by men, this did not mean that it turned men into the major providers for their wives and children, especially since most people did not work for wages and women had access to their own incomes. In fact, administrators in Nigeria until the 1950s resisted male workers' claims for wages and benefits deemed suitable for family providers, and it was Nigerian men who first raised the male breadwinner ideal. For trade unionists and individual wage earners, the image of male providers was useful for making demands from the colonial state, even if it sat uneasily with women's important economic activities. At home, steady wages and the breadwinner ideal had implications for men's marital relationships, household budgets, and self-esteem, even if those budgets were partially kept afloat through women's contributions. And in negotiations over household resources, women drew upon the fledgling male breadwinner norm to make their own claims to men's paychecks.

The ambiguity and contradictions within the male breadwinner ideal are particularly apparent in struggles over women's paid work. In the 1940s and beyond, government officials resisted the notion of Nigerian men as primary providers (who could claim improved wages and benefits) by pointing to women's independent earning and support for their children. Yet they also limited Nigerian women's access to formal sector jobs and defined market trading as something besides real employment. Women workers protested official restrictions on the grounds that they needed income to provide for themselves and their families. They received some support from trade unions, even though the unions were of course composed of men who were married to market traders and other working women. In negotiations with the colonial state over men's wages and benefits, labor activists argued that women's contributions to household budgets were insignificant—thus participating themselves in the construction of market trading as a marginal occupation. For some trade unionists, these arguments affected their stance on women in formal employment, which they resisted as a threat to male jobs. Yet other union leaders, as well as journalists and women's organizations, favored an improvement in women's employment conditions, arguing in particular that national development depended on utilizing women's labor power.[98]

Can we reconcile these different arguments and interpretations? I don't think so, nor do I think we should. Rather, it makes sense to think of gender not necessarily as something people *have* but as something people *do* in various ways. Especially in a context like colonial Nigeria—where gender was already quite malleable and a multiplicity of ideas about how different types of women and men should behave circulated with varying degrees of saliency—people could draw on gender ideologies not only to inform their sense of proper living, but also for specific strategic ends. How particular individuals *thought about* this in given contexts is a different question (and one much harder to get at). But the disjunctures as well as overlaps between discourse and practice surrounding the male breadwinner norm in southwestern Nigeria suggest not only that people shape their lives according to ideas about gender, but that they shape expressions of gender in order to better their lives.

NOTES

1. Oyèrónké Oyewùmí, *The Invention of Women: Making an African Sense of Western Gender Discourses* (Minneapolis: University of Minnesota Press, 1997), pp. 151–52 quoted.

2. Judith Butler, *Gender Trouble: Feminism and the Subversion of Identity* (New York: Routledge, 1990). Although Butler generally does not include race and class in her analysis, I find her notion of the performative nature of gender to be very useful, particularly when it is kept in mind that performances always relate to contexts, which are themselves shaped by the dynamics of race, class, and politics.

3. Karin Barber, *The Generation of Plays: Yoruba Popular Life in Theater* (Bloomington: Indiana University Press, 2000), p. 430, emphasis in the original.

4. See Sara Berry, *No Condition Is Permanent: The Social Dynamics of Agrarian Change in Sub-Saharan Africa* (Madison: University of Wisconsin Press, 1993).

5. This insight comes from James Ferguson's appreciative critique of Judith Butler. See his *Expectations of Modernity: Myths and Meanings of Urban Life on the Zambian Copperbelt* (Berkeley: University of California, 1999), pp. 93ff.

6. It is important to note here that women themselves also chose options other than wage employment, given that a self-employed seamstress or trader could earn more than females in the formal sector. I am grateful to LaRay Denzer for stressing this to me.

7. J.D. Offili to Lord Passfield, Secretary of State for the Colonies, April 26, 1931, CO 583/199/8.

8. Association of Retired Railway African Officers to Governor McPherson, June 3, 1948, SL 696.

9. Letter from "Painting Gang," Port Section, Marine Apapa to Executive Engineer, Port Section, Apapa wharf, October 8,1948, NLA/12.

10. B.S. Ramonu to Secretary, Nigerian Ex-Servicemen's Welfare Association, September 24, 1949, GMS 33/2.

11. *Nigerail: Journal of the Nigerian Railway Corporation* (December 1956), p. 4, in Edward Charles Ealey papers, MSS.Afr.s.1148, RHO.

12. S.O. Akintola, May 2, 1994, Ibadan; Mrs. Olukemi Alabi (daughter of a track foreman working in the 1930s and 1940s), April 12, 1994, Ibadan.

13. "Men Should Submit their Earnings," *WAP*, December 11, 1945.

14. See Andrea Cornwall, "Wayward Women and Useless Men: Contest and Change in Gender Relations in Ado-Odo, S.W. Nigeria," in Dorothy L. Hodgson and Sheryl A. McCurdy (eds.), *"Wicked" Women and the Reconfiguration of Gender in Africa* (Portsmouth, NH: Heinemann, 2001), p. 73. For the similar importance of "chop money" in marriages in colonial Asante, see Jean Allman and Victoria Tashjian, *"I Will Not Eat Stone": A Women's History of Colonial Asante* (Portsmouth, NH: Heinemann, 2000).

15. CvRB, Ebute Metta (Lagos) Magistrate's Court, vol. 62B, E.O. Bukola vs. L.B. Lawal, 3596/50, June 21, 1950, p. 324. Also see Lisa A. Lindsay, "Money, Marriage, and Masculinity on the Colonial Nigerian Railway," in Lindsay and Miescher (eds.), *Men and Masculinities in Modern Africa* (Portsmouth, NH: Heinemann, 2003).

16. Flora Nwapa, "A Soldier Returns Home," in *This Is Lagos and Other Stories* (Trenton, NJ: Africa World Press, 1992 [1971]), p. 114.

17. Based on my examination of divorce records from Bere Native Court, Ibadan. Also see Nigeria, *Annual Report of the Federal Social Welfare Department for the Year 1955–56*, p. 10; and Alison Izzett, "Family Life among the Yoruba in Lagos, Nigeria," in Aidan Southall (ed.), *Social Change in Modern Africa* (London: Oxford University Press, 1961). For a later period, see "Wife Divorces Husband: 'Tired of Paying His Debts,'" *WAP*, June 16, 1964.

18. Rebecca Uchefuna, February 21, 1994, Ibadan; also Raheem Balogun, head of the Lagos branch of the Railway Pensioners' Union, July 20, 1998, Lagos.

19. "Husbands and Thrift," *WAP*, November 9, 1946; "Marry the Third Class Clerk," *WAP*, April 15, 1946.

20. Nigeria, *Census of Lagos* (1950), p. 17.

21. One hundred twenty-seven men in the survey were hired before 1960; ninety-nine of their first wives were traders.

22. S. Comhaire-Sylvain, "Le travail des femmes à Lagos, Nigéria," *Zaire* 5 (1951): 169–87. Also see N.A. Fadipe, *The Sociology of the Yoruba*, edited by Francis Olu Okediji and Oladejo O. Okediji (Ibadan: Ibadan University Press, 1970 [1940]), pp. 152–57; Wambui M. Karanja-Diejomaoh, "Perceptions of Marriage, Family and Work in Nigeria: Study of Lagos Market Women," (D.Phil. thesis, Oxford University, 1980); Akin Mabogunje, "The Market-Woman," *Ibadan* 11 (1961): 14–17; Niara Sudarkasa, *Where Women Work: A Study of Yoruba Women in the Marketplace and in the Home* (Ann Arbor, MI: Museum of Anthropology, 1973).

23. Nigeria, *Urban Consumer Surveys in Nigeria: Report on Enquiries into the Income and Expenditure Patterns of Wage-Earner Households in Lagos [1953/54], Enugu [1954/55] and Ibadan [1955]* (Lagos: Federal Department of Statistics, 1957), pp. 15–16.

24. Rebecca Uchefuna, February 21, 1994, Ibadan. In my survey of railway retirees' wives, all said that their husbands had provided money for children's expenses, but 94 percent also said that they had contributed as well.

25. Sudarakasa, *Where Women Work*, pp. 118–19.

26. Felicia Adeyemi, February 11, 1994, Ibadan.

27. Bernard Aruna, December 28, 1993, Ibadan.

28. Ibid.

29. Buchi Emecheta, *The Joys of Motherhood* (New York: George Brazillier, 1979), p. 217. Compared with that of Yoruba-speakers, however, Igbo gender ideology puts more weight on the idea that a husband "owns" a wife.

30. Examples include CvRB, Ojaba I Native Court, Oke Are (Ibadan), vol. 21, 1693/30, Ayi vs. Lawani, September 8,1930, pp. 231–7; CvRB, Bere I Native Court, vol. ? (torn cover), 529/38, Moriamo vs. Raimi, June 30, 1938, pp. 16–19; CvRB, Bere I Native Court, vol. 23, 233/42, Foyeke vs. Obasawi, February 24, 1942, pp. 125–6; CvRB, Ojaba II Native Court, Oke Are, vol. 12, pp. 33/50, S.A. Akinfanda vs. Sabititu, February 7, 1950, pp. 231–7.

31. Dan R. Aronson, *The City Is Our Farm: Seven Migrant Ijebu Yoruba Families* (Cambridge, MA: Schenkman, 1978), ch. 6.

32. Ruth Adekanola, February 17, 1994, Ibadan.

33. M.O. Shofekun, April 4, 1994, Ibadan.

34. Michael Odede, December 28, 1993, Ibadan. Also Bernard Aruna, December 28, 1993, Ibadan; S.O. Akintola, May 2, 1994, Ibadan; Florence Owolabi, January 7, 1994, Ibadan; and Sudarkasa, *Where Women Work.*

35. One should avoid seeing this in Western feminist terms as some sort of "failure" on the part of women who gave up household power in order to claim some of their husbands' money. On the contrary, several interviewed women emphasized that such arrangements were welcome and beneficial. For two critiques of essentialized feminism, from different points of view, see Chandra Mohanty, "Under Western Eyes: Feminist Scholarship and Colonial Discourses," *Feminist Review* 30 (1988): 61–88; and Karen Offen, "Defining Feminism: A Comparative Historical Perspective," *Signs* 14 (1988): 119–57.

36. "Men Should Not Submit Their Earnings," *WAP*, December 21, 1945.

37. "Should I Leave Her?" *WAP*, May 6, 1946.

38. Rape cases of this nature include CRB, Ojaba I Native Court, Oke Are, vol. 49, NA vs. Alabi, 205/31, April 28, 1931, pp. 230–231; and CvRB, Ojaba III Native Court, Oke Are, vol. ? [torn cover], Okunola vs. Laduomi, 1/52, December 5, 1952, 1 ff. Also see CvRB, Ojaba Native Court, Oke Are, vol. 10, Salami vs. Lanlehin, 63/37, August 12, 1937, pp. 21–24, in which the court ruled that the man was not entitled to the return of his gifts after the engagement ended because the couple had already had sex.

39. *Sunday Times* (Lagos), February 14, 1954.

40. Luke Emejulu, "RWU Co-Operative Scheme Receives Blessing," *DTN*, May 24, 1950.

41. This is evidenced, for instance, by letters to the *West African Pilot*'s women's column, "Milady's Bower," by Miss Silva. Examples are "She Prefers an Ex-Soldier to a News Vendor," March 23, 1946, and "Girls and Presents," April 12, 1946; also see "The Housewife's Economy" (editorial), February 11, 1947. Women's alleged gold-digging is a constant theme in current Nigerian popular culture.

42. Cyprian Ekwensi, "Lokotown," in *Lokotown and Other Stories* (London: Heinemann, 1966), p. 32.

43. Victor Ifedi, "The Romance of the Lagos Pay-Week," *WAP*, September 3, 1963.

44. *Nigerail: Journal of the Nigerian Railway Corporation* (December 1956), p. 4, Edward Charles Ealey papers, MSS.Afr.s.1148, RHO.

45. Ekwensi, "Lokotown,"11.

46. "The Housewife's Economy" (editorial), *WAP*, February 11, 1947.

47. This point comes from one of Heinemann's anonymous readers, to whom I am grateful.

48. Jeune Moderniste, "The Educated Woman of To-Day," *DTN*, December 27, 1930; "Mr. Coker Lectures on Women Education and the New Africa," *WAP*, October 11–14, 1941; *WAP* August 8, 1944, cited in LaRay Denzer, *Folayegbe M. Akintunde-Ighodalo: A Public Life* (Ibadan: Sam Bookman Publishers, 2001), pp. 57–58; Nnamdi Azikiwe, "Woman . . . By a Man," *WAP*, December 20, 1945; Miss Silva, "Sex Discrimination Should Disappear," *WAP*, January 9, 1946; Sam A. Aluko, "Should Women Be Politicians? Yes, Why Should They Not?" *NT*, October 12, 1953. The women at the "Brains Trust" included Mrs. Oyinkan Abayomi, founder of the Women's Party; Mrs. H.M. Ekemode, a distinguished Ahmadiyya teacher; Mrs. A.O. Ajose; and Mrs. M. Taylore, a radio officer in the Public Relations Office.

49. LaRay Denzer, "Women in Government Service in Colonial Nigeria, 1862–1945," *Boston University Working Papers in African Studies* No. 136 (1989), p. 14.

50. Denzer, "Women in Government Service," p. 15 quoted.

51. Miss Silva, "Girls and Meagre Salary," *WAP*, November 30, 1945. For the United States, see Ruth Milkman, *Gender at Work: The Dynamics of Job Segregation by Sex during World War II* (Urbana: University of Illinois Press, 1987); and for Britain, see Penny Summerfield, *Women Workers in the Second World War* (London: Croom Helm, 1984).

52. General Secretary, Trades Union Congress to Chief Secretary to the Government, October 15, 1944, cited in Baba Oluwide, *Imoudu Biography, Part I: A Political History of Nigeria, 1939–1950* (Ibadan: Ororo Publishers, 1993), p. 277.

53. "Confidential: Trades Union Congress of Nigeria: Brief Progress Report for the Period November to February 1945, by the Acting Secretary General—Mr. R.W. Nugent," February 3, 1945, NLA /1.

54. "Report by the Committee to Consider the Question of the Employment of Women in Government Service," November 1945, CSO 26/4322, cited in Denzer, "Women in Government Service."

55. "Annual Convention of Nigerian TUC" and "Female Representative of Postal Workers Union Pleads for her Sex at TUC Confab," *WAP*, December 18, 1945. As mentioned in chapter 4, Osindero and Bankole led the trade union faction that opposed the 1945 general strike; Bankole received a headful of *gari* for his efforts.

56. "Women Workers and Our Progress" (editorial), *WAP*, December 21, 1945.

57. "Justice Ends Where Colour Begins," *DS*, June 27, 1945, quoted in Nnamdi Azikiwe, "History of the General Strike (50)," *WAP*, November 17, 1945, emphasis added.

58. This was one strategy employed by British trade unionists. See Sonya O. Rose, *Limited Livelihoods: Gender and Class in Nineteenth-Century England* (Berkeley: University of California Press, 1992); and Susan Pedersen, *Family, Dependence, and the Origins of the Welfare State: Britain and France, 1914–1945* (Cambridge: Cambridge University Press, 1993).

59. Nnamdi Azikiwe, "Woman . . . By a Man," *WAP*, December 19–20,1945.

60. "Women Workers and Our Progress" (editorial), *WAP*, December 21, 1945. The idea that the status of women in a particular country/colony indicated a general level of civilization was a widespread one. See, for example, Lata Mani, "Contentious Traditions: The Debate on *Sati* in Colonial India," in Kumkum Sangari and Sudesh Vaid (eds.), *Recasting Women: Essays in Indian Colonial History* (New Brunswick, NJ: Rutgers University Press, 1990); and Antoinette Burton, *Burdens of History: British Feminists, Indian Women, and Imperial Culture, 1865–1915* (Chapel Hill: University of North Carolina Press, 1994).

61. *Nigeria Civil Servant*, July–October 1945, 132, quoted in "Are Our Working Girls Really Serious?" (editorial), *WAP*, December 28, 1945. This echoed a story in the October 11, 1945 *WAP* about "lady railway sorters" whose work suffered from their tendency to bicker with each other.

62. Miss Silva, "Girls and Economic Insecurity," *WAP*, January 4, 1946; and "Sex Discrimination Should Disappear," *WAP*, January 9, 1946 (quoted).

63. Extract from Nigerian Gazette of February 19, 1948, Government Notice No. 297; Minute, A. Busby to Labour Officer, February 27, 1948; General Manager to Heads of Departments, May 18, 1948; all in unnumbered NRC file on recruitment. Married women

could be hired in the civil service only on a contractual basis—with most contracts terminated upon pregnancy—until 1969. Eleanor R. Fapohunda, "The Nuclear Household Model in Nigerian Public and Private Sector Policy: Colonial Legacy and Socio-Political Implications," *Development and Change* 18 (1987): 281–94, 288. These Nigerian provisions contrasted with those in the British civil service, where the "marriage bar" was removed in 1946. Other British establishments, like Barklays Bank, retained marriage bars well into the 1960s. See Robert Bennett, "Gendering Cultures in Business and Labor History: Marriage Bars in Clerical Employment," in Margaret Walsh (ed.), *Working Out Gender: Perspectives from Labour History* (Aldershot, UK: Ashgate, 1999).

64. Elizabeth Offili to Railway Labor Officer, February 24,1948, GML 313, vol. 1.

65. ComCol 3296/C.52, cited in Nina Emma Mba, *Nigerian Women Mobilized: Women's Political Activity in Southern Nigeria, 1900–1965* (Berkeley: University of California Press, 1982), p. 223.

66. Colonial Labor Advisory Committee, "Report of the Sub-Committee on Wage Fixing and Family Responsibilities," n.d. [1953], CO 859/810.

67. Letter in the *DS* from Bola Oginni, a reader in Lagos, April 4, 1953.

68. Minute by D.E. Faulkner, Social Welfare Officer, to Commissioner of the Colony, July 31, 1947, in ComCol 1/3236; Nigeria, *Annual Report of the Department of Labour for the Year 1951*, 39; *Annual Report of the Labour Office, Ibadan for 1953–54*, in Oyo Prof.1/1589/1.

69. Lagos Colony Welfare Service, Annual Report, 1952–53, 7 in Oyo Prof. 1/4108.

70. Federal Ministry of Education file /10 CADW.47, NAI, including Alison Izzett, "Financial Responsibilities of Married Women," September 17, 1948; Plummer to heads of convents in Onitsha, Akure and Ifuho, September 20, 1948; and Ag. Deputy Director of Education (Women) memorandum (missing first page). Plummer served from 1931 to 1950 and initiated many improvements in girls' education. For more on Plummer, see LaRay Denzer, "Domestic Science Training in Colonial Yorubaland, Nigeria," in Karen Tranberg Hansen (ed.), *African Encounters with Domesticity* (New Brunswick, NJ: Rutgers University Press, 1992); and Denzer, "Women in Government Service."

71. Alexander Patterson, "A Report to His Excellency the Governor of Nigeria on *Social Welfare in the Colony and Protectorate*," forwarded to the Resident, Oyo Province, July 26, 1944, in Oyo Prof. 1/4108; Nigeria, *Annual Report of the Department of Labour* (1950), p. 30.

72. H.M. Foot (chair), *Report of the Commission Appointed by His Excellency the Governor to Make Recommendations about the Recruitment and Training of Nigerians for Senior Posts in the Government Service of Nigeria* (Lagos: Government Printer, 1948), p. 17.

73. *DTN*, July 8, 1955, quoted in Denzer, *Folayegbe M. Akintunde-Ighodalo*, which portrays the expanding opportunities for women in the Western Nigeria civil service during the late colonial and early independence periods.

74. Letter from Domi-Banjul, from Apapa, *DTN*, July 23, 1955, quoted in Denzer, *Folayegbe Akintunde-Ighodalo*, p. 109; letter from B. Obeta, from Somolu, "Wanted: Women Bus Drivers," *DTN*, July 14, 1955; letter from (Miss) Z.K. Odejimi, from Ebute Metta, "Women Insulted!" *DTN*, July 23, 1955.

75. See, for instance, Heidi Hartmann, "Capitalism, Patriarchy, and Job Segregation by Sex," *Signs* 1 (1976): 137–69; and Jane Lewis, *Women of England, 1870–1950: Sexual Division and Social Change* (Bloomington: Indiana University Press, 1984), ch. 5.

76. "International Women's Day," *LC*, March 8, 1950.

77. "List of Women Employed by the Railway Corporation," n.d. [1956], GMS 302/15, vol. 2. Most (twenty-two) of these worked in the accounts department.

78. Report of the Proceedings of the Sixth Annual Delegates Conference of the Association of Railway Civil Servants at Zaria, June 7–10, 1954, GMS 28/6.

79. General Secretary's Report Presented to the Seventh Annual Delegates' Conference of the ANRCS for the Year 1954/55, June 9, 1955, GMS 28/6; Minutes of Third Stage Meeting between Railway Management and representatives of ANRCS held January 27, 1955, GMS 28/47, vol. 1.

80. For the "light repetitive" view of women's work in western Europe, see Laura Lee Downs, *Manufacturing Inequality: Gender Division in the French and British Metalworking Industries, 1914–1939* (Ithaca, NY: Cornell University Press, 1995).

81. Acting Chief Accountant to General Manager, May 26, 1955; Stores Superintendent to GM, May 31, 1955; Chief Engineer to GM, May 31, 1955; Chief Superintendent to GM, June 6, 1955; Acting Chief Mechanical Engineer to GM, June 15, 1955; all in GMS 28/47, vol. 1.

82. "Union Accuses Rail of Creating Social Problems," *DS*, September 17, 1956; "Rail Unions Say NRC's Release Is Irresponsible," *WAP*, September 17, 1956; clippings in GMS 302/15, vol. 2. During this period, the Action Group's new manpower policy included efforts to bring qualified Nigerians of both sexes into government service. See Denzer, *Folayegbe M. Akintunde-Ighodalo*.

83. M.S. Labinjo, "General Secretary's Report Presented to the Eighth Annual Delegates Conference of NTCSU [Nigerian Transportation Clerical Staff Union] at Port Harcourt, June 25–27, 1956," GMS 28/6.

84. Nigerian Railway Corporation, *Standard Conditions of Service 1957: Officers*, p. 12; General Manager's Staff Circular No. 36/1959, November 26, 1959, "Employment of Married Women," in unnumbered NRC file labeled "Staff Manual."

85. "Adora" (women's columnist), "Discrimination!" *Sunday Times*, July 10, 1955.

86. Motions/Resolutions for 5th Annual Conference of Nigerian Maritime Trades Union Federation, October 1961, NLA/30.

87. See, for instance, "Opportunity" (opinion column), *DTN*, September 13, 1963, and "Career Woman," *WAP*, October 19, 1963.

88. Simi Afonja, "Changing Modes of Production and the Sexual Division of Labor among the Yoruba," *Signs* 7 (1981): 299–313, 312. Women comprised only 13.3 percent of the wage labor force in Nigeria as late as 1981, according to the National Manpower Board. Cited in F. Ojo, "Prospects for Modern Sector Employment Generation for Women," in Tayo Fashoyin, Felicia Durojaiye Oyekanmi, and Eleanor R. Fapohunda (eds.), *Women in the Modern Sector Labour Force in Nigeria* (Lagos: Department of Industrial Relations and Personnel Management, University of Lagos, 1985), p. 200. Given the discrimination in wages and conditions women faced, and continue to face, it is no surprise that most choose self-employment.

89. See Denzer, *Folayegbe M. Akintunde-Ighodalo*, p. 127, regarding Mrs. Ighodalo's 1959 maternity leave from the Ministry of Trade and Industry.

90. "Career Woman," *WAP*, October 19, 1963.

91. Male trade unionists lamented the absence of women from their ranks at the Nigerian Labor Conference general meeting in 1950 (August 5, 1950, in NLA/15), the conference of the NTCSU in 1956 (June 25–27, 1956, in GMS 28/6), and policy statement by the president general of the Maritime Trade Union Federation in 1960 (June 20,

1960, in NLA/28). "Miss Nigerail" is referenced in GML 335/2, vol. 2, and in the article "Hail Miss Nigerail 1958," *Nigerail* 9 (September 1958), p. 14 in Ealey papers, RHO. "Miss Ports Authority" got a front-page photo spread in the October 28, 1963, *WAP*.

92. O.A. Fagbenro Beyioku, President General, "Maritime Trades Union Federation General Policy, 1960/61," NLA/28. For more on women's marginalization from trade unions, see O. Sokunbi, O. Jeminiwa and F.B. Onaeko (eds.), *Women and Trade Unionism in Nigeria* (Ibadan: NPS Educational Publishers Limited, 1995).

93. In 1975, 7.8 percent of the labor force worked for wages; in 1985 the proportion of wage earners was 10.8 percent. The first figure comes from Nigeria, *Third National Development Plan 1975–80*, p. 370, cited in Tayo Fashoyin, *Industrial Relations in Nigeria (Development and Practice)* (Ikeja: Longman Nigeria, 1980), p. 13. The 1985 statistic is from Federal Republic of Nigeria, *Fourth National Development Plan, 1981–85*, p. 426, cited in Ojo, "Prospects," p. 199.

94. The term was put forward most forcefully in R.W. Connell, *Masculinities* (Berkeley and Los Angeles: University of California Press, 1995). Critiques are in Miescher and Lindsay, "Men and Masculinities in Modern African History"; and Andrea Cornwall and Nancy Lindisfarne, "Dislocating Masculinity: Gender, Power and Anthropology," in Cornwall and Lindisfarne (eds.), *Dislocating Masculinity: Comparative Ethnographies* (London: Routledge, 1994).

95. On the idea that women do not have dependents to support while men do, see M.A. Ifaturoti, "Female Employment and Related Personnel Problems" and Moji Solanke, "Personnel Problems and Women Workers," both in Fashoyin, Oyekanmi, and Fapohunda (eds.), *Women in the Modern Sector Labour Force*, pp. 49–50, 68.

96. Folasade Tade (railway pensioner and widow, who took part in the protest), June 1, 1994, Lagos.

97. Olukemi Alabi, December 4, 1993, Ibadan.

98. Even though women have continued to make inroads into wage labor in Nigeria, the gendered discourse about work has remained remarkably constant since the 1960s. For southeastern Nigeria, see Philomena E. Okeke, "Negotiating Social Independence: The Challenges of Career Pursuits for Igbo Women in Postcolonial Nigeria," in Hodgson and McCurdy (eds.), *"Wicked" Women;* and Misty L. Bastian, "Acadas and Fertilizer Girls: Young Nigerian Women and the Romance of Middle-Class Modernity," in Dorothy L. Hodgson (ed.), *Gendered Modernities: Ethnographic Perspectives* (New York: Palgrave, 2001).

6

URBAN LABOR, EXTENDED FAMILIES, AND THE DIFFERENTIATION OF DOMESTICITY

In 1953 when the Colonial Labor Advisory Committee embraced the notion of "family wages" for African workers (see chapter 4), it had a specific notion of "family" in mind. Even if in practice wages for skilled or clerical workers were not enough to support wives and children without supplementation, colonial administrators presumed that wives and children should constitute the "family" in question. Indeed, men could only be effective breadwinners if the numbers they supported were relatively low. Yet this notion of family was a contested one in postwar Nigeria. When the Supreme Council of Nigerian Workers argued in favor of family allowances after the 1945 general strike, its first assertion was that workers had to maintain two homes—one at their place of employment and the other for family, broadly defined, elsewhere. In December 1950, at the recommendation of a government-sponsored arbitrator, Nigerian senior officers of the civil service became eligible for children's allowances, although at lower rates than those paid to expatriates. The allowances applied when a married officer with dependent children was required by the nature of his job to keep two homes and live separately from his children.[1] Over the next few years, numerous commentators complained that family allowances did not apply to relatively lower-level African civil servants.[2] "What proportion of the Nigerian Junior Civil Service men maintain one home?" wrote a columnist in the *Labour Champion*. "Does a labourer, Okere of the Survey Department (hypothetical) not maintain three homes? (Yes three homes.) Yes! Three homes! His home is at Orlu in Owerri Province, his station is at Lagos, and more often than not, he is away on tour for months on end!"[3]

In the previous chapter, I argued that a male breadwinner image flourished in the postwar period, even if that image bore a complex relationship to practices surrounding money, labor, and gender. But such an ideal was fairly new, and of fairly limited reach, in southwestern Nigeria. Adult men expected not only to educate children and keep a wife (or wives), but also to contribute to extended family members, community projects, and patronage ties. Whether they earned wages or not, most men dreamed of becoming "big" by acquiring wealth and the loyalties of many people, owning a house, and gaining prestige within their communities of origin. They provided financial support to parents, siblings, and other kin out of a sense both of obligation and of pride. Even when trade unionists and individual working men used the language of family providers, they continued to stress wage earners' involvement in hometown affairs and contributions to extended families. But often the conditions of steady labor—particularly the widespread phenomenon of migrating to find a job—made it difficult to maintain hometown ties or close relationships with kin. For many it even strained contacts with wives and children. This was largely true across income and prestige levels: even highly placed workers faced the problems of finding housing in a new city in order to bring family and getting leave and transport from work in order to visit hometowns. As shown in chapter 3, workers' activism in the 1940s related to these issues; it continued in subsequent years.

In the two decades after World War II, the labor force became increasingly stabilized, differentiated, and well paid. Although there is no doubt that hardships continued, the 1950s brought concrete improvements for many Nigerian wage and salary earners, fueled by rising commodity prices on the world market, dramatic economic expansion, and colonial political reforms. Between 1944 and 1957, exports from Nigeria increased over seven times (from a value of £17.2 million to £126.6 million) while imports increased nearly ten-fold (from £15.7 million to £151.6 million). These figures reflect a massive expansion in commercial agriculture and manufacturing, as well as the transportation and communications networks which facilitated trade. The total value of manufacturing production increased by 398 percent during the 1950s, while between 1946 and 1960 the tonnage of goods hauled by the railway more than doubled (from 1,425,000 to 3,097,000) and new construction resulted in a 65 percent increase in road mileage (from 24,920 miles to 41,065).[4] Although the overall wage labor force remained small in comparison to those engaged in agriculture, its numbers increased by about 80 percent between 1946 and 1960.[5] On the railway, in the civil service, and in other enterprises, training schemes were initiated or enlarged in order to qualify Nigerians for skilled, technical, and administrative positions; this was in addition to an expansion in primary, secondary, and university education during this period. Real wages rose and permanent positions in key industries increased, though

Photo 6.1 Apprentice Engine Drivers Training School, Lagos, 1956. Photo courtesy of A.A. Salako (back row, third from right).

in fits and starts as the government and other employers responded to strikes, union threats, and negotiations. Between 1953 and 1965, real wages in the organized sector of the Nigerian economy grew at more than twice the rate of per capita gross domestic product; between 1953 and 1960, the minimum wage paid to general unskilled labor in Lagos increased by 70.7 percent, more than twice the rise in the cost of living index for same period.[6] Railway, industrial, and other well-positioned workers earned well over minimum wages as the labor force became increasingly differentiated. In 1960, more than half (54 percent) of the 9,115 employees of the Nigerian Ports Authority were salaried members of the permanent establishment; five years later 52 percent of the railway's 29,586 workers were so designated.[7] As Cooper concluded about British West Africa generally, "a job had become something to struggle for and to keep."[8]

How did the increasing stabilization and differentiation of the labor force affect family life and domesticity in southwestern Nigeria? In general in colonial Africa, labor stabilization measures were based on officials' understandings of, and ambitions for, African families. Replacing migrant labor with a skilled, long-term, urban workforce meant relocating employees' wives and children out of the rural areas and near the workplace. Men's wages were to support wives, who would ensure the socialization of a new generation of urban workers.[9] At the same time, government and business officials in Nigeria hoped that steady urban labor would become increasingly distanced from rural ties and extended kin. As one administrator put it, when workers maintained close connections to rural families, they "may often be more easily persuaded than workers from communities depending entirely upon wages to use the strike as a means of argument and, having struck, do not have the compulsion of economic necessity to return to work, to make demands upon union funds, or even to seek a speedy settlement."[10] Even when strikes were not an issue, "[t]he economic incentive for a man to find himself a job and establish himself securely in it may be weakened if he knows that his family is bound to support him in case of need: or if he knows that financial success may mean a host of claims from poorer members of the family."[11] Into the 1960s, many employers continued to assume "that the link with the village home encourages laziness, absenteeism and uninterestedness in their jobs among Nigerian workers."[12]

Government reports and social scientists' observations beginning in the 1950s proclaimed that workers, like some elites, were becoming progressively less attached to their hometowns and extended families and were focusing their domestic energies on monogamous marriages and children. They saw this as one aspect of a generalized trend of *modernization*, an inevitable force that linked social change to technological and economic transformations. As individual Africans were exposed to European education, "modern" sector employment, and purchasable consumer goods, the assumption went, their orientations would become more individualistic, and family loyalties would increasingly be centered on spouses and children settled with them in the town of employment. While noting that education and income were important variables, they pointed to gradual but widespread trends toward more isolated conjugal units and decreasing lineage influence on couples and their offspring. As James Ferguson put it, "nuclear, conjugal family structure could serve as a metonym for the modernity of the urban African."[13]

But in contrast to colonial personnel's faith in modernization as a force to restructure African kinship, other studies show the tenacity of extended family ties and the ways in which they have been creatively adapted to changing economic circumstances. As many as 90 percent of railway workers surveyed in Lagos in 1958, for instance, sent money home on a regular basis.[14] Retirements in the hometown have been a continuous feature in the life course of wage earners through the twentieth century. Moreover, as I argue in this chapter, steady wages and a relatively comfortable standard of living allowed some workers to support a wider range of relatives than they otherwise could, bringing dependents to live with them and thus becoming, on some scale, "big." In fact, benefits like housing and medical care, which were integral to postwar labor and welfare initiatives, allowed highly placed employees to provide for their relatives with the direct assistance of the state or their employer. Thus, contrary to official plans and rhetoric, labor stabilization and differentiation allowed those at the top of employment hierarchies to fund large households and networks of financial assistance—the very opposite of the family modernization model.

Yet there are ways in which some highly placed workers did engage with modernization ideals. Notably, many long-term, relatively well-paid urban working people paid less and less attention, as time went on, to their hometown ties. Stable labor may have come with paid leave and the wages to contribute to relatives, but it made it difficult to find the time to visit and it increased the financial demands of a wide array of kin. As steadily employed, upwardly mobile men spent money on educating their children, supporting their households, purchasing consumer goods, and investing in future enterprises, they often lacked the cash for potentially expensive homecomings and preferred to spend their leave time in other places. They also relied on their pensions, personal investments, and educated children to support them in old age or incapacity, so that they had few financial incentives to make frequent hometown visits. Although many successful wage and salary earners kept in contact with relatives and others from their hometowns, increasingly they did so within the city itself, only making occasional and brief visits home.

Everywhere the term *modern* has meant something new and transformative, but its specific meaning depends on context.[15] Nigerians (and other colonized people) used the language of modernization to talk about social changes just as administrators and social scientists did. Although scholars are now more skeptical of the analytical value of terms like modernization and modernity, the people involved saw the concepts as both descriptive of the changes they observed around them and useful for making claims for a dignified and stable working- or middle-class life. Many of the retired railway men I spent time with had seen themselves as part of the cutting edge of modernity and progress in Nigeria, building a strong economy and new nation-state as well as successful nuclear families. To the extent that these were compatible with nurturing broad kinship and hometown ties, these men pursued both; but many ambitious career workers were unable or unwilling to spend significant time or money on relatively remote kinsmen. Modernization provided a language for describing, understanding, and even validating this departure from idealized norms.[16]

But just because they used the concept of modernization, this did not mean that most Nigerians accepted western social scientists' definitions of it. Postwar theories about modernization held that "the attributes of modernity form a 'package,' thus tending to appear as a cluster . . . and, consequently . . . modernization in one sphere will necessarily produce compatible ('eurhythmic') changes in other spheres."[17] Thus, for instance, an educated man in a technical job would also be monogamous and focused on his nuclear family. Instead, when Yoruba-speakers talked about "progress," "civilization," or "enlightenment," they typically used the term *ọlajú*. Through the changing circumstances of the twentieth century, as John Peel has detailed, the term has generally referred to educational and cultural competencies derived from outside the local community and then translated into both personal and communal advancement.[18] Thus, men who were relatively well placed in employment hierarchies could attribute their own success to their education and other elements of "enlightenment," which they aspired to share with their family members and townsmen. In this way, they would be contributing to the general uplift of their entire communities, which would in turn reflect well upon them. In its focus on improving education and standards of living, the widely held Yoruba ideology of *ọlajú* was thus analogous to the modernization ideals of European observers. At the same time, however, it eschewed the individualistic focus of full-fledged postwar modernization theory. Career wage and salary earners in southwestern Nigeria combined parts of their lifestyles that they associated with modernization—like highly skilled work, fewer hometown visits, and conjugal togetherness—with others that derived from other values—like *ọlajú* or the "big man" ethic of heading a large household. When they earned high salaries and gained access to perquisites such as housing and medical care—in administrators' views, the payoff for "modern" labor—they improved their abilities to selectively adopt the characteristics of "modern," "enlightened," and "big" men.

RACE, DOMESTICITY, AND DIFFERENTIATION

To understand the evolving relationship between labor stabilization, modernization, and household structures, it is necessary to establish a central premise: that domesticity was a key feature in the differentiation of the labor force.[19] In colonial Nairobi, as Luise White has shown, postwar labor reforms facilitated the construction of two male genders, separated by literacy, skills, and the kinds of home life they were allowed to lead. Stabilized workers gained access to family housing and thus their wives and children, whereas short-term, unskilled workers were housed in barracks without any domestic comforts, separated from family members who continued to live outside the city. Tim Scarnecchia has made a similar argument for Salisbury, Southern Rhodesia.[20] As I discuss later in this chapter, Nigerian workers with stable jobs and incomes also improved their access to housing and married family life during the 1950s. But there was more to the differentiation of domesticity than this. In southwestern Nigeria, "big men" were those who commanded resources of money and people. They both supported dependents and were served by them, and they designated their domestic tasks to others. Similarly, expatriates in Nigeria lived in large compounds and had their cooking, cleaning, and other domestic needs met by servants. But until the end of the colonial period, the upper ranks of the civil service were barred to Nigerians, closing off this potential route to a big man lifestyle. As Africans entered the "senior service" in increasing numbers and gained skilled positions in other employment establishments, they demanded the same perquisites as comparably placed Europeans, and these included provisions for comfortable domesticity.[21] Even outside of the top echelons, and well before the process of "Nigerianization" began in earnest, African workers agitated for the same recognition of their family lives as expatriates enjoyed. Thus, the parallels between domestic comforts and economic or employment hierarchies resulted not only from stabilization measures, but also from African assumptions about the home lives of "big men," long-standing policies for expatriates, and labor activism around extending domestic benefits to increasing numbers of Nigerian workers.

In Nigeria as elsewhere, "[w]ork and life as a colonial officer were inseparable."[22] Thus, for Europeans domesticity was an integral facet of status—both on and off the job.[23] Among colonial officials and other expatriate workers, domestic provisions came with employment and were increasingly comfortable as rank increased. An assistant district officer in the late 1950s, for instance,

> lived in various government quarters, splendidly isolated from the din and bustle of the local communities, and located on spacious grounds adorned with beautiful flowers and fruit trees. A Police orderly had constantly attended on me, carrying my files and papers and marching dutifully behind

me everywhere I went. I did not have to worry about the daily little chores; there were messengers and orderly standing at attention and anxious to please and minister unto me.[24]

Not all expatriates lived under the same conditions as assistant district officers (and the one quoted happened to be Nigerian), but generally it was taken for granted that housing and other amenities would be considerably more comfortable for Europeans than for local people.

Furthermore, and contrary to the presumed separation of public and private lives in bourgeois European cultures, Europeans in the colonies brought their home and work lives closer and closer together the higher they rose in administrative hierarchies. Highly placed civil servants, railway administrators, and commercial executives lived in quarters on the compounds of their employment establishments, allowing them to dart conveniently between the office and home. The job came with a car and driver to facilitate work-related travel, but the car was available for personal use as well. Meals, prepared and served by cooks and stewards, often functioned as work briefings or business meetings. Workplace assistants might double as domestic servants, the establishment's budget might be tapped to pay for a gardener, and prison inmates even supplied officials with firewood.[25] By the postwar period, European men could occasionally bring their children to their workplaces, in ways that would never have been acceptable for African employees. In June 1949, a Nigerian telegraph clerk was actually *arrested* for calling attention to the inappropriate behavior of a white child riding on a railway platform. Although the little boy was breaking railway rules, the policeman on duty refused to intervene because "He be our master pikin." Unfortunately for the clerk, the boy's father was the regional head of the railway police, who hauled him in front of the station master and four days later charged him with "conduct likely to cause a breech of peace."[26]

Within workplace structures as well as elsewhere, colonial, racialized hierarchies were reproduced through domestic provisions.[27] As we have seen with family allowances and the 1945 general strike, Africans resented the discrepancies between their conditions of service and those of expatriates, and they argued that measures for family life and domesticity should apply to Europeans and Africans alike. A 1941 complaint in the *West African Pilot* pointed to the differing arrangements for European and African officials proceeding on leave or transfer. Europeans were allowed to move 48 cwt. of baggage free of charge, while the highest category of African officials were allowed only 9 cwt. for the baggage of himself, his wife, and children. Moreover, Europeans had access to storage facilities for the items they did not wish to bring with them on leave or transfer, while Africans' inability to store their possessions meant they had either to transport them or risk losing them while out of town. To make matters worse, Africans had more possessions to deal with, because they had to provide their own furnishings while Europeans occupied fully furnished quarters. To compensate for the loss of such accommodations upon retirement, European pensions were supplemented with a housing allowance—a provision never considered for Africans.[28] Over a decade later, elite Africans protested that they were excluded from European recreation clubs, even those based on jobs rather than national origin, and "chased out" of housing in the exclusive white settlements.[29]

European bureaucrats, technicians, and managers were by definition migrant workers, even if that term was never used to refer to them. In order to entice them to work in Nigeria, they were offered special payments called "inducement allowances" or "expatriation pay," up to three months of leave per year, free travel for themselves and family members between Nigeria and their European homes, and of course children's allowances to compensate for the expenses of housing and educating offspring outside of Nigeria. As we have seen already, Nigerian government employees resented the "children's (separate domicile) allowance" paid to expatriates with children living in Europe. They argued that their susceptibility to transfers around the country kept them away from their homes and children just as Europeans' postings did. "There is always the problem of incessant transfer from place to place, because where you are today you might be transferred into another bush tomorrow. I had to abandon my people in the town and go."[30] In colonial Nigeria, children's educational opportunities could not be taken for granted: parents would not readily give up a child's place in secondary or even primary school in order to move to a new town, where comparable schooling may not be available. Among railway families, some wives went on transfer with their husbands until children reached school age, after which wives stayed with children either in the hometown or in some other area where the education could be continuous. Transferred employees' most frequent complaint in the 1950s and 1960s was the disruption in their children's schooling caused by new job postings.[31]

The difficulties of combining migration with the education of children were directly related to the ongoing disputes between the government and workers over family allowances. After children's separate domicile allowances were extended to senior African officials in 1950, protests continued, urging that they apply to the families of *all* African wage earners. In 1954, the All-Nigeria Trade Union Federation included children's allowances in their grievances to the Gorsuch Commission on conditions in the civil service. A memorandum submitted by the Railway Workers' Union characterized payment only to senior officials as "not only invidious but sinful in the sight of God and man. . . . All children are born equal and entitled to equal share of the wealth of the country."[32] The Gorsuch Commission recommended increasing the children's allowances paid to expatriate officials in order to better attract qualified personnel to Nigeria. It also recommended an increase in the allowances paid to those Nigerians already eligible for children's allowances. However, it emphasized that in principle it opposed subsidizing African families, but that for now it was necessary given that a transferred officer would have trouble placing a child in a new secondary school. So allowances were extended to all African "officers" (the highest broad category in government service), but only for secondary school children affected by transfers. In its response to the commission, the government staunchly rejected this recommendation, pointing out that unions had been agitating for the widespread extension of children's allowances for years and that this concession would only lead to still greater payments on behalf of Nigerian children. Rather than face a politically awkward outcry, it did not remove children's allowances from those top Nigerian officials previously eligible for them, but it also did not make them available to a wider group of Nigerians. Family allowances continued to mark a distinction between top echelons and others, a point to which I return in chapter 7.

DOMESTICITY ON TRACK

The contests over domesticity and its relationship to labor hierarchies may be illustrated with a few examples from the Nigerian Railway.[33] Railway work in particular raised such issues because its labor force was posted all over the country and because many of its workers traveled between stations as a condition of their employment. Railway workers resented the differentials between their housing and other conditions and those of European supervisors and technicians. As early as the 1930s, however, many such expatriates were phased out and replaced by Nigerians in an effort to cut personnel costs. Particularly in the postwar period, increasing numbers of Nigerians worked in such respected, skilled, and relatively well-paid positions as station masters, administrative officers, locomotive drivers, and train conductors. As I detail in the next section of this chapter, many of these and other stable, skilled employees translated their salaries and perquisites into comfortable domestic lives and some variation of "big man" status. But unlike station masters and clerical officers, drivers and conductors spent most of their working hours in transit and could spend many nights away from their usual beds. When Europeans had been in these positions, the railway administration provided them with places to sleep, eat, and rest while "on line." Not only did Nigerians demand the same concessions to their domestic needs, but also they vied with each other over access to domestic provisions, which they interpreted as indicators of their relative rank on the job.

Although few categories of workers were successful in gaining domestic provisions before the labor reforms of the postwar period, locomotive drivers

Photo 6.2 Ayo Salako and his shunting engine, Aro station (Abeokuta), 1966. Photo courtesy of A.A. Salako.

did manage to wrest some concessions from their colonial employer. Train drivers were considered to be the most crucial of the railway's African workers. It took sixteen years of training and evaluation for a man to work his way up from engine cleaner to fireman, to shunting engine driver, to locomotive driver grade I, the highest of them all. African drivers were first introduced in Nigeria early in the railway's development, although they were outnumbered by European and West Indian drivers until the early 1930s. The last West Indian drivers were recruited in 1926, and as of 1950, only one European locomotive driver remained in the service of the Nigerian Railway.[34]

Drivers spent most of their working hours "on line," and often spent the night away from their houses. Engine drivers and firemen "never failed to mention that they were strangers to their family [sic] each time they requested an increase in their salaries and allowances," even going so far as to claim that "they had to be introduced to their young ones each time they returned from a round" of driving.[35] In a 1950 request for improved salaries and working conditions for footplate staff (drivers, firemen and cleaners), their union stressed the irregular hours worked, which "make any consecutive pursuit of social, recreational, religious or domestic activities impossible. Perhaps the most readily and easily appreciated is the interference with the enjoyments of their family life."[36] Administrators did give priority in allocating living quarters to drivers and other footplate staff, largely because their services were required at short notice and all hours.[37]

Train guards, who also traveled "on line," consistently demanded the same recognition of their occupational importance and disruption of family lives as footplate staff, but they were less successful with authorities. Guards, known as conductors on other railways, oversaw the passengers and goods contained in the trains and were responsible for safety, public relations, and some financial accounts. Although guards and drivers occupied roughly analogous salary gradings, domestic conditions and other perquisites favored drivers. This generated frequent protests and in part accounts for creation of the Train Guards Union in 1946.[38] Guards petitioned to be included when drivers' salaries were revised and demanded many of the same extra allowances paid to drivers.[39] At the same time, they demanded that their salary scales should equal those of Europeans and indeed that the remaining European guards should be phased out.[40] In 1947, guards complained that drivers were included in the Harragin awards (for senior officials), but they were not, even though their conditions were analogous. Like drivers, the guards argued, they kept two homes, risked their physical safety, were exposed to harsh weather and illness, and kept irregular working hours, which caused "disintegration of family life," "non-enjoyment of community life," and "lack of recreation." The railway's general manager disagreed that the duties of guards and drivers were identical and required the same pay and benefits. Moreover, the administration was unsympathetic to the guards' claims of domestic disruption and described their alleged lack of recreation as "'Exaggerated. Guards are stationed, or break their journeys only at Depot Stations where they always manage to get a 'good time.'"[41] In fact, guards and other Traffic Section employees were notorious as womanizers, with the proverbial lady in every station, even though this stereotype was applied less frequently to drivers.[42]

Not only did drivers earn better benefits and housing than did train guards, but also they were better provided for when working "on line." Train schedules were organized around working shifts for footplate and traffic crews, who needed time and a place to rest after a given number of miles traveled or hours worked. A few rest houses were built for European railway personnel in the 1920s, and as the numbers of African drivers increased in the 1930s, the administration provided accommodation for "native" drivers as well. Normally they would spend one night per trip at the rest house, but engine men could be stranded there for up to a month if there were a train derailment, mechanical failure, or other delay. Typically they came to think of the rest house as their second home. But most other crew members had to fend for themselves until a system of rest houses for traffic personnel was constructed beginning in the mid-1940s. Until then, train guards used staff cars for rest on long-distance routes.[43]

Nigerian train guards protested the lack of provisions for their meals and sleep, even after rest houses became available to them. Guards frequently complained about the lax upkeep and poor provisions at their rest houses.[44] At its 1946 annual conference, the Station Staff Union moved that train guards should be allowed to travel with their own domestic servants "to minimize the inconveniences they were suffering." The newly formed Nigerian Train Guards Union reiterated the request several months later in a meeting with the Railway labor officer, W.A. Powell.[45] This did not come out of the blue: European guards traveled with servants, and senior officials who were required occasionally to travel on trains could bring their wives, free of passenger charges, in order to see to their feeding and other personal needs.[46] Traffic Manager D.C. Woodward's reply acknowledged that his department's rest houses were inferior to those of the Mechanical Department (in which footplate staff worked) but pointed out that caretakers were employed at the larger rest houses and soon cooks would be as well. For the meantime, cooking utensils were available at all the houses, and guards should be able to fend for themselves.[47] Two months later, in a letter alleging that they were discriminated against vis-à-vis drivers, the guards again raised the issue of servants, this time suggesting that servants would undertake a variety of tasks: helping guards with their duties, providing protection on walks in the bush between stations, and seeing to such domestic needs as cooking and laundry. In such ways, a servant would act as "small boy" for the guard. The guards argued that "a man fully exhausted whilst on duty could hardly be expected to do his own cooking." Woodward's incredulous (and disingenuous) comment was that servants were not necessary and that nowhere in the world did train guards travel with their own attendants.[48]

Yet until a system of caretakers and cooks became available throughout the rail system in 1949, the administration did allow guards to bring their "small boys" with them. The next year the Train Guards Union complained that management had revoked guards' right to travel on limited trains with personal servants. Instead, the railway provided two cooks in the staff cars. The union complained that so few cooks could hardly provide food and act as servants for the ten guards assigned to them. Further, the cooks allegedly were ignorant of regional diets and refused to wash singlets and shoes. The administration did not budge this time, though, on the grounds that improved rest house facilities made servants unnecessary. Guards were no longer to bring their servants on trains.[49]

The train guards' request for servants should be understood in the context of both the links between workplace status and domesticity, and of the concessions to domestic needs that applied to more highly ranked personnel.

European guards and ticket collectors were attended by servants, senior officials could bring their wives to work, and locomotive drivers and firemen were met at each station by a porter who carried their boxes of food and personal effects to the rest house.[50] Even if administrators did not acknowledge it, guards commanded enough prestige and resources among Nigerians that they delegated their domestic tasks to "small boys."[51] The fact that Nigerian train guards did bring servants to work with them for a few years reveals an official acknowledgment that such workers' domestic needs could not be separated from their employment conditions, and that the railway's provisions were insufficient. But by the 1950s, the administration moved to reduce the private arrangements for domesticity made by its workers and instead to make "welfare" provisions generally available. Still, as the next section describes, highly ranked salary earners continued to enjoy "big man" domesticity—in part through their work benefits.

THE DIFFERENTIATION OF HOUSING AND HOUSEHOLDS

The move toward a more regular system of rest houses and caretakers was part of a larger trend of labor reforms in the 1950s. Staff welfare became a key concern, with major employers building recreation areas and canteens, sponsoring sports teams, offering first aid training, and sometimes extending housing to employees even below the top echelons. Wages rose, and in many industries the opportunities for training and promotion increased. A major focus was to keep workers healthy and contented so as to raise labor productivity and quell discontent.[52] Many of these changes in labor regimes reinforced the domestic distinctions among workers differently placed in job hierarchies. Not only did higher salaries and steady wages allow some workers to make more credible claims to "breadwinner" status than others could, but job-related housing and other benefits could be used to accommodate and provide for a range of relatives and dependents.

As discussed in chapter 3, migrants to Lagos, and to a lesser extent other cities, faced formidable challenges in securing housing. Although there were enormous differences between the housing conditions of the rich and the poor, the vast majority of Lagosians lived in housing that was crowded and expensive. Households contained, on average, three to four people, most often living in one room—and this was true whether the main income earner was a clerk, artisan, or laborer.[53] As the demand for housing continued to increase after the war, landlords subdivided existing houses or erected "tenements" consisting of numerous private rooms surrounding a central hallway, with shared kitchen and bath facilities. The lowest-paid employees often ate and slept at the workplace, unable to afford private accommodation: domestic workers might put a mat on their employer's floor or, if they worked for Europeans or elite Nigerians, inhabit small "boys' quarters" in their employers' compounds; craft apprentices stayed in the workshop; trading assistants slept in the market stall; motor drivers and touts inhabited the motor park.[54]

Difficult housing conditions naturally had an impact on marriages. Migrants to Lagos and other cities waited for improved accommodation before marrying, or before bringing wives and children from the hometown to join them.[55] In the meantime, men without domestic help bought cooked food from market sellers, while those who could afford it hired "small boys" to assist with their domestic needs like shopping, cooking, and washing clothes. Some married women objected to being left behind when their husbands took jobs in, or were transferred to, other towns: the wife of a man transferred from Lagos to Jos flatly refused to go back to their hometown, remaining in his relative's compound in Lagos over the family's objections.[56] Others requested help from the Lagos and Ibadan welfare officers in locating husbands who left home seeking work and never returned to wives and children.[57] On the other hand, men were nervous about bringing wives to live in places shared with other roommates, and even rooms occupied by family members were generally very crowded.[58] As the Railway Workers Union argued before the Gorsuch Commission, "An average Nigerian lives in a room of twelve feet by ten feet with a family of about four to six with a bed in one side, food safe in another, tables and chairs all crowded in. He does not live in a healthy atmosphere."[59]

Railway workers were just one group of many that continually agitated for better and more housing through the colonial period. In 1951, the Railway Workers Union of Nigeria complained that the entire senior service, already earning large salaries and benefits, was provided with housing "with all modern amenities," and railway police were housed as well, while junior workers who needed it the most were denied quarters in Lagos. If official funds were not available, the Union suggested, then prospective tenants were prepared to contribute fifteen shillings per month toward construction, to be refunded later. Such a proposal was not feasible, according to the reply, because neither funding nor land for building in Lagos were available. The following year, in response to a union request for housing for workshop and running shed staff, especially at Ebute Metta, the management stressed that it was not government policy to provide housing for servants in the Lagos area and funds for such a program did not exist. By the early 1960s, as ethnic tensions within the railway mounted, critics and disgruntled applicants alleged bribery and favoritism in the allocation of staff quarters.[60]

The lowest level workers, of course, never were eligible for quarters. Track and road crews, often working in the "bush," slept in makeshift "beater" camps because "[i]f we work in a place today, tomorrow we could be transferred to another station which might be another twenty miles to our former station."[61]

In the late 1950s, representatives of the Permanent Way Workers Union requested that suitable beater camps be built for track men throughout the railway system, but many track workers remained unhoused. The chief engineer stressed that "management is under no obligation whatsoever to house any of its servants," and quarters were provided only as "a matter of administrative convenience."[62] Although administrators generally did not expect workers' families to live with them in the road and rail "beater camps," and there were no schools outside of the towns, wives or dependents were necessary in order to fetch water, collect firewood, and take care of other arduous tasks of social reproduction in isolated areas.[63] Under these conditions, some track workers engaged in serial marriages, leaving wives with children behind upon transfer to a new station because of the lack of facilities, but finding another woman in the new station for companionship and domestic help.[64]

Such low-level employees were not even allowed to eat near the workplace, even though they had no other provisions. If their jobs brought them near the railway stations, work crews scouted for a spot in a depot building to spend the night and consume a meal. Yet new railway regulations in 1954 prohibited track workers from station offices, passenger waiting rooms, and goods sheds, although they were allowed to sleep on station verandahs at the discretion of the local station master. Workers were not allowed there during the day, however, "as it is undesirable to have food cooked and eaten in the vicinity of the office." At that point, the Railway Workers Union threatened that its members would not work at outstations unless accommodations were provided. The chief engineer replied sympathetically, although he declined to allocate funds for permanent quarters. Rather, he reported that traveling bunk vans were on order, and ten were due for delivery in June 1955. Further, the railway purchased on a trial basis ten prefabricated portable aluminum houses for track men to sleep in. But when these arrived, workers unanimously rejected them as far too hot and badly ventilated. Instead, they suggested that they live in rooms at wayside stations or reconditioned wooden wagon bodies with windows and concrete floors.[65]

In the postwar period, the railway and other establishments did expand the housing available to employees. Between 1953 and 1960, the government built a small number, 477, of new junior service quarters in Lagos for employees of the railway, Nigerian Port Authority, and railway police. In the 1950s, the railway administration constructed 912 new staff quarters throughout the system, the vast majority of which contained two rooms and were targeted for junior staff.[66] In addition, the Nigerian government began to offer loans for building or buying a house in Lagos to pensionable employees of the Nigerian government or Lagos Town Council earning greater than £150 per year, who had been in ten years continuous employment. In 1957, the Nigerian Railway liberalized its requirements, granting advances of up to four years' salary to

Photo 6.3 Railway housing quarters, Ibadan, 1998.

pensionable employees with at least five years of service to build a house, buy land for a house, or buy a house in Lagos. These provisions were expanded over the next decade to include building or buying outside of Lagos, the repair of existing houses, and the NRC's guarantee of private loans.[67] These new initiatives were still insufficient to meet the housing needs of the urban labor force, and the railway, for one, constantly reiterated that it had no intention of housing all of its Lagos workers. But senior officials and many in so-called "essential" posts were guaranteed housing or were paid in lieu of quarters. In the Nigerian Port Authority, all senior service staff were eligible for quarters, and, if none were available, they were paid a housing allowance. Although nearly all port facilities included some quarters for junior staff, these housed only a small minority of employees and favored those whose services were determined to be most essential.[68]

Even housing built by the government for the Lagos public, which expanded dramatically in the 1950s, largely accommodated those with the highest incomes. It was senior personnel who benefited from the extension of the Apapa and Ikoyi Government Reserve Areas and the low-density housing developed on Victoria Island. These costly initiatives limited the resources available for low-income housing. Among the projects of the Lagos Executive Development Board (LEDB), which oversaw slum clearance and housing projects, the largest and most controversial was the housing estate at Surulere (a name that means "patience is rewarded"). This complex scheme was first proposed in 1951, to supply housing for people of all income levels and to accommodate homeowners from central Lagos who were displaced by slum clearance measures. Between 1957 and 1966, the LEDB built 6,714 units. Of these, roughly a third were for rehousing, although these new houses did not replace all the accommodation demolished in central Lagos. Almost none of the rest ended up housing low income earners. Seventy-seven percent of the funding went to freehold houses for medium and high income families. A total of 913 "low cost" houses were built, each having one to four rooms, water and electricity. Although the rents were subsidized, the price was still higher than many former residents of central Lagos, and others on lower incomes, could afford. They in turn subleased to others with greater means, leaving the estate for cheaper parts of the city.[69]

Increased access to housing, either through higher wages or job-related quarters, meant that better-paid wage and salary earners could more easily than otherwise accommodate their families. This was, of course, a crucial component of plans to stabilize urban labor and "modernize" cities. But there were important differences between planners' and Nigerians' conceptions of who entailed *family*. Peter Marris's study of the effects of rehousing for those Lagosians resettled at Surulere stresses the disruption of their social and economic networks. The new houses were designed for relatively small households, and the layout of the suburb left many families socially isolated.[70] Still, consumer surveys from the late 1950s and into the 1960s show clearly that rising incomes brought bigger households. In Lagos in 1960, the average household size ranged from seven to nine people, increasing directly with income. On average, the lowest paid wage earners in Ibadan lived in households of three or four people, while those at the highest salary levels accommodated eight people. The average household size for junior employees of the Nigerian Tobacco Company was 3.3 people in Lagos and 4.5 people in Ibadan, rising to 5.9 and 5.7, respectively, for "intermediate" level employees. A 1968 survey found that professionals and administrators had four times as many dependents in their households as did unskilled manual workers.[71]

Although new migrants and those earning small incomes struggled to accommodate a wife in town, greater resources meant that husbands could offer housing to their wives, sometimes more than one at a time. One of the old cliches about modernization in Nigeria (and Africa) was that it made polygyny economically untenable.[72] When the Harragin Commission rejected African family allowances in 1946 through reference to large families and polygyny, one trade union response had been that urban workers did not engage in polygyny because it was too expensive for them (see chapter 4). Indeed, the railway pensioners I surveyed seem to have been more monogamous than

Photo 6.4 Locomotive fireman Ayo Salako (front, center), his immediate family, and other members of his residential compound, Kano, c. 1960. Photo courtesy of A.A. Salako.

typical men of their generations. While 78 percent of those who had been working for the railway establishment during the 1950s remained monogamous through their lives, monogamy rates were only 35 percent for the men surveyed in cocoa farming areas and 62 percent for householders in central Lagos.[73] There are several possible explanations. The majority of pensioners in my survey (77 percent) were Christians, and while only 37 percent of married Muslims had one wife, 62 percent of Christians did. Another possibility comes from the fact that the monogamous pensioners had, on average, slightly more education than their polygynous counterparts. Moreover, my examination of railway personnel records indicates that pensioners were more likely to be monogamous than those railway employees who were not in pensionable appointments, making monogamy associated with upward mobility in salaried employment.[74] Through much of the twentieth century, as Karin Barber writes, monogamy "represented an ideal of 'enlightenment' associated with education, white-collar jobs, and middle-class status."[75]

But this view was not ubiquitous. In my overall sample of railway pensioners hired before 1965, 44 percent of the men were or had been polygynous. Similarly, a 1964 survey in Lagos found that one-third of female respondents lived in polygynous households. Although better educated men tended toward monogamy, 17 percent of the husbands in administrative and professional jobs and 25 percent of those in clerical and related work made polygynous marriages.[76] Among railway workers at least, a second or even third marriage was occasioned in some cases by a job transfer that necessitated leaving children and their mother in one town while the man's job took him elsewhere. In the new place, the man would marry a new wife. But in other cases, men rose sufficiently in income and rank so that they could accommodate more than one wife, and their offspring, all together. From the 1950s on, it was not unusual to find polygynous households occupying the detached bungalows of senior employee housing, as well as one- and two-room railway quarters. A satirical newspaper article "reported" that European civil servants were complaining of discrimination, since "[a] polygamously married Nigerian officer may house in Government quarters as many of his wives as he finds necessary to his well-being while the expatriate officer is frowned upon for having more than one wife at home."[77]

Secure incomes also translated into greater numbers of children living at home, beyond the simple correlation between wealth and health. Yorubaland has a tradition of child fostering, and in the 1950s and 1960s the exchange of children between relatives was common in Lagos and elsewhere.[78] But many railway pensioners related proudly that their offspring lived only with them or in boarding schools. "I did not allow any of my father's brother or relatives to train my children," one retiree bragged, explaining that when money is tight, "it is then you give out your children as wards to uncles, neighbors or brothers."[79] But who would care for children when wives worked outside the home, even in flexible occupations like trading, especially if the family had relocated to places where they lacked local relatives? Particularly under these conditions, both elderly and young relations were brought in to help. Live-in relatives helped take care of children in nearly two-thirds of railway homes in my sample.[80]

Because of the nature of their working lives, some railway workers were more likely to become big men at home, with many dependents, than others. Station masters, for instance, were the top managers in their workplaces and often lived there with their families and some staff as well. A sense of station masters' positions relative to their households and underlings can be gleaned from a 1966 exchange between E.E. Okojie, head of Iwo station (between Ibadan and Oshogbo), and his district superintendent, J.A. Sobowale. Okojie requested permission to sue for damages and criminally charge his staff clerk, Francis Akinlabi, who had seduced and impregnated Okojie's sixteen-year-old sister. The girl had been part of Okojie's household for thirteen years, and while marriage to Akinlabi was never raised as an option, Okojie did want the clerk to take responsibility for expenses associated with the pregnancy and child rearing. Part of his hostility could have been related to the political tensions of the period and the fact that, based on their surnames, Okojie was from eastern Nigeria and Akinlabi was Yoruba. But Okojie's letters indicated that he was most offended by Akinlabi's disrespectful conduct toward him as big man in the station and household. "I have to point out here," he wrote to Sobowale,

> that the human trust that should exist between two people in the same place is already dented.... If a youngman next in rank in a place could be so bold as to go into a house in which he is supposed to be a regent to commit himself with impure and insincere motives, then everything else like *trust* in the handling of Ticket Tube, Ticket Stock or Station administration if I am sick or otherwise out of station when he is supposed to take over temporarily is punctured.[81]

"Big man" status, reflecting domestic dominance and control over subordinates, was linked with workplace hierarchies and responsibilities. Okojie saw the station as an extension of his household, and he expected deference in one just as in the other. In 1958, signal man Sumonu Animasaun was charged with setting up communications in a new railway station north of Ibadan. His new posting came with quarters in which he could house his wife, children, and other dependents. Summing up both his work and domestic lives decades later, Animasaun recalled, "I was a big man at that time."[82]

Not only did employer-provided housing allow some workers to accommodate large households, but other employee benefits could be channeled to families and a range of dependents as well, with and without official approval. Once the staff canteen opened at Ebute Metta in the mid-1950s, for instance, railway workers had to be reminded not to entertain relatives and guests there, because prices were subsidized as a worker welfare measure.[83] Occasionally, railway police enforced regulations against private trading at stations, housing compounds, and near the workshops—an important source both of livelihood for market women and of goods and services for railway men and others employed nearby.[84] These official efforts at controlling space, limited and sporadic as they were, often singled out the relatives, friends, and dependents of lower paid workers and tolerated identical practices among dependents of more highly paid employees. In 1959, members of the Transport Staff Union and Lagos's Union of Domestic Servants complained that railway police were arresting family members and friends of workers when they came to the railway compound to visit or do domestic work. Although the administration insisted that all nonemployees were prohibited from the railway compound, the servants, friends, and relatives of senior staff members were never turned away.[85] There was even a minor scandal when in 1961 a senior administrator recruited his young mistress to kick off a ceremony inaugurating the first diesel long-distance train in the system—making it clear to outraged employees that *his* social life could be relevant to official business.[86]

Medical benefits were another example of the stratified ways in which differently ranked railway employees could provide for their dependents, with official assistance. In 1956, administrators agreed to establish a medical service separate from the facilities for other government employees. Railway workers in the permanent establishment, but not their wives and children, were eligible for free treatment in railway dispensaries located throughout the system and the railway hospital in Lagos.[87] Three years later Olaolu Oduleye of the Nigerian Union of Railwaymen (Federated) complained to the corporation's chief medical officer that workers' young children were not included in the medical benefits. Oduleye argued that work time would be wasted if fathers had to take their children elsewhere for health care.[88] By 1961, free medical care was extended to the families of railway officers and members of the established staff. But "family" was defined as one wife and children under eighteen, explicitly excluding domestic servants and pensioners. The NUR(F) noted that the exclusion of nonestablished and daily paid workers' families was particularly regretful, because these were the people who needed free medical services the most and could least afford them. Arguing that extending the benefit would be in the best interest of the NRC, Union leader Oduleye stressed that an employee needed "peace of mind" in order to be a good worker, and this was impossible "when his wife is ridden with disease and he has no money to treat her." The secretary of the Union's Eastern Division echoed Oduleye, writing, "It would be tragic to sacrifice healthy family life for financial stringency."[89] Four years after an investigation into the costs of treating families of unestablished staff, the general manager ordered the extension of free medical services to the families of daily rated employees.[90] Highly ranked employees continued to be treated at the "officers' clinic," while others attended the regular Ebute Metta dispensary.[91]

LOCALIZING THE FAMILY

Even as steadily employed men were housing, feeding, and securing medical care for dependents in town with them, they were also contributing money to rural relatives, as men with jobs had done throughout the history of wage labor in Nigeria. In the 1950s, according to one source, wage earners spent 25 percent to 30 percent of their annual incomes on "family commitments under the extended family system." In another estimate, from the early 1960s, most bachelors sent home about one-fifth of their wages and approximately one-sixth were assisting relatives financially.[92] Ninety-six percent of the pensioners I surveyed reported giving regularly to their parents while they were employed, and about three-quarters sent money to their parents-in-law and siblings as well (74 percent and 73 percent, respectively). About half sent money to other relatives. The fact that nearly all of the railway pensioners I talked with reported that they had sent money to relatives during their careers also suggests the normative value of such behavior. Interviewed men responded to the question about remittances as if it were obvious that they would have sent money to relatives. That was part of being steadily employed, and it helped to build up self-esteem as a financially capable and responsible member of the community. It also translated into material benefits like a portion of each harvest on the family farm—an important resource given the high food prices in cities.

Although earners at all levels contributed money to their parents and hometown relatives, the amounts increased as wages and salaries rose. Indeed, those with greater resources were generally expected to share with kin and townsmen in need. According to a 1961 survey in Ibadan, those defined as middle income earners spent more than eight times as much on monetary transactions—including gifts to relatives and others—as did those in the lower income group. More strikingly, wage earners made more monetary contributions than the self-employed. A survey of Nigerian Tobacco Company employees in Lagos and Ibadan in 1967 concluded in general that the "dependency burden"—meaning financial obligations to dependents—rose in tandem with incomes.[93]

Yet even if higher incomes could be translated into remittances, the requirements of steady work and the attractions of urban living often meant that workers did not spend a lot of time actually in their hometowns. Ideally, migrants in the 1940s and 1950s visited their hometowns at least once a year. A 1958 survey found that two-thirds of workers in the Lagos railway workshops had visited home at least once in the previous year, even though only 58 percent had been eligible for annual leave.[94] Yet such visits could be difficult, even for those entitled to paid leave. Rufus Awoboyade, a train guard based in Lagos, complained in 1958 that it had been eleven years since his last visit to his hometown of Ikola-Ekiti, even though he had been part of the permanent establishment for four years already.[95] In my survey, Lagos and Ibadan pensioners—who by definition had been in mid- to high-levels—were asked how often they had visited their parents when they were working in their longest railway job. Although already more than half of those who entered the railway service in the 1940s saw their parents on annual leave or less often, that number had jumped to over three-fourths for those who were hired in the 1960s, reflecting both the ubiquity of transfers and the difficulties of visiting the hometown. During the same period, the percentage that visited home at least weekly declined from a third to zero.[96]

It is also useful to attend to the *amount* of leave time spent at home. In 1955, the railway clerical staff union requested that established employees be granted free train passes to travel throughout the rail system while on leave for "broadening their general knowledge of the Railways." In subsequent years salaried workers would often spend one or two weeks of their month-long leave with hometown relatives, and then use their free train passes to spend the rest of the time visiting friends or exploring unfamiliar parts of Nigeria. According to one former locomotive driver, railway work

> affords someone the chance to serve the nation and know it better. For instance, if you traveled from here [Ibadan] to Kano you will bypass so many towns and villages along the line and you will know and be used to them more than someone who works and stays in Lagos or Enugu. At the time they were running the Lagos–Port Harcourt train I could travel from Lagos to the North then to the East during my annual leave. So I can tell more of these places than someone who has not traveled.[97]

A former train ticket collector who had worked in Lagos, Port Harcourt, Zaria, and Ibadan recalled that his annual leave could last for one to two months. During that time he typically visited his relatives in Ijebu and then used his "privilege tickets" to visit friends living all over Nigeria.[98] More than most other occupations, railway work gave men a base of friends and colleagues posted all over the country, from all of Nigeria's regions and ethnic groups. Such social networks and nationwide travel were part of railway men's modern, cosmopolitan self-images, and indeed several pensioners said that the opportunity for travel was one of the appeals of their jobs.

Moreover, some who were entitled to paid leave did not always use it. T.M. Yesufu mentioned that more than half of workers he surveyed in 1958 took vacation leave in the past year, yet railway policies in force during the time of his research were for all employees—permanent and casual—to have some paid annual leave. The discrepancy can be partly explained by the fact that workers could forgo leave in exchange for extra money, which many of them did.[99] People delayed leave for several years until they saved enough money for presents, patronage, and showing off when they got home. In a context in which material exchanges formed an important component of social relations, one could not show up for a visit empty-handed, and workers tended to travel to see their families only when they were in a position to dispense gifts. While uneducated migrants visited hometowns as often as possible, "the educated and smart young men and women" in urban employment, as the Department of Labor put it, saw "the village as a place to spend vacation leave if he or she can accumulate sufficient money with which to make presents in cash or kind to elderly parents and a number of relatives." One former locomotive driver found hometown visits distasteful because, he said, as soon as he arrived in Ogbomosho people would come from high and low to greet and flatter him. "Before you know it, you have already finished your money. Home is just a place you have to go once in a while and when going you have to take with you some money."[100]

In addition, for those who had worked to provide their new homes with comfortable furnishings and entertainment such as radios and gramophones, hometown accommodations could be less than ideal. The 1961/62 Ibadan consumer survey revealed marked differences in the standard of living between wage earners and the traders and farmers who made up the largest group of self-employed people. More than twice as many homes of wage earners were equipped with electricity than others were (47 percent of wage earner households as opposed to 20 percent of the self-employed). Average monthly expenditures even for laborers with a wage job were higher than for each occupational group among the self-employed. In 1958, a railway employee at the Ebute Metta workshops told a researcher that "so far as workers are concerned, bicycles, gramophones, radios, nylon clothes for the wife, the use of electricity in the home, and attendance at cinemas, were a mark of social distinction." Decades later, a retiree recalled that when he had visited his hometown on leave from work, his family did not even have chairs to sit on, and they only used plates and forks when he provided them.[101]

By the late 1950s, many strains of public discourse suggested that urban working people were spending less and less money on their hometown relatives, for various reasons. A Nigerian economist claimed in 1959 that increasing overall prosperity had affected rural as well as urban areas, causing families to rely less than before on remittances from wage-earners. "As prosperity also percolates to the countryside over the years, and as old customs decay under the influence of a rapidly growing monetary economy, the burden of the extended family on the wage of the worker is being lightened."[102] The Department of Labor remarked with approval that a stable urban labor force had developed, relatively cut off from rural relatives and dependent on regular wage employment.[103] Labor activists generally agreed with this description, although they saw it less as cause for celebration. According to a political advertisement, "the old men of today are getting less assistance from their children not necessarily because the children of today are less kindhearted than those of generations ago but mainly because the social and economic needs of the men and women of today have become complex and more abundant."[104] A fictional railway worker from the early 1960s Nigerian novel *Blade among the Boys* refused to make a hefty payment to become head of his lineage, arguing to his uncle: "When I started to earn a salary you made me give a large portion of my earnings to you, under the pretext that when I am old others will look after me. What guarantee is there that they will do it, now that our economy is fast changing into a cash economy? . . . I am sick of this forced loyalty to the lineage and I am going to have no more of it."[105]

It is important to note that this type of attitude was particular to those with steady, significant incomes, who were less needy than others of rural networks as safety nets. The lower the wage, of course, the more a worker would rely on income from other sources like trading, part-time work, and remittances from others. While the wages of "junior" employees of the Nigerian Tobacco Company accounted for about three-fourths of the money they actually spent, for instance, "intermediate" employees' wages comprised 84 percent to 88 percent of their expenditures. In Lagos in 1954, laborers' wages accounted for only 55 percent of their incomes, while for clerks the wage represented 66 percent of income; in Ibadan the next year, laborers' and clerks' wages accounted for 61 percent and 77 percent of income, respectively.[106]

Moreover, the steadily employed counted on savings, pensions, and educated children to sustain them in retirement more than resources recruited through kinship networks. Although inflation continually undermined the security of pensions, steadily employed wage and salary earners frequently had the means to make other investments in their futures. The 1961 survey in Ibadan showed that wage earners saved three times as much money as the self-employed. They used this money to build houses, educate children, and form businesses intended to support their retirements. A Marine Department pensioner featured in a 1962 *Drum* magazine article, for instance, used his savings to buy a house during his first year of retirement. His family lived in one wing and tenants rented the other. "I rake my rental and pension incomes together to meet the entire family's health and feeding problems," he explained. "A man in my position, if he has not got his own house, would surely be a burden on his relatives and friends."[107] In addition, steady workers, like all Nigerians, looked to their educated children to support them in old age. Paying educational expenses was crucial in helping to define steadily employed men as family providers. Daniel Mowela, a Lagos fitter about to retire after twenty-seven years, wrote to the Railway labor officer in 1948 to urge that his son be reconsidered for an apprenticeship. "After all, this [his son's job] is the only material benefit I would receive from Government for my long service," Mowela argued. Nearly fifty years later, former locomotive driver D.A. Owolabi made a similar point about his own retirement: "You must struggle at the earlier stage to train your children and get them well established so at old age the children will rally round you and will not abandon you to hunger or starvation." Owolabi, like others, emphasized that his financial strategies for retirement were not based on family networks. "And with the little pension," he went on, "you can cope so you won't rely on any of the family's property, because as for me I like to be on my own. That is my prayer for my children too: not to be a burden on anybody."[108] These days,

Urban Labor, Extended Families, and the Differentiation of Domesticity 159

Photo 6.5 D.A. Owolabi, Ibadan, 1998.

in fact, Owolabi maintains his own business in Ibadan, whose customer base comes primarily from his railway contacts.

It is this type of self-reliance, along with other considerations, which has drawn many career wage earners to spend their retirements outside of their hometowns, in marked contrast to most older Nigerians. In Flora Nwapa's story about the Civil War, "A Soldier Returns Home," an Igbo train guard leaving Jos says he is going to

> Port Harcourt and then retirement. I am due now at home. . . . But my fear is, what will I do at home? I have worked in the railways for the past twenty-six years. Occasionally, I went home, during my leave to see home people. But I have never belonged to home people. I don't understand their ways, and I don't think they understand mine.[109]

For many railway workers, the situation was similar to this idealized one. Adetunji Adeyemi, who was hired by the Railway in 1955, is from Ijebu-Ode, but he and his wife continue to occupy their comfortable quarters in Ibadan.

> To go back and live there [Ijebu-Ode], well my father has a building there and I do go there for a day, two or three on visiting but to stay there permanently, no way. For instance, I want to establish here. I don't want to establish at home.... Here I have friends and connections unlike home where I did not stay much because we schooled in Lagos and all my own children were born in Lagos. I don't want to go back to Lagos because of the problems there.... That is why I prefer to stay here and visit my people at home when necessary.[110]

M.O. Shofekun was born in 1920 to Ijebu parents in Shagamu and became a railway clerk in 1942. Throughout his career he saw his relatives frequently, sent money to his siblings, and maintained kin in his hometown. But in 1975, two years before his retirement, he built a two-story house in Odo Ona, a neighborhood in Ibadan with a large Ijebu population. When asked why he did not retire in Ijebu, he answered, "I would become a foreigner in my own town."[111]

Personnel files indicate that within the overall Railway workforce, nearly two-thirds of former employees went home for retirement. But what is striking is the difference between "pensioners" (those eligible for pensions—generally long-term, higher-level employees) and "annuitants" (those not eligible for pensions but who were paid a lump sum upon retirement). In the general pool of employees, annuitants retired in their hometowns at nearly twice the rate of pensioners. Among those from southwestern Nigeria, annuitants were more than three times as likely to retire in the hometown as pensioners were. Only about a quarter of career Yoruba railway workers chose to retire in their hometowns, far less than the general body of railway workers, other pensioners, and other Yoruba railway men.[112] Of the 138 pensioners I surveyed who now live in Ibadan, only twenty-six were born there. Yoruba railway pensioners seem to lend credence to the proverb collected in the late 1960s, "One who knows English never dies at the place of his birth" (*Agb' oyinbo ki i ku s'ile*).[113]

FAMILY MODERNIZATION?

In the 1950s and 1960s, it seemed for many in southern Nigeria that their country was entering the modern world. By the mid-1950s, the three regions were achieving self-government, and it was clear that national independence would follow shortly. In government departments, parastatal corporations, and some large businesses, Nigerians of ability were replacing expatriates in ever-increasing numbers. The Action Group, the political party that controlled the

Western Regional government after it became autonomous in 1954, promised "life more abundant" and embarked upon ambitious schemes for economic development, improved infrastructure, and social services—the most exciting, costly, and popular of which was the program of universal primary education launched in 1955. Newspaper articles were full of praise for each step in the region's, and the country's, march to what was envisioned as a future of dignity and prosperity. Wage-earners, particularly on the railway, identified with the mission of advancing their new country just as civil servants, politicians, and businessmen did.[114] In the 1950s to the early 1960s, according to a former engine driver, "somebody would either work in the Railway, in Marine, or in the PWD. Anybody who got job in any of the three departments would consider himself or herself working in a nice place." Why? "The salary was nice, there was promotion prospect and there was the feeling too of serving one's country because all of them were government ministries." Another pensioner agreed: "The railway was serving as a developer in the country then."[115]

Nigerians used the language of modernization to describe their family and social relationships as well as their contributions to the new nation. A newspaper article entitled "The Modern Nigerian Home," for example, suggested that being modern entailed having access to private space and amenities like piped water and electricity, as well as housing only the nuclear family.[116] But local versions of modernization were more complicated than the idealized versions promulgated by western social scientists and government officials. Even as literate Nigerians read about what supposedly made someone "modern," they also insisted on the importance of extended families, patronage relationships, and ties to the hometown. Many struggled with the seemingly intractable conflicts between "traditional" family values and the circumstances of "modern" urban living. An article on the women's page of the *West African Pilot* began, "The new family pattern emerging in many parts of the world can bring increased freedom to the individual, more rights to women, greater happiness to children or it can disrupt the family, plunging its members into a misery greater than even the most isolated village has known."[117] Local commentators repeatedly pointed to the conflicts between kinship loyalties and the security these could bring, and the desire for individual accumulation and advancement. The extended family, as one observer put it, "acts as a serious obstacle to economic progress. A Nigerian on a high income scale finds it difficult to save and invest when he has many distant relatives to maintain."[118]

An article published in 1961 in the journal of the Railway Technical Staff Association starkly reveals trade unionists' attempts to grapple with issues surrounding family obligations and stable employment. "The Social Background of Industrial Relations," by F.O. Majekodunmi, the union's Western district secretary, began with the question, "Can the new forces released by economic development be harmonized with earlier social ideas and customs?" The answer is ambiguous, but the author seems to lean toward a "no." "Modern industry," he wrote,

> implies individual and utilitarian attitudes of mind: The kinship obligations common in one form or another throughout West Africa stand in the way of this stimulation of individual effort. Under tribal conditions work was largely motivated by family and social incentives. The economic incentive, for a man to find himself a job and establish himself securely in it may be weakened if he knows that his family is bound to support him in case of need; or if he knows that financial success may mean a host of claims from poorer members of the family.[119]

This is not far from the arguments of colonial administrators in the 1940s. But Majekodunmi also noted that family ties might encourage a worker to greater effort in order to meet financial obligations. Nevertheless, he pointed out that some "awkward problems in industrial relations arise from the African concept of the family and the home," which included polygamy, separate residences for spouses, financial responsibilities to extended families, and child fostering. "Under these conditions some apparently simple questions are puzzling in West Africa," the article continued.

> What is a "house" for the purpose of assessment a room, or rooms, or a compound? Where is the "home" if the first and second wife reside at different places? What is a family and can a "family budget" be drawn up to calculate "the cost of living"? . . . The answers to such questions are seldom simple in West Africa. An increase of wages may mean an increase of dependents. An improved housing standard may invite uncontrollable over-crowding.

This is how the article ends, with no proposed resolution to the issue. Like others, Nigerian workers were consciously grappling with the apparent contradictions between modernization—as a "package" heavily laden with Western European social norms—and African family ideals.

CONCLUSION

Earlier chapters of this book have argued that working men actively played with competing ideologies of masculinity to suit situational interests. The material in this chapter supports that broad idea as well, although here the frame of reference has shifted in part from wives and children to a larger group of relatives and hometown associates. Masculine ideals in postwar southwestern Nigeria stretched from the "big man," heading a large household and participating in a range of patronage relationships, through the man of ọlajú ("enlightenment") to the "modern" monogamous father, typically Christian and always focused on the nuclear family at the expense of extended kin. But it is inaccurate to think of these as points on a temporal continuum. As Barber has put it, we are not seeing "a short-lived transitional phase between 'tradition' and Western-type modernity; on the contrary, it is a functioning mode which could perpetuate itself indefinitely."[120] The progressivist tone of modernization theory was one of its biggest conceits, and real people made their real lives in a variety of ways that defied, and also creatively used, social scientists' categories. The trade union publication quoted earlier is only one indication of urban workers' simultaneous attraction to and critique of modernization models.

One of the key ironies here centers on the implication of labor stabilization policies in the complex "modernization" of workers' families. The differentiation of the workforce, along with the provision of housing and other benefits, allowed long-term skilled workers as well as top administrative and technical officers to develop large households composed of a range of dependents—the opposite of what postwar social engineering was supposed to bring. While many such employees did rely on savings and investments more than on family safety nets, and while they did visit their hometowns relatively rarely, they also continued to support parents and other kin, frequently by bringing or allowing these relatives to live with them in their urban housing.

Throughout the colonial period and into the 1960s, workplace hierarchies, social status, and material wealth continued to be reflected in domestic life. While those at the top used their incomes and job perquisites to grow ever "bigger" in their households and communities, men at the lower ends of employment structures, even those who were steadily employed, continued to struggle for *any* family life. In 1964, their resentment of the differentials between their domestic circumstances and those of the upper echelons—including the ability to provide for wives, children, and other relatives—exploded in the second massive general strike in Nigeria's history, the subject of the next chapter.

NOTES

1. General Manager's Staff Circular No. 11/50, December 6, 1950, GMS 335, vol. 1.

2. See "Wanted: Children's Allowance for Junior Servicemen," *DS*, March 12, 1953; "Union Urges Pay Increase for Juniors," *DTN*, November 1, 1954; Gogo Chu Nzeribe, "Secretary-General's Report to the First General Council Meeting of the All-Nigeria Trade Union Federation," NLA/19, 1954.

3. Chukuwa Okola, "A Simple Analysis of the Economic [*sic*] and Incidence of the COLA Award," *LC*, April 11, 1950.

4. R. Olufemi Ekundare, *An Economic History of Nigeria, 1860–1960* (New York: Africana Publishing Co., 1973), pp. 8, 311, 262, 266.

5. In the late 1950s, 75 percent of Nigeria's economically active population was engaged in agriculture, forestry, and animal husbandry, mainly on an independent basis. T.M. Yesufu, *An Introduction to Industrial Relations in Nigeria* (London: Oxford University Press, 1962), p. 4. The increase in the size of the wage labor force is extrapolated from Ekundare, *Economic History*, p. 362. The total number of people in wage-earning occupations in 1946 was given as 236,000; in 1960, the total employed by government was 184,224, and the number in nongovernment wage labor was 238,650.

6. Peter Kilby, *Industrialization in an Open Economy: Nigeria, 1945–1966* (Cambridge: Cambridge University Press, 1969), p. 281; Ekundare, *Economic History*, p. 363. The cost of living index in Lagos rose 32 percent between 1953 and 1960.

7. NPA, *Fifth Annual Report for the Year Ended 31st March 1960* (NPA, 1960); NRC, *Report and Accounts for the Year Ended 31st March 1965* (NRC, 1965). The differentiation among Lagos port workers is detailed in Peter Waterman, *Division and Unity amongst Nigerian Workers: Lagos Port Unionism, 1940s–60s* (The Hague: Institute of Social Studies, 1982).

8. Frederick Cooper, *Decolonization and African Society: The Labor Question in French and British Africa* (Cambridge: Cambridge University Press, 1996), p. 461.

9. Frederick Cooper, "Industrial Man Comes to Africa," in Lisa A. Lindsay and Stephan F. Miescher (eds.), *Men and Masculinities in Modern Africa* (Portsmouth, NH: Heinemann, 2003).

10. Memorandum by A.H. Couzens, Nigerian Commissioner of Labor, May 22, 1950, Albert Harry Couzens papers, MSS.Afr.s.1377, RHO.

11. J.I. Roper, *Labour Problems in West Africa* (London: Penguin, 1958), p. 27.

12. Yesufu, *Introduction*, p. 121.

13. James Ferguson, *Expectations of Modernity: Myths and Meanings of Urban Life on the Zambian Copperbelt* (Berkeley: University of California Press, 1999), p. 175. For colonial officials and early modernization theory, see Cooper, *Decolonization*, ch. 9; and "Modernizing Bureaucrats, Backward Africans, and the Development Concept," in Frederick Cooper and Randall Packard (eds.), *International Development and the Social Sciences: Essays on the History and Politics of Knowledge* (Berkeley: University of California, 1997). On the links between family life and modernization, see William J. Goode, *World Revolution and Family Patterns* (New York: Free Press, 1963). For a general review of the literature on this theme, see Tamara K. Hareven, "Modernization and Family History: Perspectives on Social Change," *Signs* 2 (1976): 190–206. For an overview of the application of modernization theory to Nigerian families, see Sheilah Clarke Ekong, "Continuity and Change in Nigerian Family Patterns," in Simi Afonja and Tola Olu Pearce (eds.), *Social Change in Nigeria* (London: Longman, 1984). Examples of the modernization view of Nigerian social change include Mary E.C. Bird, "Social Change in Kinship and Marriage among the Yoruba of Western Nigeria" (D.Phil. dissertation, University of Edinburgh, 1958) and "Urbanization, Family and Marriage in Western Nigeria," in M. Ruel (ed.), *Urbanization in African Social Change* (Edinburgh: Edinburgh University Centre for African Studies, 1963); Alison Izzett, "Family Life among the Yoruba, in Lagos, Nigeria," in Aidan Southall (ed.), *Social Change in Modern Africa* (London: Oxford University Press, 1961); Ukandi Godwin Damachi, *Nigerian Modernization: The Colonial Legacy* (New York: Third Press, 1972).

14. Yesufu, *Introduction*, p. 120. The "adaptation" thesis was a strong one in the urban African anthropology of the 1950s. See Cooper, *Decolonization,* pp. 370–74.

15. Introduction to Jean Comaroff and John Comaroff (eds.), *Modernity and Its Malcontents: Ritual and Power in Postcolonial Africa* (Chicago: University of Chicago Press, 1993).

16. Ferguson, *Expectations*, makes an analogous point for mineworkers on Zambia's Copperbelt, linking a self-conscious adoption of a "cosmopolitan" style to modernist ideologies and a political economy which made it possible, for a while, for urban workers to neglect their rural relatives.

17. Dean C. Tipps, "Modernization Theory and the Comparative Study of Societies: A Critical Perspective," *CSSH* 15 (1973): 199–226, p. 215.

18. J.D.Y. Peel, *"Olaju*: A Yoruba Concept of Development," *Journal of Development Studies* 14 (1978): 139–65.

19. On domesticity as a prop and index of class status in Africa, see Karen Tranberg Hansen (ed.), *African Encounters with Domesticity* (New Brunswick, NJ: Rutgers University Press, 1992).

20. Luise White, "Separating the Men from the Boys: Constructions of Gender, Sexuality, and Terrorism in Central Kenya, 1939–1959," *IJAHS* 23, no. 1 (1990): 1–25; Luise White, *The Comforts of Home: Prostitution in Colonial Nairobi* (Chicago: University of Chicago Press, 1990); Timothy Scarnecchia, "The Politics of Gender and Class in the Creation of African Communities, Salisbury, Rhodesia, 1940–56" (Ph.D. dissertation, University of Michigan, 1993), and Timothy Scarnecchia, "Poor Women and Nationalist Politics: Alliances and Fissures in the Formation of a Nationalist Movement in Salisbury, Rhodesia, 1950–56," *JAH* 37 (1996): 283–310.

21. See the Minority Report by C.O. Nwokedi and O.I. Akinkugbe, Appendix to the Report of the Commission on the Review of Wages, Salary and Conditions of Service of the Junior Employees of the Governments of the Federation and in Private Establishments (Morgan Report), 1963–64. Africans' appropriation of the housing and servants previously reserved for European officials can be seen in the memoir of Augustus Adebayo, who became in 1955 one of the first Nigerian district officers, *White Man in Black Skin* (Ibadan: Spectrum Books, 1981).

22. Helen Callaway, *Gender, Culture and Empire: European Women in Colonial Nigeria* (Urbana: University of Illinois Press, 1987), p. 17.

23. In addition to Hansen, *African Encounters* and Callway, *Gender, Culture*, see Nancy Rose Hunt, *A Colonial Lexicon of Birth Ritual, Medicalization and Mobility in the Congo* (Durham, NC: Duke Press, 1999).

24. Adebayo, *White Man*, 80.

25. Ibid., p.53. At the Enugu Colliery until World War II, employees carried the white managers from their residences to work in hammocks. Carolyn A. Brown, "A 'Man' in the Village is a 'Boy' in the Workplace: Colonial Racism, Worker Militance and Igbo Notions of Masculinity in the Nigerian Coal Industry, 1930–1945," in Lindsay and Miescher (eds*.), Men and Masculinities*. Also see Callaway, *Gender, Culture*, and Hunt, *A Colonial Lexicon*.

26. "Incident Leading to My Arrest on the 25th of June 1949" by Emman E. Nweze, telegraph clerk, Minna, GMS 33/2.

27. Indeed, Carolyn Brown insists that historians of West African labor need to pay more attention to race. See "A 'Man' in the Village" and *"We Were All Slaves": African*

Miners, Culture and Resistance: The Enugu Government Colliery, Nigeria, 1914–1950 (Portsmouth, NH: Heinemann, 2003).

28. "Reader Compares Transport Facilities in Govt. Civil Service," *WAP*, November 24, 1941.

29. "Senior Railway Staff Plan to Form Their Own Trade Union," *WAP*, January 8, 1953.

30. Michael Odede, retired railway yard supervisor (formerly porter and shunter), December 28, 1993, Ibadan.

31. Francis Jaekel (former Chief Superintendent of the NRC), personal communication, July 22, 1994. Also see letter from Zaria Osubu ("able-Seaman") to Harbor Master, Apapa wharf, August 11, 1948, NLA/11, protesting the effects his impending transfer will have on his children's schooling, and a similar letter from train guard Theophilus T. Ojumo, February 9, 1964, WP 9362, Ibadan Pension Office, NRC.

32. Memorandum submitted by the RWU to Gorsuch Commission, November 1, 1954, GMS 337/8. Also see "Union Urges Pay Increase for Juniors," *DTN*, November 1, 1954.

33. Also see Lisa A. Lindsay, "'No Need . . . to Think of Home'? Masculinity and Domestic Life on the Nigerian Railway, c.1940–61," *JAH* 39 (1998): 439–66.

34. Francis Jaekel, *The History of the Nigerian Railway* (Ibadan: Spectrum Books Ltd., 1997), vol. 3, pp. 97 and 104–5. This driver, Thomas Shacklady, retired in 1954.

35. Wale Oyemakinde, "Railway Construction and Operation in Nigeria, 1895–1911: Labour Problems and Socio-Economic Impact," *JHSN* 7 (1974): 303–24, 320.

36. Appendix A: ALDFAWN Memorandum of the Association's Claim in Respect of Salaries and Conditions of Footplate Staff and Allied Workers, in Minutes of Third Stage Meeting between Management and ALDFAWN in June, July, September, October 1957, GMS 26/23.

37. A.U. Nnodua (retired locomotive driver), February 1, 1994; Jaekel, *History*, vol. 3, p. 114.

38. Animosity and competition for status between conductors, who were in charge of passengers and baggage, and engineers, who actually drove the machines, were legendary on other railroads. Walter Licht, *Working for the Railroad: The Organization of Work in the Nineteenth Century* (Princeton, NJ: Princeton University Press, 1983), p. 235.

39. Train Guards Union to GM, March 26, 1947, and C.B. Mosanya, General Secretary of the Train Guards Union to GM, November 12, 1947, both in GM 27, vol. 1.

40. "Annual Report of the Railway Station Staff Union Presented to the Sixth Annual Conference (2)," *WAP*, March 25, 1946. Train guards and workshop foremen were the lowest rank occupied by European railway men in Nigeria; in 1940 there were 194 Europeans in these grades. Jaekel, *History*, vol. 3, pp. 97–98.

41. C.B. Mosanya, General Secretary, Train Guards' Union to GM, November 12, 1947; minute, nn., nd; GM to General Secretary, TGU, December 22, 1947, all in GM 27, vol. 1.

42. M.O. Nola, NRC Ibadan Pension Office, personal communication, 1994.

43. D.A. Owolabi (former locomotive driver), January 20, 1994, Ibadan; Jaekel, *History*, vol. 3, pp. 140–41.

44. W.J. Lardner, Stores Superintendent to Traffic Manager, W.H. Best, December 30, 1947, GM 27, vol. 1; General Secretary, Train Guards Union to GM, December 16, 1952, GML 27/5, vol. 1.

Urban Labor, Extended Families, and the Differentiation of Domesticity 167

45. The request for servants was first reported in "Station Staff Gives the Sum of £21 to Zik's Press Fund," *WAP*, March 13, 1946. Minutes of meeting between Railway Labor Officer, W.A. Powell, and representatives of the Train Guards Union on November 19, 1946, GM 27, vol. 1. Descriptions of rest houses and cooking facilities in the 1940s and 1950s are in the same file.

46. "Officers on Line Accompanied by Wives," Ref. No. GMS 195/5/B1/2269, March 14, 1956, GMS 335 vol. 1.

47. Acting Traffic Manager to GM, January 24, 1947, GM 27, vol. 1. Woodward became general manager of the Nigerian Railway later that year.

48. Train Guards Union to GM, March 26, 1947, and Acting Traffic Manager to GM, April 4, 1947, GM 27, vol. 1.

49. General Secretary, Train Guards Union to GM, D.C. Woodward, December 20, 1951, and Chief Superintendent to Chief Secretary to the Organization, March 5, 1952, GMS 27, vol. 2; Jaekel, *History*, vol. 3, p. 113.

50. Railway Labor Officer to Traffic Manager, November 25, 1946, GM 27, vol. 1.

51. Similarly, at the Enugu Colliery, "pick boys" had their tools carried to work each day by "small boys." C.H. Croasdale, "Report on Labour at the Enugu Government Colliery" (1938), cited in Brown, "A 'Man' in the Village."

52. An overview is in Cooper, *Decolonization*.

53. In 1953, 79 percent of all Lagos households and 58 percent of wage earner households in Ibadan comprised one room. Nigeria, *Report on Enquiries into the Income and Expenditure Patters of Lower and Middle Income Households in Lagos, 1959–60* (Lagos: Federal Office of Statistics, 1963), p. 7; Nigeria, *Report on Enquiries into the Income and Expenditure Patters of Lower and Middle Income Households at Ibadan* (Lagos: Federal Office of Statistics, 1961/2), p. 6; Nigeria, *Urban Consumer Surveys in Nigeria: Report on Enquiries into the Income and Expenditure Patterns of Wage-Earner Households in Lagos [1953/54], Enugu [1954/55] and Ibadan [1955]* (Lagos: Federal Department of Statistics, 1957), p. 26.

54. Court cases sometimes reveal sleeping arrangements. Examples include CRB, Oke Are Court, vol. 20, 41/65, SGP v. Audu Sanni and eleven others, March 12, 1954, p. 47; and CvRB, Ojaba III Native Court, Oke Are (Ibadan), vol. ? [torn cover], 1/52, Okunola vs. Laduomi, December 5, 1952, p. 1.

55. On this phenomenon among migrants to Ife and Oshogbo in the 1960s, see A. Adepoju, "Some Aspects of Migration and Family Relationships in South-West Nigeria," *Legon Family Research Papers* 3 (1975): 148–56; on the women left behind in the town of Awe, see Niara Sudarkasa, *Where Women Work: A Study of Yoruba Women in the Marketplace and in the Home* (Ann Arbor: Museum of Anthropology, University of Michigan, 1973), pp. 129–30.

56. CvRB, Lagos Magistrate's Court 60B, 3485/49, E. Ibejianya vs. Samual Opara, September 20, 1949, p. 329.

57. In 1960, a pregnant woman by the name of Cecilia Ewezor brought her two children to the Ibadan Welfare Office to solicit help in locating her husband. They had moved to Ibadan from eastern Nigeria, and he worked for a time as a servant for a European official. After he went home on leave, he traveled to Lagos in search of work, promising to come back for his family after he found another job. He was employed by the NRC but never returned. This case prompted Jean Williams, a Lagos social welfare

officer, to meet with her counterpart in the NRC to discuss the rising number of cases in which railway staff neglected their wives and children, especially on transfer. Her estimate was that the Lagos Welfare Office was currently dealing with about forty such cases. Although the NRC officer, T.O. Songunuga, pledged his cooperation in tracking down renegade railway men, he also stressed that the corporation had no machinery for doing so and suggested that it was none of its business. J.O. Sowunmi, Family Welfare Officer, Ibadan Province to Family Welfare Officer, Family Welfare Office in Lagos, October 7, 1960, forwarded to NRC Welfare Officer, October 15, 1960; L. Jean Williams, Social Welfare Officer, Family Welfare Services, Lagos to NRC Welfare Officer, October 15, 1960; minute to NRC Senior Labor Relations Officer from T.O. Songunuga, Welfare Officer, October 28, 1960; all in GMS 360, vol. 3. See Lisa A. Lindsay, "Putting the Family on Track: Gender and Domestic Life on the Colonial Nigerian Railway" (Ph.D. dissertation, University of Michigan, 1996), pp. 220–21.

58. A dispute between a Lagos port worker and his wife, which ended up in court, revolved around accusations of improper relations between the wife and a townsman of the husband who shared their Apapa Road room with them. CvRB, Yaba Magistrate's Court No. 1, vol. ? [torn cover], 2545/59, Eunice E. Emmanuel vs. Dennis Okpara, March 10, 1961, pp. 21–34.

59. Memorandum by the RWU to the Gorsuch Commission, November 1, 1954, GMS 337/8.

60. Acting General Secretary, RWUN to GM, July 9, 1951 and Acting GM to Acting General Secretary, RWUN, August 1, 1951, GML 24/9 vol. 1; "Railwaymen Want their Own Quarters," *DTN*, July 24, 1951; Minutes of Third Stage Departmental Council held between representatives of management and the RWU, September 11–October 8, 1952, GMS 24/18, vol. 1; S. Olaolu Oduleye, Secretary General of NUR to GM, July 10, 1962, GMS 302/5, vol. 1.

61. Francis Soetan (railway trackman from 1932 to 1945, and thereafter an inspector in the Permanent Way department until retirement in 1970), April 12, 1994, Ibadan.

62. Minutes of meeting of Departmental Staff Council between Chief Engineer and representatives of the Permanent Way Workers Union held on April 12, 1958, GML 29/2, vol. 1.

63. Luke Emujulu, Acting General Secretary, RWUN to GM, September 12, 1946, SC 24.12; Olukemi Alabi (daughter of railway track foreman, who died in 1952), March 3, 1994, Ibadan; C. Okei-Achamba, General Secretary, Nigerian Railway Permanent Way Workers' Union to GM, March 21, 1963, GMS 29/14, vol. 12.

64. Eunice Soetan (wife of a career railway track worker), April 19, 1994, Ibadan.

65. Acting Chief Superintendent to District Superintendents, June 18, 1954, GML 24/9, vol. 1; GM to CME, June 26, 1958, and Acting General Secretary, RWUN to Chief Engineer, October 8, 1954, both in unmarked SLRO (Senior Labor Relations Officer) file.

66. Jaekel, *History*, vol. 3, p. 112; Extract from Minutes of Joint Industrial Staff Council between NRC and NUR(F) on April 28–May 6, 1959, GMS 302/5, vol. 1.

67. African Staff Housing Scheme Regulations, 1948–50, CSO 26/2 10056/S.3, vol.1; Staff Housing Scheme Regulations, 1957, GMS 302/5, vol. 1; Acting GM to Heads of Departments, January 12, 1960, unnumbered SLRO file; Secretary to NRC to GM and Heads of Departments, October 18, 1963, and GM to Heads of Departments, December 31, 1969, GML 302/33, vol. 1.

68. Nigerian Maritime Trade Unions Federation, "Memorandum submitted to the Morgan Commission for Salaries Revision," n.d. [1963], NLA/42.

69. Margaret Peil, *Lagos: The City Is the People* (Boston, MA: G.K. Hall, 1991), pp. 158, 167–69; Akin Mabogunje, *Urbanization in Nigeria* (London: University of London Press, 1968), p. 302.

70. Peter Marris, *Family and Social Change in an African City: A Study of Rehousing in Lagos* (Evanston, IL: Northwestern University Press, 1962).

71. *Report on Enquiries . . . Lagos (1959/60)*, p. 25; *Report on the Enquiry . . . Ibadan (1961/62)*, p. 23; T.M. Yesufu, "Consumption Patterns and Living Conditions of Employees of the Nigerian Tobacco Company Ltd." (Lagos: NTCL, 1967), p. 23; P.O. Ohadike, "Urbanization: Growth, Transitions and Problems of a Premier West African City, Lagos, Nigeria," *Urban Affairs Quarterly* 3 (1968): 69–90, 83. Also see Adepoju, "Some Aspects," p. 150, and Kenneth Little, "Some Urban Patterns of Marriage and Domesticity in West Africa," *Sociological Review* 7 (1959): 65–82.

72. For Nigeria, see Bird, "Social Change," and a critique in Ekong, "Continuity and Change." For Africa more generally, see Goode, *World Revolution*, and M. Osmond, "Correlates of Types of Marriage," *Social Forces* 44 (1965): 8–15.

73. R. Galletti, K. D. S. Baldwin, and I. O. Dina, *Nigerian Cocoa Farmers: An Economic Survey of Yoruba Cocoa Farming Families* (London: Oxford University Press, 1956), p. 72; Marris, *Family and Social Change*, p. 158.

74. Lindsay, "Putting the Family," pp. 202–5.

75. Karin Barber, *The Generation of Plays: Yoruba Popular Life in Theater* (Bloomington: Indiana University Press, 2000), p. 283.

76. P.O. Ohadike, "A Demographic Note on Marriage, Family and Family Growth in Lagos, Nigeria," in J.C. Caldwell and C. Okojo (eds.), *The Population of Tropical Africa* (London: Longman, 1968), p. 381.

77. Folasade Tade (who lived in such a household herself), June 1, 1994, Lagos; "Timesman Report," *DTN*, July 1, 1955.

78. In Marris's survey, 25 percent of central Lagos households included the children of relatives. Marris, *Family and Social Change*, p. 161. For Ibadan, see Barbara Lloyd, "Indigenous Ibadan," in P.C. Lloyd, A.L. Mabogunje and B. Awe (eds.), *The City of Ibadan* (Ibadan: Institute of African Studies, 1967), p. 68. For fostering in the small Yoruba town of Awe, see Sudarkasa, *Where Women Work*, pp. 139–40.

79. Ayo Salako, February 15, 1994, Ibadan.

80. Forty-six percent received child care assistance from live-in relatives, as opposed to 24 percent from unrelated live-in help, 16 percent from nonresident kin, and 18 percent from unrelated nonresident help.

81. Okojie to Sobowale, November 18, 1966, and other correspondence in Francis Akinlabi's personnel file, WP 9097, Ibadan Pension Office, NRC, emphasis in the original. See Lindsay, "'No Need.'"

82. N.I. Sumonu Animasaun, July 6, 1998, Ibadan.

83. Mechanical Department Staff Circular No. 52/1960, "Canteen Facilities: Irregular Use," GML 335/2 v. 2.

84. This is substantiated by interviews and observations as well as by the story of Mrs. D.O. Fowokan, recounted in R.S. Ourbo Eze, General Secretary of the Association of Nigerian Railway Clerical Staff, to GM, September 22, 1954, GML 28/13. Mrs. Fowokan was the wife of a clerk who became embroiled in a dispute over railway housing. Allegedly in an attempt to reallocate their quarters to a member of the station staff, the couple was evicted on the grounds that Mrs. Fowokan was selling food on the station premises to laborers working there. In defense, the union official representing Mr.

Fowokan argued that such activity was a general practice throughout the railway system and no one had ever been evicted for it before. Eventually the eviction order was rescinded, but Mr. Fowokan was ordered to ensure that his wife no longer traded on railway premises.

85. Transport Staff Union to General Manager, September 30, 1959; Union of Domestic Servants to GM, October 21, 1959; and Railway Police Superintendent to GM, October 27, 1959, GMS 360, vol. 3.

86. "Union Leaders Mob Railway Chief," *WAP*, November 7, 1961; "Imoudu and Adebola in New Uproar," *MP*, November 7, 1961, and editorial, *DTN*, November 8, 1961; personal correspondence from Francis Jaekel (former Chief Superintendent, Nigerian Railway), March 17, 1995.

87. H.R. Rishworth, *A Report on Medical and Sanitary Conditions on the Nigerian Railway with Recommendations for a Railway Medical Service*. Wightman Mountain Ltd., 1955.

88. S. Olaolu Oduleye, Secretary-Treasurer of NUR(F) to John A. Dryden, Chief Medical Officer, August 4, 1959, GMS 302/22 vol. 1. This request and the response to it reveals starkly different visions of what fatherhood entailed. Dryden, the Chief Medical Officer, wrote to General Manager Emerson, "It does not appear to me that it should normally be necessary for the fathers to take the children. . . . Why cannot the mothers undertake these responsibilities and not waste Corporation's time?" Emerson agreed, telling the union that fathers should not take their children for medical treatment. "Where it became necessary for this to be done," he wrote, "their mothers can undertake these responsibilities, and the older children within the age-group mentioned can always attend such clinics [un]accompanied." Dryden to Emerson, Confidential, August 12, 1959, and Emerson to Oduleye, August 20, 1959, both in GMS 302/22, vol. 1. See Lindsay, "'No Need.'"

89. General Manager's Staff Circular 6/1961, June 13, 1961, GMS 335/3, vol. 9. Oduleye, Secretary-General, NUR(F) to GM, July 11, 1961, and W.E. Mornu, District Secretary, NUR(F) Eastern District, to Oduleye and GM, July 20, 1961, GMS 302/22, vol. 1. "Railway Union Protests Against Medical Ban," *DTN*, July 25, 1961.

90. Acting GM to Chief Medical Officer, August 29, 1961, GMS 302/22, vol. 1; Acting GM to Heads of Departments, June 29, 1965, unnumbered SLRO file labeled "Staff Manual"; "Free Medical Care for Daily Paid Men," *DTN*, May 19, 1964; "Railway Medical Centre a Waste," *DTN*, March 3, 1965. As of December 1965, additional wives were treated at 25 percent of hospital fees. GMSC No. 9/1965, December 13, 1965, unnumbered SLRO file labeled "Staff Manual."

91. Press Release 71, July 17, 1961, "Railway Medical Service," GMS 335/3, vol. 9.

92. Ekundare, *Economic History*, p. 364; Peter Kilby, "The Nigerian Labourer," *Ibadan* 10 (1960): 23–24. Also see Yesufu, *Introduction*, p. 120.

93. Yesufu, "Consumption Patterns," p. 24.

94. Yesufu, *Introduction*, p. 120.

95. Personnel file of Rufus Adewale Awoboyade, WP 6330, Ibadan Pension Office, NRC.

96. For more details, see Lindsay, "Putting the Family," pp. 245–48.

97. Report of the Seventh Annual Delegates Conference of Nigerian Transport Clerical Staff Union held in Lagos, 9–11 July 1955, GMS 28/6; M.O. Shofekun, April 4, 1994, Ibadan; A.U. Nnodua, February 1 1994, Ibadan, quoted.

98. M.O. Shofekun (employed by the Nigerian Railway from 1942 to 1977), April 4, 1994, Ibadan.

99. Felix Elue, April 8, 1994, Ibadan. It also could be that the small amount of leave for which casual workers were eligible in 1958 (a week, in most cases) was insufficient time for many to travel home and back.

100. Nigeria, *Annual Report on the Department of Labor for the Year 1957–58*, p. 53; Ayo Salako, April 12, 1994, Ibadan. Also see Adrian J. Peace, *Choice, Class and Conflict: A Study of Southern Nigerian Factory Workers* (Brighton, Eng.: Harvester Press, 1979), ch. 3, which describes the attempts of migrant workers in Lagos to evade financial responsibilities in their hometowns.

101. *Report on the Enquiry . . . Ibadan (1961/62)*; Yesufu, *Introduction*, pp. 11–12; Ayo Salako, April 12, 1994, Ibadan.

102. Asuquo O. Ita, "Labour Disunity in Nigeria," *WAP*, January 21, 1959.

103. *Annual Report on the Department of Labour, Nigeria, for the Year 1958–59*, pp. 22–23.

104. "Advertiser's Announcement: Action Group Welfare Series (9): Old Age Pension," *DTN*, September 24, 1959.

105. Onuora Nzekwu, *Blade among the Boys* (London: Heinemann, 1972 [1962]), p. 156.

106. Yesufu, "Consumption Patterns," p. 13; *Urban Consumer Surveys in Nigeria*, pp. 15–16.

107. David Omoruyi, "Long Day in the Life of a Pensioner," *Drum* (December 1962): 31–32.

108. Daniel Mowela, Tally No. 9, Carriage and Wagon fitter, Ebute Metta to Railway Labor Officer, July 15, 1948, in unnumbered file marked "recruitment"; D.A. Owolabi, January 20, 1994, Ibadan.

109. Flora Nwapa, "A Soldier Returns Home," in *This is Lagos and Other Stories* (Trenton, NJ: Africa World Press, 1992 [1971]), p. 113.

110. Adetunji and Felicia Adeyemi, February 11, 1994, Ibadan. Also see Dan R. Aronson's examination of Ijebu migrants in Ibadan, *The City Is Our Farm: Seven Migrant Ijebu Yoruba Families* (Cambridge, MA: Schenkman, 1978).

111. M.O. Shofekun, April 4, 1994, Ibadan. In Ghana as well, by the early 1970s railway retirees stayed in Sekondi rather than returning home. Richard Jeffries, *Class, Power and Ideology in Ghana: The Railwaymen of Sekondi* (Cambridge: Cambridge University Press, 1978), 17. For more on hometown retirements in Yorubaland, and the particular importance of owning a house, see Margaret Peil, Stephen K. Ekpenyong, and Olotunji Y. Oyeneye, "Going Home: Migration Careers of Southern Nigerians," *International Migration Review* 22 (1988): 563–85.

112. Pension office files indicated that a former railway employee had retired in his hometown either by the authorization for repatriation assistance or by the fact that the current address matched the reported hometown. See Lindsay, "Putting the Family," pp. 272–74, and also "'No Need.'"

113. Bernth Lindfors and Oyekan Owomoyela, *Yoruba Proverbs: Translation and Annotation*, Papers in International Studies, Africa Series No. 17 (Athens: Ohio University Center for International Studies, 1973).

114. For one personal account of the excitement of that period, see Chief Simeon O. Adebo, *Our Unforgettable Years* (Lagos: Macmillan, 1984). Adebo was then head of the Western Region's civil service.

115. A.U. Nnodua, February 1, 1994, Ibadan; M.O. Shofekun, April 4, 1994, Ibadan. Wale Oyemakinde has asserted that the basis of railway men's sense of occupational community from its earliest years was this modernizing ethos. "The Railway Workers and Modernization in Colonial Nigeria," *JHSN* 10 (1979): 113–24.

116. "The Modern Nigerian Home," *DTN*, May 30, 1964.

117. "The Changing Family Pattern," *WAP*, January 17, 1959. Respondents to John Peel's 1974 survey in Ilesha also highlighted the detrimental, as well as liberating, effects of *ọ̀lajú*. One opined, "There's no respect for us elders as there used to be—our children are 'enlightened' beyond measure" (*Eè si ibọ 'ọ fun ian agba mọ bi ti atijọ—ian ọmọ ria ti laju aala odi*). Peel, *"Olaju,"* p. 143.

118. James Ojiako, "More Money: Do Workers Deserve It?" *DTN*, October 29, 1963.

119. F.O. Majekodunmi, "The Social Background of Industrial Relations," *The Railway Technician (Monthly Journal of the Railway Technical Staff Association)* 43 (September 1961): 7, 11, 12, in GMS 31, vol. 1; see Lindsay, "'No Need.'"

120. Barber, *Generation of Plays*, p. 235.

7

DOMESTICITY AND DIFFERENCE RECONFIGURED: THE 1964 GENERAL STRIKE

For thirteen days in June 1964, approximately 800,000 Nigerian wage-earners participated in a general strike.[1] The strike took place in the context of palpable discontent with Nigeria's first national government, regional political instability, escalating ethnic tensions, and widespread corruption. After more than a year of agitation, trade unionists called the work stoppage to press for improved wages and a mitigation of the enormous gaps between the top echelons and the rest of the employment structure. Strikers accused the government and elites of greed and of neglecting the needs of workers. They made explicit reference to the general strike of 1945, which had forced significant wage and benefit concessions from the British colonial government.

As I detailed in chapter 4, during the general strike of 1945 gender, nationalism, and economic demands were intimately connected, although in some contradictory ways. Striking men demanded wages and benefits by referring to themselves as family providers, even though most married women contributed to household budgets and the support of market women was critical in the strike's success. Trade union leaders demanded that the government pay family allowances to workers, not only because these were necessary to facilitate social reproduction, but also because European officials in Nigeria received them and Nigerian activists claimed that they were family providers just as expatriate men were. In response, the colonial government stressed the differences between African and European families, suggesting that Nigerian workers were not eligible for breadwinner wages and family allowances because they did not really support their families. Thus the demands of Nigerian workers and the responses of the government centered on particular notions of working class masculinity.

Most Nigerian workers did not receive family allowances after the 1945 strike, as we have seen. But in 1950 certain senior Nigerian officials became eligible for them, and in the decade before independence, as expatriates were phased out of top governmental and business positions, increasing numbers of highly placed Nigerians gained access to the type of perquisites previously reserved for Europeans. Many of these benefits—like family allowances, subsidized housing, and free medical care for dependents—allowed top officials and highly skilled workers to support a kind of family life aspired to, but beyond the reach of, most Nigerian wage earners. In the general strike of 1964, not only did workers demand increased wages, job security, and promotion prospects, but they also called for the *abolition* of family allowances and other such benefits for top officials. What had been in 1945 a symbol of the common masculinity of all employed men—African and European alike—changed within two decades into one of several representations of the differences between the *haves* and *have nots*. Further, in 1945 workers argued, somewhat optimistically, that they *did* support wives and children and therefore needed family allowances in addition to wage increases. In 1964, the lowest-paid workers argued that they *wanted to* support families but could not do so, although other men could. The national government could not respond, as colonials had done in 1945, that top families were inherently different than bottom ones. Instead, political leaders focused on the government's ability to pay and the need for unified patriotism. By trying to paint the strikers as selfish and unwilling to make sacrifices on behalf of the new nation, the administration implied that those on the lowest pay scales would have to forego certain kinds of highly valued masculinity in the national interest.

What kind of family the striking workers wanted to support had also changed since 1945. In the earlier strike, Nigerian trade unionists compared their conditions with those of expatriates. This tactic made it necessary to stress working men's support for wives and children, since European family allowances were focused on such family members. But in 1964, the point of comparison for striking workers was instead Nigerian top officials. Trade unionists now talked about family commitments as extending to a broad range of relatives, such as those helped along by local "big men." Moreover, trade unionists no longer insisted so strongly that workers were breadwinners for wives and children, now that they were negotiating with other Nigerians who knew very well that most men's wages were inadequate to support entire households and that the dependents to be funded included parents and kinsmen as well as wives and children. In this strike as always, the political context shaped the articulation of masculinity.

One irony in 1964 was that working men stressed their financial linkages to a broad range of people, but the community support for the strike was far less unanimous than it had been in 1945, when strikers had insisted that their financial support went to a fairly narrow group in the nuclear family. This is exemplified by the role of women. As I have argued, market women were indispensable to the success of the 1945 strike, in spite of the unions' insistence that men supported nonworking wives. But women had their own grievances against the colonial government, and these contributed to a strong coalition between nationalist parties, market women's organizations, and trade unions. Nearly twenty years later, many market women also opposed the federal government, and some of their leaders expressed support for the strike. But the main financial support for strikers came from their own resources, international contributions, and from political groups opposed to the government. Moreover, in the end the strike lasted less than two weeks, as opposed to six in 1945, and strikers won the major concession of being paid for the period they refused to work. The differentiation and professionalization of the labor force meant that strikers did not need resources from market women as badly in 1964 as they had in 1945. It also meant that the government could point to the differences between wage earners and other segments of the population—in particular, "housewives" and farmers—in an effort to isolate the strikers from potential support networks. That this strategy did not work to contain the strike does not negate the point that the differentiation of the wage labor force had undermined its previous links across lines of gender and wealth.

POLITICS AND LABOR IN THE FIRST REPUBLIC

What had happened to the optimistic predictions about Nigeria's independence? The political failures of the First Republic have become infamous. As Nigeria's federal structure solidified during the 1950s, the three regions became closely linked with three major parties: the Northern People's Congress (NPC) in the north; the National Council of Nigerian Citizens (NCNC), led by Nnamdi Azikiwe and based in the east but aspiring for national prominence; and the Action Group (AG), led by Obafemi Awolowo, in the west. Each of these parties controlled its respective region's government. The federal elections of 1959 brought in a central administration led by the NPC in coalition with the NCNC, with Abubakar Tafawa Balewa as prime minister and Azikiwe as a largely ceremonial president. But by 1961 the NPC had a working majority in the federal parliament, and its alliance with the NCNC fell apart. Political strength translated into patronage, both for the region of the party in power and for individuals who used access to the government for their own enrichment. Since both electoral strength and the allocation of national revenue among the regions were based upon population figures, the census—begun in 1962 but then re-done in 1963—was heavily contested and politicized. Meanwhile, politics in the Western Region became openly chaotic. After Awolowo resigned as regional premier in 1959 to compete in the federal arena, Chief S.L. Akintola succeeded him and consolidated his own power. The developing rivalry between the two was based on personal and ideological differences, as well as Akintola's willingness to ally with the NPC. When Akintola's AG opponents attempted to remove him as premier in May 1962, his supporters in the regional House of Assembly staged a riot in order to disrupt the proceedings. The federal government dissolved the House, proclaimed an emergency, suspended the governor, and appointed an administrator to run the regional government. In November 1962, Awolowo was arrested and charged with treason. In June 1963, he was sentenced to ten years' imprisonment, by which time Akintola had been reinstated as premier.[2]

Wage earners, along with numerous others, resented the conspicuous displays of opulence by the elites, particularly rich parliamentarians and government ministers. Politicians and businessmen erected expensive buildings and bought luxury cars for themselves, their family members, and even their mistresses. As far as many workers were concerned, they had merely replaced the old colonial masters with comparable nationalist politicians. As the pamphlet of even a moderate trade union put it in 1962, "Independence Day, October first 1960, freed us from colonial domination. It did not, unfortunately, free us automatically from colonial institutions. The edifice of privilege remains; only its proprietors are different."[3]

Organized labor's grievances against the government concerned both its role as employer and as the administration. First, wage labor continued to be concentrated in the public sector, with 54 percent of all wage earners employed by the federal, regional, and local governments of the federation. Thus, workers looked to the state for improvements in wages and benefits, and private sector employees usually demanded that their employers follow practices set in government establishments. But the leaders of the First Republic resisted granting improvements to wage earners. Though the cost of living had been going up constantly, wages stayed the same through the early 1960s. When the government launched the six-year development plan in 1962, it openly declared that pay increases would have to be deferred in order to nourish capitalist profits and investment. Yet the administration was paying European-type salaries to higher civil servants, and in 1963, top officials received a 10 percent pay increase. Organized labor's second broad grievance concerned the 38 percent of the labor force employed in European-owned private firms. When the government did not back workers' demands for higher wages from European employers, it became vulnerable to accusations of corruption and neocolonialism.[4]

Although wage earners still were a small minority of the economically active Nigerian population (about 3 percent in 1963), their significance was magnified in the cities. In 1963, wage earners comprised, on average, about a quarter of the urban population in the two southern regions and about 30 percent of the population of Lagos.[5] But organized labor was in a weak position to demand wage increases and structural changes, largely because through the 1950s and into the 1960s it had become highly factionalized. Soon after the 1945 general strike, the pan-union Trade Union Congress disintegrated into two factions, prefigured by the dispute over strategy between Imoudu and Bankole (see chapter 4). The TUC managed to survive until 1949, when it finally broke up over the issue of affiliation with the NCNC—a step favored by the Imoudu faction and opposed by a more politically moderate group. This pattern of splitting and regrouping and then splitting all over again then became a constant element in the Nigerian labor movement, with basically the same individuals fighting over the same issues, but with ever-changing and proliferating organizations. Through the 1950s the divisions in the trade union movement were exacerbated by the ideological conflicts of the Cold War, most frequently articulated in disputes about whether and with whom the unions should make international affiliations. Critics accused trade union leaders of lacking interest in the health of the constituent unions, self-serving rivalry for leadership, and a desire for a personal share in funds coming from abroad.[6] The weakness of the unions was further compounded by the fact that wage and benefit gains were often made through political agitation and government commissions, making politics and political networks the operative sphere for unionism rather than industrial relations.[7] And as Nigeria's formerly broad movement of anticolonialism disintegrated into political rivalries, nationalist sentiment no longer helped to unify unions and members. As one commentator wrote in 1959, "the alliance between unionism and nationalism has been broken for good."[8]

DIFFERENTIATION AND DISCONTENT

As much as they disagreed over international affiliation and personal politics, the unions did share a broad critique of the imbalances in the wage structure and the resulting hardships for junior level and unestablished workers. The Independence Manifesto of the moderate Trade Union Congress of Nigeria (TUCN) included broad recommendations on the national economy, foreign policy, development programs, and the trade union movement. It particularly condemned the inequalities in the wage structure and reaffirmed the union's demands for improved conditions of employment, a national minimum wage, increased labor stabilization, and equal pay for work of equal value without discrimination on account of sex. The more radical Nigerian Trade Union Congress (NTUC) made largely the same demands, but in addition called attention to workers' concerns about housing, Nigerianisation, vocational training, and unemployment.[9]

Both of these umbrella unions consistently argued that the living conditions of the lowest paid workers were untenable, and they contrasted these to the extravagant salaries, allowances, and benefits paid to senior officials. In January 1961 the TUCN set up a committee to investigate the structure and pay of wage employment. The resulting report of the "Zudonu Committee" argued that the wage structure caused resentment among personnel in the junior segment of the public services and that the gap in pay and benefits between the junior and senior services had only grown over time. The committee argued that the wage structure should be reconstituted so as to guarantee a living wage for the lowest class of workers, based on monthly budget devised for an "average worker" plus extra amounts necessary to maintain family members. Further, it suggested increased public transport and expanded provisions for low-cost housing in order to ease the financial burdens of the lowest paid. The commission argued that the country could afford its recommended minimum wage and other reforms by cutting the salaries and perquisites attached to top posts. A memorandum by the NTUC, submitted the same month, went even further. In calling for a national minimum wage, it asserted that "there are some workers in our Federation today whose policy is to eat only a single meal a day because their pay is incapable of sustaining anything beyond this. Others, with their families, share the same under-sized rooms with several working families because they cannot maintain one room exclusively." The union demanded wage increases and some job reclassifications, the establishment of a Ministry of Housing, and rapid Nigerianization of senior posts. Finally, the NTUC memorandum called for more job opportunities for the unemployed, the abolition of daily paid labor, and the provision of transport, leave, and free medical facilities for workers currently ineligible for them.[10]

The major labor organizations spent the next two years making unsuccessful attempts to join together. By 1963, the central unions had been reconfigured again, intensifying their agitation as the federal government became increasingly authoritarian.[11] The politically moderate United Labor Congress (ULC), led by H.P. ("Horse Power") Adebola and L.L. Borha, published in July 1963 an open letter to all political leaders, legislators, and the governments of the federation. The union reminded the political elite "that in the long-drawn struggle for national independence, the workers of Nigeria fought side-by-side with you," and then sharply condemned the recently passed Preventive Detention Act and the proposal for a "national government" which would remove official opposition from the federal parliament. Its final area of focus was the "Economic Distress of the Workers," reminding the government that "there is enough for the need of all but not for the greed of the few." The union warned that class polarization could have political consequences: "In your luxurious surroundings, in your residential palaces far removed from the squalor of the worker's living conditions, from his privation and generally depressed economic condition, you, dear compatriots, may be sitting on a powder-keg. . . . We want you to understand the present, and live it in accordance with the tenets of social and economic justice, so that we can all avoid the catastrophes of tomorrow."[12] The ULC demanded a commission of inquiry into the wage structure, as the unions had been doing since independence, pointing out that parliamentarians and members of the senior service had received direct salary increases of between 64 and 100 percent since 1955, whereas the average worker had received increases of not more than 25 percent. These calculations did not even include additional allowances added to the pay of the senior service. As O. Zudonu, the industrial relations expert who had written the 1961 memorandum for the TUCN, pointed out, "Under the present obnoxious wage structure a foreman or work supervisor earns at least 8 times more than the skilled worker he supervises and about 14 times more than the semi-skilled worker he supervises. Besides, the foreman draws a chain of allowances. Yet both the foreman and those he supervises buy from the same market and have identical basic responsibilities to their families and to the nation."[13]

Indeed, allowances had become a major symbol of the differences between the upper ranks of the employment structure and the rest, and protests over inequities in allowances bridged the colonial and independence periods. As already mentioned, in 1954 the colonial government reaffirmed the eligibility of certain top Nigerians for children's allowances but resisted pressure to extend them to all Nigerian employees (as was done in French West Africa in 1956[14]). At a 1957 mass meeting of 5,000 Lagos railwaymen centered on wage levels, the keynote speaker also stressed that lower echelon workers should be entitled to the children's, food, and other allowances enjoyed by senior officials. Taking up the demand trade unions had been making for nearly twenty years, the Action Group included family allowances for all workers in its 1959 "Welfare State Proposals."[15] But the children's allowance system remained unchanged during the First Republic, and between 1960 and 1963, the federal and regional governments paid a combined total of nearly £1.5 million on them.

The greatest expenditures on allowances, however, were for cars. The governments of the federation offered loans to senior civil servants so that they could purchase vehicles, on the grounds that poor public transport and their job requirements made cars necessary. Then the governments paid these officials a supplement called the Motor Car Basic Allowance to enable them to repay the loans, and in addition paid a mileage allowance when they used their cars in executing official duties. Car allowances alone were often higher than the monthly salary of a clerk or technician in government service. In the first three years of independence, the governments of the federation paid out over £4 million in Motor Car Basic Allowances.[16]

Senior administrative and technical officials also received a range of other allowances as well as, frequently, government housing provided at subsidized rates. The Nigerian Railway Corporation was often singled out as the establishment with the most profligate spending on allowances and perquisites for senior officials. At the prompting of the Nigerian Union of Railwaymen, the labor officer in 1957 drew up a list of staff allowances—an impressive testament to the differentiation of the labor and benefit structure on the railway—yet no reforms were made (see Table 7.1).[17]

The rank-and-file's resentment of the differences between what the railway administration spent on salaries and additions for its top officials (nearly all Europeans), and what it paid the rest of the workforce came to a head in the closing days of the colonial period. In the December 1959 "Emerson Must Go" demonstration, between 5,000 and 10,000 railway workers and their supporters (depending on whose figures one uses) clashed with riot police in and around the Ebute Metta (Lagos) railway headquarters. The Nigerian Union of Railwaymen (NUR) made three basic demands: the removal of the corporation's chairman, Ralf Emerson, because he lived in Britain and his travel and salary expenses were far beyond what a Nigerian in his place would have required; an acceleration of the NRC's slow policy of Nigerianization; and an end to the massive retrenchment of daily-paid workers and Africans in the permanent establishment, begun in September in response to financial crisis. The bloody demonstration led to the appointment of a commission of inquiry whose report strongly criticized the NRC for mismanagement, corruption, and poor labor relations. Among its recommendations were the replacement of top officials with Nigerians, a halt to the retrenchment program until a new one could be worked out with the participation of the labor unions, and a careful review of the allowances paid to senior staff.[18]

In August 1961, the new NRC chairman, Dr. Okechukwu Ikejiani, announced that many of the allowances formerly granted to senior officials, including children's allowances for non-expatriates, would be abolished as part of a general austerity drive. Other allowances were to be limited, including the car basic allowance, and paid leave was curtailed to one month for senior officials and two weeks for clerks. Ikejiani described such allowances and benefits as a "colonial hand over and privilege" and estimated that these reforms would save the NRC over £500,000 per year.[19] Yet two months later, the railway administration announced plans to lay off 2,000 railway men in an effort to lower wage costs.[20]

Over the next two years, the grievances as well as the squabbling of the major trade union organizations were mirrored within the railway labor force, whose unions vied with one another even as they protested the injustices of the employment structure. In fact, several of the most prominent leaders of the central trade union organizations in the early 1960s were based in railway unions: Alhaji H.P. Adebola represented the Railway and Ports Transport and Clerical Staffs Union, L.L. Borha came from the Locomotive Drivers

Table 7.1 Railway Staff Allowances, 1957

Allowance	To Whom
baggage	officers
rent	officers
children (separate domicile)	officers
assisted passages (children)	officers
hospitality/guest of government	officers
outfit	officers
home-port of embarkation	officers
personal	officers
rest house or catering	officers
refund of airport service	officers
visit to factory	officers
entertainment	officers
acting	officers/servants
traveling or night	officers/servants
detention	officers/servants
lecture	officers/servants
transport	officers/servants
ex-gratia (lieu of overtime)	officers/servants
subsistence	officers/servants
overtime	servants
shed duty	servants
aggregation	servants
motor vehicle	officers
motor mileage	officers
ex-gratia payment	officers
nonpensionable	officers
higher grade duty	servants
shorthand	servants
fire protection (pay office)	servants
pay-rip	servants
tools	servants
height	servants
compensation (track gang)	servants
machine (press)	servants
brick factory	servants
dirt	servants
heat	servants
mileage	servants
rest	servants
breach of rest	servants
on call	servants
cancellation of trains	servants
torch	servants
"no accident" (drivers, mechanics)	

Union, and Michael Imoudu was legendary as head of the Railway and Port Workers Union. Other leaders were based in other public sector trade unions: Wahab Goodluck in the Public Utility and Public Works Departments and Gogo Nzeribe as general secretary of the Posts and Telegraphs Workers' Union.

MASCULINITY AND WORKER DIGNITY: THE MORGAN COMMISSION

Although women's participation in wage labor doubled in the first years of independence (from 3.5 percent of the formal sector workforce in 1959 to 7.2 percent in 1963),[21] paid employment and trade unionism in Nigeria remained largely masculine preserves. Precise statistics on the numbers of female trade union members in the early 1960s are not available, but all commentators on the subject agree with A.O. Okoronkwo that "trade unionism has been regarded as the prerogative of men" since official Nigerian unionism began. In part this was due to the small numbers of women in unionized jobs, but sex discrimination, women's household obligations and thus lack of free time for meetings, and the rough and confrontational style of many unions also discouraged women from taking part in labor organizations.[22] The practical equation of organized labor and masculinity meant that workers' concerns could be articulated through reference to men's roles and obligations as a matter of course. Indeed, through the early 1960s trade unionists elaborated a vision of the working class that included women not as members but as dependents.

Through the early 1960s, labor's demands focused on the dignity and economic security of wage earners; and as in 1945, these were often expressed through reference to men's ability to support their families. In a 1962 memorandum, for instance, Michael Imoudu argued that the government needed to set wages which would reduce the income gap between upper and lower level earners "because the senior service wives and the junior service wives buy from the same market."[23] The ULC's July 1963 letter to the politicians began, "Our fight for freedom was dedicated to the proposition that every worker, every citizen, in independent Nigeria must be a man of dignity with the right to the pursuit of, and guaranteed the means to attain, happiness in individual liberty and freedom." Then the union detailed what it meant by this: "that he will be a man who can raise a family in congenial surroundings, in a comfortable home, assured that his children will possess equal opportunity in education, in business and in politics; that he and his family will enjoy a fair share of the national prosperity, secure and free from hardship, privation and wants; that he must know he is the happy citizen of a great new nation."[24] In this document the ULC explicitly elided being a worker with masculinity, citizenship, and fatherhood. A contributor to the *West African Pilot* enumerated similar basic goals for Nigerian workers: a fair salary, the ability to feed and educate children, decent housing, medical care for oneself and one's offspring, and protection from victimization at work. Yet, this commentator argued, insufficient wages and living conditions, along with poor political and union leadership, undermined wage-earners' abilities to provide for their families. "Nigerian workers . . . want bread and butter and not only speeches and conferences," he concluded.[25] As a letter to another newspaper put it, "As a Nigerian, the Prime Minister should know that an average worker lives from hand to mouth. He should know that an average worker occupies one room with his wife, five children. It is from the worker's meagre salary that he buys medicine and food for his family and pays the monthly exorbitant rents." Under these circumstances, workers needed not only wage increases but also rent and price controls.[26] Another columnist called not only for revision of the wage scale, but also for family allowances for married wage-earners who had children, at levels set according to the scale of "responsibilities." Like the previous commentator, he emphasized the financial importance of fathers, not mentioning any contributions likely provided by their wives. Poor wages and unemployment, he wrote, create "disorder" in the family and potentially lead to crime, as workers with many dependents need more money than their wages can provide.[27]

The agitation for wage increases intensified through the middle of 1963. On October 1, 1963, Nigeria became a republic. As this day approached, a rumor spread among junior government employees that they would receive a cash bonus as part of the celebrations. When Prime Minister Balewa summarily dismissed this possibility, workers talked of boycotting the celebrations, or even going on strike to embarrass the government. At this point, the trade union leaders took command of the protest movement, forming themselves into the Joint Action Committee (JAC), an ad hoc agglomeration of the existing central labor organizations and the major national unions. The JAC went beyond the agitation for a one-time wage bonus, and instead demanded that the federal government set up an enquiry into wages and salaries. If this were not done, the JAC threatened to call a strike for September 27—which it did. The strike lasted until October 3 before the government, concerned with its international image on an occasion when many foreign visitors were present, agreed to institute a wage commission.

The original JAC demand had been for a review of the entire wage and salary structure, anticipating reductions for the highest paid along with gains for the lowest paid. The government, however, confined the inquiry's terms of reference to junior employees. An independent commission headed by Chief Justice Adeyinka Morgan of the Western Region High Court began its hearings in October. Over the next seven months, the commission received

258 memoranda and heard testimony from fifty-five people representing the JAC, other unions, the governments and statutory corporations of the federation, and the expatriate-dominated Nigerian Employers' Consultative Association. The employers essentially argued that investments were dependent on low wages and threatened to withdraw capital if the unions' demands were met. For its part, the government expressed no intention of accepting the unions' positions. Its memorandum endorsed the employers' view, argued that wage setting should happen exclusively through industrial relations mechanisms, and dismissed all of the workers' claims. It even ridiculed the unions' demands for fundamental reforms: "This is only possible in Utopia; incidentally, Nigeria is not Utopia."[28] Michael Imoudu countered with some levity of his own, dramatically drinking a cup of *gari* as he stood before the commissioners. Then he threw down his cup and spoon, clutched his abdomen, and complained of a stomachache. One of his JAC compatriots impersonated a doctor and gave Imoudu some pills to swallow, as the hall erupted in laughter. Imoudu's intention was to dramatize the acute poverty and inadequate diet (or lack of bread) of an average Nigerian laborer.[29]

The JAC memorandum to the Morgan commission was drafted with the assistance of sympathetic leftist intellectuals, some of whom had worked with Awolowo on the Action Group program. The document combined statistical evidence on wages and the cost of living with a strong attack on the pay differentials between top administrators and other workers. It traced the gap in wages and benefits to the colonial period, when expatriates had to be enticed to come to Nigeria with high salaries and allowances. One of the goals of the independence movement had been to open this "privileged caste" to Nigerians, many of whom—ironically—won their privileges through popular strikes in the 1940s and 1950s like the "Emerson Must Go" demonstration. But ordinary workers, the JAC argued, were still living on colonial wages. While an unskilled worker in the state-controlled sector of the economy earned £36–78 per year, a government minister or managing director earned more than £3,500, or 50 to 100 times as much. "There was a pronounced master-servant relation expressed not only in a prestige income structure but in social snobbishness. All this has been carried into the new period." To close the gulf between the two poles of the wage and salary structure, the JAC recommended a minimum annual wage of £180 and an upper income scale varying from £500 to £960.[30]

Submissions to the commission continued the pattern of linking the wage structure to men's positions within households, showing that employees were even less able to support dependents than they had been in the 1940s. The Nigerian Maritime Trade Unions Federation compared workers' household expenses in 1963 with those compiled by the Supreme Council of Nigerian Workers in 1946 to show a dramatic increase in the cost of living relative to wages and a corresponding drop in the standard of living of the average wage earner. Whereas the lower classes of workers in 1946 listed the rent they paid for accommodation of the "room and parlour" type, in 1964, such people and their families lived in only one room. Budget submissions in the 1940s listed the wages an employed man would pay to a "small boy," but by 1964, none of the lowest-paid workers could afford a household servant. In addition, the Federation argued, the budget that the Supreme Council compiled in 1946 was for a very junior staff member living without any family. But the comparable figures submitted for 1964 had to entail a laborer along with "his wife, his average of four children, his parents and his immediate relatives," since limited opportunities for upward mobility or transfer to the permanent establishment meant that "numbers of the labour grade . . . would remain on such a rate for a period of from 15 to 20 years and may . . . retire on the rate."[31] The Federation thus urged the Morgan Commission to "set aside completely the existing colonial structure and to substitute it with one which will reflect the manliness of this great Republic." *Manliness* here referred to national strength and justice, but the unions' economic demands also were designed to make possible a particularly gendered vision of working class domestic life.

In this vision, unlike the one promulgated in the 1940s, family responsibilities were broadly construed. In 1945 and after, as we have seen, much of the argument between trade unionists and the government over family allowances centered on the nature of African families and Nigerian men's putative status as providers. I have argued that trade unionists and other men used the language of male breadwinners not necessarily because working men *did* provide exclusive financial support for their households, but in part because these arguments were politically expedient in the colonial context. In response, colonial administrators pointed to extended family commitments and women's income earning to argue that working men did not deserve the wages and benefits of breadwinners. Nearly twenty years later, trade unionists dropped the stance that workers had families just as Europeans did, and instead made Nigerian big men the point of reference. The 1961 Zudonu Committee argued that wages must be pegged even higher than a man's own minimum budget requirements because a worker would have a range of people to support. "A young man beginning life as a worker expects sooner or later to be coupled," Zudonu wrote. "In the meantime he may have a girl-friend to care for, who may later become his wife. Or he may have an old mother or father, brother or sister, nephew or niece who, by reason of our custom and tradition, he is also expected to look after."[32] Another commentator pointed out in 1963 that "Every Minister, every Member of Parliament, and even Mr. Justice Morgan himself knows" that a Nigerian worker "has obligations towards a much larger number of people than in British and American communities." Indeed, he suggested, "It is this institution of extended family which is the root of labour unrest in Nigeria." This time, the argument was one that had been floated in 1945 but had not gone very far: that extended family responsibilities made necessary either a serious government investment in social security or family wages in the very broadest sense, recognizing the far-flung commitments of urban wage earners.[33]

On April 30, the Morgan Commission presented its findings, with two minority reports, to the government. But the politicians delayed publishing the report for nearly a month, and only did so when the JAC threatened a general strike. As expected, it was largely favorable to the workers, although its recommendations were less than the JAC had asked for.[34] In general, the commission recommended increases of about 25 percent at the lowest ends of the wage scale, ranging to 2–7 percent salary increases at the top. In addition, the commission recommended minimum wages for each of four zones in the country (to replace the seven zones currently in use) and a phasing out of the daily paid category of workers. Of particular interest to the workers, wage arrears were to be paid retroactively to October 1, 1963. Morgan also suggested that the minimum wages be applicable to private employers, who should adhere to or exceed the recommended salary levels for junior employees. While the commission did not make specific recommendations on rent and price controls, it did note the "utter inadequacy and appalling conditions of the houses inhabited by workers whose houses we inspected in Lagos." Finally, in the opinion of the commission, the entire industrial relations machinery was in need of reappraisal given the importance of wages in employers' budgets and in workers' lives. "Whatever may have been the position in the past, the Nigerian worker has reached the point where, as in the more developed economies, his remuneration in the form of a salary or wage determines the standard of living and welfare, not only of himself but of his whole family."[35]

Indeed, the Morgan Report was the first official attempt in Nigeria to take seriously the notion of a family wage, although with the more narrow understanding of *family*. Although the colonial government had replied to a query from the secretary of state in 1954 that "the bachelor wage is unknown in Nigeria," the reality was that wage calculations reflected political pressures and market forces, not any acknowledgment of workers' financial obligations to family members.[36] Quoting the 1941 Bridges Commission with approval, Morgan reiterated that

> even if a man is not "his brother's keeper" in so far as his extended family is concerned, he is very much the provider for his family, i.e. his wife or wives and children. And it must be borne in mind that the fact that a man has no education or special training to enable him to undertake employment other than at the bottom of the ladder does not and should not debar him from getting married and raising a family.

Thus, the commission based its minimum wage calculations on the notion of a "living wage," which "should be high enough to enable a wage earner who does a full day's work to support himself and his family out of his wages." More specifically, the minimum wage "should be the level of income which should be earned by a young unskilled labourer entering wage employment for the first time, and sufficient to meet the following requirements of himself, a wife and child": one-room housing, food, clothing, transport, a mat and blanket, tax, entertainment once a week, cigarettes or tobacco, fuel and soap, and savings at 5 percent of earnings.[37]

Morgan suggested that the governments could pay the increased labor costs called for in the report through a "rigorous pruning of expenses" and suggested an examination of senior servants' motor car and children's allowances. Two minority reports submitted along with Morgan's went even further. The first, by C.O. Nwokedi and O.I. Akinkugbe, agreed with the unions that the existing salary structure was "colonial in outlook": "We advocate a complete break with this humiliating past and would recommend one which would be a challenge to our *Nationhood* and *Patriotism*."[38] While favoring the wage and salary revisions in the main report, Nwokedi and Akinkugbe also suggested a drastic reduction in spending in the public corporations, particularly in the salaries and benefits for the upper ranks of their employees; the complete abolition of government-sponsored car allowances; and changes in government housing policy. According to this minority report, a senior official earning a salary of over £2500 per year paid rent of about £150 per year for a house on an acre of gardens, with maintenance provided by the government, while a subordinate directly under him on salary of under £700 per year paid roughly £240 annually for a small, unfurnished flat in a crowded neighborhood. "This is the worst hangover from the colonial past." The authors recommended that the government stop providing housing, especially since only a minority of junior and senior employees had access to it, and instead sell the quarters and use the money to build accommodations for lower-paid workers.[39]

The second minority report was written by an industrial relations expert, Dr. T.M. Yesufu, and was the most radical. Like the first minority report, this one largely agreed with Morgan on the revisions of wages and salaries. But Yesufu argued that Morgan should have gone further on both housing and allowances, since the government needed sources of funds to implement the increased wages, and because these issues were particularly important to the workers. "From the evidence submitted to the Commission," Yesufu wrote, "it is clear that there is great resentment against the continued payment of certain allowances to a class of public servants who many people, rightly or wrongly, regard as already being overpaid. Most Economists in Nigeria consider the allowances as economically indefensible; to the ordinary worker, they are patently unethical."[40] Like Nwokedi and Akinkugbe, Yesufu recommended the abolition of car allowances and also hoped that the government would get out of the business of providing quarters, instead using its housing funds to provide loans so that workers might purchase their own houses. In addition, Yesufu recommended the abolition of inducement allowances for Nigerian officers, along with the children's separate domicile allowance. In his view,

> This is one allowance for which, in my opinion, no adequate reason has yet been advanced, especially as it applies to indigenous officers. It may be plausible to pay something to compensate an officer for the additional expense which he may be compelled to incur if, in mid-term, he is required to proceed on transfer and he has to leave his children behind in school. The payment of such an allowance should clearly be temporary—normally for a period not exceeding six months. It is certainly difficult to justify the payment of an allowance to a parent who voluntarily sends his children to school away from his normal place of work.[41]

Together with the two minority reports, the Morgan document forcefully recommended an overhaul of the pay and benefit structure for wage and salary earners in Nigeria. In essence, the reports called for a significant rise in the standard of living—and ability to support dependents—among the lower ranks, to be paid for by drastic reductions in the salaries and benefits of opulent "big men." The commissioners and the trade union movement together presented a critique of government policies based not only on notions of democracy and some form of a welfare state, but also including an attack on the self-aggrandizement of the ruling elite. They demanded that the trend by which new leaders assumed the benefits and luxuriant lifestyles of colonial personnel be reversed. But would the administration reorient its priorities, and cut its own salaries, so dramatically?

THE GENERAL STRIKE

When the government published the Morgan and two minority reports, it did not, however, append any statement of its reaction to them. The omission of the official White Paper was as frustrating to the unions as the delay in publishing the report had been. Two days after the report was issued, the JAC threatened a general strike unless the government issued its response. On Saturday, May 30, veteran trade union leaders Michael Imoudu and H.P. Adebola led a milelong procession from the United Labor Congress headquarters at Ebute Metta to the Carter Bridge, which connected the mainland to Lagos Island. According to regulations in effect since 1962, mass meetings were banned in the federal territory of Lagos. In a scene reminiscent of that before the 1945 strike, the two leaders differed over whether or not to proceed in defiance of the government ban. As in the earlier strike, Imoudu's rowdy faction prevailed, and the entire procession headed toward the bridge.

The police were waiting there, and in the resulting clash many in the procession, including Imoudu and Adebola, suffered from tear gas and beatings. The next day, six labor leaders—including Imoudu, Adebola, and Wahab Goodluck—were arrested and later released on bail. From his sick bed, where he was surrounded by police, Adebola announced that the general strike would commence on Monday morning.

The strike began in Lagos on June 1 and hit nearly all government offices and industrial undertakings. As in 1945, transport and communications workers were key to its success and geographic spread, shutting down the port and railroad systems. Civil servants stayed home, leaving soldiers detailed to run post offices and other government services. In addition to the public sector, the strike affected big department stores and small companies in retail and distribution trades. The three regional capitals of Ibadan, Kaduna, and Enugu were largely shut down in the first few days, as was Lagos, and similar stoppages occurred in other large cities like Port Harcourt, in eastern Nigeria. By the third day an estimated 750,000 workers nationwide were taking part in the strike and nearly everything was closed except some schools, hospitals, and petrol stations. By the end of the first week, teachers and hospital workers had joined, closing schools and curtailing health services. Besides wage- and salary-earners, other supporters included domestic servants and a number of the unemployed who joined demonstrations in the towns. Daily mass rallies kept workers informed of each day's events and exhorted them to continue the strike and to remain nonviolent. Indeed, the strike was remarkably peaceful, both because of workers' discipline and because the government called in troops to maintain essential services and guard against sabotage.

The government tried on June 3 to contain the strike by releasing its White Paper on the Morgan Report. In a departure from established practices in Nigerian wage fixing, the administration refused to pay the wage and salary scales recommended, on the grounds that this was financially impossible. Instead, it offered about half of the recommended improvements, and not retroactively. While Morgan had recommended a minimum monthly wage of £12, the government offered £10. The White Paper insisted on maintaining the current seven national wage zones, refused to extend minimum wage requirements to the private sector, and opposed Morgan's labor stabilization measures. The JAC staunchly rejected these terms, and in fact the primary effect of the White Paper was to make the Morgan report seem even more attractive to workers than it had previously.

During the first week, government officials seemed remarkably unconcerned about the strike. The minister of labor flew to New York to attend a conference on youth problems, while the prime minister vacationed at his home in Bauchi. On June 8, back in Lagos to receive a visiting diplomat from Basutoland, Balewa issued an order that the strikers return to work or be fired.

The following day, striking workers of two major private employers—Union Trading Company and United Africa Company—were fired, and directors of the Nigerian Railway Corporation gave notice that they would follow suit the next day.

In mass meetings, particularly in the south, strike leaders derided Balewa's call for a return to work without offering any concessions and heated up their explicitly political rhetoric. Strikers chanted "Balewa must go," and NTUC leader Wahab Goodluck asked crowds: "What is the meaning of independence for a worker? Did he fight for independence so that only the pot-bellied politician will continue to grow fatter and more secure, while he vegetates in insecurity?"[42] Another union leader charged that the conflict was no longer between employer and employee but between the whole nation and a few greedy people who constitute the government.[43] At a mass meeting in Ibadan, the JAC's Western Regional Branch adopted a resolution giving Balewa a forty-eight-hour ultimatum to resign his position, a sentiment repeated on handbills distributed in the streets of Lagos.[44] The next day at a rally in Lagos JAC leaders repeated that there would be no negotiations and no end to the strike unless the government accepted the recommendations of the Morgan commission. Imoudu led the crowd in hisses when, referring to police animals, he reminded listeners that "some dogs earn more than human beings in this country." Workers sang a new song, whose lyrics began, "Stand up, stand up for Morgan, you soldiers of Imoudu. Raise high your valiant request. It must not suffer loss."[45] The rally was disbanded when police teargassed the crowd.[46]

The government's actions produced an even greater solidarity among the strikers and expressions of support from nonstrikers who also opposed the government. In one large British-owned establishment in Ibadan, policemen played football with workers who had reluctantly returned to the job, while the sergeant defended the former strikers to the management: "They did actually report for work, sir." Strike solidarity committees were formed on university campuses in Ibadan and Ife, and at night ostensibly neutral commercial printers secretly produced strike literature. Leftist elements in the two opposition parties, the NCNC and the AG, donated money and strategic expertise. In Port Harcourt and several other towns in Eastern Nigeria, politicians as well as businessmen demonstrated their sympathy with workers by carrying palm fronds—an action that soon became a recognized sign of solidarity with the strikers. Church leaders in Lagos declared their support for the Morgan recommendations, which they described as reasonable.[47]

In the opinion of left-wing participants and observers, the strike constituted part of a broad movement in opposition to the government, based not on ethnicity or origin but on economic concerns and a demand for democracy. Yet there was an important regional dimension as well. The JAC was led by southerners, most of whom supported the Action Group or the NCNC, and it was in confrontation with a government dominated by the Northern Peoples' Congress. Federal parliamentary elections were scheduled for later that year, and it seemed clear that the NPC would use its control of government to ensure its reelection. Still, even the British High Commissioner in Nigeria saw the strike as "an unprecedented Nigeria-wide, non-tribal protest by the urban proletariat." The JAC continually pointed out that the government was siding with expatriate employers rather than Nigerian workers. In response, Balewa blamed the strike on communist agitators, thereby ignoring economic questions altogether.[48] Wole Soyinka's firsthand description of the political context of the strike deserves to be quoted at length:

> Back and forth it all went, back and forth, just like the various agents moving from Lagos to Enugu to Kaduna, Kano and Ibadan, stiffening up labour resolve; Michael Imoudu's flaming rhetoric lighting up the labour rallies . . . confidently predicting the downfall of the Balewa Government unless it yielded to workers' demands, while the Government . . . infiltrated their ranks with money and tribal suspicions, shrewdly reminding its adherents that this labour action was not without its political motivation—recent election results had, after all, been fiercely contested, and the nation had teetered on the verge of a violent power tussle. Nor did its propaganda machine neglect to accuse the sympathy of the "progressives" for Awolowo and his radical lieutenants who were languishing in prison cells all over the country, convicted of treasonable felony. Radicalism was a disease of the South, and the strike was only another attempt by the South to spread its poison and achieve what Awolowo had failed to do—snatch political power from the North through non-democratic means.[49]

But government economic advisers warned about the serious economic consequences of allowing the strike to drag on, and finally a reconciliation committee was set up under the chairmanship of the minister of finance, Chief Festus Okotie-Eboh, with which the JAC agreed to cooperate. The government seems to have been motivated in part by pressure from the British high commissioner working in tandem with the (largely expatriate) employers' union, which feared the economic consequences of a prolonged strike and associated political instability. More significantly, federal officials were responding to the announcement by the Eastern regional premier, Dr. Michael Okpara of the NCNC, that his administration would implement the Morgan recommendations if the other governments of the federation did the same. The NPC probably calculated that it could not afford to concede this political position to the NCNC.[50]

Thus on June 13 the government abruptly announced that the strike had been called off. Workers celebrated when the terms were read at a meeting that afternoon: there would be no victimization of participants; the period of the strike was to be treated as leave with full pay; and a negotiating body representing the government, private employers, and the JAC would begin deliberations on the basis of the Morgan Report. But meanwhile, under intense pressure because of the census crisis and upcoming federal elections, the government continued to press the labor movement. During the post-strike negotiations, police conducted a sweep of trade unionists' homes, rounding up labor leaders in connection with an alleged coup plot. A visiting British sociologist studying trade unionism was arrested and subsequently held for nearly a year.[51] Most other unionists were released, but government harassment and rumors of clandestine payoffs delayed the wage negotiations and increased the air of tension and mistrust.[52]

The Okotie-Eboh negotiating committee worked for two weeks and ultimately produced an agreement that was in general closer to the original Morgan proposals than to the stipulations of the government White Paper. The June 29 "Workers' Charter," as it became known in some quarters, created a new system of salary scales and labor grades; set minimum wages in six geographic areas, at rates between those advocated by the Morgan Report and the government White Paper; provided for the gradual abolition of the daily wage system; and applied both to government and private sector junior employees. The new wage rates were retroactive to the first of the year. The government also agreed to set up a rent and price control tribunal for Lagos and to examine the payments of car, children's, and inducement allowances to senior officials. The Okotie-Eboh agreement was widely seen as a victory for the unions, although inflation soon undermined the rise in wages. As labor historian Robin Cohen argues, the strike contributed to the collapse of the First Republic two years later by challenging the legitimacy of the government and revealing its precarious authority. "Many workers during the strike were not simply begging for their share of the national cake, but were explicitly threatening the political system itself."[53]

WOMEN AND LABOR DIFFERENTIATION

In 1945, women were vital supporters of the general strike, in spite of the male breadwinner rhetoric of trade unionists. In 1964, the relationship between strikers and women was more complex. A major difference in 1964 was that the strike lasted two weeks instead of six, and ultimately workers were paid for the period of missed work. In addition, the NCNC and the Action Group provided material assistance to the striking workers, who also received some clandestine contributions from abroad. Among other things, these resources paid for the twenty vans that carried members of Wahab Goodluck's eight strike-organizing commandos from industry to industry to generate support.[54]

Thus, strikers had less need for material help from community members, including market and other women, than they had in 1945. Moreover, the economic differentiation of the late colonial period had affected women as well as men. While market women's organizations expressed support for strikers, as a previous generation had done, women as wives both favored wage increases for their "breadwinners" and opposed measures that would raise prices for themselves as consumers. The government could point to cleavages between wage earners and other groups like housewives and farmers in an attempt to isolate the strikers. The differentiation of the wage labor force had reinforced its association with masculinity and threatened its previous solidarities across gender lines.

By the second week of the strike, female traders in Lagos and elsewhere were publically behind it. Interviewed by a roving reporter, one "shy market woman" clearly blamed the administration for the impasse: "The Government is causing all this trouble by refusing to give as much as the Morgan Commission recommended."[55] On June 11, 10,000 workers at a Lagos rally cheered a representative of the Market Women's Association when she threatened that market women would stage a protest demonstration against the government's rejection of the Morgan recommendations. If the government did not adopt the Morgan Report within forty-eight hours, she asserted, Lagos traders would desert the markets in sympathy with striking workers.[56]

This sympathy, as in 1945, resulted at least in part from market traders' own political and economic concerns, particularly price inflation and perceived persecution by state authorities. A June 17 meeting of the Lagos Market Women's Association called on the prime minister both to stop Lagos City Council officials from harassing traders with arbitrary sanitary regulations and high water rates and to recognize "our husbands' just demands" by granting the wage increases set out in the Morgan Report. Abibatu Mogaji, president of the association, threatened that the government will "feel our presence if the demands of the workers are not granted" and reiterated that "We are behind the workers." Mogaji pointed out that since the strike, sales in the market had dropped drastically and that prices had soared by as much as 75 percent. Therefore she urged a speedy resolution to the wage negotiations. Finally, she thanked the workers for returning to work.[57] Market women were especially gratified by the termination of the strike, since it had paralyzed all rail and most road transport in Nigeria, leaving traders unable to receive new supplies. But they blamed the NPC government, not strikers, for the disruption, particularly since market women's organizations in Lagos were at the time openly allied with the Action Group.[58]

Some women vocally supported the strike *as wives* dependent on husbands' earnings. On Saturday, June 13, the press vaguely reported that "housewives" were planning a march to Lagos on the coming Monday to present a petition to the prime minister. The women would urge the government to pay the Morgan award so "as to give us a living wage."[59] The march never took place, however, as the strike was called off over the weekend. Later that week, Mrs. E.A. Sheppard protested the government's claims that it could not afford to pay the benefits recommended by the Morgan Commission, given that top officials earned huge salaries. "We are not asking for the ministerial scale of salaries for our husbands," she wrote to the *West African Pilot*, "but we maintain that Morgan's 'Living Wage' must be guaranteed." Sheppard went on to emphasize that not just market women but women in general favored the workers' cause, since wages helped to support them. "If the Prime Minister fails to grant the workers of this country decent wages upon which to live, he should regard such failure as an invitation to the entire [*sic*] housewives, spinsters and children to visit him at his lodge in the very near future. Consequent upon that, I charge the women of this country not market women alone to be at alert for the clarion call."[60] The term *housewife* was not even used in the press in the 1940s; its deployment by the early 1960s testifies to the rise of the male breadwinner ideal traced in chapter 5. But the inclusion of *spinsters* is important, too, signifying that working men contributed to the upkeep of their sisters and others in addition to wives and children.

Further, the term *housewife* points to economic differentiation among working families. While market women's interests in some ways paralleled those of the strikers and some wives saw the wages earned by men as sources of their own support, other—particularly elite—women also approached the strike as consumers inconvenienced by its economic disruptions. The government-recognized National Council of Women's Societies defined itself as a nonpolitical body and worked to represent the interests of its elite, educated leadership, as well as their "less fortunate sisters." During the second week of the strike, the NCWS sponsored a rally of all the local women's organizations in Ibadan. It later issued a statement asking the government to pay "adequate salaries and wages which will enable them [workers] to live above subsistence level," but also appealing "to the trade union leaders to co-operate in order to eliminate the sufferings of all Nigerians caused by the strike."[61] Other elite women took up this theme. Tokunbo Ajose, the women's columnist for the *Daily Times*, wrote that "[m]ost of us are more than happy that the strike is now over." She detailed the hardships suffered by housewives during the strike, including increased food prices and interrupted garbage collection. "I for one am certainly very, very glad that our men folk have settled their quarrel at last. Now perhaps we women can settle down to the difficult task of trying to make ends meet, caring for the children and home without having the extra worry of strike." To that end, Ajose went on to announce a lecture sponsored by the Christian Mothers' Association of St. Mary's Cathedral Church in Ibadan and a fashion parade to be held in Lagos.[62]

Opponents of the strike sought to exploit the cleavages between wage-earners and other segments of society by pointing to the hardships suffered by consumers and farmers. In particular, they identified women as wives and mothers who would be adversely affected, painting workers as irresponsible husbands and fathers as well as greedy Nigerians. On the second day of the strike, the *Morning Post*, owned and controlled by the federal government, ran the following commentary:

> Yesterday, our children sweated and panted as they walked miles from home to school. Pregnant women stood fainting as they waited in vain at bus stop; or precariously hung to mammy wagons in the anxious bid to keep their dates with their doctors. Market women were kept from their daily rounds, could not go after their merchandise. Such workers as were still prepared to remain faithful to their charge [sic] were deprived the means of transport, and lost hours waiting, or trekking to work. The farmers' harvest lay waste. As for the nation, it stood paralysed by the doings of its own children, its economic life-lines cut, its ports dead, its workshops silent.[63]

The *Daily Times* followed similar lines in its editorial of June 6, stressing that wage earners' interests were not the same as those of farmers and traders, and that strikers were shirking their duties both to the new nation and to the families they provided for. The enormous costs of implementing the Morgan recommendations, the article went on, would lead to layoffs, with the result that "millions of housewives and children and old age people who depend on retrenched workers for their living will be thrown into penury and misery." This, of course, rather contradicts the previously articulated view that workers' concerns were separate from those of the general public. Then the *Times* editorial turned against the JAC the unions' claims that workers had similar family demands but grossly different resources than elites: "There are millions of traders, farmers and peasants who are not wage earners; but who buy in the same markets and shops with the small percentage of wage earners who are getting more pay now. If prices are inflated because a few thousand workers get wage increases what happens to these millions of non wage-earners?"[64] A few days later in the same newspaper, a woman calling herself "Auntie Yetunde" wrote a letter to the editor detailing the hardships caused by the strike, including scarce food and transport and interrupted public services. "Babies die in hospitals and expectant mothers are in danger. . . . Let all work for the purpose of the nation so that there may be more wealth for us all to share," she concluded. "A strike does not help."[65]

In yet another permutation of the relationship between women and the strike, labor spokesmen cast some elite women as the very embodiments of their grievances. Big men's abilities to provide for extended family members and offer luxuries to wives and children earned the resentment of working men unable to provide the same for their dependents. As the general secretary of the union of United Africa Company workers argued, "Why do private employers continue to bring more of their brothers here and sack our own brothers under the pretense that they have no money? Do you know that the wives and children of our foreign employers can go on leave twice within a tour at the same company's expense? Do you know that our small almighties have raised their car allowances and are now owning mighty buildings but pay very little for government rented blocks?"[66] In the post-strike negotiations, the JAC demanded the wage and salary structure recommended by the Morgan Report, and in addition called for the abolition of the allowances and perquisites for senior officers spelled out in the two minority reports. The JAC also added another demand, reflecting again workers' resentment of government big men's abilities to provide patronage to family members and women: the termination of the appointments of wives and girlfriends of ministers and permanent secretaries who worked part time in certain government establishments, earning fabulous salaries. "There are secondary school girls who can do the jobs better than these wives and girl friends who waste most of the time in chatting and putting powder on their faces. This is the opportune time to clean our society of civic impurities."[67] Indeed, an earlier commentator had pointed to the irony in paying family allowances to senior officials, who were "the leading authors" of the current "state of sexual promiscuity."[68]

CONCLUSION

The general strike of 1964 was in many respects a mirror image of the one in 1945. While in the first strike workers demanded family allowances through reference to their common masculinity with expatriate men, during the second, strikers called for the abolition of family allowances and pointed to the differences in lifestyles between themselves and elites. Ironically, strikers used discourse identifying themselves with colonial rulers in 1945, which they did not do in 1964 when the national leadership was Nigerian. In 1945, the alliance between strikers and market women belied the men's claims to be household and community breadwinners; in 1964, market and other women referred to the wage needs of their "husbands," but strikers argued that their low wages made it impossible for them to be family providers. Their commonalities with the general public translated into broad community support for strikers in 1945, even as they made wage and benefit demands that centered on claims to support fairly narrowly defined families. Nineteen years later, strikers' claims were based on the necessity of contributing to a broad range of relatives and dependents, yet their material support came largely from a narrow group of political and trade union allies.

How do we explain these differences? What had changed in the labor-gender nexus over the late colonial and early independence periods? First, wage labor continued to be identified as a male preserve, even as increasing numbers of women undertook paid employment. Many women and men could use the discourse of *housewives* and male *breadwinners* unreflexively, and this reinforced the notion that men were on strike on behalf of their families but also undermined the practical alliances between labor unions and market women's associations. The second and related point is that the differentiation of the labor force was inseparable from domesticity and male gender. This differentiation had helped well-placed, highly paid men to be "big" by supporting dependents and living comfortably, often at public expense; it had allowed more middle-level administrative and technical personnel to function somewhat as breadwinners in their households; and it had left those without skills or job security with few prospects for accommodating or feeding wives and children, let alone incurring any additional comforts or assisting relatives. This differentiation helps to explain strikers' insistence on their domestic needs, which included providing for wives, children, and other relatives. It helps to explain why some women described their husbands as providers while others had little sympathy for strikers. And most significantly, the stark differentiation of the economic structure explains workers' passionate condemnation of the fringe benefits, like car and children's allowances, enjoyed by the senior service. In Wale Oyemakinde's analysis, what seemed most "strange" about the strike "was the extent to which workers carried their disapproval of the differential" in living conditions between the top and bottom of the wage and salary scale.[69] But this hardly seems surprising when one considers the links between wage labor, domesticity, and male roles in historical context.

A comparison of the two general strikes also points to a broader issue: the malleability of discourse about gender. The *work* that employed men did with gender was different in 1945, when they strategically argued that they were breadwinners for wives and children, than in 1964, when they argued that they stretched their meager resources to help a broad range of relatives even as they were unable to provide housing and food for their closest dependents. The different historical circumstances were crucial. In the late colonial period, it was nationalism that was most on the agenda, and the 1945 strike brought together issues of worker dignity, masculinity, and citizenship in a critique of the racialized economy of colonial rule. During the First Republic, the pressing public questions—at least in southern Nigeria—most centered on the overlap between politics and class differentiation, on the linkages between access to the state and living the good life as a big man. Although in both strikes workers based their claims on gendered visions of who a worker was and what he (always a he) needed, they articulated these points in ways calculated to be most effective given the prevailing relations of power. Labor's discourses of gender were shaped perhaps as much by the intended audience as by concrete practices within households.

NOTES

1. My account of the strike draws on the following sources: Wogu Ananaba, *The Trade Union Movement in Nigeria* (New York: Africana Publishing, 1970); Emile R. Braundi and Antonio Lettieri, "The General Strike in Nigeria," *International Socialist Journal* 1 (1964): 598–609; Francis Cumming-Bruce (British High Commissioner in Nigeria), "Federation of Nigeria: The General Strike," submitted to the Secretary of State for Commonwealth Relations, June 30, 1964, DO 195/291; Robert Melson, "Nigerian Politics and the General Strike of 1964," in Robert I. Rotberg and Ali A. Mazrui (eds.), *Protest and Power in Black Africa* (New York: Oxford University Press, 1970); Wale Oyemakinde, "The Nigerian General Strike of 1964," *Genève-Afrique* 13 (1974): 53–71; Peter Kilby, *Industrialization in an Open Economy: Nigeria, 1945–1966* (Cambridge: Cambridge University Press, 1969), pp. 286–89; Robin Cohen, *Labour and Politics in Nigeria* (London: Heinemann, 1974), pp. 164–68; Larry Diamond, *Class, Ethnicity and Democracy in Nigeria: The Failure of the First Republic* (New York: Macmillan, 1988), ch. 6; and coverage in the *Daily Times of Nigeria* and the *West African Pilot*.

2. An accessible account of these intrigues is in Toyin Falola, *The History of Nigeria* (Westport, CT: Greenwood, 1999), ch. 7. For more detail, see Diamond, *Class, Ethnicity and Democracy*.

3. United Labor Congress Policy Statement, "A Programme for the Future," May 25, 1962, quoted in Melson, "Nigerian Politics," p. 776. For a dark, funny, and only semi-fictitious elaboration of the same points, see Chinua Achebe, *A Man of the People* (New York: Anchor Books, 1989 [1966]).

4. Melson, "Nigerian Politics," p. 775.

5. Ibid., p. 773.

6. Kilby, *Industrialization*, p. 286; T.M.Yesufu, *An Introduction to Industrial Relations in Nigeria* (Oxford: Oxford University Press, 1962), p. 155; S.O. Osoba, "The Development of Trade Unionism in Colonial and Post-Colonial Nigeria," in I.A. Akinjobgin and Segun Osoba (eds.), *Topics on Nigerian Economic and Social History* (Ile-Ife: University of Ife Press, 1980), p. 202.

7. Besides the Tudor Davies and Harragin wage revisions of 1945 and 1946, government wage and salary commissions prompted wage revisions in 1955 and 1959–1960. See Cohen, *Labour and Politics*, p. 191, for a summary. Scholars of Nigerian labor engaged in a vigorous debate in the 1960s and early 1970s over the extent to which union pressure influenced government wage setting. A summary of the debate is in Cohen, *Labor and Politics*, pp. 197–209, and an extended statement of one position is in Kilby, *Industrialization*, ch. 9.

8. Asuquo O. Ita, "Labour Disunity in Nigeria: Corruption in Union Leadership (2)," *WAP*, January 22, 1959.

9. Ananaba, *Trade Union Movement*, pp. 196–207.

10. Ananaba, *Trade Union Movement*, pp. 200–207. The author served as secretary to the Zudonu committee.

11. In 1964, there were approximately 300,000 trade union members organized into about 300 active unions, which were in turn organized into five central labor organizations. The two politically moderate organizations were the United Labor Congress (ULC), led by Alhaji H.P. Adebola and L.L. Borha and officially sanctioned by the government, and the Nigerian Workers' Council, led by N. Chukwwra and E. Okongwu. More radical were the Nigerian Trade Union Congress (NTUC), led by Wahab Goodluck and S.U.

Bassey; the Labour Unity Front, led by Michael Imoudu and Gogo Nzeribe; and Ibrahim Nock's Northern Federation of Labor. See Melson, "Nigerian Politics," p. 774; Cohen, *Labour and Politics*, ch. 3; Kilby, *Industrialization*, p. 286; and Diamond, *Class, Ethnicity and Democracy*, pp. 162–67. For the ebb and flow of central trade union bodies over time, see "Summary Chart of Central Trade Union Organizations," in Cohen, *Labour and Politics*, pp. 104–7.

12. Ananaba, *Trade Union Movement*, pp. 231–36, 235 quoted.

13. O. Zudonu, "The Case of Wages," *DTN*, September 24, 1963.

14. Frederick Cooper, *Decolonization and African Society: The Labor Question in French and British Africa* (Cambridge: Cambridge University Press, 1996), ch. 7.

15. "Rapson Recommendations: Rail Workers to Lead Delegation to Government," *DS*, August 5, 1957. A commentary on the AG proposal is in "Welfare State Proposals for Nigeria," *DTN*, September 2, 1959.

16. Adeyinka Morgan, chair, *Report of the Commission on the Review of Wages, Salary and Conditions of Service of the Junior Employees of the Governments of the Federation and in Private Establishments, 1963–64* (Lagos: Federal Ministry of Information, 1964), p. 47.

17. "List of Allowances," n.d. [November 1957], GML 302/2, vol. 1. The distinction between "officers" and "servants" replaced that between the "senior" and "junior" service at the recommendation of the Gorsuch Commission in 1955.

18. Nigeria, *Report of the Elias Commission of Enquiry into the Administration, Economic and Industrial Relations of the Nigerian Railway Corporation* (Lagos, 1960); "News from Nigeria: A Twice-Weekly Summary of News from All Parts of the Federation," No. 96/59, December 12, 1959, CO 554/2501. Also see Ananaba, *Trade Union Movement*, ch. 15.

19. "Railway to Abolish Special Allowances," *DTN*, August 8, 1961; "New Economy Drive: No More Car Advance for Railwaymen," *WAP*, August 8, 1961; NRC, *Report and Accounts for the Year Ended 31st March, 1962* (Lagos: NRC, 1962), p. 8.

20. "Ikejiani Uses Axe in Drastic Economy Drive: 2,000 Railmen to Go," *WAP*, October 10, 1961.

21. Nigeria, *Annual Report of the Federal Ministry of Labour, Labour Division, for 1963–64* (Lagos: Federal Ministry of Information, 1966), p. 18.

22. A.O. Okoronkwo, "Women [sic] Participation in Trade Unions," in Tayo Fashoyin, Felicia Durojaiye Oyekanmi and Eleanor R. Fapohunda (eds.), *Women in the Modern Sector Labour Force in Nigeria* (Lagos: University of Lagos, 1985), p. 84, as well as other contributions to the same volume and to O. Sokunbi, O. Jeminiwa, and F.B. Onaeko (eds.), *Women and Trade Unionism in Nigeria* (Ibadan: NPS Educational Publishers, 1995).

23. "A Memorandum to his Excellency the Governor-General of the Federation, and the Prime Minister of the Federation: On Behalf of Nigerian Workers" by M.A.O. Imoudu, President of the IULC [Independent United Labour Congress], n.d. [1962], in GML 307 vol. 1.

24. Ananaba, *Trade Union Movement*, p. 232.

25. Henry Nwigwe, "Workers Want Bread," *WAP*, September 13, 1963.

26. Letter to the editor, *DTN*, October 22, 1963.

27. Jerome K. Okuru, "The Wage Structure," *WAP*, October 4, 1963.

28. Quoted in Braundi and Lettieri, "General Strike in Nigeria," p. 603.

29. H.H. Dosu-Oyewole, *Narrative History of the Great Strike* (Lagos: Charity Printers, 1964), p. 26.

30. Joint Action Committee Memorandum to the Morgan Commission, United Labor Congress, 1963, p. 10 (quoted), excerpted in Melson, "Nigerian Politics," p. 781; and also summarized in Braundi and Lettieri, "General Strike in Nigeria."

31. Nigerian Maritime Trade Unions Federation, "Memorandum to the Morgan Commission for Salaries Revision," n.d. [1963], NLA/42.

32. Quoted in Ananaba, *Trade Union Movement*, p. 202.

33. James Ojiako, "More Money: Do Workers Deserve It?" *DTN*, October 29, 1963.

34. Morgan, *Report of the Commission*.

35. Ibid., para. 78, 83.

36. Colonial Labour Advisory Committee, Report of the Sub-Committee on Wage Fixing and Family Responsibilities, CO 859/810.

37. Morgan Report, para. 44, 47.

38. Minority Report I by Messrs. C.O. Nwokedi and O.I. Akinkugbe, in Morgan Report, para. 7 quoted, emphasis in original.

39. Ibid., para. 61 (quoted), para. 72–77.

40. Minority Report II by Dr. T.M. Yesufu, para. 5.

41. Ibid., para. 12.

42. Braundi and Lettieri, "General Strike," p. 608.

43. "PM's Talk Angers Union," *WAP*, June 9, 1964.

44. "Quit, PM Is Told," *DTN*, June 11, 1964; "Workers Stay Put, Say Defense Committee Ultimatum to Govt," *WAP*, June 11, 1964.

45. "No Morgan, No Talks, Say JAC," *DTN*, June 11, 1964. Dogs really did earn more than some Nigerians: in 1949, the United Africa Company paid its laborers 7.5 pence to 1 shilling a day, while the English dogs in its employment were allocated £3 per month, or two shillings a day, for maintenance. Mokwugo Okoye, *Storms on the Niger: A Story of Nigeria's Struggle from the Arab Influx to the Election Crisis* (Enugu, 1965), p. 171, cited in S.O. Osoba, "The Development of Trade Unionism in Colonial and Post-Colonial Nigeria," in I.A. Akinjogbin and Segun Osoba (eds.), *Topics on Nigerian Economic and Social History* (Ile-Ife: University of Ife Press, 1980), p. 193.

46. "Police Use Teargas at Workers' Rally," *DTN*, June 11, 1964; "Police Teargas Workers," *WAP*, June 11, 1964.

47. Cohen, *Labour and Politics*, p. 167; Wole Soyinka, *Ibadan: The Penkelemes Years, A Memoir: 1946–1965* (Ibadan: Spectrum Books, 1994), pp. 260–61; Melson, "Nigerian Politics," p. 786; "Church Leaders Back Morgan," *WAP*, June 11, 1964.

48. Braundi and Lettieri, "General Strike"; Melson, "Nigerian Politics"; Oyemakinde, "Nigerian General Strike"; Francis Cumming-Bruce, "Federation of Nigeria: The General Strike."

49. Soyinka, *Ibadan*, pp. 261–62.

50. Cumming-Bruce, "Federation of Nigeria: The General Strike."

51. Dr. Victor Allen was a senior lecturer in Industrial Relations at the University of Leeds, in Nigeria interviewing workers for a research project. British documents relevant to his detention are in DO 195/329–336.

52. On government bribes to labor leaders after the strike, see Soyinka, *Ibadan*, p. 263.

53. Cohen, *Labour and Politics*, p. 168.

54. "AG Supports the Strike," *DTN*, June 6, 1964; Melson, "Nigerian Politics," p. 786; M.A. Tokunboh, *Labour Movement in Nigeria: Past and Present* (Lagos: Lantern Books, 1985), p. 62. On Goodluck and the vans, see Oyemakinde, "Nigerian General Strike," p. 68, citing the *Daily Express*, June 5, 1964. According to Dosu-Oyewole (*Narrative*

History, pp. 31–32), "Mr. Wahab Goodluck was here, there and everywhere during the strike. In all the firms where the workers heard his voice they stopped work and joined the strike."

55. Pat Uriesi, "Strike Families Pull in Belts," *DTN*, June 8, 1964.
56. "We Stand with Workers—Market Women," *WAP*, June 12, 1964.
57. "Women Protest to PM," *DTN*, June 17, 1964. In October, market women were teargassed along with striking educators when they joined a demonstration on behalf of the Nigerian Union of Teachers. "As Women Tear-Gassed in Lagos . . . Govts Pipe Down," *NT*, October 9, 1964.
58. Nina Emma Mba, *Nigerian Women Mobilized: Women's Political Activity in Southern Nigeria, 1900–1965* (Berkeley, CA: Institute of International Studies, 1982), p. 232.
59. "Housewives Plan March on Balewa," *WAP*, June 13, 1964.
60. Mrs. E.A. Sheppard, "Morgan: Women to Demonstrate?" *WAP*, June 19, 1964.
61. Nina Mba writes both that the NCWS was inaugurated in Ibadan in 1959 (p. 188) and that it was founded in Lagos in 1957 (p. 232). Its officers included Lady Ademola, wife of the Chief Justice of the Western Region; Mrs. Adetowun Ogunsheye, a lecturer at the University of Ibadan; Mrs. Akran, wife of the Western Region Minister of Social Welfare; and Lady Oyinkan Abayomi, who had been active in women's welfare work since 1920. While the NCWS never openly demonstrated support for any political party, many of the executive members in the Ibadan and Lagos branches were AG activists. Mba, *Nigerian Women*, pp. 188–91, 232; "Women Speak on the Strike," *DTN*, June 11, 1964.
62. Tokunbo Ajose, "Women's Corner," *DTN*, June 25, 1964.
63. *MP*, June 2, 1964, quoted in Oyemakinde, "Nigerian General Strike," p. 63.
64. "National Interest" (editorial), *DTN*, June 6, 1964.
65. Auntie Yetunde, "No One Likes the Strike" (letter to the editor), *DTN*, June 10, 1964.
66. Paid announcement by F.N. Kanu, General Secretary, U.A.C. & Associated Companies African Workers' Union, *WAP*, June 12, 1964.
67. "JAC: No Compromise on £12 for Labourers," *WAP*, June 16, 1964. Also see "JAC Won't Budge on £144 Minimum Pay," *DTN*, June 16, 1964.
68. Mrs. Fola Ogunsola, "Welfare State Proposals for Nigeria," *DTN*, September 2, 1959.
69. Oyemakinde, "Nigerian General Strike," p. 66.

8

CONCLUSION: THE FALL OF THE "MODERN" BREADWINNER?

Before and through the era of stabilization, colonial commentators, planners, and officials took it for granted that certain types of labor and certain types of families went together. In Nigeria before World War II, the "target" labor model assumed that extended families would care for workers in periods of unemployment, sickness, and retirement, and that wives supported themselves and their children. But by the mid-1940s and beyond, European observers no longer favored workers' kin as sources of security that could justify low wages, and instead began to see the extended family as a drain on employees' resources and wives' financial autonomy as problematic for reproducing a working class. By the 1950s and into the 1960s, the expansion and stabilization of urban labor coincided with the flourishing of modernization ideology. The stabilization and modernization ideals held that a committed urban wage earner would focus on his nuclear rather than extended family and that breadwinner wages would make earning a male activity and reproducing (in its broadest sense) a female one.

The social history of urban wage labor in southwestern Nigeria takes these top-down views as context, but encompasses far more complexity and human drama. In contrast to the idea that all wage labor before World War II was temporary and for specific financial goals, the evidence points to large numbers of men who made long careers in the formal sector. Although their goals did include "targets" like marriage money, they also helped support a range of family members even as they lost many of their hometown safety nets. But during the 1945 general strike, trade unionists argued that they had wives and children to support and therefore they were entitled to family allowances and breadwinner wages. In the postwar era, some career wage and salary earners did earn enough to make credible claims to "breadwinner" status, even though most of their wives earned incomes too. Some long-term employees also loosened their ties to hometowns and extended families and talked about their new family values as part of a commitment to modernity. But this was a differentiated domesticity: while these colonial and postcolonial "middles" (to use Nancy Hunt's term)[1] were in some senses becoming self-styled "modern" breadwinners, new elites were using the benefits of their jobs to distinguish their families and lifestyles from those of other men, and the urban masses were struggling for any family life at all. This differentiation was the driving force behind the 1964 general strike, in which workers demanded, among other things, the abolition of family allowances.

How does this story affect our understandings of the relationships between wage labor, gender, and colonialism? On one hand, the ways that career workers' domestic lives did *not* conform to the stabilization/modernization ideals resonates with James Ferguson's observations of Copperbelt households in the 1980s.[2] In spite of male breadwinner rhetoric, wives of wage- and salary-earners were economically active, and even trade unionists who talked about working men as financial providers sometimes defended women's access to paid employment. Extended families remained important sources of support for many working men, while those who could afford it made contributions to their relatives and townspeople. These arrangements point to the limited power of colonial labor policies and gender ideologies to shape Nigerian families according to European-derived models.

On the other hand, however, what seems remarkable is the extent to which many career railway men and others *did* make domestic arrangements that resembled colonial and modernization ideals. Career wage- and salary-earners became associated with a distinct type of masculinity, in large part through their regular access to cash, which in the context of preexisting links between money, seniority, and power, brought them new status with their wives and extended families. They increasingly defined themselves as breadwinners, both at home in relation to household members and in union representations calling for a family wage. Many steadily employed men based their plans for the future on educated children and a government pension, so they did not feel absolutely compelled to maintain claims to family land or goodwill among extended kin. They have retired in their hometowns to a much lesser extent than other Nigerians of their age. Moreover, this occurred in "old" urban areas, where there were always close ties with extended or rural families and where the state was in a relatively weak position to interfere with workers' domestic arrangements.

The evidence in this book points to several overlapping explanations for such transformations. First, there were concrete changes in labor processes and structures. Travel around the country, particularly in the case of railway men, and, more crucially, relatively high wages steadily earned were instrumental in focusing household strategies on a man's wage. Already in Yoruba cultures money was an important marker of status, power, and alliances. In this context, steady wages increased men's desirability, smoothed marital relationships, and helped to create the image of the male household head as family provider. Because nearly all colonial-era wage-earners were male, this affected the ways people thought and talked about masculinity and money. These developments seem, in rough outline, to parallel the gendered history of wage labor and the development of the male breadwinner ideal in Britain and elsewhere.[3] Since the expansion and then partial stabilization of wage labor in Nigeria was a colonial phenomenon, to some extent we can trace the gendering of the Nigerian working class to colonial impositions.

But Nigerians were not passive in the construction of the male breadwinner ideal or in the transformation of working people's households. A second explanation for the gender and domestic changes charted in this book is the performative nature of gender, or rather, the potential instrumentality of gender discourse. Nigerian trade unionists, individual workers, Yoruba women, and colonial administrators talked about gender in particular ways for particular purposes. In the circumstances of late colonial Nigeria, wage earners found it useful to employ the language of male breadwinners for relatively small families in their interactions with employers and government administrators. Men and women within families could use this same discourse in their negotiations over household resources and power. Later, trade unionists stressed the wide range of dependents supported by wage earners. The fact that the gendered discourse of striking workers could be so different in 1964 than it was in 1945 only underscores its malleability and responsiveness to circumstances.

Judith Butler has stressed the performative nature of gender, and James Ferguson has shown how this concept can be applicable to postcolonial Africa. In particular, he notes that one cannot just adopt a certain style of behavior arbitrarily; the range of choices is limited by material contexts and by the ideologies that make sense therein.[4] In colonial and postcolonial Nigeria, the range of gender choices included those with local *and* colonial origins: the big man, the "enlightened" new elite, the monogamous Christian, and many other ways of living that did not fall neatly into these categories. The array of models underscores how difficult it is to rank masculinities in colonial Africa. This book does not describe masculinities as "hegemonic" or "subordinate."[5] Not only were there a variety of competing models for men to aspire to, but these models were neither coherent nor unchanging. The sheer proliferation of possibilities is partly what allowed people to "work with gender" so persistently and effectively.

To the extent that practices did shift over time, there was also a third explanation. Family and gender transformations resonated with workingmen's sense that they were part of a grand process of modernization. While the 1950s saw the early elaboration of modernization theory among social scientists and colonial administrators, this was also the era in which Nigerians looked forward to independence and increased prosperity. Many wage- and salary-earners took pride in their contributions to capitalist development, as well as their abilities to spread education and improve conditions within their own families. At the time and in hindsight, they described themselves as part of a movement of national modernization whose markers included a certain kind of family life: monogamous marriage, husband and father as family provider, and relatively loose ties with rural relatives. An awareness of being "modern" has shaped many pensioners' gendered self-representation, both in the sense of being different from women and being different from other men in other types of occupations.[6]

Yet even as many Nigerians in the mid-twentieth century embraced the notion of modernization, their definitions of it did not fit neatly with those of Western social scientists and administrators. To some extent, their aspirations seem consistent with the long-standing appeal of *ọlajú*, or seeking "enlightenment" by gaining access to resources in part through the adaptation of skills and values derived from outside the local community and then distributing some of the benefits through communal networks. Yet modernity in its Western-derived sense laid far more emphasis on the rational, autonomous individual, focused on his (yes, "his") nuclear family at the expense of wider connections. By the early 1960s, as the ideologies associated with colonialism increasingly came under criticism, trade unionists among many others searched for appropriately local ways of modernizing such institutions as the workforce and the family. The continuous evaluation and modification of different ways of living—those associated with foreign impositions as well as those seen as "traditional"—may be, as Karin Barber suggests, what most defines Yoruba, or even West African, modernity.[7] But even as the content of "modernity" was multivalent, it remained appealing as a marker of what was happening to people's lives and as a promise of good things to come.

Similarly, the ideological equation of wage earning with men and home making with women was always fraught with complexities and contradictions, but this did not prevent that equation from persisting. Today in Nigeria wage labor still is generally thought of as a male preserve, in spite of women's important income earning and the elusiveness of wages for most men.[8] According to a report produced in the mid-1980s by a coalition of female academics and activists, women comprised only 8 percent of the waged workforce, even though wage labor was highly desirable for women because it offered secure incomes and benefits. Female wage earners were concentrated at the lowest end of employment scales and were frequently denied benefits available to male employees. Trade unions generally ignored women's concerns and discouraged women's participation. And the "assumption that men are the bread-winners" remained both pervasive and deeply flawed.[9]

In a 1993 public address, for instance, a state chairman of the Nigerian Labor Congress likened the relationship between employers and workers to that of husbands and wives. "Even a housewife's loyalty and productivity in the family will be affected by her welfare," the trade union official said.

> At the best of times, she is the enterprising wife that holds the heart of the husband, serving and caring for her husband and children. . . . But at the other extreme, you would need to remind her that you need water after taking a meal and when she fetches the water, don't be surprised that the same water would be poured on you. This same relationship goes between the worker and his employer.[10]

The speaker's point was that employers should consider welfare provisions as important investments in employee productivity. His speech also reveals the normative ideal that wage earning is for men and unreflexively highlights the linkages between labor and domestic life that this book has traced. But at the same time, the reference to the wife's potential disrespect indicates the tensions beneath both the vision of male workers and female housewives and the ideal of committed workers and paternalistic employers.

These tensions have intensified since the 1964 general strike, the ending point of this book. Oil was discovered in southeastern Nigeria in the 1950s and exploration and exportation got underway in the 1960s. In the 1970s, the oil industry brought rapid economic growth and transformed Nigeria into a regional power, an emerging industrializing country, and the home of a prosperous middle class and an increasing number of conspicuous millionaires. The oil boom funded two government-mandated wage increases, in 1970–1971 and in 1974–1975. The latter, known as the Udoji awards, was a one-time windfall for workers, bringing a 100 percent wage increase, a lump-sum payment of arrears, and the addition of car allowances to many job categories. But at the same time, military governments worked to gain control of the labor unions. A 1976 commission of inquiry into trade union activities led to the arrest and banning of left-wing labor leaders, the dissolution of the central trade union organization that had been formed the previous year, and the appointment of a trade union administrator. Two years later, the government reorganized the existing unions and drastically reduced their number. The administration then sanctioned only one trade union center, the Nigerian Labor Congress. It was this organization which called Nigeria's third general strike, in May 1981. Wages and salaries had been frozen in the more austere economy of the late 1970s, and in 1979 vehicle loans and other allowances were cancelled, even as legislators in the Second Republic (1979–1983) voted themselves huge pay raises. The 1981 general strike lasted only a few days, but it involved an estimated 700,000 workers and succeeded in raising the minimum wage, forcing the reintroduction of car loans and basic allowances, and increasing pension rates by 60 percent.[11]

Nigeria suffered astronomical inflation in the 1980s as the price of oil declined on the world market and the administration of General Ibrahim Babangida (1985–1993) adopted structural adjustment policies. The cost of living index, pegged at zero for 1975, skyrocketed to 1,107 by the end of 1989. Pay cuts were imposed for the civil service and the army in 1985, and wages in other sectors declined as well. In 1989, the official minimum wage was 150 naira per month, and many did not even earn that. With 150 naira, as Margaret Peil has detailed, one could buy a half tin of local rice, a tin of *gari*, a tin of powdered milk, a liter of groundnut oil, two small loaves of bread, and six eggs—and this would have to last the month, with nothing left for other expenses such as rent, transport, clothing, or vegetables.[12] Needless to say, this was *not* a family wage. Few wage earners intended to make a career of it, and especially those at the bottom of the pay scales needed alternative sources of income simply to survive.

By the early 1990s when I started spending time in Nigeria, people seemed positively nostalgic for the previous decade, tough as it had been. Prices continued to rise, and the cruelty of the Abacha regime (1993–1998) softened the memories of foregoing governments, even military ones. There were two general strikes during the year I conducted dissertation research in Lagos and Ibadan: the NLC called a one-week walkout in August 1993 to protest the abrogation of the June 12 election, which would have installed Moshood Abiola as a civilian president; and in mid-November there was another short general strike to protest the government's removal of subsidies on the price of gasoline. This strike was ended by the military coup in which General Sani Abacha took power. There have been subsequent, short general strikes as well, including a protest against increased fuel prices in July 2003.

Economic deterioration and political chaos formed the context of my conversations with retired workers and their family members. The fortunes of the Nigerian Railway Corporation had been in decline since the 1960s because of mismanagement, increasing road competition, and Nigeria's economic orientation toward the oil sector at the expense of agriculture. Layoffs and inadequate pension provisions regularly plagued the workforce in the post-independence decades. Repeatedly through the late 1980s and 1990s, the NRC's financial problems caused it to defer salary payments to employees, pensions to retirees, and gratuities to the workers retrenched in successive waves.[13] Under these circumstances, as the wife of a former locomotive driver put it, "It was so hard to maintain the house, so terrible to feed ourselves and

Photo 8.1 Former locomotive driver Anthony Nnodua (right) and Hannah Nnodua in front of their shop adjacent to the railway compound, Ibadan, 1994.

the children—to talk less of the payment of the children's school fees."[14] In interviews, former locomotive drivers, senior station personnel, managers, and skilled craftsmen expressed anger and frustration with an employer they felt had cheated them, along with humiliation and anxiety because many were financially destitute. Men who were once "big," or who could previously afford to let hometown connections wane, now could not face their extended families because of financial "embarrassment" and certainly could not look to them for help.[15] Indeed, very few pensioners whom I surveyed were receiving any support from relatives. Most pinned their hopes on educated and employed children, many of whom schooled abroad or had emigrated from Nigeria. Yet only about half (54 percent) of those surveyed reported actually receiving support from their offspring. Others started small businesses, often using urban contacts forged during their years of formal employment.

Most pensioners, however, depended on their wives for money. Women who thirty to fifty years ago were able to shape their own careers around a husband's steady paycheck were now unable to retire from trading because they largely supported their households.[16] One pensioner's wife told me that although her husband used to give her money regularly, "since his retirement things have changed because all the allowances he used to give me were no more forthcoming."[17] This woman, like many others, was now shouldering

Photo 8.2 Ironic sign in front of the Pensioners' Union headquarters, Ebute Metta, Lagos, 1998.

more financial burdens than ever before. According to a former locomotive driver, "I live at the mercy of my wife [who] runs up and down going to farms to buy some fruits . . . that she sells to get us food." The wife of another railway pensioner agreed: "You know his [her husband's] income could not be enough like before. It's me that now struggles to give him money at times."[18] While some couples seemed resigned to this arrangement, in others the shift in the economic balance of power brought new tensions. Some pensioners' wives continued to earn for their own upkeep but no longer would feed their husbands.[19] According to the press, they were divorcing pensioners, as well as currently employed railway men, in droves.[20] In chapter 5, I showed that steadily earned incomes helped men to woo women and form relatively harmonious marriages; the absence of those wages over the past decade seems to be having the opposite effect.

Nigeria has no government-sponsored retirement plan, few employers offer pension schemes, not many individuals are even eligible for pensions, and—as with the railway men—those who are eligible are rarely paid.[21] So in fact, railway pensioners are in similar straits to most other Nigerian men their age, facing "retirement" without any financial security. And they share with men of all ages the sense that they have little to offer women who can or must fend for themselves.²² Yet their story is particularly poignant because they worked for, and expected, something different. Part of the pensioners' tragedy has to do with the rise and fall of their particular ideal of modern masculinity: they became self-styled breadwinners only to live out their retirements depending on their wives' trading incomes; they became self-styled "moderns" only to have the political and economic underpinnings of modernization, as they saw it, disintegrate. In the end, the ideal of modernization—and with it, modernizing families—helped to shape gendered aspirations that simply cannot be fulfilled under present political economic circumstances. Thus it is important to remember that gender transformations are not necessarily linear, and they must be considered within their material contexts.

The rise and fall of the modern male breadwinner in Nigeria points to the power and also the limits of colonial influence in Africa.²³ If this masculine model came into being in part through foreign impositions in the labor process and in the realm of ideology, it seems to be losing saliency as those influences disappear. Moreover, if new masculinities were associated with colonial capitalism, the story of the male breadwinner's rise and fall reminds us that capitalist structures, including a defined wage labor force with particular social relations, have beginnings and endings. What comes next is very much in question, both in terms of Nigeria's political and economic configuration and in terms of the arrangements individuals and families make to live within it. For now in southwestern Nigeria, the image of the working-class male breadwinner, however ambiguous and contradictory, persists more in discourse than in practice, and even as an elusive image it may not last much longer.

NOTES

1. Nancy Rose Hunt, *A Colonial Lexicon of Birth Ritual, Medicalization, and Mobility in the Belgian Congo* (Durham, NC: Duke University Press, 1999).

2. James Ferguson, *Expectations of Modernity: Myths and Meanings of Urban Life on the Zambian Copperbelt* (Berkeley: University of California Press, 1999), ch. 5.

3. See Laura L. Frader and Sonya O. Rose (eds.), *Gender and Class in Modern Europe* (Ithaca, NY: Cornell University Press, 1996).

4. Judith Butler, *Gender Trouble: Feminism and the Subversion of Identity* (New York: Routledge, 1990); Ferguson, *Expectations*, pp. 94–99.

5. R.W. Connell, *Masculinities* (Berkeley: University of California Press, 1995).

6. On this point, see Dorothy L. Hodgson, "Of Modernity/Modernities, Gender, and Ethnography," in Hodgson (ed.), *Gendered Modernities: Ethnographic Perspectives* (New York: Palgrave, 2001).

7. Karin Barber, *The Generation of Plays: Yoruba Popular Life in Theater* (Bloomington: Indiana University Press, 2000), pp. 236 and 424.

8. The International Labour Organization's 1993 *Yearbook of Labour Statistics* (Geneva: ILO), p. 54, classified 18.8 percent of Nigeria's economically active population

(5,783,500 out of 30,765,500) as "employees," of which 15 percent (876,500) were women.

9. Women in Nigeria, *The WIN Document: Conditions of Women in Nigeria and Policy Recommendations to 2,000 AD* (Zaria: Ahmadu Bello University Press, 1992 [1985]), pp. 17–20.

10. "Between Workers Welfare and Their Productivity," *The Guardian*, December 7, 1993.

11. Abubakar Sokoto Mohammed, "The Working Class," in Yusufu Bala Usman (ed.), *Nigeria since Independence: The First 25 Years;* vol. 1: *The Society* (Ibadan: Heinemann, 1989); Dafe Otobo, "The Nigeria General Strike of 1981," in Dafe Otobo and Morakinyo Omole (eds.), *Readings in Industrial Relations in Nigeria* (Lagos: Malthouse Press, 1987).

12. Margaret Peil, *Lagos: The City Is the People* (Boston, MA: G.K. Hall, 1991), pp. 101–2.

13. The situation is no better under the current administration. According to an April 29, 2002, letter to the editor of the online *Guardian* newspaper (www.ngrguardiannews.com) from Chuma Ifedi in Lagos, "The highest death rate among public service pensioners has been recorded during the current democratic regime. According to recent statistics, about 7,000 Railway pensioners have died in the last three years due to misery and destitution. The Federal Government owes Railway pensioners' arrears of 20 months pensions yet President Olusegun Obasanjo has no immediate plans to settle these outstanding dues. Patriotic citizens are shocked at the insensitivity of the President towards the deplorable plight of his fellow senior colleagues."

14. Hannah Nnodua, January 6, 1994, Ibadan.

15. Bernard Aruna, December 28, 1993, Ibadan; Emmanuel Erewa, January 23, 1994, Ibadan; M.A. Folarin, February 1, 1994, Ibadan.

16. This is a pervasive phenomenon in southern Nigeria, not restricted to the railway community. For men's financial dependence on their wives in a small Yoruba town, see Andrea Cornwall, "Wayward Women and Useless Men: Contest and Change in Gender Relations in Ado-Odo, S.W. Nigeria," in Dorothy L. Hodgson and Sheryl A. McCurdy (eds.), *"Wicked" Women and the Reconfiguration of Gender in Africa* (Portsmouth, NH: Heinemann, 2001), p.79. For southeastern Nigerian men's inability to be breadwinners in hard economic times, see Philomena E. Okeke, "Negotiating Social Independence: The Challenges of Career Pursuits for Igbo Women in Postcolonial Nigeria," in the same volume, p. 246.

17. Hannah Nnodua, January 6, 1994, Ibadan.

18. A. A. Salako, "Autobiography of Mr. Ayo-Ade Adeleke Salako, Retired Locomotive Engine Driver Grade I, 1951–1987," handwritten, June 1994, copy in author's possession; Olukemi Alabi, April 12, 1994, Ibadan.

19. Ruth Adekanola, February 17, 1994, Ibadan.

20. Ademola Adeyanju, Peter Ajayi Dada and Idowu Adelusi, "Non-Payment of Salaries: Divorce Rate Soars in Railways," *NT*, May 30, 1993.

21. Williams Ekanem, "For Pensions! It's Goodbye Tomorrow," *Post Express* (September 1, 1999), on-line at www.postexpresswired.com.

22. Andrea Cornwall, "To Be a Man Is More Than a Day's Work: Shifting Ideals of Masculinity in Ado-Odo, Southwestern Nigeria," in Lisa A. Lindsay and Stephan F. Miescher (eds.), *Men and Masculinities in Modern Africa* (Portsmouth, NH: Heinemann, 2003).

23. As Jacob Ajayi famously noted, "[I]n any long-term historical view of African history, European rule becomes just another episode." J. F. Ade Ajayi, "The Continuity of African Institutions under Colonialism," in T.O. Ranger (ed.), *Emerging Themes of African History* (Dar es Salaam: East African Publishing House, 1968), p. 194. A more recent and subtle rendering of both the power and the limitations of African colonialism is in Frederick Cooper, "Conflict and Connection: Rethinking Colonial African History," *AHR* 99 (1994): 1516–45.

BIBLIOGRAPHY

ARCHIVAL SOURCES

Nigerian National Archives, Ibadan

CADW: Federal Ministry of Education files
COMCOL 1: Commissioner of the Colony Office, Lagos files
CSO 26: Chief Secretary's Office, Lagos files
IBADAN DIV 1: Ibadan Divisional Office files
MED (FED) 1: Federal Ministry of Economic Development files
MLG (W): Ministry of Local Government Papers, Ibadan
OYO PROF: Oyo Provincial Office files
African Civil Servants Union, "Memorial Submitted to the Secretary of State Praying for the Amelioration of Salary and Other Service Conditions of the African Staff," May 1, 1943.
G. C. Whiteley, "Memorandum: Rates of Pay of Laborers and Employees in the Southern Provinces," Acting Chief Secretary's Office, Lagos, September 3, 1935.

Kenneth Dike Library, University of Ibadan, Nigeria

Herbert Macaulay Papers

Nigerian Railway Corporation (NRC) Headquarters, Ebute Metta

Senior Labor Relations Officer's files, labeled GM, GML, GMS, SC, and SL

NRC Pension Office, Ebute Metta

Personnel files of pensioners and annuitants, NRC headquarters

NRC Pension Office, Ibadan

Personnel files of pensioners and annuitants, Western Region

Obafemi Awolowo University Library, Ife

Civil Record Books, Agodi Customary Court, 1961–1964
Civil Record Books, Bere Native Court, 1930–1958
Civil Record Books, Ibadan Customary Court (Mapo Hall), 1958–1959
Criminal Record Book, Judicial Council of Ibadan, 1931–1934
Criminal Divorce Record Book, Ibadan City Customary Court (Mapo Hall), 1959–1965
Civil Record Books, Ibadan Customary Court (Ojaba), 1959
Criminal Record Books, Ibadan Customary Court (Ojaba), 1949–1958
Civil Record Books, Ojaba Native Court, 1930–1957
Criminal Record Book, Ojaba Native Court, 1931–1958
Civil Record Books, Ibadan City Customary Court (Oke Are), 1960–1965
Criminal Record Books, Ibadan City Customary Court (Oke Are), 1959–1965
Divorce Record Book, Ibadan Customary Court (Oke Are), 1960

Yaba Magistrate's Court, Lagos

Civil Record Books, Ebute Metta Magistrate's Court, 1948–1961
Civil Record Books, Lagos Magistrate's Court, 1949
Civil Record Books, Yaba Magistrate's Court, 1953–1961
Criminal Record Books, Ebute Metta Magistrate's Court, 1943–1961
Criminal Record Books, Lagos Magistrate's Court, 1957
Criminal Record Books, Yaba Magistrate's Court, 1961

Public Record Office, London

CO 554: West Africa Original Correspondence
CO 583: Nigeria Original Correspondence
CO 657: Nigeria Administrative Reports
CO 847: Africa Original Correspondence
CO 859: Social Service Correspondence
CO 888: Colonial Labor Advisory Committee Papers
DO 195: Commonwealth Relations Office and Commonwealth Office: West and General Africa Department and Successors: Registered Files

Rhodes House Library, Oxford, U.K.

Albert Harry Couzens Papers, MSS.Afr.s.1377
Edward Charles Ealey Papers, MSS.Afr.s.1148
Campbell Leach Waide Papers, MSS.Afr.s.757

Schomburg Center for Research in Black Culture, New York Public Library, United States

Nigerian Labor Archive, 1943–1975, collection of Chief O.A. Fagbenro Beyioku

Bibliography

INTERVIEWS AND RELATED MATERIAL

M.O. Adegbite, December 28,1993, Ibadan
Ruth Adekanola, February 17, 1994, Ibadan
E.A. Adelani, December 28, 1993, Ibadan
Victoria Adelani, December 28,1993, Ibadan
Adetunji Adeyemi, February 11, 1994, Ibadan
Felicia Adeyemi, February 11,1994, Ibadan
Ganiyu Adeyemi, May 6, 1994, Lagos
S.O. Akintola, May 2, 1994, Ibadan
Olukemi Alabi, March 3 and April 12, 1994, Ibadan
N.I. Sumonu Animasaun, July 6, 1998, Ibadan
Bernard Aruna, December 28, 1993, Ibadan
A.O. Bakare, May 6, 1994, Lagos
Raheem Balogun, July 20, 1998, Lagos
Emanuel Erewa, January 23, 1994, Ibadan
Mudasiru Folarin, January 11 and February 1, 1994, Ibadan
G.E. Gbenoba, March 22, 1994, Ibadan
Isaac Jokodola, February 11, 1994, Ibadan
L.A. Kassim, December 30, 1993, Ibadan
A.U. Nnodua, February 1, 1994, Ibadan
Hannah Nnodua, January 6, 1994, Ibadan
M.A. Odede, December 28, 1993, Ibadan
D.A. Owolabi, January 20, 1994, and July 13, 1998, Ibadan
Florence Owolabi, January 7, 1994, Ibadan
Dr. Wale Oyemakinde, October 5, 1993, Ibadan
A.S. Rufai, December 30, 1993, Ibadan
A.A. Salako, February 15, March 3, and April 12, 1994, and July 10, 1998, Ibadan
M.O. Shofekun, April 4, 1994, Ibadan
Francis Soetan, April 12, 1994, Ibadan
Eunice Soetan, April 19,1994, Ibadan
Folasade Tade, June 2 and June 9, 1994, Lagos
Rebecca Uchefuna, February 21, 1994, Ibadan
Salako, A.A. "Autobiography of Mr. Ayo-Ade Adeleke Salako, Retired Locomotive Engine Driver Grade I, 1951–1987." Handwritten and unpublished, 1994. Copy in author's possession.

PUBLISHED PRIMARY SOURCES

Reports

Bridges, A.F.B. (chair). *Report of a Committee Appointed to Consider the Adequacy or Otherwise of the Rates of Pay of Labour and of African Government Servants and Employees in the Township of Lagos.* Cost of Living Committee, Lagos: Published for the Government by the Crown Agents, 1942.
Federation of Nigeria. *Conclusions of the Government of the Federation on the Report of the Commission on the Public Services of the Governments in the Federation of Nigeria, 1954–55.* Lagos: Federal Government Printer, 1955.

———. Federal Census Office. *Population Census of Nigeria, 1963.*
———. Federal Census Office. *Population Census of Nigeria, 1963, Western Region.*
———. Federal Department of Statistics. *Urban Consumer Surveys in Nigeria: Report on Enquiries into the Income and Expenditure Patterns of Wage-Earner Households in Lagos [1953/54], Enugu [1954/55] and Ibadan [1955].* Lagos: Government Printer, 1957.
———. Federal Ministry of Labor. *Annual Reports* (1959–1964).
———. Federal Office of Statistics. *Report on Enquiries into the Income and Expenditure Patterns of Lower and Middle Income Households at Ibadan.* Lagos: Federal Office of Statistics, 1961/2.
———. Federal Office of Statistics. *Report on Enquiries into the Income and Expenditure Patterns of Lower and Middle Income Households in Lagos, 1959–60.* Lagos: Federal Office of Statistics, 1963.
Foot, H.M. (chair). *Report of the Commission Appointed by His Excellency the Governor to Make Recommendations about the Recruitment and Training of Nigerians for Senior Posts in the Government Service of Nigeria.* Lagos: Government Printer, 1948.
Gorsuch, L.H. (chair). *Report of the Commission on the Public Services of the Governments in the Federation of Nigeria 1954–55.* Lagos: Federal Government of Nigeria, 1955.
Harragin, Walter (chair). *Report of the Commission on the Public Services of the Governments in the Federation of Nigeria 1954–55.* Lagos: Federal Government of Nigeria, 1955.
Hoskyns-Abrahall, T. *Report of the Lagos Town Planning Commission with Recommendations on the Planning and Development of Greater Lagos.* Lagos: Government Printer, 1946.
International Labour Organization. *African Labour Survey.* Geneva: ILO, 1958.
———. *Yearbook of Labour Statistics.* 52nd issue. Geneva: ILO, 1993.
Leese, C.W. (chair). *Report of the Committee Appointed by His Excellency the Governor to Enquire into the Question of Unemployment.* Nigeria Legislative Council Sessional Paper 46/1935. Lagos: Government Printer, 1935.
Miller, E.A. (chair). *Report on Unestablished and Daily-Rated Government Servants.* Lagos: Government Printer, 1947.
Morgan, Adeyinka (chair). *Report of the Commission on the Review of Wages, Salary and Conditions of Service of the Junior Employees of the Governments of the Federation and in Private Establishments, 1963–64.* Lagos: Federal Ministry of Information, 1964.
Nigeria. *Annual Report on the Colony* (1946).
———. *Annual Report of the Federal Ministry of Labour, Labour Division* (1963–64).
———. *Annual Report on the General Progress of Development and Welfare Schemes* (1946–53).
———. *Annual Report on the Government Railway and Colliery of Nigeria* (1934–37).
———. *Annual Report on the Government Railway* (1937–55).
———. *Annual Report on the Nigerian Marine* (1945–53).
———. *Annual Report of the Public Works Department* (1944–47).
———. *Annual Report on the Social and Economic Progress of the People of Nigeria* (1931–38).
———. *Annual Reports of the Department of Labor* (1942–59).
———. *Blue Books* (1930–45).
———. *Census of Nigeria*, 1931.
———. *Guide Book for Trade Union Officials.* Lagos: Government Printer, n.d. [1950?].
———. *Marine Department Annual Report* (1929–38).

———. *Report of the Elias Commission of Enquiry into the Administration, Economic and Industrial Relations of the Nigerian Railway Corporation*. Lagos: Government Printer, 1960.

———. Department of Statistics. *Population Census of Lagos, 1950*. Kaduna: Government Printer, 1951.

———. Department of Statistics. *Population Census of Nigeria, 1952–53*.

———. Department of Statistics. *Population Census of the Western Region of Nigeria, 1952*. Lagos: Government Printer, Western Region, 1956.

Nigerian Ports Authority. *Annual Reports* (1956–60).

Nigerian Railway and Udi Coal Mines. *Annual Reports* (1931–33).

Nigerian Railway Corporation. *Notes on Industrial Relations Submitted to the Elias Commission of Enquiry*. Lagos: Government Printer, 1960.

———. *Report and Accounts for the Year Ended 31st March 1962*. Lagos: NRC, 1962.

———. *Report and Accounts for the Year Ended 31st March 1965*. Lagos: NRC, 1965.

———. *Standard Conditions of Service, 1957. Officers*. Ebute Metta: Railway Printer, 1957.

Orde Browne, G. St. J. *Labour Conditions in West Africa*. Cmd. 6277. London: HMSO, 1941.

Rishworth, H.R. (chair). *A Report on Medical and Sanitary Conditions on the Nigerian Railway with Recommendations for a Railway Medical Service*. Wightman Mountain Ltd., 1955.

Tudor Davies, W. (chair). *Enquiry into the Cost of Living and the Control of the Cost of Living in the Colony and Protectorate of Nigeria*. Colonial No. 204. London: HMSO, 1946.

Yesufu, T.M. *Consumption Patterns and Living Conditions of Employees of the Nigerian Tobacco Company Ltd*. Lagos: Nigerian Tobacco Company Ltd., 1967.

Newspapers and Magazines

Daily Service (Lagos)
Daily Times (Lagos)
Drum
The Guardian (Lagos)
The Guardian online (www.ngrguardiannews.com)
Labour Champion
Nigerail, the Journal of the Nigerian Railway Corporation
Nigeria (Lagos)
The Nigerian Worker
Nigerian Tribune
Post Express (online at www.postexpresswired.com)
The Railway Technician, Monthly Journal of the Railway Technical Staff Association
Sunday Times (Lagos)
The Times Survey of the British Colonies (London)
West African Pilot

BOOKS, CHAPTERS, DISSERTATIONS, AND ARTICLES

Achebe, Chinua. *A Man of the People*. New York: Anchor Books, 1989 [1966].

Adebayo, Augustus. *White Man in Black Skin*. Ibadan: Spectrum Books, 1981.

Adebo, Chief Simeon O. *Our Unforgettable Years*. Lagos: MacMillian Nigeria Publishers Ltd., 1983.

Adepoju, A.A. "Some Aspects of Migration and Family Relationships in South-West Nigeria." *Legon Family Research Papers, Institute of African Studies* 3 (1975): 148–56.
Afonja, Simi. "Changing Modes of Production and the Sexual Division of Labor among the Yoruba." *Signs* 7 (1981): 299–313.
Ajayi, J. F. Ade. "The Continuity of African Institutions under Colonialism." In *Emerging Themes of African History*, ed. T.O. Ranger. Dar es Salaam: East African Publishing House, 1968.
Akinola, R.A. "The Growth and Development of Ibadan, the Largest Yoruba Town." *Bulletin of the Ghana Geographical Association* 11 (1966): 48–63.
Aladesanmi, Daniel Anirarẹ. *My Early Life: An Autobiography*. Privately published in Nigeria, 1977.
Allman, Jean and Victoria Tashjian. *"I Will Not Eat Stone": A Women's History of Colonial Asante*. Portsmouth, NH: Heinemann, 2000.
Amadiume, Ifi. *Male Daughters, Female Husbands: Gender and Sex in an African Society*. London: Zed Books, 1987.
Ananaba, Wogu. *The Trade Union Movement in Nigeria*. New York: Africana Publishing, 1970.
Aronson, Dan R. *The City Is Our Farm: Seven Migrant Ijebu Yoruba Families*. Cambridge MA: Schenkman, 1978.
Awe, Bolanle. "The Economic Role of Women in a Traditional African Society: The Yoruba Example." In *La Civilisation de la Femme dans la Tradition Africaine*. Paris: Presence Africaine, 1975.
Azikiwe, Nnamdi. *My Odyssey: An Autobiography*. London: C. Hurst, 1970.
Baker, Pauline. *Urbanization and Political Change: The Politics of Lagos, 1917–67*. Berkeley: University of California Press, 1974.
Barber, Karin. *The Generation of Plays: Yoruba Popular Life in Theater*. Bloomington: Indiana University Press, 2000.
———. *I Could Speak until Tomorrow: Oriki, Women, and the Past in a Yoruba Town*. Edinburgh: Edinburgh University Press, 1991.
———. "Money, Self-Realization, and the Person in Yoruba Texts." In *Money Matters: Instability, Values and Social Payments in the Modern History of West African Communities*. Edited by Jane I. Guyer. Portsmouth, NH: Heinemann, 1994.
Barnes, Sandra T. *Patrons and Power: Creating a Political Community in Metropolitan Lagos*. Bloomington: Indiana University Press, 1986.
Baron, Ava. "Introduction" to *Work Engendered: Toward a New History of American Labor*. Edited by Ava Baron. Ithaca, NY: Cornell University Press, 1991.
Barrett, M., and M. McIntosh. "The 'Family Wage': Some Problems for Socialists and Feminists." *Capital and Class* 9 (1980): 51–72.
Bascom, William. *The Yoruba of Southwestern Nigeria*. New York: Holt, Rinehart & Winston, 1969.
Bastian, Misty L. "Acadas and Fertilizer Girls: Young Nigerian Women and the Romance of Middle-Class Modernity." In *Gendered Modernities*. Edited by Dorothy L. Hodgson.
Beier, H.U. "The Position of Yoruba Women." *Presence Africaine* 1 (1955): 39–46.
Beinart, William. *The Political Economy of Pondoland, 1860–1930*. Cambridge: Cambridge University Press, 1982.
Bennett, Robert. "Gendering Cultures in Business and Labor History: Marriage Bars in Clerical Employment." In *Working Out Gender: Perspectives from Labour History*. Edited by Margaret Walsh. Aldershot, U.K.: Ashgate, 1999.

Bibliography

Berry, Sara. *Cocoa, Custom, and Socio-Economic Change in Rural Western Nigeria.* Oxford: Clarendon Press, 1975.

———. *Fathers Work for their Sons: Accumulation, Mobility, and Class Formation in an Extended Yoruba Community.* Berkeley: University of California, 1985.

———. *No Condition is Permanent: The Social Dynamics of Agrarian Change in Sub-Saharan Africa.* Madison: University of Wisconsin Press, 1993.

Bird, Mary E. C. "Social Change in Kinship and Marriage among the Yoruba of Western Nigeria." D. Phil. thesis, University of Edinburgh, 1958.

———. "Urbanization, Family and Marriage in Western Nigeria." In *Urbanization in African Social Change.* Edited by M. Ruel. Edinburgh: Edinburgh University Centre for African Studies, 1963.

Bloch, Maurice, and Jonathan Parry. "Introduction." In *Money and the Morality of Exchange.* Edited by J. Parry and M. Bloch. Cambridge: Cambridge University Press, 1989.

Braundi, Emile R., and Antonio Lettieri. "The General Strike in Nigeria." *International Socialist Journal* 1 (1964): 598–609.

Bravman, Bill. *Making Ethnic Ways: Communities and Their Transformations in Taita, Kenya, 1800–1950.* Portsmouth, NH: Heinemann, 1998.

Brown, Carolyn A. "A 'Man' in the Village Is a 'Boy' in the Workplace: Colonial Racism, Worker Militance and Igbo Notions of Masculinity in the Nigerian Coal Industry, 1930–1945." In *Men and Masculinities.* Edited by Lisa A. Lindsay and Stephan F. Miescher.

———. *"We Were All Slaves": African Miners, Culture and Resistance: The Enugu Government Colliery, Nigeria, 1914–1950.* Portsmouth, NH: Heinemann, 2003.

Burton, Antoinette. *Burdens of History: British Feminists, Indian Women, and Imperial Culture, 1865–1915.* Chapel Hill: University of North Carolina Press, 1994.

Butler, Judith. *Gender Trouble: Feminism and the Subversion of Identity.* New York: Routledge, 1990.

Byfield, Judith. "Women, Marriage, Divorce and the Emerging Colonial State in Abeokuta (Nigeria), 1892–1904." *CJAS* 30 (1996): 32–51.

Caldwell, J. C., I. O. Orubuloye, and P. Caldwell. "The Destabilization of the Traditional Yoruba Sexual System." *Population and Development Review* 17 (1991): 229–62.

Callaway, Helen. *Gender, Culture and Empire: European Women in Colonial Nigeria.* Urbana: University of Illinois Press, 1987.

Carrigan, Tim, R. W. Connell, and John Lee. "Toward a New Sociology of Masculinity." *Theory and Society* 14 (1985): 551–604.

Chauncey, George Jr., "The Locus of Reproduction: Women's Labour in the Zambian Copperbelt, 1927–1953." *JSAS* 7 (1981): 135–64.

Clark, Anna. "Manhood, Womanhood, and the Politics of Class in Britain, 1790–1845." In *Gender and Class in Modern Europe.* Edited by Laura L. Frader and Sonya O. Rose.

———. "The New Poor Law and the Breadwinner Wage: Contrasting Assumptions." *Journal of Social History* 34 (2000): 261–81.

———. *The Struggle for the Breeches: Gender and the Making of the British Working Class.* Berkeley: University of California Press, 1995.

Clark, Gracia. "Gender and Profiteering: Ghana's Market Women as Devoted Mothers and 'Human Vampire Bats.'" In *"Wicked" Women and the Reconfiguration of Gender in Africa.* Edited by Dorothy L. Hodgson and Sheryl A. McCurdy.

———. *Onions Are My Husband: Survival and Accumulation by West African Market Women*. Chicago: University of Chicago Press, 1994.

Cohen, Robin. *Labour and Politics in Nigeria, 1945–71*. London: Heinemann, 1974.

———. "Michael Imoudu and the Nigerian Labour Movement." In *The Nigerian Class Structure*. Edited by Oshomha Imoagene. Ibadan: Evans Brothers, 1989.

———. "Nigeria's Labour Leader No. 1: Notes for a Biographical Study of M.A.O. Imoudu." *JHSN* 5 (1970): 303–8.

Coleman, James S. *Nigeria: Background to Nationalism*. Berkeley: University of California Press, 1971.

Comaroff, Jean, and John Comaroff, eds. *Modernity and Its Malcontents: Ritual and Power in Postcolonial Africa*. Chicago: University of Chicago Press, 1993.

Comaroff, John. "Introduction." In *The Meaning of Marriage Payments*. Edited by J.L. Comaroff. London: Academic Press, 1980.

Comhaire-Sylvain, S. "Le travail des femmes á Lagos, Nigèria." *Zaire* 5 (1951): 169–87.

Connell, R.W. *Gender and Power: Society, the Person and Sexual Politics*. Stanford, CA: Stanford University Press, 1987.

———. *Masculinities*. Berkeley: University of California Press, 1995.

Cooper, Barbara M. "Women's Worth and Wedding Gift Exchange in Maradi, Niger, 1907–89." *JAH* 36 (1995): 121–40.

Cooper, Frederick. "Conflict and Connection: Rethinking Colonial African History." *AHR* 99 (1994): 1516–45.

———. *Decolonization and African Society: The Labor Question in French and British Africa*. Cambridge: Cambridge University Press, 1996.

———. "From Free Labor to Family Allowances: Labor and African Society in Colonial Discourse." *American Ethnologist* 16 (1989): 745–65.

———. "Industrial Man Goes to Africa." In *Men and Masculinities in Modern Africa*. Edited by Lisa A. Lindsay and Stephan F. Miescher.

———. "Modernizing Bureaucrats, Backward Africans, and the Development Concept." In *International Development and the Social Sciences: Essays on the History and Politics of Knowledge*. Edited by Frederick Cooper and Randall Packard. Berkeley: University of California Press, 1997.

———. "The Senegalese General Strike of 1946 and the Labor Question in Post-War French Africa." *CJAS* 24 (1990): 165–215.

Cooper, Frederick, and Ann L. Stoler, eds. *Tensions of Empire: Colonial Cultures in a Bourgeois World*. Berkeley: University of California Press, 1997.

Cornwall, Andrea. "To Be a Man Is More Than a Day's Work: Shifting Ideals of Masculinity in Ado-Odo, Southwestern Nigeria." In *Men and Masculinities in Modern Africa*. Edited by Lisa A. Lindsay and Stephan F. Miescher.

———. "Wayward Women and Useless Men: Contest and Change in Gender Relations in Ado-Odo, S.W. Nigeria." In *"Wicked" Women and the Reconfiguration of Gender in Africa*. Edited by Dorothy L. Hodgson and Steryl McCurdy.

Cornwall, Andrea, and Nancy Lindisfarne. "Dislocating Masculinity: Gender, Power and Anthropology." In *Dislocating Masculinity: Comparative Ethnographies*. Edited by Andrea Cornwall and Nancy Lindisfarne. London: Routledge, 1994.

Creighton, Colin. "The Rise of the Male Breadwinner Family: A Reappraisal." *CSSH* 38 (1996): 310–37.

Damachi, Ukandi Godwin. *Nigerian Modernization: The Colonial Legacy*. New York: Third Press, 1972.

Denzer, LaRay. "Domestic Science Training in Colonial Yorubaland, Nigeria." In *African Encounters with Domesticity*. Edited by Karen Tranberg Hansen.
———. *Folayegbe M. Akintunde-Ighodalo: A Public Life*. Ibadan: Sam Bookman Publishers, 2001.
———. "Women in Government Service in Colonial Nigeria, 1862–1945." *Boston University Working Papers in African Studies* No. 136 (1989).
———. "Yoruba Women: A Historiographical Study." *I JAHS* 27 (1994): 1–39.
Diamond, Larry. *Class, Ethnicity and Democracy in Nigeria: The Failure of the First Republic*. New York: Macmillan, 1988.
Dosu-Oyewole, H.H. *Narrative History of the Great Strike*. Lagos: Charity Printers, 1964.
Downs, Laura Lee. *Manufacturing Inequality: Gender Division in the French and British Metalworking Industries, 1914–1939*. Ithaca, NY: Cornell University Press, 1995.
Ducker, James H. *Men of the Steel Rails: Workers on the Atchison, Topeka and Santa Fe Railroad, 1869–1900*. Lincoln: University of Nebraska Press, 1983.
Ekong, Sheilah Clarke. "Continuity and Change in Nigerian Family Patterns." In *Social Change in Nigeria*. Edited by Simi Afonja and Tola Olu Pearce. London: Longman, 1984.
Ekundare, R. Olufemi. *An Economic History of Nigeria, 1860–1960*. New York: Africana Publishing, 1973.
Ekwensi, Cyprian. *Lokotown and Other Stories*. London: Heinemann, 1966.
Emecheta, Buchi. *The Joys of Motherhood*. New York: George Braziller, 1979.
Emejulu, L.M.E. *A Brief History of the Railway Workers Union*. Lagos: Railway Printer, 1949.
Etherington, Norman. "Natal's Black Rape Scare of the 1870s." *JSAS* 15 (1988): 2–53.
Fadipe, N.A. *The Sociology of the Yoruba*. Edited by F.O. Okediji and O.O. Okediji. Ibadan: University of Ibadan Press, 1970.
Fafunwa, A. Babs. *History of Education in Nigeria*. London: George Allen and Unwin, 1974.
Falola, Toyin. *The History of Nigeria*. Westport, CT: Greenwood, 1999.
Falola, Toyin, and Akanmu Adebayo. *Culture, Politics and Money among the Yoruba*. New Brunswick, NJ: Transaction Publishers, 2000.
Fapohunda, Eleanor R. "The Non-Pooling Household: A Challenge to Theory." In *A Home Divided: Women and Income in the Third World*. Edited by Daisy Dwyer and Judith Bruce. Stanford, CA: Stanford University Press, 1988.
———. "The Nuclear Household Model in Nigerian Public and Private Sector Policy: Colonial Legacy and Socio-Political Implications." *Development and Change* 18 (1987): 281–94.
Fashoyin, Tayo. *Industrial Relations in Nigeria*. London: Longman, 1980.
Fashoyin, Tayo, Felicia Durojaiye Oyekanmi, and Eleanor R. Fapohunda, eds. *Women in the Modern Sector Labour Force in Nigeria*. Lagos: Department of Industrial Relations and Personnel Management, University of Lagos, 1985.
Felski, Rita. *The Gender of Modernity*. Cambridge, MA: Harvard University Press, 1995.
Ferguson, James. *Expectations of Modernity: Myths and Meanings of Urban Life on the Zambian Copperbelt*. Berkeley: University of California Press, 1999.
Forde, C. Daryll, ed. *Social Implications of Industrialization and Urbanization in Africa South of the Sahara*. Paris: UNESCO, 1956.
Frader, Laura L. "Engendering Work and Wages: The French Labor Movement and the Family Wage." In *Gender and Class in Modern Europe*. Edited by Laura L.Frader and Sonya O. Rose.

Frader, Laura L., and Sonya O. Rose. "Gender and the Reconstruction of European Working-Class History." In *Gender and Class in Modern Europe*. Edited by Laura L. Frader and Sonya O. Rose.
Frader, Laura L., and Sonya O. Rose, eds. *Gender and Class in Modern Europe*. Ithaca, NY: Cornell University Press, 1996.
Galletti, R., K. D. S. Baldwin, and I. O. Dina. *Nigerian Cocoa Farmers: An Economic Survey of Yoruba Cocoa Farming Families*. London: Oxford University Press, 1956.
Gaonkar, Dilip Parameshwar. "On Alternative Modernities." *Public Culture* 11 (1999): 1–18.
Goode, William J. *World Revolution and Family Patterns*. New York: Free Press, 1963.
Grillo, R. D. *African Railwaymen: Solidarity and Opposition in an East African Labour Force*. Cambridge: Cambridge University Press, 1973.
Gutkind, P.C.W. "African Urban Family Life: Comment on an Analysis of Some Rural-Urban Differences." *Cahiers d'etudes africaines* 3 (1962): 149–217.
Guyer, Jane I. "Lineal Identities and Lateral Networks: The Logic of Polyandrous Motherhood." In *Nuptiality in Sub-Saharan Africa: Contemporary Anthropological and Demographic Perspectives*. Edited by Caroline Bledsoe and Gilles Pison. Oxford: Clarendon Press, 1994.
———. "Wealth in People, Wealth in Things—Introduction," *JAH* 36 (1995): 83–90.
Guyer, Jane I., ed. *Money Matters: Instability, Values and Social Payments in the Modern History of West African Communities*. Portsmouth, NH: Heinemann, 1995.
Guyer, Jane Mason. "The Organizational Plan of Traditional Farming: Idere, Western Nigeria." Ph.D. dissertation, University of Rochester, 1972.
Hansen, Karen Tranberg, ed. *African Encounters with Domesticity*. New Brunswick, NJ: Rutgers University Press, 1992.
———. *Distant Companions: Servants and Employers in Zambia, 1900–1985*. Ithaca, NY: Cornell University Press, 1989.
Hareven, Tamara K. "Modernization and Family History: Perspectives on Social Change," *Signs* 2 (1976): 190–206.
Harries, Patrick. *Work, Culture, and Identity: Migrant Laborers in Mozambique and South Africa, 1860–1910*. Portsmouth, NH: Heinemann, 1994.
Hartmann, Heidi. "Capitalism, Patriarchy, and Job Segregation by Sex." *Signs* 1 (1976): 137–69.
Hodgson, Dorothy L. "Of Modernity/Modernities, Gender, and Ethnography." In *Gendered Modernities*. Edited by Dorothy L. Hodgson.
Hodgson, Dorothy L., ed. *Gendered Modernities: Ethnographic Perspectives*. New York: Palgrave, 2001.
Hodgson, Dorothy L., and Sheryl McCurdy, eds. *"Wicked" Women and the Reconfiguration of Gender in Africa*. Portsmouth, NH: Heinemann, 2001.
Hopkins, A.G. "The Lagos Strike of 1897: An Exploration in Nigerian Labour History." *Past and Present* 35 (1966): 133–55.
———. "A Report on the Yoruba, 1910," *JHSN* 5 (1969): 67–100.
Hughes, Arnold and Robin Cohen. "An Emerging Nigerian Working Class: The Lagos Experience, 1897–1939." In *African Labor History*. Edited by P.C.W. Gutkind, Robin Cohen and Jean Copans. London: Sage, 1979.
Hunt, Nancy Rose. "Le Bebe en Brousse': European Women, African Birth Spacing and Colonial Intervention in Breast Feeding in the Belgian Congo." *IJAHS* 21 (1988): 401–32.

———. *A Colonial Lexicon; of Birth Ritual, Medicalization, and Mobility in the Congo.* Durham, NC: Duke University Press, 1999.
———. "Introduction." In *Gendered Colonialisms in African History*. Edited by N.R. Hunt, T.P. Liu, and J. Quataert. Oxford: Blackwell, 1997.
———. "Noise over Camouflaged Polygamy, Colonial Morality Taxation and a Woman-Naming Crisis in Belgian Africa." *JAH* 32 (1991): 471–94.
Ifaturoti, M.A. "Female Employment and Related Personnel Problems." In *Women in the Modern Sector Labour Force*. Edited by Tayo Fashoyin, Felicia Durojaiye Oyekanmi, and Eleanor R. Fapohunda.
Izzett, Alison. "Family Life among the Yoruba in Lagos, Nigeria." In *Social Change in Modern Africa*. Edited by A. Southall. London: Oxford University Press, 1961.
Jaekel, Francis. *The History of the Nigerian Railway*. 3 vols. Ibadan: Spectrum Books Ltd., 1997.
Jeater, Diana. *Marriage, Perversion, and Power: The Construction of Moral Discourse in Southern Rhodesia, 1894–1930*. Oxford: Clarendon Press, 1993.
Jeffries, Richard. *Class, Power and Ideology in Ghana: The Railwaymen of Sekondi*. Cambridge: Cambridge University Press, 1978.
Joby, R.S. *The Railwaymen*. London: David and Charles, Ltd., 1984.
Johnson, Cheryl. "Madam Alimotu Pelewura and the Lagos Market Women." *Tarikh: Grass Roots Leadership in Colonial West Africa* 7 (1981): 1–10.
———. "Towards a Conceptual Framework for the Study of African Women: A Case Study of Pre-Colonial and Colonial Yoruba Women." *Red River Historical Journal of World History* 55 (1979): 52–63.
Karanja-Diejomaoh, Wambui M. "Perceptions of Marriage, Family and Work in Nigeria: A Study of Lagos Market Women." D. Phil., Oxford University, 1980.
Kilby, Peter. *African Enterprise: The Nigerian Bread Industry*. Stanford, CA: Hoover Institution on War, Revolution, and Peace, 1965.
———. *Industrialization in an Open Economy: Nigeria, 1945–1966*. Cambridge: Cambridge University Press, 1969.
———. "The Nigerian Labourer." *Ibadan* 10 (1960): 23–24.
Killingray, David and Richard Rathbone, eds. *Africa and the Second World War*. New York: St. Martin's Press, 1986.
Kingsford, Peter. *Victorian Railwaymen: The Emergence and Growth of Railroad Labour, 1830–70*. London: Frank Cass, 1970.
Lewis, Jane. *Women of England, 1870–1950: Sexual Division and Social Change*. Bloomington: Indiana University Press, 1984.
Licht, Walter. *Working for the Railroad: The Organization of Work in the Nineteenth Century*. Princeton, NJ: Princeton University Press, 1983.
Lindfors, Bernth, and Oyekan Owomoyela. *Yoruba Proverbs: Translation and Annotation*. Papers in International Studies, Africa Series No. 17. Athens: Ohio University Center for International Studies, 1973.
Lindsay, Lisa A. "Domesticity and Difference: Male Breadwinners, Working Women, and Colonial Citizenship in the 1945 Nigerian General Strike." *AHR* 104, no. 3 (1999): 783–812.
———. "Money, Marriage and Masculinity on the Colonial Nigerian Railway." In *Men and Masculinities in Modern Africa*. Edited by Lisa A. Lindsay and Stephan F. Miescher.
———. "'No Need . . . to Think of Home'? Masculinity and Domestic Life on the Nigerian Railway, c. 1940–61." *JAH* 39 (1998): 439–66.

———. "Putting the Family on Track: Gender and Domestic Life on the Colonial Nigerian Railway." Ph.D. dissertation, University of Michigan, 1996.
Lindsay, Lisa A., and Stephan F. Miescher, eds. *Men and Masculinities in Modern Africa*. Portsmouth, NH: Heinemann, 2003.
Little, Kenneth. "Some Urban Patterns of Marriage and Domesticity in West Africa." *Sociological Review* 7 (1959): 65–82.
Lloyd, Barbara. "Indigenous Ibadan." In *The City of Ibadan*. Edited by P.C. Lloyd, A.L. Mabogunje, and B. Awe. Ibadan: Institute of African Studies, 1967.
Lloyd, P.C. "The Status of the Yoruba Wife." *Sudan Society* 2 (1963): 35–42.
Low, D.A., and J.M. Lonsdale. "Introduction: Towards the New Order, 1945–1963." In *History of East Africa*, vol. 3. Edited by D.A. Low and Alison Smith. Oxford: Oxford University Press, 1976.
Mabogunje, Akin. "The Market-Woman." *Ibadan* 11 (1961): 14–17.
———. *Urbanization in Nigeria*. London: University of London Press, 1968.
Macnicol, John. *The Movement for Family Allowances, 1918–45: A Study in Social Policy Development*. London: Heinemann, 1980.
Mani, Lata. "Contentious Traditions: The Debate on *Sati* in Colonial India." In *Recasting Women: Essays in Indian Colonial History*. Edited by Kumkum Sangari and Sudesh Vaid. New Brunswick, NJ: Rutgers University Press, 1990.
Mann, Kristin. *Marrying Well: Marriage, Status and Social Change among the Educated Elite in Colonial Lagos*. Cambridge: Cambridge University Press, 1985.
———. "Owners, Slaves and the Struggle for Labor in the Commercial Transition at Lagos." In *From Slave Trade to "Legitimate" Commerce: The Commercial Transition in Nineteenth-Century West Africa*. Edited by Robin Law. Cambridge: Cambridge University Press, 1995.
———. "The Rise of Taiwo Olowo: Law, Accumulation, and Mobility in Early Colonial Lagos." In *Law in Colonial Africa*. Edited by Kristin Mann and Richard Roberts. Portsmouth, NH: Heinemann, 1991.
———. "Women's Rights in Law and Practice: Marriage and Dispute Settlement in Colonial Lagos." In *African Women and the Law: Historical Perspectives*. Edited by Margaret Jean Hay and Marcia Wright. Boston, MA: Boston University, 1982.
Mark-Lawson, Jane, and Anne Witz. "From 'Family Labour' to 'Family Wage'? The Case of Women's Labour in Nineteenth-Century Coalmining." *Social History* 13 (1988): 151–74.
Marris, Peter. *Family and Social Change in an African City: A Study of Rehousing in Lagos*. Evanston, IL: Northwestern University Press, 1962.
May, Martha. "Bread before Roses: American Workingmen, Labor Unions, and the Family Wage." In *Women, Work, and Protest: A Century of U.S. Women's Labor History*. Edited by Ruth Milkman. Boston, MA: Routledge and Kegan Paul, 1985.
Maynard, Steven. "Rough Work and Rugged Men: The Social Construction of Masculinity in Working-Class History." *Labour/Le Travail* 23 (1989): 159–69.
Mba, Nina Emma. *Nigerian Women Mobilized: Women's Political Activity in Southern Nigeria, 1900–1965*. Berkeley, CA: Institute of International Studies, 1982, 232.
McClelland, Keith. "Masculinity and the 'Representative Artisan' in Britain, 1850–1880." In *Manful Assertions: Masculinities in Britain Since 1800*. Edited by Michael Roper and John Tosh. London: Routledge, 1991.
———. "Rational and Respectable Men: Gender, the Working Class, and Citizenship in Britain, 1850–1867." In *Gender and Class in Modern Europe*. Edited by Laura L. Frader and Sonya O. Rose.

———. "Some Thoughts on Masculinity and the 'Representative Artisan' in Britain." *Gender and History* 1 (1989): 164–77.

———. "Time to Work, Time to Live: Some Aspects of Work and the Re-Formation of Class in Britain, 1850–1880." In *The Historical Meanings of Work*. Edited by Patrick Joyce. Cambridge: Cambridge University Press, 1987.

Melson, Robert. "Nigerian Politics and the General Strike of 1964." In *Protest and Power in Black Africa*. Edited by Robert I. Rotberg and Ali A. Mazrui. New York: Oxford University Press, 1970.

Miescher, Stephan F. "The Life Histories of Boakye Yiadom (Akasease Kofi of Abetifi, Kwawu): Exploring the Subjectivity and 'Voices' of a Teacher-Catechist in Colonial Ghana." In *African Words, African Voices: Critical Practices in Oral History*. Edited by Luise White, Stephan F. Miescher, and David William Cohen. Bloomington: Indiana University Press, 2001.

———. "The Making of Presbyterian Teachers: Masculinities and Programs of Education in Colonial Ghana." In *Men and Masculinities in Modern Africa*. Edited by Lisa A. Lindsay and Stephan F. Miescher.

Miescher, Stephan F., and Lisa A. Lindsay. "Men and Masculinities in Modern African History." In *Men and Masculinities in Modern Africa*. Edited by Lisa A. Lindsay and Stephan F. Miescher.

Milkman, Ruth. *Gender at Work: The Dynamics of Job Segregation by Sex during World War II*. Urbana: University of Illinois Press, 1987.

Mohammed, Abubakar Sokoto. "The Working Class." In *Nigeria Since Independence: The First 25 Years*, Vol. 1: The Society. Edited by Yusufu Bala Usman. Ibadan: Heinemann, 1989.

Moodie, T. Dunbar with Vivienne Ndatshe. *Going for Gold: Men, Mines and Migration*. Berkeley: University of California Press, 1994.

Moore, Sally Falk. *Anthropology and Africa: Changing Perspectives on a Changing Scene*. Charlottesville: University Press of Virginia, 1994.

Murray, Colin. *Families Divided: The Impact of Migrant Labour in Lesotho*. Cambridge: Cambridge University Press, 1981.

Nelson, Scott. *Iron Confederacies: Southern Railways, Klan Violence, and Reconstruction*. Chapel Hill: University of North Carolina Press, 1999.

Nwapa, Flora. *This Is Lagos and Other Stories*. Trenton, NJ: Africa World Press, 1992 [1971].

Nzekwu, Onuora. *Blade among the Boys*. London: Heinemann, 1972 [1962].

Oberst, Timothy Sander. "Cost of Living and Strikes in British Africa, c. 1939–1948: Imperial Policy and the Impact of the Second World War." Ph.D. dissertation, Columbia University, 1991.

Offen, Karen. "Defining Feminism: A Comparative Historical Perspective." *Signs* 14 (1988): 119–57.

Ohadike, P.O. "A Demographic Note on Marriage, Family and Family Growth in Lagos, Nigeria." In *The Population of Tropical Africa*. Edited by J.C. Caldwell and C. Okojo. London: Longman, 1968.

———. "Urbanization: Growth, Transitions and Problems of a Premier West African City, Lagos, Nigeria." *Urban Affairs Quarterly* 3 (1968): 69–90.

Ojo, F. "Prospects for Modern Sector Employment Generation for Women." In *Women in the Modern Sector Labour Force in Nigeria*. Edited by Tayo Fashoyin, Felicia Durajaiye Oyekanmi, and Eleanor R. Fapohunda.

Okeke, Philomena E. "Negotiating Social Independence: The Challenges of Career

Pursuits for Igbo Women in Postcolonial Nigeria." In *"Wicked" Women and the Reconfiguration of Gender in Africa*. Edited by Dorothy L. Hodgson and Sheryl McCurdy.

Okoronkwo, A.O. "Women [*sic*] Participation in Trade Unions." In *Women in the Modern Sector Labour Force in Nigeria*. Edited by Tayo Fashoyin, Felicia Durajaiye Oyekanmi, and Eleanor R. Fapohunda.

Oldfield, G.A. "The Native Railway Worker in Nigeria." *Africa* 9 (1936): 379–402.

Olusanya, G.O. *The Second World War and Politics in Nigeria, 1939–1953*. Lagos: Evans Brothers, 1973.

Oluwide, Baba. *Imoudu Biography, Part I: A Political History of Nigeria, 1939–1950*. Ibadan: Ororo Publishers, 1993.

Omolewa, Michael, Gbolagade Adekanmbi, Larinde Akinleye, Kemi Adeola, and MBM Avose. *Michael Imoudu: A Study in the Nigerian Labour Movement*. Ilorin: Michael Imoudu Institute for Labour Studies, 1992.

Oppong, Christine. *Marriage among a Matrilineal Elite*. Cambridge: Cambridge University Press, 1974.

Osmond, M. "Correlates of Types of Marriage." *Social Forces* 44 (1965) 8–15.

Osoba, S.O. "The Development of Trade Unionism in Colonial and Post-Colonial Nigeria." In *Topics on Nigerian Economic and Social History*. Edited by I.A. Akinjobgin and Segun Osoba. Ile-Ife: University of Ife Press, 1980.

Otobo, Dafe. "The Nigeria General Strike of 1981." In *Readings in Industrial Relations in Nigeria*. Edited by Dafe Otobo and Morakinyo Omole. Lagos: Malthouse Press, 1987.

Oyemakinde, O. "A History of Indigenous Labour on the Nigerian Railway, 1895–1945." Ph.D. dissertation, University of Ibadan, 1970.

Oyemakinde, Wale. "The Impact of the Great Depression on the Nigerian Railway and Its Workers." *JHSN* 8 (1977): 143–60.

———. "Michael Imoudu and the Emergence of Militant Trade Unionism in Nigeria, 1940–1942." *JHSN* 7 (1974): 541–61.

———. "The Nigerian General Strike of 1945." *JHSN* 7 (1975): 693–710.

———. "The Nigerian General Strike of 1964." *Genève-Afrique* 13 (1974): 53–71.

———. "The Pullen Marketing Scheme: A Trial in Food Price Control in Nigeria, 1941–1947." *JHSN* 6 (1973): 413–23.

———. "Railway Construction and Operation in Nigeria, 1895–1911: Labour Problems and Socio-Economic Impact." *JHSN* 7 (1974): 304–25.

———. "The Railway Workers and Modernization in Colonial Nigeria." *JHSN* 10 (1979): 113–24.

Oyewùmí, Oyèrónké. *The Invention of Women: Making an African Sense of Western Gender Discourses*. Minneapolis: University of Minnesota Press, 1997.

Oyono, Ferdinand. *Houseboy*. London: Heinemann, 1966.

Parpart, Jane L. "Class and Gender on the Copperbelt: Women in Northern Rhodesian Copper Mining Communities, 1926–1964." In *Women and Class in Africa*. Edited by Claire Robertson and Iris Berger.

———. "The Household and the Mine Shaft: Gender and Class Struggles on the Zambian Copperbelt, 1926–64." *JSAS* 13 (1986): 36–56.

———. "Sexuality and Power on the Zambian Copperbelt: 1926–1964." In *Patriarchy and Class: African Women in the Home and in the Workforce*. Edited by Sharon Stichter and Jane L. Parpart. Boulder, CO: Westview Press, 1988.

———. "'Where Is Your Mother?': Gender, Urban Marriage, and Colonial Discourse on the Zambian Copperbelt, 1924–1945." *IJAHS* 27 (1994): 241–71.

———. "'Wicked Women' and 'Respectable Ladies': Reconfiguring Gender on the Zambian Copperbelt, 1936–1964." In *"Wicked" Women and the Reconfiguration of Gender in Africa*. Edited by Dorothy L. Hodgson and Sheryl McCurdy.

Peace, Adrian J. *Choice, Class and Conflict: A Study of Southern Nigerian Factory Workers*. Brighton, Sussex: Harvester Press, 1979.

Pedersen, Susan. "The Failure of Feminism in the Making of the British Welfare State." *Radical History Review* 43 (1989): 86–110.

———. *Family, Dependence, and the Origins of the Welfare State: Britain and France, 1914–1945*. Cambridge: Cambridge University Press, 1993.

———. "Gender, Welfare, and Citizenship in Britain during the Great War." *AHR* 95 (1990): 983–1006.

Peel, J.D.Y. *Ijeshas and Nigerians: The Incorporation of a Yoruba Kingdom, 1890s–1970s*. Cambridge: Cambridge University Press, 1983.

———. "*Olaju*: A Yoruba Concept of Development." *Journal of Development Studies* 14 (1978): 139–65.

———. *Religious Encounter and the Making of the Yoruba*. Bloomington: Indiana University Press, 2000.

Peil, Margaret. *Lagos: The City Is the People*. Boston, MA: G.K. Hall, 1991.

Peil, Margaret, Stephen K. Ekpenyong, and Olotunji Y. Oyeneye. "Going Home: Migration Careers of Southern Nigerians." *International Migration Review* 22 (1988): 563–85.

Pheffer, Paul. "Railways and Aspects of Social Change in Senegal, 1877–1933." Ph.D. dissertation, University of Pennsylvania, 1975.

Robertson, Claire C. *Sharing the Same Bowl: A Socioeconomic History of Women and Class in Accra, Ghana*. Bloomington: Indiana University Press, 1984.

Robertson, Claire and Iris Berger, eds. *Women and Class in Africa*. New York: Africana Publishing Co., 1986.

Roper, J. I. *Labor Problems in West Africa*. London: Penguin, 1958.

Roper, Michael, and John Tosh, eds. *Manful Assertions: Masculinities in Britain since 1800*. London: Routledge, 1991.

Rose, Sonya O. "Gender at Work': Sex, Class and Industrial Capitalism." *History Workshop* 21 (1986): 113–31.

———. *Limited Livelihoods: Gender and Class in Nineteenth-Century England*. Berkeley: University of California Press, 1992.

———. "Respectable Men, Disorderly Others: The Language of Gender and the Lancashire Weavers' Strike of 1878 in Britain." *Gender and History* 5 (1993): 382–97.

Rosenthal, Anton. "Controlling the Line: Worker Strategies and Transport Capital on the Railroads of Ecuador, Zambia and Zimbabwe, 1916–1950." Ph.D. dissertation, University of Minnesota, 1990.

Scarnecchia, Timothy. "The Politics of Gender and Class in the Creation of African Communities, Salisbury, Rhodesia, 1937–1957." Ph.D. dissertation, University of Michigan, 1994.

———. "Poor Women and Nationalist Politics: Alliances and Fissures in the Formation of a Nationalist Movement in Salisbury, Rhodesia, 1950–56." *JAH* 37 (1996): 283–310.

Schmidt, Elizabeth. *Peasants, Traders, and Wives: Shona Women in the History of Zimbabwe*. Portsmouth, NH: Heinemann, 1992.

Scott, Joan Wallach. *Gender and the Politics of History*. New York: Columbia University Press, 1988.
Scully, Pamela. *Liberating the Family? Gender and British Slave Emancipation in the Rural Western Cape, South Africa, 1823–1853*. Portsmouth, NH: Heinemann, 1997.
Seccombe, Wally. "Patriarchy Stabilized: The Construction of the Male Breadwinner Wage Norm in Nineteenth-Century Britain." *Social History* 2 (1986): 53–76.
Sinha, Mrinalini, *Colonial Masculinity: The "Manly Englishman" and the "Effeminate Bengali" in the Late Nineteenth Century*. Manchester: Manchester University Press, 1995.
Sokunbi, O., O. Jeminiwa, and F.B. Onaeko, eds. *Women and Trade Unionism in Nigeria*. Ibadan: NPS Educational Publishers Limited, 1995.
Solanke, Moji. "Personnel Problems and Women Workers." In *Women in the Modern Sector Labour Force*. Edited by Tayo Fashoyin, Felicia Durojaiye Oyekanmi, and Eleanor R. Fapohunda.
Southall, Aidan (ed.). *Social Change in Modern Africa*. London: Oxford University Press, 1961.
Soyinka, Wole. *Aké: The Years of Childhood*. New York: Random House, 1982.
———. *Ibadan: The Penkelemes Years, A Memoir: 1946–1965*. Ibadan: Spectrum Books, 1994.
———. *Isara: A Voyage around Essay*. Ibadan: Fountain Publications, 1989.
Stoler, Ann Laura. *Race and the Education of Desire: Foucault's History of Sexuality and the Colonial Order of Things*. Durham, NC: Duke University Press, 1995.
———. "Rethinking Colonial Categories: European Communities and the Boundaries of Rule." *CSSH* 31 (1989): 134–61.
Sudarkasa, N. *Where Women Work: A Study of Yoruba Women in the Marketplace and in the Home*. Ann Arbor: Museum of Anthropology, University of Michigan, 1973.
Summerfield, Penny. *Women Workers in the Second World War*. London: Croom Helm, 1984.
Tipps, Dean C. "Modernization Theory and the Comparative Study of Societies: A Critical Perspective." *CSSH* 15 (1973):199–226.
Tokunboh, M.A. *Labour Movement in Nigeria: Past and Present*. Lagos: Lantern Books, 1985.
Tosh, John. *A Man's Place: Masculinity and the Middle Class Home in Victorian England*. New Haven, CT: Yale University Press, 1999.
———. "What Should Historians do with Masculinity? Reflections on Nineteenth-Century Britain." *History Workshop* 38 (1994): 179–202.
Ward, E. *Marriage among the Yoruba*. Washington, DC: Catholic University of America, 1937.
Ward, Edward. *The Yoruba Husband-Wife Code*. Washington, DC: Catholic University of America, 1938.
Waterman, Peter. *Division and Unity amongst Nigerian Workers: Lagos Port Unionism, 1940s–60s*. The Hague: Institute of Social Studies, 1982.
White, Luise. *The Comforts of Home: Prostitution in Colonial Nairobi*. Chicago: University of Chicago Press, 1990.
———. "Matrimony and Rebellion: Masculinity in Mau Mau." In *Men and Masculinities in Modern Africa*. Edited by Lisa A. Lindsay and Stephan F. Miescher.

———. "Separating the Men from the Boys: Constructions of Gender, Sexuality, and Terrorism in Central Kenya, 1939–1959." *IJAHS* 23 (1990): 1–25.

———. *Speaking with Vampires: Rumor and History in Colonial Africa*. Berkeley: University of California Press, 2000.

Wolpe, Harold. "Capitalism and Cheap Labour-Power in South Africa: From Segregation to Apartheid." *Economy and Society* 1 (1972): 425–56.

Women in Nigeria. *The WIN Document: Conditions of Women in Nigeria and Policy Recommendations to 2,000 A.D.* Zaria: Ahmadu Bello University Press, 1992 [1985].

Yesufu, T.M. *The Dynamics of Industrial Relations: The Nigerian Experience*. Ibadan: University Press Ltd., 1984.

———. *An Introduction to Industrial Relations in Nigeria*. London: Oxford University Press, 1962.

INDEX

Abacha, Sani, xi, 208
Abeokuta, 16, 35, 43, 63, 65, 143
Abiola, Moshood, xi, 208
Accra, Ghana, 7–8
Action Group, 131 n.82, 160, 175–76, 179, 184, 190–93
Adebayo, Akanmu, 31–2
Adebo, Simeon, 41, 50 n.49
Adebola, H.P., 178–80, 188–89, 198 n.11
Administrators: colonial, 2–3, 5–6, 9, 12, 22, 34, 36, 46, 68, 78, 98, 105, 133, 136–38, 162, 185, 203, 205–6; Nigerian, 53–56, 58, 61, 63, 70, 72, 80, 82–3, 85–7, 90, 116, 120, 125, 161, 188–89; railway, 18, 140, 142, 144–48, 154, 180
Ado-Odo, 40
Africa: central, 5, 12; colonial, 1, 13, 31, 77, 124, 136, 205, 211; east, 12, 71; French, 8, 96–97; southern, 5; west, 6, 9, 33, 59, 93–94, 97, 118, 136, 162, 179
African Civil Servants Technical Workers Union (ACSTWU), 62, 79, 84–87, 92–93
Agriculture, 6, 34
Akinkugbe, O.I., 187
Akintola, S.L., 175–76
All-Nigeria Trade Union Federation, 95, 141

Allowances: children's, 95, 133, 141–42, 179–80, 187–88, 192, 197; family, 22–23, 77–78, 84, 89–97, 105, 116–17, 133, 140–42, 150, 173–74, 179, 183, 185, 196, 203–4; housing, 149; inducement, 141, 188, 192; local, 79, 92; motor car, 179–80, 187, 192, 196–97, 207–8; for railway staff, 144, 180–81; separation, 77–80, 84, 89, 91–5
America: north, 4, 11, 89; south, 91; United States of, 21, 116
Annuitants, 20, 160
Anthropologists, colonial, 6, 36
Apapa, 58, 149
Aronson, Dan, 111
Artisans, 16, 18, 33, 109–10, 146
Association of Nigerian Railway Civil Servants, 56, 121
Associations, 14, 42
Awolowo, Obafemi, 175–6, 184, 191
Azikiwe, Nnamdi, 62, 67, 84, 86–7, 101 n.46, 115, 117, 175

Babangida, Ibrahim, 208
Balewa, Abubakar Tafawa, 175, 183, 189–91
Bankole, T.A., 85, 87–88, 117, 129 n.55, 177
Barber, Karin, 31, 37, 106, 151, 163, 206
Baron, Ava, 3

Begging fees, 45, 51 n.77, 110
Benefits: employment, 15, 18, 23, 54–5, 57, 77, 95, 107, 109, 116, 122, 137, 144, 146, 153, 163, 173–4, 176–8, 184, 187–8, 194, 196–7, 204, 206; medical, 23, 138, 154, 174, 178
Beveredge Report, 89, 92, 102 n.64
"Big man," 15, 33, 41–43, 45–46, 50 n.59, 59, 134, 137–9, 142, 146, 152–3, 163, 174, 185, 188, 195–7, 205, 209
Borha, L.L., 178, 180, 198 n.11
Bourdillon, Bernard, 56, 61, 79
Breadwinner, male, 5, 9–10, 14, 21–22, 33, 43, 46, 72, 77–78, 88–89, 92, 97, 105–26, 133–34, 146, 174, 185, 193–4, 196–7, 203–11, 212 n.16
Brideprice, 37–39. *Also see* Marriage, money for
Bridges Commission, 62–63, 70–71, 79, 90–91, 186
Brown, Carolyn, 12, 23 n.6
Businessmen, 42, 110, 161, 176, 190
Butler, Judith, 11, 126 n.5, 205

Calabar, 33
Cash crops, 33–35, 41
Census, 110, 175, 192
Chiefs, 14, 43, 80–81, 85
Child care, 20, 152
Children, 38, 41, 43–44, 92, 114, 119, 140, 195–6, 203; fostering of, 152, 162; of workers, 4, 83–84, 90–91, 98, 107, 109–12, 117, 124, 133, 136–7, 139, 141, 147–8, 152, 154, 158, 162, 174, 182–3, 194, 197, 204, 209
Christianity, 8, 10, 14, 35, 37, 43, 151, 163, 205
Cities, 5, 8–9, 11, 34, 54, 63, 71–2, 176, 204
Citizenship, 22, 64, 91–92, 115, 182–3, 197
Civil Servants Union, 65–6, 69, 79, 118
Civil service, 33, 35, 55, 64, 78–9, 92–3, 95, 116, 122–3, 133, 139, 141, 161, 176, 179, 208

Class, 11, 101 n.46, 197
Clerks, 16, 18, 33, 35, 40–41, 53, 59, 109–10, 118, 121, 146, 158, 160
Cocoa, 9, 33–35, 37, 41–44, 151
Cohen, Robin, 192
Cold War, 177
Colonial period, 4, 7, 9, 12, 16, 33, 65, 106, 139, 147, 163, 179–80, 184, 193, 196–7
Colonial Labour Advisory Committee, 96, 133
Colonial Office, 57–60, 63, 68, 71, 96, 118
Colonialism, 9, 12, 14, 78, 88, 97, 105, 197, 204–5, 213 n.23
Conditions, of employment, 65–6, 121, 140, 146, 177
Congo, Belgian, 5, 8
Connell, R.W., 13
Consumer goods, 34, 86, 137, 157
Cooking, 139, 145, 147–8
Cooper, Frederick, 2–3, 14, 27 n.59, 60, 77, 136
Copperbelt, 5–7, 23 n.6, 165 n.16, 204
Corruption, 173, 176, 180
Cost of living, 54, 61, 69, 72, 78–80, 97, 162, 176, 184; adjustments, 61–3, 78, 84, 94, 96, 107; allowance, 62, 67, 84–7, 89; index, 79, 82, 92, 136, 164 n.6, 208
Court: cases, 31, 37–9, 44–5, 109, 111; records, 20, 36, 112

Daily Comet, 86
Daily Service, 117
Daily Times, 58, 115, 120, 194–5
Denzer, LaRay, 126 n.6
Department of Labor, 63, 119–20, 156–7
Depression, Great, 54–60, 68, 72, 90
Development, 6, 86, 125, 161, 206
Differentiation, 7–8, 22–23, 133–163, 175, 177–82, 192–97, 204
Discourse, 4, 106–7, 110, 112, 114–15, 126, 157, 196–7, 205, 211
Divorce, 38, 44–45, 94, 109, 210

Domesticity, 15, 23, 77–8, 97, 133–63, 173–97, 204
Drum, 158

Ebute Metta, 16–18, 56, 59, 147, 153, 157, 180, 188, 210
Education, 7–8, 33, 41–3, 46, 53, 59, 64–5, 98, 110, 138, 141, 151, 206; of girls, 115; government provision of, 69, 91, 134; of women, 115, 118–19, 122; universal primary, 161; Western, 10, 14, 16, 35, 43, 106, 136–7
Ekiti, 34
Ekwensi, Cyprian, *Lokotown*, 17, 113–14
Elders, 5, 40, 45
Elites: African, 5, 115; Christian, 10; new, 14, 32, 42–43, 204–5; Nigerian, 23, 136, 173, 176, 178, 188, 195–6; urban, 7; women, 80, 87, 194–5
Emecheta, Buchi, *The Joys of Motherhood*, 50 n.54, 68, 111
Emejulu, Luke, 55, 92–3
Emerson, Ralf, 121, 80
"Emerson Must Go" demonstrations, 180, 184
Employers, 79, 89, 116, 118, 136, 146, 176, 186, 190, 192, 196, 205, 207, 209–10; colonial, 2–4, 12, 22, 46, 57, 62, 65, 68–9, 106–8; European, 5, 12, 105, 176, 191
Employment: daily-paid, 178; formal, 209; permanent, 59; wage, 58, 109, 124, 157; women's, 97, 106–7, 114–26, 204. *Also see* labor
Engine drivers, railway, 17–18, 113–14, 142, 156; African, 53, 143–4; conditions for, 143–5; European, 143–4; West Indian, 67, 143
English language, 18, 160; pidgin, 18
Enugu, 16, 18, 60, 110, 156, 165 n.25, 167 n.51, 189, 191
Erinle, J.O., 85
Ethnicity, 7, 18, 20, 28 n.66, 147, 153, 156, 173, 190
Europe, 4, 11–12, 69–70, 89, 91, 97, 116, 131 n.80

European: businesses, 33; families, 77; officials, 79, 91, 152, 173, 180; workers, 140–41, 144, 166 n.40
Expatriates, 139, 42, 160, 174–5, 184
Eze, Nduka, 121

Fadipe, N.A., 35, 37, 39–41
Falola, Toyin, 31
Family: African, 6, 77, 90, 94, 173; extended, 3–4, 9, 44, 57–9, 63–70, 85, 92, 95, 112, 133–63, 185–6, 195, 203–4, 209; life, 2, 4, 14–15, 21, 98, 174, 204; modern, 4, 14; nuclear, 4, 7, 23, 72, 138, 161, 163, 203, 206; obligations to, 36; railway, 20; urban, 7; workers', 4, 6, 9, 21–22, 40–41, 53–72, 85, 97, 106, 148, 150–63, 174, 178–9, 182–3, 185–6, 195–7, 203, 206
Farmers, 44, 79, 82, 108, 110, 157, 175, 193, 195
Fatherhood, 3, 22, 38, 97, 170 n.88, 183
Fathers, 39–40, 83, 163, 183, 195, 206
Femininity, 3
Ferguson, James, 7, 15, 137, 204–5
Fiction, 20
First aid, 146
First Republic, 175–77, 179, 192, 197
Food, 5, 37–38, 44, 62, 98, 147, 183, 187, 197; expenses, 59, 108–10, 194; shortages, 80–83, 195
France, 6, 89, 97

Galletti, R., 43
Gari, 82–3, 85, 87–9, 129 n.55, 184, 208
Geary, Sir William, 56, 58, 60, 66
Gender, 21, 78, 85, 97, 105, 139, 173, 175, 193, 197, 204, 211; as performance, 11, 22, 106, 125, 126 n.2, 205; definition of, 4, 11–12; ideology, 5, 9, 18, 23, 126, 204; norms, 13, 32; policies about, 1–2; relations, 2–3, 9–10, 12, 32, 78, 80, 98
Generations, 36, 39–40
Ghana. *See* Gold Coast

Gifts, 37–9, 42, 44, 48 n.26, 51 n.77, 110, 112–14, 155–56
Gold Coast, 7–8, 13, 33, 50 n.65, 99 n.4, 171 n.111
Goodluck, Wahab, 182, 189–90, 192, 198 n.11, 201 n.54
Gorsuch Commission, 95–6, 141–2, 147, 199 n.17
Government: colonial, 62, 77, 95, 115, 173, 175, 179, 186; military, 207–8; Nigerian, 57, 68, 71, 79, 82, 84, 86, 88, 93–4, 97, 107, 136, 141–2, 148–9, 173–97, 212 n.13; opposition to, 190–92; Western Regional, 161
Great Britain, 5–6, 8, 11, 60, 79, 89–90, 95–7, 121, 205

Harragin Commission, 93–96, 144, 150, 198 n.7
History: African, 12; gender, 105; labor, 12, 15, 77, 203
Hometowns, 14, 42–43, 109, 141, 147, 161; retirement in, 159–60, 204; visits to, 14, 57, 155, 163; workers' connections with, 22, 54–55, 59, 64–70, 134, 136–8, 155–60, 203–4, 209
Hopkins, A.G., 34, 58
Hoskyns-Abrahall, T., 71
House, 36, 59; building a, 37, 41–2, 46, 149, 158
Households, 23, 36, 41–43, 98; finances within, 43–46, 88, 108–14, 125; polygynous, 152; size of, 59, 69, 78; of workers, 4–5, 12, 89–90, 106, 137, 146–54, 163, 184–5, 197, 204–5, 209
Housewives, 111, 114, 175, 193–5, 197, 207
Housing, 141, 162, 174, 178–9; in Lagos, 54, 62, 70–2; railway, 16, 142–44; urban, 7–9, 91, 134; of workers, 5, 7, 22, 55, 64, 138–40, 146–54, 163, 183, 186–8, 197
Hunt, Nancy Rose, 204
Husbands, 9, 44, 108–14, 195–6, 206–7

Ibadan, 8–9, 16–17, 19–20, 34, 37–40, 43–44, 60, 63–4, 68, 81, 88, 108, 110–11, 119, 123–4, 147, 150, 153, 155–60, 189–91, 194, 208–9
Identity, 10–11, 45–6, 78
Ife, 34, 43, 190
Igbo, 16, 23 n.1, 23 n.6, 109–10, 127 n.29, 159
Ijebu, 156, 160
Ijebu-Ode, 72, 160
Ikejiani, Okechukwu, 180
Ikoyi, 149
Ilesha, 34–35, 39, 48 n.28, 63
Imoudu, Michael, 58, 60, 63, 79, 84–88, 177, 182, 188–91, 199 n.11
Independence, Nigerian, 117, 160, 174–6, 178–9, 182, 184, 186
Indirect rule, 5
Industrialization, 11
Industrial relations, 78, 86, 95, 161–2, 177, 184, 186
Influx controls, 8–9, 69
Inter-African Labor Conference, 96
International Labor Organization, 8
Interviews, 4, 19, 21, 108, 111, 113, 124, 209
Islam, 10, 37, 151
Izzett, Alison, 119

Johannesburg, South Africa, 5
Joint Action Committee, 183–4, 186, 188–92, 195–6
Jos, 60, 109, 147, 159
Juvenile delinquency, 7, 119

Kaduna, 16, 189, 191
Kano, 16, 18, 60, 151, 156, 191
Kenya, 6, 8, 99 n.4

Labor: casual, 18, 54–55, 58; migrant, 5–6, 72, 95, 136, 141; policies, 3, 60–63, 96, 204; shortages, 33–34; "target," 31, 39, 41, 47 n.11, 54, 58, 203; urban, 1, 133–63; wage, 3–6, 8–10, 16, 20–22, 31, 53–55, 65, 105,

Index

108, 115, 124, 176, 197, 203–6, 211. *Also see* Stabilization
Laborers, 33–35, 53, 55, 68, 109–10, 146, 157–8, 184, 187
Labour Champion, 121, 133
Lagos, 8–9, 16–20, 33–34, 40, 55–58, 60–62, 64, 66–72, 79–82, 84, 86–8, 108, 110–12, 115, 119, 134, 136–7, 146–58, 176, 179–80, 186, 188–94, 208, 210
Lagos City Council, 193
Lagos Executive Development Board, 149–50
Lagos Market Women's Association, 80, 193
Lagos Town Council, 67, 71, 80, 148
Lagos Women's League, 80, 115
Leave from work, 55–57, 65, 72, 134, 140–41, 155–57, 159, 178, 196; disputes over, 4, 65–66; maternity, 121, 123; with pay, 54, 61, 137, 180, 192
Liberia, 33
Literacy, 43, 139
Love, 38, 44, 46, 112
Lugard, Frederick, 34

Macaulay, Herbert, 80, 84, 100 n.15, 100 n.26
MacDonald, Malcolm, 56
Maiduguri, 16, 60
Marine Department, 55, 58, 72 n.2, 158, 161
Maritime Trade Union Federation, 122, 124
Marriage, 21, 42–46, 94, 118; and housing, 7, 147; money for, 36–40, 45, 203; "Ordinance," 10; process of, 36, 38; urban, 7; women's employment after, 109; of railway workers, 148, 210
"Marriage bar," 116–18, 122, 129–30 n.63
Marris, Peter, 150
Masculinity, 3, 21, 23, 31–46, 60, 80, 109, 112, 117, 193, 197, 205, 211; adult, 36–41; African, 13; hegemonic, 13, 124, 205; and labor, 10–12, 86; multiple, 13, 15, 21, 162, 205; working class, 91, 97, 123, 173–4, 182–88, 204, 211
McEwen, J.H., 56, 63
Men: adult, 12, 134; ideals about, 3; senior, 41–43; Yoruba, 42–3; young, 31, 36, 39, 41, 43, 46. *Also see* Big men
Miescher, Stephan, 13, 124
Migration, 10, 22, 35; chain, 55, 71–2; labor, 39, 54, 60, 63–68, 105, 134
Miller Commission, 75 n.50
Missionaries, 7–8, 14, 33, 35, 106
Modernization, 2, 12–15, 22, 115, 136–9; as colonial project, 6–7; and families, 160–63, 206, 211; ideals, 1, 10, 203–4; of Nigeria, 21, 121, 211; and Railway, 18; theory, 14, 150, 163, 206
Money, 10, 21, 31–46, 111–14, 1156–7, 204–5
Monogamy, 43, 136, 150–52, 163, 206
Morgan Commission, 182–96
Morning Post, 195
Mothers, 195

Nairobi, Kenya, 5, 7, 9, 139
National Council of Nigerian Citizens (NCNC), 175, 177, 190–2, 201 n.61
National Council of Women's Societies, 194
National Union of Railwaymen (Federated), 122, 154
Nationalism, 6, 77, 80, 101 n.46, 173, 177, 197
Newspapers, 20, 40, 59, 83, 86, 88, 101 n.43, 108, 112, 114, 152, 161, 183, 195
Niger Delta, 33
Nigerail, 108, 113–14
Nigerian Employers' Consultative Association, 184, 191
Nigerian Labor Congress, 207–8

Nigerian Maritime Trade Unions Federation, 184
Nigerian National Democratic Party (NNDP), 80–81, 100 n.15
Nigerian Ports Authority, 124, 136, 148–9
Nigerian Railway Corporation, 19–20, 107, 122, 124, 149, 154, 180, 190, 208
Nigerian Tobacco Company, 150, 155, 158
Nigerian Trade Union Congress (NTUC), 190, 198 n.11
Nigerian Union of Railwaymen (NUR), 180
Nigerian Youth Movement, 117
Nigerianization, 139, 178, 180
Northern People's Congress (NPC), 175–76, 191, 193
Northern Rhodesia. See Zambia
Nwapa, Flora, "A Soldier Returns Home," 109, 159
Nwokedi, C.O., 187
Nzekwu, Onuora, *Blade Among the Boys*, 40, 157
Nzeribe, Gogo, 182, 199 n.11

Officials. See Administrators
Ogbomosho, 157
Oil industry, 1, 207–8
Okotie-Eboh, Festus, 191–92
Okpara, Dr. Michael, 191
Okuku, 37
Ọlajú, 14–15, 138, 163, 172 n.117, 206
Omagle, A.O., 117
Ondo, 34, 37, 43
Orde Browne, G. St. J, 59, 63
Oshogbo, 39, 63
Osindero, J. Marcus, 85, 117, 129 n.55
Overcrowding, 22, 55, 68, 71–2, 162
Oyemakinde, Wale, 18, 100 n.21, 197
Oyewùmí, Oyèrónké, 105
Oyo, 64

Parpart, Jane, 7, 23 n.6
Passfield, Lord, 60

Patronage, 15, 23, 42, 46, 59, 134, 156, 161, 163, 175, 196
Paychecks, 4, 31, 40, 44, 59, 109, 112, 114, 125, 209
Pedersen, Susan, 89
Peel, J.D.Y., 14, 138, 172 n.117
Peil, Margaret, 208
Pelewura, Alimotu, 80–82, 84, 87–8, 100 n.15, 100 n.23
Pensioners, 19–21, 108, 110–11, 150–52, 154–6, 158, 160, 206, 208–11, 212 n.13
Pensions, 14, 18, 21, 54–7, 65, 67, 69, 72, 91, 95, 122, 124, 137, 158, 204, 208, 210
Permanent establishment, 18, 56–7, 61–2, 65–6, 136, 154–5, 180, 185
Permanent Way Workers Union, 148
Personnel files, railway, 20, 28 n.66, 58, 151, 160
Plummer, Gladys, 119–20, 130 n.70
Police, railway, 140, 148, 153
Policy-makers. See Administrators
Politics, 80–83; First Republic, 175–7; Lagos, 8; local, 42; nationalist, 85; and organized labor, 175–7
Polygyny, 43, 778, 92, 94–5, 150–2, 162
Popular culture, 113, 128 n.41
Port Harcourt, 16, 86, 156, 159, 189–90
Port workers, 5, 107, 165 n.7
Poverty, 57, 70
Practice, of gender, 4, 106, 126, 211. *Also see* Gender
Pregnancy, 152; as grounds for job termination, 118, 129 n.63
Preventive Detention Act, 178
Price controls, 62, 78–84, 86, 101 n.46, 183, 186, 192
Promotion, job, 61, 64, 146, 161, 174
Prostitution, 5, 120
Proverbs, 31, 38, 42, 87, 160
Provident funds, 57–8, 61, 67
Providers, men as, 4, 44, 46, 78, 88, 107, 173, 186, 196–7, 204–6. *Also see* Breadwinners

Public Works Department, 55, 58, 60, 72 n.2, 161, 182, 185
Pullen marketing scheme, 80–83, 87

Race, 12, 53, 77, 139–42; discrimination, 22, 78–80, 91, 97–8, 117. *Also see* Racism
Racism, 2, 56, 61
Railway: division of labor on, 17–18; Nigerian, 15–21, 34, 39, 41, 55, 63, 72 n.2, 109–10, 121–4, 134, 142–9; retirees, 111, 138, 209–10, 212 n.13; workers, 1, 4–5, 15–21, 35, 40, 53, 56–7, 60–62, 65, 67, 77, 85–6, 88, 95, 109–10, 123, 136–7, 142–6, 152–6, 159–62, 179–80, 204, 210
Railway and Port Workers Union, 180, 182
Railway Technical Staff Association, 161
Railway Workers Union, 55–56, 58, 60–63, 66, 79, 84, 141, 147–8
Rape, 112
Relatives, of workers, 15, 41, 45, 56, 59–60, 85, 87, 92, 137, 146, 152–6, 160, 162–3, 174, 185, 196–7, 204, 206
Religion, 20; Yoruba, 37, 43
Remittances, 85, 118, 137, 154–5, 157–8
Rent, 70–71, 110, 114, 150, 183, 185–7, 192, 208
Reproduction: of labor, 5–6, 72, 89–90, 97; social, 22, 24 n.14, 91, 148, 173
Respectability, 7, 12, 77, 90
Rest houses, railway, 144–46
Retirement, 57–8, 64, 67, 98, 107, 137, 158–60, 203, 209–11
Richards, Arthur, 79
Rooke, C.E., 63
Rose, Sonya, 11
Royal Niger Company, 58

Salaries, 21–22, 40, 57–8, 69, 94, 109–11, 138, 142–4, 146, 161, 176–80, 183–4, 186–9, 192, 194, 196–7, 207–8

Salisbury, Southern Rhodesia, 9, 139
Scarnecchia, Timothy, 139
Schools, 17, 35, 141–2148, 188; fees for, 85, 87, 108, 110–12, 209
"Second colonial occupation," 6
Second Republic, 207
Seniority, 42, 46, 204
Servants: of Europeans, 12, 139–40; in households, 59, 154, 185, 189; on trains, 145–6
Sex, 5, 112, 128 n.38; discrimination, 104, 117, 131 n.88, 177, 182
Shagamu, 160
Shonekan, I.S.M.O., 91
Sierra Leone, 8, 33
Slavery, 8, 32–35, 42, 47 n.9
Slum clearance, 71, 149–50
"Small boy," 12, 36, 42, 145–7, 167 n.51, 185
Social security, 64, 68, 186
South Africa, 6
Southern Rhodesia. *See* Zimbabwe
Soyinka, Wole, 18, 88, 191
Stabilization, labor, 6–9, 15, 18, 22, 90, 134, 136–7, 139, 163, 177, 189, 203–5
State, 89, 96, 204; colonial, 10, 53–72, 105–6, 125; Nigerian, 15, 176, 197
Station masters, railway, 17, 53, 142, 152
Station Staff Union, 145
Stooke, G. Bereford, 71–2
Strikes, 56, 58, 62–3, 124, 136, 183–4, 186; 1941 threat of, 61; 1945 general, 6, 22–23, 71–2, 77–98, 105, 107, 112, 117, 129 n.55, 133, 140, 173–5, 177, 188, 192–3, 196–7, 203; 1964 general, 23, 173–97, 204, 207; 1981 general, 207–8; Dakar general, 97; recent, 208; wave of, 6, 77, 99 n.4
Structural adjustment programs, 21, 208
Subjectivity, 4, 11, 106
Supreme Council of Nigerian Workers, 91–2, 98, 133, 184–5
Surulere, 150

Surveys, 19, 88, 108–10, 137, 150–51, 155–58, 209

Taxes, 34, 46, 59, 69, 80–1, 100 n.23, 187
Trade, 14, 68; palm oil, 8, 33; in railway compounds, 169–70 n.84; slave, 8, 92; women's, 1, 9, 20, 44, 80, 88, 120
Trades Union Congress (TUC), 70, 91, 102 n.62, 116–17, 177
Trade Union Congress of Nigeria (TUCN), 177–79
Trade unions, 1–3, 5, 12, 18, 22–23, 46, 54, 60, 62, 69, 72, 84–5, 89, 97, 107, 116, 124–5, 134, 142, 173–80, 182–8, 192, 196–7, 198 n.11, 204, 206–7. *Also see* individual unions, listed by name
Traders, 32–33, 157, 195; female, 46, 78, 87, 109–11, 193; *osomaalo*, 35, 39
Train conductors (guards), 17–18, 142, 144–46, 155, 159
Train Guards Union, 144–45
Training, job, 65, 134, 146
Transfers, job, 4, 64–65, 70, 140–41, 152, 155, 168 n.57, 188
Transport: for hometown leave, 54, 61, 64–6, 72, 134; public, 178–9; to work, 187, 195, 208
Transport Staff Union, 153
Travel, 4, 18, 20, 156, 204
Tudor Davies Commission, 86, 89, 91–4, 198 n.7

Udoji awards, 207
Unemployment, 22, 55–57, 60, 65, 68–9, 71–2, 81, 83, 95, 118, 183, 189, 203
Union of Domestic Servants, 153
Union Trading Company, 190
United Africa Company, 66, 81, 190, 196, 200 n.45
United Kingdom. *See* Great Britain
United Labor Congress, 178–9, 182, 188, 198 n.11

United States. *See* America
Urbanization, 7, 16, 64

Victoria Island, 149

Wages, 35–7, 40–41, 54–5, 58, 60, 62, 65, 68–9, 85, 98, 107, 110, 116–17, 125, 134, 136–7, 146, 158, 162, 173–4, 176–9, 182–9, 193, 195–7, 198 n.7; family, 2, 4–6, 14, 90–91, 96–7, 133, 186, 204, 208; "living," 178, 187, 194; minimum, 62, 79, 84, 136, 178, 184, 186–7, 189, 192, 208
Ward, Edward, 36–7, 42
Warfare, 8–9, 34, 47 n.9
Wealth in people, 31, 42–3
Welfare: measures, 55, 57, 69, 86, 146, 153, 207; social, 120
West African Pilot, 40, 58, 61–2, 64–5, 67, 80, 83, 86, 94, 110, 115, 117–18, 124, 140, 161, 183, 194
Western Region, 9, 16, 175
White, Luise, 3, 12, 139
Wilson, W.G.W., 61
Wives, 9, 36–7, 43, 195–6, 207; as dependents, 105, 108; expectations of, 44; "outside," 10; of railway employees, 108, 124, 141, 148, 154, 208–11; of workers, 4–5, 7, 54, 77, 87, 90, 92, 95, 106–14, 123, 133, 136, 139, 147, 150, 162, 174, 182, 193–4, 197, 203–4
Women, 35, 39; and 1945 general strike, 78, 80–85, 87–89, 101 n.43, 192; and 1964 general strike, 174–5, 192–7; as dependents, 1, 182, 193–4; financially independent, 6–7, 10, 43, 78, 118–20, 206; market, 22, 77–8, 80–85, 87–89, 100 n.15, 110, 124, 153, 173, 175, 193–7, 201 n.57; in trade unions, 123–24, 132 n.92, 182, 207; urban, 7; as wage earners, 4, 22, 97, 114–26, 182, 197, 206; Yoruba, 1, 9, 31, 205
Women's Party, 118, 128 n.48

Workers: African, 5–6; casual, 58, 177; daily-paid, 54, 57–8, 66, 180, 186; Nigerian, 78, 179; permanent, 58; skilled, 60; unskilled, 40, 184; urban, 6–7. *Also see* Labor; Employment

World War II, 1, 3, 6, 22, 53–4, 60, 63, 68, 70, 72, 79, 81, 84–6, 92, 107, 109, 116, 134, 165 n.25, 203

Yesufu, T.M., 156, 187–8
Yoruba, 9–10, 16, 105, 205
Yorubaland, 21, 31–46, 88

Zambia, 5, 7–9, 15, 99 n.4, 165 n.16
Zaria, 16, 18, 156
Zimbabwe, 7–8
Zudonu Committee, 178–9, 185, 198 n.10

About the Author

LISA A. LINDSAY is Assistant Professor of History at the University of North Carolina, Chapel Hill. Along with Stephan F. Miescher, she is co-editor of *Men and Masculinities in Modern Africa*.